ILLUMINATING THE BLACKNESS

ILLUMINATING THE BLACKNESS

Blacks and African Muslims in Brazil

Habeeb Akande

RABAAH
PUBLISHERS

Copyright © 2016 by Habeeb Akande
All rights reserved
First Published in England by Rabaah Publishers
7 Granary Square
Epping Place
London, N1 1FA
www.rabaah.com
sales@rabaah.com

No part of this publication may be reproduced, stored in any retrieval system, or transmitted in any form or by any means, electronic, mechanical, photocopying, recording or otherwise, without the prior written permission of the copyright owner.

Written by: Habeeb Akande
Edited by: Abdassamad Clarke
Cover design and Typeset by: Ian Whiteman

Printed and bound by: CPI Group (UK) Ltd, Croydon, CR0 4YY
A catalogue record of this book is available from the British Library
ISBN: 978-0-9574845-2-8

Front cover image: Africano Bahia, Rodolphe Lindemann /Portrait of a man with tribal scarification, Bahia, Brazil, 1860 © Schomburg Center for Research in Black Culture

Back cover image: Book with Islamic supplications written in the Arabic language found attached to the neck of an African male after the revolt in Bahia, 1835

ACKNOWLEDGEMENTS

Every effort has been made to contact copyright holders of material reproduced in this book. Any omissions will be rectified in subsequent printings if notice is given to the publisher.

All the internet addresses (URLs) given in this book were valid at the time of going to press. However, due to the dynamic nature of the internet, some addresses may have changed, or sites may have changed or ceased to exist since publication. While the author and publisher regret any inconvenience this may cause readers, no responsibility for any such changes can be accepted by either the author or the publisher.

IN THE NAME OF ALLAH,
THE MOST BENEFICENT, THE MOST MERCIFUL.

'Leave a legacy'

AZEEZ AKANDE

Contents

ACKNOWLEDGMENTS XI

PREFACE XIII
Meeting the Sultan of Sokoto in Northern Nigeria xvi
Trips to Brazil xvii
Perceptions and Misconceptions of Brazilian Women xx
Final Thoughts on Being Black and Muslim in Brazil xxiii
Twenty Facts About Brazil That Many People Do Not Know xxv

INTRODUCTION 1
Brazil's Enslavement of Black Africans 4
Brazil's Denial of Anti-Black Racism and White Supremacy 11
Fighting Racism Through Education and Activism 21
Who is Black? What is Blackness? 22
African Influences on Brazilian Culture 33
Islam in the History of Brazil 41
Contributions of African Muslims to Brazil 48
The Islamic Revival in Brazil 53
Why are Brazilians Embracing Islam? 57
The Structure of the Book 66

PART ONE

RACE-RELATIONS IN BRAZIL

CHAPTER 1
RACE, ETHNICITY AND SKIN COLOUR IN BRAZIL 73

The Miscegenation Ideology 74
The Whitening Ideology 80
The Ideology of Racial Democracy 86
The Census' Racial Categories 92
Conclusion 100

CHAPTER 2
BLACK BEAUTY IN BRAZIL 103

Colourism 104
Skin Bleaching 107
Interracial Marriages 109
The Politics of Black Hair 114
The Media and the Fashion Industry 122
Appreciation of Black Beauty 134
Conclusion 143

CHAPTER 3
AFFIRMATIVE ACTION IN BRAZIL 147

Advocates and Benefits 148
Opponents And Criticisms 155
A Problem for the White Elite 157
Conclusion 162

PART TWO

BRAZIL'S AFRICAN MUSLIM HERITAGE

CHAPTER 4
AFRICAN MUSLIMS IN BRAZIL BEFORE THE PORTUGUESE 167

North African Moors in Brazil 168
West African Mandinkas in Brazil 171
Africans in Renaissance Europe 177

CHAPTER 5
SLAVE REVOLTS IN BAHIA, 1807–1835 181

Yoruba 182
Hausa 184
West African Culture 184
Bahia's Slave Revolts 186
Was the Malê Revolt a Success 204
Comparisons with the 869 Zanj Revolt in Baghdad 205
Conclusion 211

CHAPTER 6
WEST AFRICAN MUSLIMS IN RIO DE JANEIRO, PERNAMBUCO AND ALAGOAS 213

Muslim Communities 214
Literacy and Qur'ānic Schools 220
Women and Marriage 229
Black Heroines 235
Return to Africa 236

CHAPTER 7
AFRICAN PERSONALITIES 239

Rufino José Maria 239
Mahommah Gardo Baquaqua 243
Efunroye Tinubu 245

CONCLUSION
The Racial Democracy Of Islam In Brazil 247

APPENDIX 1
CATEGORIES OF WHITENESS AND BLACKNESS IN BRAZIL 251

APPENDIX 2
CHRONOLOGY OF SLAVE REVOLTS IN BAHIA, 1807 – 1835 255

APPENDIX 3
INDEX OF IMAGES 257

BIBLIOGRAPHY 265

INDEX 279

ABOUT THE AUTHOR 287

ACKNOWLEDGMENTS

"He who has not thanked people, has not thanked Allah."[1]
PROPHET MUḤAMMAD

I HAVE ACCUMULATED many debts to people who have influenced my thinking, many more than I can possibly thank in these pages. They include academics, activists, everyday Brazilians and close friends. After Allah who deserves all praise and acts of gratitude, I would like to express by deepest thanks to my parents who instilled in me from a young age the importance of faith, education and to have pride in my blackness.

It is a great pleasure to thank my teachers, tutors and mentors at the Winnie Mandela pan-African Saturday School in Camden, London which I attended in my pre-teens. Special thanks to the Sultan of Sokoto, Muhammadu Sa'adu Abubakar III, the *Shehu* (traditional ruler) of the Borno Emirate, Abubakar ibn Umar Garbai el-Kanemi, Brazilian historian João José Reis, Shaykh Abdul Hameed Ahmad of the *Centro Cultural Islâmico da Bahia* (Islamic Cultural Center of Bahia), Misbah Wale Akanni of the Nigerian Cultural House in Salvador, the staff of the *Centro de Estudos Afro-Orientais* (Center for Afro-Oriental Studies), Thiago and Mirella from the *Museu AfroBrasil* (Afro-Brazil Museum) in São Paulo, the staff of MAFRO - *Museu Afro-Brasileiro UFBA* (Afro-Brazilian Museum) in Salvador, David A Wilson co-founder of *the Grio* news website, Denis Mola (Mola Photography) and Marques Travae, the curator of the *Black Women of Brazil* blog for helping me with the research of this book. I would also like to extend my warmest thanks to the wonderful people of Salvador, São Paulo and Rio de Janeiro,

---

[1] Al-Bayhaqī, *Shuʿab al-īmān,* and Ibn Abi'd-Dunyā narrating from an-Nuʿmān ibn Bashīr. Aḥmad and at-Tirmidhī from Abū Hurayrah. Ad-Daylamī from Jābir. Al-Khaṭīb and Ibn ʿAsākir from Ibn ʿAbbās.

especially Ricardo, Max Wianna, Anete Freitas, Jucy Silva, Michelly Ramos, Érica de Paula, Claudia Poliana da Silva, Maurício Arcanjo, Ronan Araujo, Wallace Barbosa, Camilla Oliveira, Cristina Karima, Camila Velame, Rita Bacelar, Geisa Correia, Milena Simões, Marina Rocha, Debora Cordeiro, Carla Santos Santana, Ivone Alves, Ana Luiza Duarte and Munik Mota who were all very helpful to me in gaining an understanding of the female and black experience in Brazil. Last but most definitely not least I would like to thank the Muslim community in Salvador for their warm hospitality and allowing me to interview them for the purpose of this book.

Just like every successfully completed book, this one would not have come into fruition without the help, guidance, and support of Abdassamad Clarke (editor), Ian Whiteman (typesetter and cover designer), my older brother and business adviser, Azeez Akande (Mansa), and my two younger sisters, Azeezat and Yasmin Akande for their creative input. I would like to thank them all for their assistance in publishing this book with Rabaah Publishers.

PREFACE

The incredible history of African Muslims in Brazil should be a great area of interest to all black and Muslim educators in rewriting a world history which has hitherto had a Eurocentric perspective.

GROWING UP IN London, England in a proud Nigerian Muslim household,[2] I fondly remember seeing the Second World Black and African Festival of Arts and Culture (commonly known as FESTAC) 1977[3] framed banner hung on a corridor wall with "I am black and proud" written in large letters. The banner was next to framed Qur'ānic verses in Arabic calligraphy about the oneness of God and the Messengership of the Prophet Muḥammad ﷺ. Looking back, these framed texts made a deep impression on my consciousness, a consciousness of my black identity and my belief in the one God, Allah, that I would not fully realise nor appreciate until decades later.

As a British-born Muslim of Yoruba extraction, I have always had a keen interest in learning about the history of Yoruba Muslims and the impact that they had on other cultures and peoples. Historians have documented that many of the Africans brought to Brazil in the nineteenth century, particularly Yoruba Muslims, were more literate and sophisticated than their Portuguese masters. A fiercely proud people, the Yorubas fought against their enslavement with singular determination

---

2 Originally from Oyo state, my grandfather on my father's side was from Porto Novo in Benin, my grandmother on my father's side was from Lagos and my grandparents on my mother's side were from Ogun state in southwestern Nigeria.

3 FESTAC '77 refers to the Second World Black and African Festival of Arts and Culture that was held in Lagos, Nigeria in 1977. The festival was attended by more than 17,000 people from over 50 countries. FESTAC '77 was the largest cultural event ever held on the African continent. I saw the same FESTAC '77 calendar in the Afro-Brasil museum in São Paulo in January 2015.

and sought liberation for themselves and their fellow Africans.⁴

When people speak about the religion of Afro-Brazilians, the traditional Yoruba religion (*Candomblé*) and its divinities (*orixás*) often comes up. Strangely the religion of Islam and the contribution of West African Muslims to modern-day Brazil are often neglected. The heroic exploits of West African Muslims, particularly the Yoruba and Hausa, who established communities, taught literacy and were determined to hold onto their faith, should not be forgotten as they are just as inspiring as they are educational.

Prior to my first visit to Brazil in February 2014, I was already aware of the country's African heritage from the time I spent learning about black history at a Pan-Africanist Saturday school. The now-closed Winnie Mandela School situated in north-west London taught history from an African perspective, something lacking in my state schooling. At the tender age of ten I fondly remember learning about the history of African peoples in Africa, Brazil and the United States. Reading the autobiography and watching the film of the inspirational African-American Muslim activist Malcolm X was a catalyst in awakening my desire to know more about my Islamic and African heritage. I attended the Saturday school for a few years where I was awarded the Child of the Year award for two consecutive years. Upon reflection, the school gave me the grounding I needed when studying history and other subjects at secondary school, where the schooling was always taught from a culturally biased European perspective.⁵

Over time, one thing I could not help but notice as I read more and met people from various backgrounds was that the black experience was similar, whether in Europe, the Americas, Asia and even Africa. Blackness is often denigrated, as is African culture. With the exception of sports, music and other forms of entertainment, where blacks were lauded, it was evident that in the minds of other races, blacks were inferior and destined to be at the bottom. Even today blacks are noticeably absent from positions of power in multicultural countries, where fairer-skinned peoples have created and maintained a racial hierarchy positioning blacks at the bottom. Fortunately my time studying at the Winnie Mandela

---

4 http://www.newsafrica.net/component/k2/item/213-58soul-legacy/213-58soul-legacy

5 Malcolm X encouraged peoples of African descent to identify with oppressed people in the world and connect with their blood brothers in Brazil, Venezuela, Haiti and Cuba. He remarked, "Not one black man is prominent in Brazil. The Negroes there are still at the bottom."

Preface

School, for which I am eternally grateful, gave me an understanding from a very young age of the systematic racism that has been perpetuated against people of African descent. As Afro-Caribbean students, we were instructed to learn our history and not be ashamed of our cultural heritage. Fate would have it, that I travelled to Nigeria that summer after the end of the school year.

TRIPS TO NIGERIA

When I visited Nigeria for the first time in 1994, the trip left a favourable impression upon me, as I saw positive depictions of Africans first hand. Beautiful and confident Nigerian women who were not ashamed of their blackness. and rich, hardworking male entrepreneurs who took pride in their culture, religion and polygamous relationships, were in stark contrast to the perception of Africans I was accustomed to in the UK. It was in Nigeria that I began to want to learn more about the history of Yoruba Muslims, especially after hearing about the Yoruba Muslims in Brazil during my time at the Winnie Mandela School.

It wasn't until 2005, just before I visited Nigeria again, that I came upon *Rebelião Escrava no Brasil* (Slave Rebellion in Brazil), an excellent book by Brazilian historian João José Reis about the 1835 Yoruba Muslim revolt in Brazil. Unlike previous books I had read about African slavery, the author spoke about the merits of the Yoruba as traders and warriors rather than focusing on their plight as slaves. This refreshing book demonstrated that there was indeed more to black history than slavery and persecution.

In 2002, as part of my Film Studies and Business Studies undergraduate degree I studied the critically acclaimed Brazilian feature film *Cidade de Deus* (City of God). The gritty film highlighted the plight of black Brazilians lying behind the romanticised images of Brazil's beautiful women, paradisiacal beaches, lively street carnivals, beautiful natural scenery and majestic football players that previously came to mind when one thought about Brazil. The film showed the harsh realities of the anti-black racism that exists in the most racially-mixed country in the world. Brazil's racial inequalities were further underlined in the film *Bus 174* and the Brazilian TV series, *Cidade dos Homens* (City of Men),[6] where the recurring theme of the Brazilian black experience is

---

[6] The directors of *City of God* went on to create a TV series called *Cidade dos Homens* (City of Men). The drama series focuses on the the lives of two black Brazilian teenagers living in the favelas of Rio de Janeiro. A feature film of the same name

that of discrimination and poverty. Anecdotes in the drama series *City of Men* demonstrated the daily struggles that black Brazilians face: "If you're black and you're poor, you have to paint yourself white [to be successful]." "Do you know what '*boa aparência* (decently presentable)' means [in a job advertisement]? It means you must be white."[7]

A few years later, anti-black racism would be brought to my attention again when I travelled to North Africa to further my studies in Islamic education after graduation from Kingston University in 2006. During my time in Cairo, Egypt, I was shocked by the mockery of blackness which I witnessed, especially considering the fact that Egyptians are Africans and many of its peoples are brown or dark in complexion. The events in Egypt, along with the inferiority complex I noticed that some Muslims of dark complexion had begun to develop, was the catalyst for me to write my first book, *Illuminating the Darkness: Blacks and North Africans in Islam*. In the book I wanted to address some misconceptions about blackness, from an Islamic perspective.

MEETING THE SULTAN OF SOKOTO IN NORTHERN NIGERIA

In February 2013, after my book's launch event in Lagos, Nigeria, I was invited to meet the Sultan of Sokoto, Muhammadu Sa'adu Abubakar III[8] at his palace in the state of Kaduna in north-western Nigeria. During the meeting with the man who is the spiritual leader of Nigeria's 74.5 million Muslims, he told me that he was impressed with my book and that he would like me to write more about the history of West African Muslims. Mansa Kankan Mūsā of Mali, the city of Timbuktu and the Sultan's own great grandfather Uthman dan Fodio were some of the topics we spoke about as potential subjects. The Sultan gave me an open invitation to Sokoto to carry out research on manuscripts there.

In addition to education, we spoke about the importance of financial empowerment for Africans after he heard how I self-funded my trip to Nigeria. The Sultan was particularly impressed by this which seemed to earn his respect. I was also fortunate enough to meet Abubakar ibn Umar Garbai el-Kanemi, the *Shehu* (traditional ruler) of the Borno Emirate, along with other traditional Nigerian rulers at the Sultan's palace.

---

was later released in 2007. The TV series and film touch upon the issue of racism in Brazil where, "If you're black and you're poor, you have to paint yourself white."
7 The phrase '*boa aparência*' can also refer to "an exuberant morena (light brown complexioned woman) with long hair and fine features." Caldwell, 2007, p. 67
8 Sa'adu Abubakar III's great grandfather is the revered Muslim reformer of the nineteenth century, Uthman dan Fodio.

Preface

Whilst in Nigeria, I was also asked repeatedly by well-wishers if I was going to write another book about Yoruba Muslims as they did not feature in my first book. It was then that I started to think seriously about writing a book about Yoruba Muslims in nineteenth-century Brazil. I had already planned to visit Brazil in the following year for a holiday, but at the time I was undecided about whether I would write another book.

TRIPS TO BRAZIL

When I travelled to Brazil for the first time in February 2014, the first city I visited was Rio de Janeiro. Whilst there during the *Carnaval* (Carnival), I was struck by the striking similarities between black *cariocas* (residents of Rio) and Yorubas from Nigeria; culturally, physically and in terms of religious devotion. The African influence in Brazil is undeniable; unfortunately so is the clear colour hierarchy in the country where I witnessed firsthand the perceived inferiority of blackness and discrimination against blacks which still exists in Brazil's ethnically diverse society. I was also informed by some Brazilians of a sinister effort by some people in the country's educational system and commercial world to undermine the achievements of black Brazilians in history. Denigration of blackness normally started at an early stage in the educational system, as political scientist Michael Hanchard notes:

> From the first years of formal education, blacks are confronted by a panoply of images and representations of themselves, which can only be characterized as negative. Numerous studies of children's primary textbooks depict blacks as more sexually promiscuous and aggressive, intellectually inferior to whites, and rarely in positions of power. Specifically, black males are often represented as brawny types, long on stamina and physical strength and short on intellect. Black women are portrayed as a form of "superwoman," an image found in evocations of women of African descent throughout the Western literature.[9]

A chance meeting I had with a stunning bronze-complexioned lady from Salvador, called Tamires, in Ipanema beach fuelled my desire to learn more about Brazil's African Muslim heritage. Fluent in English, she spoke at length about the socio-economic plight of black Brazilians and Brazilian history, in which she repeatedly recommended me to visit Salvador. She later remarked that she actually thought that I was

---

9 Hanchard, 1994, p. 60

from Salvador because of my Yoruba facial features, such is the strong resemblance of the people of Salvador and the Yoruba people. I was also slightly embarrassed somewhat when this beautiful and also intelligent woman spoke Yoruba to me which I did not understand fully and she then went about explaining the origin of these words. I must say, I was extremely impressed by her and felt a need to learn more about the history of Brazil's African Muslims.

Thus, after much thought and discussion I finally decided to write a follow-up book to *Illuminating the Darkness* which I entitled *Illuminating the Blackness: Blacks and African Muslims in Brazil*.[10]

When I travelled to Brazil for a second time, I journeyed to the city of Salvador in the northeast state of Bahia and the city of São Paulo. During my visit to Salvador, at times I felt as if I was in Nigeria. Some of the Bahian cuisine and a number of the customs are from West Africa. Many Bahians informed me that they were proud *negros/negras* (black) and are connected to their African history. Many *morenos/morenas*, (brown, mixed-race) Brazilians who phenotypically were European- or Asian-looking, even spoke with fondness of their African roots. Bahia is truly an amazing city, especially for an African, as you will see beautiful black women proudly rocking their natural hair, hear African-inspired Brazilian music, and experience wonderful hospitality accompanied with pleasant smiles. Although I was aware that my experience was due to the privilege of coming from Britain and that some people were probably cordial to me for commercial reasons, I can say that I never felt threatened or in danger even when I visited some of the *favelas* and impoverished areas. Perhaps this was because I was able to blend in as I dressed casually like a local without wearing the jewellery and branded fashion clothes that I sometimes wear. To fit it as a black person in Brazil, particularly in Bahia, is very easy and a comfortable experience for me. Strange to say, even though I did not at the time understand the language, I felt more at home in Bahia than in most places in London, where I was born and bred. Oftentimes it wasn't until I spoke that people knew that I was a *gringo* (foreigner). As I wanted to find out more about the country from the perspective of black Brazilians who were fluent in English, I headed for the cosmopolitan city of São Paulo to visit a female friend that I had met in Rio and also to visit the Afro-Brazil Museum in São Paulo.

At the museum I met Thiago, an employee of the Afro-Brazil Museum in São Paulo who spoke fluent English and his colleague, Mirella, both

---

10 The book's subtitle 'Blacks and African Muslims in Brazil' refers to Brazil's *negros/pretos* (dark-skinned 'blacks') and *mulatto/moreno/pardo* (brown-skinned 'blacks.')

Afro-Brazilians who were committed to black activism in Brazil. They informed me that Brazil's African Muslim heritage is often underplayed or completely excluded from the educational system and that many Brazilian abolitionists of African ancestry are depicted as white in paintings and television commercials. As Thiago and Mirella gave me a personal guided tour of the museum, I saw paintings of Castro Alves (d. 1871) and Machado de Assis (d. 1908), two great historic Afro-Brazilian figures in the abolition movement, who were portrayed as white men with European phenotypes.

I was also informed by Thiago of a recent commercial for the Brazilian bank *Caixa Econômica Federal*, in which de Assis was depicted as a white man, which caused outrage amongst Brazil's black community.[11] After protests, the commercial was removed with the bank issuing a statement, "The bank apologises to the entire population and, in particular, movements linked to racial causes for not having characterised the writer [de Assis], who was Afro-Brazilian, with someone of the same racial origin."[12] This attempt to whiten de Assis and erase blacks from history is not the first in Brazil and will probably not be the last. The change brought about by those who protested demonstrates the importance of resisting white appropriation of black culture and history.[13]

---

11 http://exame.abril.com.br/marketing/noticias/caixa-se-explica-apos-branquear-machado-de-assis-em-comercial

12 http://g1.globo.com/economia/negocios/noticia/2011/09/caixa-tira-do-ar-progaganda-que-mostra-machado-de-assis-branco.html

13 "To appropriate" means to take (something) for one's own, typically with the owner's permission. White appropriation generally refers to black culture, music and religion being used by whites for their own financial gain or pleasure with little regard for blacks. What was previously known as 'black music or culture' eventually becomes 'white music or culture.' Rock 'n' Roll is an example of such an appropriation, and the same is being said about Hip-Hop. The more commercially successful something whose cultural origins lie among black people, the whiter it will be projected in the commercial world.

A recent example of "white appropriation" in Brazil can be seen with the public criticism of a Brazilian advertising agency called *Africa*. According to the company's website the name "the name Africa has been chosen to be understood internationally and also to pay homage to people who lent its culture to Brazil." Interestingly there aren't any black or Afro-Brazilians of the 32 people featured on the website who manage the advertising agency. The agency has been accused of appropriating itself in the name of the black continent as an identity for itself but there hardly any black staff in its publicity photographs.

ILLUMINATING THE BLACKNESS

During my final trip to Brazil in November 2015 - the month of black consciousness in Brazil, I went to the cities of Rio de Janeiro, São Paulo and Salvador again. Whilst in Salvador, a popular *pagode*[14] singer, Max Wianna, accompanied me whilst I interviewed a number of Afro-Brazilians to gain an insight into their perspectives of blackness and being black in Brazil. I spoke at length with a number of self-identified "*negroes*" and "*morenas*," including academics, university students, entertainers, models, *capoeiristas* and activists about what it is like to be black in Brazil.

What was encouraging in Salvador was the racial pride of the black and mixed-race Brazilians that I encountered. Many self-identified as *negro/negra* (black) and were active in promoting a positive image of black beauty, which they acknowledged is not present on Brazilian television. Walking in the streets of Salvador and speaking to Brazilians of various hues, I was pleasantly surprised by the interest they showed in learning about their African-Muslim ancestry, when I mentioned the topic of the book I was researching. Although many were not aware of the contribution of the African Muslims in 19th century Brazil, they expressed an eagerness to know more about this untold history. It was also nice to see confident Afro-Brazilian women of various hues and hair textures, who embraced their blackness and took pride in the beauty of their God-given African features.

PERCEPTIONS AND MISCONCEPTIONS OF BRAZILIAN WOMEN

For many men the primary reason why they are intrigued and interested in Brazil is because of the women. Brazilian women are widely known for their beauty, sensuality, exoticness and femininity. Whilst there is obviously more to Brazil than its women, the allure of Brazilian women captivates the imagination of a number of heterosexual men when Brazil is brought up. Whilst Brazilian women are unquestionably very attractive and held in high esteem, they are also perceived by many in a negative light due to their affectionate behaviour and attitudes towards sexuality.

In regards to female sexuality, it can be argued that there are two Brazils when it comes to Brazilian women: those who are sexually very liberal and those who are very conservative. Of course this not to say that every Brazilian woman falls into one of these two categories, as many are clearly somewhere in between. Nevertheless it is interesting

---

14 Pagode is a Brazilian style of music which is a sub-genre of samba.

to see women who are very open about their sexuality and women who are somewhat traditional living side by side one another in this tolerant country.

Many westerners have an inaccurate perception of Brazil being a land filled with beautiful half-naked women ready to fulfil the every needs of a male suitor. In many cases, foreign tourists who have had a lot of "success" with women in Brazil have actually paid to receive sexual favours. Brazilian women who dress half-naked at the beach for example are not all promiscuous as some foreigners mistakenly believe. Clothing is not a determining factor of a woman's sexuality in Brazil or anywhere else in the world.

Whilst I can't deny that some of the most beautiful women you will ever see reside in Brazil, the perception that is held by many outside of the country that all Brazilian women are easy and promiscuous is false. Despite their exceptional beauty, many Brazilian women are surprisingly very humble and uphold traditional values in regards to gender roles and sexuality. Something which I do find interesting is the halo effect that Brazilian women seem to have upon men who have never been to Brazil or spent a considerable amount of time with a Brazilian woman. Women are women at the end of the day and Brazilian women are no different to other women in that respect. That being said, Brazilian women seem to conjure up either a very positive or negative perception from outsiders. This was something which I noticed bothered many Brazilian women themselves whom I came across.

The misrepresentation of Brazilian women was an issue which regularly came up in conversations I had with a number of locals whilst in Rio, Salvador and São Paulo. They told me of countless stories of foreign men coming to Brazil expecting easy sex and showing such contempt for the women as if they could buy their sexual favours. Unfortunately, many of these women, who were Afro-Brazilian and from poor backgrounds, felt that their bodies were the only commodities that were of value in the eyes of the *gringos*.

Sexual Tourism

Sadly sexual tourism is rampant in several parts of Brazil, particularly in poorer areas where brown and black women are often targeted for sexual exploitation.[15] The country's erotic reputation, beautiful women and sexual freedom has long been attracting sex tourists, many of whom share

---

15 Sexual tourism is travel to engage in sexual activity, particularly with prostitutes.

similar characteristics to sex offenders and rapists.[16] The issue of sexual tourism in Brazil was explored in the 2009 documentary *Cinderelas, Lobos e um Príncipe Encantado* (Cinderellas, Wolves and a Prince Charming). Although not the focus of the documentary, the filmmaker Joel Zito Araújo noted that "75% of the object of desire of foreign tourists are *afrodescendentes* (African descendants) women".

Carnival

During the Carnival, sexual tourism and sexuality in Brazil goes into overdrive with excessive drinking of alcohol and casual sexual relations, mainly amongst young people. There are also some strange practices which take place during the Carnival such as that it is considered customary for men to kiss random women on the lips, even at times against their will. The widespread public kissing which often takes place between complete strangers during the Carnival, has also contributed to the perception of Brazilian women being promiscuous. In addition the large number of prostitutes working the streets has also contributed to the notion that Brazilian women lack sexual restraint. Whilst experiencing the lively Carnival in the streets, it was also noticeable the great number of men who would resort to strange and sexually aggressive tactics to gain the attention of women rather than approaching them like ladies.

Some of these tactics include cat calling, grabbing women by force and wearing sexually controversial costumes to gain female attention.

---

16 Men who pay for sex share similar traits to rapists and sex offenders, according to new research from the University of California, Los Angeles (UCLA). The online study published online August 31 2015 in the *Journal of Interpersonal Violence* claims that men who have sex with female sex workers feel less empathy for them than men who do not buy sex. Part of this reason is due to the fact that they view them as "intrinsically different from other women," according to the authors of the study. The study also reported that men who buy sex are more likely themselves, to have raped or committed violent sex acts against women. The "key characteristics" that men who buy sex and men who commit acts of sexual violence shared were: "a preference for impersonal sex, a fear of rejection by women, a history of having committed sexually aggressive acts and a hostile masculine self-identification," according to the study's co-author and UCLA professor Neil Malamuth. The study's lead author and executive director of Prostitution Research and Education, Melissa Farley said, "We hope this research will lead to a rejection of the myth that sex buyers are simply sexually frustrated nice guys." http://newsroom.ucla.edu/releases/men-who-buy-sex-have-much-in-common-with-sexually-coercive-men

Preface

It is very common for men, both heterosexual and homosexual men, to dress in drag, and to even wear body suits with exaggerated female anatomy. Women, on the other hand, are expected to dress in traditional female clothing, and commonly in revealing outfits or swimsuits. Unfortunately sexual harassment of women, both verbal and physical is a frequent occurrence during this festive period. In fact, many *cariocas* (residents of Rio) leave the city for two weeks in order to escape the chaos that comes with the Carnival.

The Carnival does provide an interesting insight into Brazilian culture and female sexuality. Although some of the popular practices such as cross-dressing by heterosexual men to gain women's favours, which I witnessed were incomprehensible to me, they were similarly shared by many other Brazilians as demonstrated by a conversation I had with an elderly woman whilst waiting for a taxi at my hotel near the *bloco* (street party). She bluntly told me, "Do not think all Brazilian women are like this! People go crazy just for the Carnival!" Many Brazilian women are in fact very religious with a strong faith in God and are virtuous in their sexual conduct. Although Brazil is a very liberal and tolerant country with regards to sexuality, conservative attitudes are still maintained by many people, especially in regards to women where they are expected to be monogamous and uphold traditional gender roles.

FINAL THOUGHTS ON BEING BLACK AND MUSLIM IN BRAZIL

One thing I have noticed about black people is that we love and accept other races and cultures before we love and accept our own. We love anything and everything that is not black and non-African. Anything that reminds us of our African ancestry is perceived to be inferior and shameful. Our physical features, our culture and our history. Sadly, we as black people have a deep inferiority complex which many of us do not want to admit but it is something which runs deep in our consciousness. As a Muslim of West African descent, I considered myself to be Muslim first and foremost, but my blackness and African heritage is part of my identity and it is not something I believe I should feel ashamed about as so many black and brown Muslims of African descent unfortunately do. I do not consider black people to be a superior race, nor do I consider black people to be an inferior race. We have our differences and unique qualities but ultimately we are all part of the one race – the human race. Our differences should be embraced and celebrated. After all didn't Allah say in the Qur'an,

> "*Mankind! We created you from a male and female, and made you into peoples and tribes so that you might come to know each other. The noblest among you in Allah's sight is the one with the most* taqwā. *Allah is All-Knowing, All-Aware*"[17]

As more people become conscious of the issue of blackness and the religion of Islam, I hope this book will be a useful source for those interested in learning about Afro-Brazilian and Muslim history. In this age, in which we are constantly reminded that Europe is the pinnacle of civilisation and that all great ideas and people of stature originate there, it is only natural that non-European peoples will rarely look to their own histories expecting greatness. Thus, it is imperative for people of African descent to learn their history in order not to develop inferiority complexes and feel as though they need to look outside their religious and cultural traditions for inspiration.

Europeans and their descendants in the Americas have done a phenomenal job in mentally enslaving non-white peoples, particularly those of African descent. Whether you look at North America, the Caribbean, South America or even Africa, black and mixed-race people of African descent aspire to whiteness and to renounce their Africanness. In Brazil, this is most certainly the case and has been for decades, but there has been pushback among Brazil's black and mixed-race community who are embracing their blackness and their African heritage.

It is also important for people of African descent and Brazilian Muslims to establish their own educational institutions, businesses and media platforms so that they can project positive depictions of themselves, rather than having someone else dictate who and what is black and beautiful, as well as highlighting the great contribution Muslims have made and are continuing to make to Brazil.

The heroic battles of former slave warriors for free black communities in 19th century Brazil is often untold in Brazil's education system. Instead European colonisers and immigrants are venerated for their role in shaping Brazilian culture. This book will present how African culture came to shape Brazilian culture, in its language, music, food and religious customs. In addition, it will depict how Afro-Brazilian culture in turn impacted West African communities following the return of former slaves to their lands of origin.

I ask Allah that this book will be beneficial for many years to come, even when I leave this world, and that by it I may earn His grace as the

---

17 Qur'an 49:13. *Taqwā* is piety and the fearful awareness of Allah.

Preface

Prophet Muḥammad ﷺ said, "When a man passes away, his good deeds will also come to an end except for three: *ṣadaqah jāriyah* (a perpetual charity), knowledge which is beneficial, or a virtuous descendant who prays for him."[18]

TWENTY FACTS ABOUT BRAZIL THAT MANY PEOPLE DO NOT KNOW

1. North and West African Muslims travelled to Brazil hundreds of years before the Portuguese 'discovered' the country.
2. Ten times as many black Africans were transported to Brazil than to the United States during the transatlantic slave era.
3. In the 19th century, an estimated 30% of the West Africans (mainly Yoruba and Hausa) transported to Brazil were Muslims.
4. The country's racial mixture is built upon white Portuguese men fathering children with black African and indigenous women during the slave period, often times by coercion.
5. Runaway African slaves created an independent *quilombo* (maroon society) community in Palmares that endured for almost a hundred years.
6. In Bahia and Rio de Janeiro, unlike their Portuguese colonisers, African Muslims were literate and established Qur'ānic schools known as *madrasas*.
7. Between 1807 and 1835, African Muslims, men and women, in Bahia took part in and led a series of slave revolts, which contributed towards the abolition of slavery in 1888.
8. After the revolts, many African Muslims bought their freedom and travelled back to Africa to live out their lives as Muslims.
9. Afro-Brazilians Muslims who travelled back to West Africa built mosques that are still standing today.
10. After the abolition of slavery in 1888, Brazil's white elite wanted to eradicate the country's black population by encouraging mass immigration of white Europeans and Asians to the country. This official government policy is known as 'whitening', in which the government encouraged its white population to have children with blacks in order to decrease the country's black population.
11. Today over half of Brazil's population identify themselves as black or mixed-race, making it the second largest "black" population in the world after Nigeria.

---

18 Related by Muslim ibn al-Ḥajjāj in an authentic prophetic tradition.

12. Anti-black racism still exists in Brazil despite the country's large mixed population and the presentation of the country as a "racial democracy."
13. Racism is subtle in Brazil towards Afro-Brazilians, particularly those who are dark skinned.
14. Brazilians describe themselves by skin colour not race or ethnicity.
15. Colourism is arguably more of an issue than racism in Brazil as most Brazilians are mixed-race but Brazilian society still favours whiteness and European features.
16. Brazil's white elite continue to dominate the greater part of the country's resources and wealth, whilst most prisoners in Brazil are black or mixed-race.
17. Brazil's university lecturers and students are overwhelmingly white even in predominantly black states such as Bahia.
18. Yoruba influence in Bahia remains strong in the state's cuisine (*acarje*), music (Olodum), religion (*Candomblé*) and culture (*Ilê Aiyê*).
19. The black-consciousness movement in Brazil, in which activists embrace their blackness and history, has been growing since the 1970s. African-Americans were influential in reawakening the Brazilian black-consciousness movement.
20. Islam has been growing in Brazil since the 1990s, particularly amongst Brazilians of African descent, whose first contact with Islam was through African-American Muslim activists and hip-hop music.

INTRODUCTION

"There is a history of black people without Brazil but there is no history of Brazil without black people."

JANUÁRIOS GARCIA

TO THE PORTUGUESE elite in nineteenth century Brazil, Islam and blackness were a dangerous combination.[19] They felt threatened by the presence of African Muslim slaves due to their strong faith, literacy and experience in military warfare in their homeland. Inspired by Qur'ānic injunctions to fight oppression and by the Haitian slave revolt, a group of West African Yoruba Muslims unified multi-ethnic African Muslims, under the banner of Islam, and unified non-Muslim Africans, under the banner of their tribal affiliations, to lead a revolt in Bahia in 1835. Though unsuccessful, the revolt led to the abolition of slavery in 1888, which, however, resulted in the exclusion of black and mixed-race Brazilians from participation in the nation's wealth and resources. Today, in their modern-day struggle against anti-black racism and white supremacy, many black Brazilian activists draw inspiration from the courage of the African Muslims warriors who valiantly fought for their freedom in nineteenth century Brazil.[20] In a country as ethnically mixed as Brazil, white remains the colour of aspiration and success, whilst black continues to be the colour of poverty and a history that some would prefer to forget. This book examines that history.

Illuminating the Blackness presents the history of Brazil's race-relations and African Muslim heritage. The book is divided into two parts. Part I explores the issue of race, anti-black racism, white supremacy, colourism,

---

19 Gomez, 2005, p. 40; Aidi, 2014, p. 27
20 Brazilian black activist groups Posse Hausa and *Ilê Aiyê* (meaning 'House of Life' in Yoruba) draws inspiration from Brazil's "black slave revolts which strongly contributed to the process of ethnic identity and [raising] the self-esteem of blacks."

black beauty and affirmative action in contemporary Brazil. Part II examines the reports of African Muslims' travels to Brazil before the Portuguese colonisers, slave military revolts in Bahia and West African Muslim communities in nineteenth century Brazil. The historical significance of the slave revolts remains an important spiritual inspiration and a rallying point for what is regarded as black identity in Brazil.

Today, Brazil is the largest and most populous country in South America. Its diverse population includes more persons of African descent than any country except Nigeria, though many Afro-Brazilians are marginalised in Brazilian society. Black activists in Brazil are campaigning to reawaken the nation's black consciousness by taking pride in African religion, culture and aesthetics. The government of Brazil is also trying to address the nation's socio-economic imbalance between whites and non-whites by enacting affirmative action laws with the intention of promoting racial equality. In 2012, Brazilian President Dilma Rousseff signed *Lei de Cotas Sociais* (The Law of Social Quotas) which requires public universities to reserve half of their admission spots for Brazilian public school students, who are primarily of African descent and poor. The quota system is intended to increase the number of students of African descent from 8,700 to 56,000 within ten years, after which the racial quota system will be discontinued. Other government initiatives were also introduced to address the legacy of slavery that has influenced and shaped current-day race-relations in Brazil, where whites control the vast majority of the nation's wealth and resources.

Although much has been written by anthropologists, historians and sociologists alike regarding Brazil's racist history, the contribution and perspectives of African-Muslims in Brazil is often overlooked, as is that of the religion of Islam. The exploits of the Hausa and Yoruba Muslims in the 1814 and 1835 slave revolts of Bahia remind us that Islam played a crucial role in unifying multi-ethnic African Muslims and was seen as a form of resistance amongst non-Muslim African slaves in their struggle against the racial and religious oppression they had suffered at the hands of the Portuguese. Many within the *Movimento Negro* (Black Movement) of Brazil draw inspiration from the courage of African Muslims who fought for their freedom.

In order to understand modern day race-relations in Brazil it is important to gain an understanding of its early history during which indigenous and black Africans were enslaved by the Portuguese.

Since time immemorial slavery has existed, but not to the extent nor with the appalling conditions with which Europeans carried out

Introduction

during the transatlantic slave trade between the sixteenth and nineteenth centuries. During this period, an estimated four million Africans were transported to Brazil by Europeans.[21] Brazil received approximately ten times more slaves than the United States of America.

The slavery of African peoples in the Americas was a destructive process of oppression and dehumanisation. Many people are aware of the enslavement of African peoples in the United States, but little is known about the massive and brutal enslavement of Africans in South American countries such as Brazil. Although slavery in the United States was brutal, it was even worse in Brazil, where the Portuguese treated African slaves barbarically for over three hundred years. In comparison to Brazil, Africans and their descendants were better treated in the United States, because the Portuguese were able to obtain new slaves easily and cheaply, since Brazil was considerably closer to Africa than North America was. The Portuguese would work slaves to death and then pick up more slaves in West and Central Africa. Slave labour was free labour and it was the foundation on which Brazil's modern-day society is built.

Though many Brazilians do not like to admit this historical fact, as historian and expert on Brazilian slavery, João José Reis said, "slavery is an inconvenient history for the Brazilian elite," who try to portray an image of racial harmony. Despite the government's attempts, when it comes to the issue of race, it can be argued that Brazil has not been able to move forward because it has yet to fully acknowledge its shameful history. The more than four centuries of barbaric treatment by Portuguese colonisers towards African and Amerindian[22] slaves have ramifications even today. The large wealth disparity that currently exists between Brazil's whites and non-whites is largely due to the country's horrific past. Brazil owes a debt to its black and mixed-race population, whose ancestors built the country with their free labour.

---

21 Former West African slave (in modern day Nigeria) and writer Olaudah Equiano (d. 1797) published *The Interesting Narrative of the Life of Olaudah Equiano or Gustavus Vasa, the African* in 1789. In the book, Equiano described how the experience of slavery differed in West Africa and the Americas and how slaves were treated more humanely in Africa, where they were considered to be like an extended family member. In contrast, the treatment of slaves, which he witnessed first-hand and experienced at the hands of the white Europeans in America was brutal and vicious. He was himself beaten and witnessed European slave owners' rape of African women, acts he had not seen whilst a slave in West Africa.

22 Amerinidians are the indigenous peoples of the Americas, commonly known as American Indians or Native Americans.

BRAZIL'S ENSLAVEMENT OF BLACK AFRICANS

The Portuguese first landed on Brazilian shores in 1500, and, after creating *engenhos* (sugar plantations) in the country's northeastern region, they went about trying to establish an economy. Initially they enslaved the native population to provide the work-force necessary for labour-intensive sugar crops. But the enslaved indigenous population was soon decimated by wars and European diseases. Some of the natives fled to the interior of the country to escape the Portuguese for whom it was unnavigable. The Portuguese then turned to Africa as an alternative source of labour to build their economy.

In 1538, the first group of African slaves were herded ashore in northeastern Brazil. The decision to exploit imported and unpaid black labour had partly been in response to the Papal Bull of 1537, which forbade the enslavement of indigenous Brazilians, and partly because the African's more robust constitution, greater immunity to 'white man's diseases' and their being accustomed to hard, physical work in a tropical environment made them potentially more suitable as slaves than the natives.[23]

From the 1580s, with the expansion of the sugar industry, the importation of Africans to Brazil increased dramatically. A century later, the discovery of gold in Minas Gerais further increased the demand for slave labour. The economy then shifted to mining and cattle raising in the eighteenth century and finally to coffee growing in the nineteenth century. In the seventeenth and eighteenth centuries, the vast majority of slaves were imported from Angola.[24] The influx of slaves from Angola was so great in numbers that the African country remained virtually depopulated for a generation. The Brazilian slave trade, which spanned from the mid-1500s to the 1850s, brought approximately four million enslaved Africans to the Portuguese territories in South America that were to become, after 1822, independent Brazil.[25] By 1800, a demographic survey revealed that *gente de cor* (people of colour) constituted over two-thirds of the population, twenty per-cent of whom were slaves.[26] The majority of the population were of African origin.

Although Central Africa contributed more than three-quarters of the slaves in the beginning of the nineteenth century, the slave trade from

---

23 See John Geipel's *Brazil's African Legacy*
24 See John Geipel's *Brazil's African Legacy*
25 Reis and Mamigoniam, "Nagô and Mina: The Yoruba Diaspora in Brazil" in *The Yoruba Diaspora in the Atlantic World*, p. 77
26 See John Geipel's *Brazil's African Legacy*

Introduction

West Africa constituted an important part of the total. While most slave trading was conducted from ports in and around the Portuguese colony of Angola, in the eighteenth century merchants in Bahia established trade directly with the Bight of Benin, which would change the population profile in the colony.[27]

At the turn of the nineteenth century, Bahia's export economy was booming. The number of *engenhos* (sugar plantations) expanded significantly, followed by an intensification of the African slave trade to the region.[28] The sugar trade then diminished and, although slaves were distributed among other parts of Brazil, many slaves remained in Bahia and worked in the capital, Salvador. In the 1690s, gold was found in Minas Gerais, tripling the demand for slaves; of the estimated 1.7 million slaves brought to Brazil in the late 17th and early 18th century, almost a million went to the gold and diamond mines.

By 1760, the slowdown in gold and diamond mining coincided with sugar's second wind, causing a renewed influx of African slaves to the northeast of Brazil. In the 1830s, coffee came to prominence in southern Brazil, and 1.3 million slaves eventually made their way to the coffee plantations. Slaves were also sent to major cities and, by the late 18th century, 40-50% of households in São Paulo, Ouro Preto (in the state of Minas Gerais and Salvador) owned slaves.

Over the centuries, Portugal exploited different parts of Africa. In the 16th century, Senegambia provided most of Brazil's slaves; in the 17th century, Angola and the Congo rose to dominance; and in the 18th century, slaves were coming from the Mina Coast[29] and Benin. "Without Angola no slaves, without slaves no sugar, without sugar no Brazil" was a common expression during the 17th century. During the last fifty years of the slave trade, large numbers of Yoruba people were brought to the

---

27 Reis and Mamigoniam, "Nagô and Mina: The Yoruba Diaspora in Brazil" in *The Yoruba Diaspora in the Atlantic World*, p. 77
28 Reis and Mamigoniam, "Nagô and Mina: The Yoruba Diaspora in Brazil" in *The Yoruba Diaspora in the Atlantic World*, p. 80
29 The term 'Mina' has often been considered to be a port and not an ethnic designation by historians. They have widely assumed that Africans listed as Mina were brought from the Gold Coast via the slave trade post of San Jorge de Mina (commonly referred to as Elmina), or that they were Gold Coast slaves living near this port but perhaps exported from another port. However in Latin America, the term Mina was normally used as an ethnic designation and not a port. The Mina Coast used by Brazilians refers to the coast east of Elmina, and most especially the Bight of Benin or the Slave Coast east of the Volta River.

northeastern region of Brazil, making a lasting impact on the culture of that region.

When Brazil gained independence in 1822, slavery was such an entrenched part of the economy that the elites who structured the new nation never seriously debated the issue. Brazilians believed that the prosperity of their country depended on the institution of slavery, since they so desperately needed the labour, but slavery was rarely defended on racial grounds.

Contrary to popular belief, slaves in the United States were better housed, clothed and fed than they were in Brazil. As the voyage from Brazil to Africa was shorter than from the United States, Portuguese plantation owners in Brazil could import African slaves easily and cheaply. For the Portuguese, slavery meant enormous wealth. This being the case, it was more beneficial for the Portuguese to replace slaves than to maintain them. Thus the average slave had a shorter life-span in Brazil due to the demanding work they had to do to satisfy the world's growing demand for sugar.[30] Life expectancy in Brazil for newly arrived slaves was a mere six or seven years, and, on average, slaves born in Brazil lived only into their early twenties.[31]

White Europeans later devised racist theories to justify their brutal treatment of black Africans. These theories about the inferiority of blacks and their African culture are perpetuated by some white Brazilians today, though often disguised in the form of modern-day capitalism. Europeans' enslavement of millions of black Africans was motivated by monetary greed and lust for power. Like other non-white Europeans, black Africans were seen as items of trade to enrich the wealth of whites. More than anything else, the trans-Atlantic slave trade was an economic enterprise but one which the Europeans needed to justify, since the enslavement of people had never been done on such a scale before with such horrendous and inhuman treatment.

Trafficking in slaves was at its most intense between 1825 and 1850, amounting to 32% of the total number of Africans imported into Brazil since the start of the transatlantic slave trade. The majority of slaves imported during this period were from the Bight of Benin, in modern day Benin and Nigeria. According to historian John Giepel, "it was these comparative latecomers who were to leave their indelible imprint on the culture of their new home."[32] A large number of these

---

30 See Henry Gates, Jr.'s *Black in Latin America*
31 See *Brazil: An Inconvenient History*, 2010, BBC
32 See John Geipel's *Brazil's African Legacy*

'latecomers' were imported West-African slaves of Hausa and Yoruba origin. Predominately Muslims, they were literate and well-versed in the Qur'ān. The Hausa were esteemed as house slaves for their courteous manners, and they were intellectually superior to many of their illiterate Portuguese masters. Many Hausas were erudite and taught the tenets of Islam to other Muslims in secret Islamic schools.

Although there are no official records of the number of African Muslims transported to Brazil, some researchers believe that "several thousands" Muslims were brought to the Americas, while others, such as Raimundo Nina Rodrigues, believe that 30% of Africans enslaved in Bahia were Muslims. Some slave masters appointed their Muslim slaves as drivers and farm managers, or placed them in other positions of trust. They believed, as did many West African European colonial administrators, that African Muslims were more trustworthy and intelligent than other African people.[33] Other masters were afraid that Muslim slaves would undermine the establishment, a fear that was not without grounds because African Muslim slaves had a reputation for rebelliousness.[34] In many cases, Islam became the catalyst for revolt and resistance in Brazil, particularly in the city of Salvador.[35]

Despite being numerically inferior to the non-Muslim Bantu and Yorubas, West African Muslims had the "greatest impact on the ultimate destiny of Brazil's slave population: for it was they who spearheaded the insurrections which punctuated the eighteenth and nineteenth centuries and accelerated the end of bondage," according to historian John Geipel.[36]

In 1850, due to pressure from the British government, the Brazilian government abolished the traffic in African slaves. Britain had outlawed slavery in the British colonies in 1833, and rising labour costs in the colonies made it difficult to compete with the slave economies of countries like Brazil and Cuba. Beginning in the 1830s, Britain's Royal Navy began to intercept slave ships headed for Brazil in order to free enslaved Africans. While the British were not very successful at first, increased efforts between 1845 and 1850 allowed them to seize almost four hundred ships. Subsequently, Brazil was forced to close down the transatlantic slave trade.

The abolitionist movement in Brazil began to gain widespread support in the late 1860s, due in part to pressure from the outside world. After

---

33 Miller and Smith, *1988*, p. 371
34 Genovese, 1979, p 29
35 Junne, Jr., 1995, p. 19
36 See John Geipel's *Brazil's African Legacy*

the end of the slave trade in 1850, Brazil experienced a labour shortage because slavery had been sustained by continued imports of slaves rather than reproduction among the slave population. The slaves were also becoming harder to control, and slave owners feared revolts such as the major uprising of 1835.

A number of slave revolts took place in Bahia during the early decades of the nineteenth century, but the insurrection of 1835 is arguably the most famous. Primarily led by West-African Yoruba Muslims, they were referred to by the ethnonym 'Malê', which is from the Yoruba word *imale* meaning 'add knowledge' but which refers specifically to Muslims.[37] In Bahia during the 1830s, the word *Malê* was used to identify Muslims who were brought to the Bight of Benin in general but particularly Yoruba Muslims.[38] The 1835 revolt is often referred to as the *Revolta Malê* (*Malê* revolt) due to the significant role that Yorubas played in the armed struggle. Experienced in the art of warfare from their participation in *jihāds* and civil wars in Yorubaland, the Yoruba Muslims made use of their military skills and tactical nous to create havoc in Bahia's capital city of Salvador.[39] The uprising was well organised by highly-motivated Muslims, whose strong faith inspired their armed resistance. Involving both enslaved and freed Africans, the 1835 rebellion was the most formidable slave uprising in the history of Brazil.[40]

Although the 1835 uprising was ultimately quelled by the establishment, it left a lasting impression upon other African slaves and the Portuguese, which eventually led to the abolition of slavery in 1888, though a series of government reforms before then gradually emancipated slaves.[41]

---

37 I was informed by the Nigerian Muslim cleric of Salvador, Abdul Hameed Ahmad that the Yoruba word *imale* means 'add knowledge'. French sociologist Roger Bastide was of the opinion that the term *Malê* is a corruption of the country Mali. According to Bastide, the *malê* were Mandingas, though later scholars such as João José Reis disagreed and said that the word *Malê* is derived from the Yoruba word *imale* for a Muslim.

38 Cairus, 2014, p. 185

39 http://www.newsafrica.net/component/k2/item/213-58soul-legacy/213-58soul-legacy

40 Isfahani-Hammond, 2014, p. 163

41 Historian Paul E. Lovejoy argued that the experience of the Hausa and *Nagô* (Yoruba) slaves with religiously-inspired revolt and West African *jihād* prior to enslavement contributed to the rise of a slave rebellion culminating in the 1835 *Malê* revolt in Bahia. See Lovejoy, Paul, E., 'Background to Rebellion: The Origins of Muslim Slaves in Bahia', in *Slavery and Abolition*.

Introduction

In 1871, Brazil passed the *Lei do Ventre Livre* (Law of Free Birth), also known as the Rio Branco Law., which granted freedom at birth to every child born of a slave. Fourteen years later in 1885, the Sexagenarian Law (also known as the Saraiva-Cotegipe Law) was passed, which freed slaves who were over sixty years old. Average life expectancy for field slaves ranged from seven to fifteen years, and thirty-year old slaves were more of a liability for the slave owner than an asset. Thus, the sexagenarian law favoured slave owners rather than slaves, as a slave who was over sixty years old was barely productive, and by freeing them the slave owner was freed of responsibility for them.[42]

Finally, on 13th May 1888, Princess Isabel signed the 'Golden Law' that officially abolished slavery in Brazil, granting no compensation to slave owners. At the time, approximately 700,000 slaves out of a total population of about 15,000,000 were set free.[43] Though white abolitionists have been given the credit for the end of slavery, the slave revolts were influential, as an 1898 editorial in Brazilian newspaper *Rebate* stated:

> Had the slaves not fled en masse from the plantations, rebelling against their masters...Had 20,000 of them not fled to the famous *quilombo* [community] of Jabaquara, they might still be slaves today...Slavery ended because the slave didn't wish to be a slave any longer, because the slave rebelled against his master and the law that enslaved him...The May 13th [abolition] law was no more than the legal sanctioning, so that public authority wouldn't be discredited, of an act that had already been consummated by the mass revolt of the slaves.[44]

The myth that benevolent Christians were the sole reason for the abolition of slavery, attempts to exonerate Christians in general and the Catholic church in particular from being implicated in the violent racism upon which slavery was based during European colonial expansion. An examination of Catholic doctrine, however, quickly shows the true nature of the Church's attitudes toward black Africans.[45] In 1633, the famous Jesuit of Bahia, Antônio Vieira, sang the praises of black bondage in a sermon directed to the enslaved African people of Bahia:[46]

---

42 http://www.lac.ox.ac.uk/sites/sias/files/documents/Schwarcz47.pdf
43 http://www.britannica.com/EBchecked/topic/504187/Rio-Branco-Law
44 Andrews, 1994, p. 90
45 Nascimento, 1989, p. 67
46 Nascimento, 1989, p. 68

> You should give infinite thanks to God for giving you the knowledge of yourselves, and for having taken you away from your lands, where your parents and you lived as heathen, and having brought you to this one, where, instructed in the faith, you live as Christians and save yourselves.[47]

Vieira further counselled:

> Slaves, you are subjected and obedient in everything to your master, not only to the good and modest one, but also the bad and unjust ... because in this state in which God has put you, it is your vocation similar to that of his son, who died for us, leaving you the example that you must imitate.[48]

Although slavery came to an end, and blacks and mulattos were set free, many were excluded from the nation's wealth and resources. Today, Brazil is said to have the second largest black population in the world, and the country is portrayed as a 'racial democracy'.[49] Although the majority of people are of mixed ancestry, black and mixed-race Brazilians of African descent are still far more likely to be subject to racial discrimination and colour prejudice than white Brazilians of European and Asian ancestry. The legacy of slavery in modern Brazil consists in racial inequalities and disenfranchised blacks who are mostly poor and who are not as well educated as whites. Black activists argue that many non-white Brazilians are unaware of the complexities of the systemic racism which operates in Brazil. "We blacks need to become conscious of our situation, but Brazilian society needs to change too – in the way it looks at blacks, the way it treats blacks and the way it receives blacks in Brazilian society," said Maria de Lourdes of the *Unified Black Movement*. "We are the great excluded people – the great marginalised people."

In recent times as more Brazilians acknowledge their African heritage, there has been growing interest in tackling the taboo of racism in Brazil. This is in part due to the work of Afro-Brazilian groups in Bahia, who have preserved their African culture and distinctive identity just like their African ancestors, who fought for them during the slave revolts of the early nineteenth century. The *Malê* revolt in particular was not only instrumental in the abolition of slavery, but continues to serve as a

---

47 Vieira, 1969, pp. 23-24
48 Vieira, 1969, pp. 399-400
49 The 'black' population refers to the *preto* (black) and *pardo* (brown) population of Brazil.

Introduction

source of inspiration for black Brazilians today in their struggle against racism.

The *Malê* revolt may have been inspired by other great slave revolts in Latin America and the Muslim world, which the learned Yoruba and Hausa Muslims are likely to have been aware of, since they were voracious readers. Some of the rebellions which may have been a source of inspiration for African Muslims in Brazil were: the ninth century slave revolts in Baghdad, Iraq by East African Zanj Muslims; the Palmares revolts in northeastern Brazil in the seventeenth century, which led to the creation of an independent state with their inspirational leader Zumbi of Palmares; and the infamous Haitian-led slave revolts of the late eighteenth and early nineteenth centuries that culminated in the elimination of slavery there and the founding of the Republic of Haiti. In the African Diaspora, these revolts are considered a symbol of resistance in the struggle against white supremacy, racism and religious discrimination. The issue of anti-black racism, however, remains an issue that Brazil has long struggled to come to terms with.

BRAZIL'S DENIAL OF ANTI-BLACK RACISM AND WHITE SUPREMACY

Racism is a big problem in Brazil. Despite the rhetoric of racial democracy, it can be argued that racism is worse in Brazil than racism in the United States and South Africa. The fact that most Brazilians are mixed race does not exonerate Brazil from racism. The denial of racism is an issue Brazil must confront if it really wants to make any progress with its race problem. However before any discussion about racism and white supremacy, it is important to define what is meant by these terms and concepts.

Racism as defined by the Oxford dictionary is:

> The belief that all members of each race possess characteristics, abilities or qualities specific to that race, especially so as to distinguish it as inferior or superior to another race or races.[50]

Institutional racism as defined by the Macpherson Report is:

> The collective failure of an organisation to provide an appropriate and professional service to people because of their colour, culture, or ethnic origin. It can be seen or detected in processes, attitudes and behaviour which amount to discrimination through unwitting

---

50 Oxford Dictionary

prejudice, ignorance, thoughtlessness and racist stereotyping which disadvantage minority ethnic people.

According to A. Sivanandan, Director of the Institute of Race Relations:

> Institutional racism is that which, covertly or overtly, resides in the policies, procedures, operations and culture of public or private institutions – reinforcing individual prejudices and being reinforced by them in turn.

White supremacy or white supremacism is defined as:

> a form of racism centred upon the belief, and the promotion of the belief, that white people of European descent are superior in certain characteristics, traits and attributes to people of other racial/ethnic backgrounds. White supremacists believe that white people should politically, economically and socially rule non-whites.

The ideology of white supremacy stems from 'scientific' racism, which was developed by white European intellectuals in order to subjugate non-whites. White supremacy is a significant factor in the dominant power structure and system in many powerful nations today such as Brazil and the United States of America. H. R. Halderman, Richard Nixon's chief of staff, said:

> [President Nixon] emphasized that you have to face the fact that the whole problem is really the blacks. The key is a system that recognizes this while not appearing to.

Brazil's elite similarly had a 'negro problem' in the late nineteenth century. During slavery and afterwards, Brazil's elite set out a plan to whiten the population that was endorsed by 'scientific' racism theories. In the words of a leading Brazilian intellectual, Sílvio Romero, "My argument is that future victory in the life struggle among us will belong to the white race."[51] Paraense writer José Veríssimo (d. 1916) also commented:

> As ethnographers assure us, and as can be confirmed at first glance, race mixture is facilitating the prevalence of the superior race here. Sooner or later it will eliminate the black race. Here this obviously already is happening.[52]

---

51 Skidmore, 1974, p. 36; Nascimento, 1989, p. 60
52 Skidmore, 1974, p. 73

Introduction

Brazilian intellectuals, largely white, have often claimed that Brazil is able to solve its race problem by means of the physical and cultural mixing of the races. The notion of racial democracy that is central to modern day Brazil's national identity often obscures the social hierarchy that exists in the country, in which Brazilian whites disproportionately prosper.[53]

In a 1988 survey of attitudes to racism that was conducted in São Paulo, 97% of respondents claimed that they were not racist, while 98% of them claimed to know someone who was racist. In another survey conducted in São Paulo, the majority of respondents denied being victims of racial discrimination but said that they knew of friends and family members who had been discriminated against because of race. The results of the survey are interesting as they suggest that whilst Brazilians recognise that there is an issue with racism in their country, most people deny harbouring any prejudices or being victims of racial discrimination. The conclusion of the study was, "every Brazilian feels like an island of racial democracy surrounded on all sides by a sea of racists".[54]

In a more recent survey, 92% of respondents acknowledged that there is racism in the country but only 1.3% of respondents considered themselves to be racist. The research carried out by the Data Popular Institute reported that the majority of Brazilian adults have witnessed a white Brazilian refer to a black Brazilian as a *macaco* (monkey).[55]

The ombudsman of the Secretariat for the Promotion of Racial Equality, Carlos Alberto Júnior said about the cancer of racism in Brazil:

> Racism is a crime with no father and no mother. They say that it exists, but they don't admit that they are racist. People want to make out that this (racial democracy) is part of Brazilian culture, but it is a lie. It's a farce created and every day, we need to deconstruct it. It is important that society sees that citizenship and democracy will never be developed as long as we live with this type of crime.[56]

Brazilian sociologist Antonio Sérgio Alfredo Guimarães said about racism in Brazil:

---

53 Jones de Almeida, *2003, pp. 41-63*
54 http://www.lac.ox.ac.uk/sites/sias/files/documents/Schwarcz47.pdf
55 Monkey (*macaco*) is a racial slur directed at people of African descent, which stems from theories of scientistic racism and human evolution, even though the theory of evolution would logically apply the epithet to people of all races.
56 http://blackwomenofbrazil.co/2014/04/21/racist-who-me-92-of-brazilians-believe-racism-exists-but-only-1-3-consider-themselves-racist/

> Any study of racism in Brazil must begin by reflecting on the very fact that racism is a taboo subject in Brazil. Brazilians imagine themselves as inhabiting an anti-racist nation, a "racial democracy." This is one of the sources of their pride and, at the same time, conclusive proof of their status as a civilized nation.[57]

A former black Brazilian professional footballer spoke of the disingenuous of Brazil's media after reporting the racial abuse he received whilst playing in a football match in another South American country:

> In Brazil we talk about equality, but we hide our prejudice ... we pretend that everyone is equal.[58]

The footballer's comments reflect the feeling of many Brazilians of African descent who say that there is an issue of anti-black racism in the country, though many white Brazilians deny its existence. According to a popular Brazilian blog, *Black Women of Brazil*, "Brazil remains a country that is ruled by an obsession with *branquidade* (whiteness) and European supremacy which leads many Afro-Brazilian children (and later adults) to a lack of confidence, a profound shame of assuming racial identity, having no knowledge of self and thus identifying with white figures that often contribute to their sense of invisibility".[59] In regards to the responses that are usually given by Brazilians who deny the existence of racism, the blog cites the following:

> 1) Some Brazilians consistently claim that racism doesn't exist in Brazil (*"racismo não existe no Brasil"*) although studies over the past few decades show that this response is ridiculous.
> 2) Many Brazilians proclaim another slogan: "We are all equal (*Somos todos iguais*)", which really means that when a racist incident occurs, people believe that this type of behaviour shouldn't exist and that in some ways it is almost un-Brazilian.

---

57 Guimarães, Antonio Sérgio Alfredo, 1995, p. 208

58 Comments were made by Tinga, a former professional footballer for the Brazilian national football team.

59 A popular blog dedicated to Brazilian women of African descent, *Black Women of Brazil* addresses many of the misconceptions regarding stereotypical hyper-sexual Afro-Brazilian woman by showcasing Afro-Brazilian women in a variety of endeavours, from academia to modelling, politics to singing. The blog does an excellent job in chronicling the Afro-Brazilian perspective on racism in Brazil. Featuring articles from numerous sources, it is dedicated to raising awareness of the issue of racism and colourism in Brazil. http://blackwomenofbrazil.co/2014/11/28/november-is-the-month-of-black-consciousness-but-where-are-the-black-heroes-in-the-history-of-brazil/

Introduction

3) Many accept that racism does indeed exist but are comforted by believing that at least it is not as bad as in the United States.

4) Some scholars believe that American-styled racism is more blatant but that its counterpart in Brazil is more subtle.[60]

American professor Anthony B. Pinn asserts that the reason many Brazilians deny the existence of racism in Brazil is because, "racism is associated, in the Brazilian mind, with physical segregation as exemplified by the United States. Without this type of segregation currently present, Brazilians often overlook the presence of harmful racial attitudes."[61]

The racial mixture of Brazil's population is also cited as evidence for the non-existence of racism. The Portuguese had sexual relations with indigenous and black African women so how could they have been racist? Such polemics ignore the fact that Brazil's early miscegenation was often the result of rape and coercion. Even today, many white Brazilians deny the existence of racial discrimination because they themselves have had sexual relations with a black person. A white Brazilian woman who was caught on camera calling a black Brazilian footballer a *macaco* (monkey at a football match, denied any form of racism. Protesting her innocence when questioned, "I know I'm not racist, I've already been with a black guy."[62] Although the woman's words may sound absurd, it is not an unusual response from people who deny harbouring any racist sentiments. Many white people in Brazil who harbour such prejudices are oblivious to the issue because they have not personally experienced discrimination or because they lack education in the topic.

As Charles M. Mill puts it in his book *The Racial Contract*, denial of racism is all-pervasive amongst white Brazilians. In Brazil's colour-coded social hierarchy, whites are situated at the top and darker-skinned Brazilians are rooted at the bottom of Brazilian society. White supremacy is so engrained in the Brazilian subconscious that little attention is paid towards the existence of white privilege in Brazilian society.[63] It is important to note that the concept of white supremacy is not restricted

---

60 http://blackwomenofbrazil.co/2011/12/05/natural-black-hair-and-the-politics-of-good-appearance-in-brazil/n

61 http://digitalcommons.macalester.edu/cgi/viewcontent.cgi?article=1114&context=macintl

62 http://blackwomenofbrazil.co/2014/09/26/im-not-racist-ive-already-been-with-a-black-guy-the-privilege-of-white-racism-contradiction-of-black-pride-and-other-peculiarities-of-how-brazil-deals-with-race/

63 http://www.obv.org.uk/news-blogs/world-cup-brazil-2014-racial-divide-behind-beautiful-game

to white people alone; black people can also believe subconsciously in it. There are many black people in Brazil as in other parts of the world who believe in the supposed inferiority of blackness/Africanness and the superiority of whiteness/Europeanness. In an attempt to escape their blackness and Africanness, Afro-Brazilians who have 'white blood' are seen as superior, particularly if they are light-skinned and have European features. In Brazil, whether someone identifies themselves as black or not, the darker-skinned and more African-looking a person is, the more likely it is that they will be discriminated against, Brazilian historian João José Reis informed me during our discussion about Brazil's race problem.

One of seven children, Reis, would be considered 'white' in Brazil due to his fair complexion and straight hair, though he is actually mixed-raced. The son of a white father and light brown (*morena*) mother, Reis informed me of the complexities of racial identification in Brazil and how "racism is growing in Brazil" since President Lula introduced affirmative action policies to help address Brazil's social and economic inequalities. According to Reis, a number of white Brazilians are upset that blacks are not "staying in their place" due to the rise of black and mixed-raced students at universities and prominent positions in Brazilian society.

One thing which Reis did emphasis during our conversation was that Brazil's racial classification is very different to the United States model, which some African-Americans have found difficult to comprehend when trying to understand Brazil's race-relations. As most Brazilians are in fact mixed-raced, it can be argued that colourism is more of an issue than racism, as many fair skinned Brazilians who have African blood deny their blackness as it has many negative connotations. One Brazilian saying, Reis informed me illustrates this, "if you see a white person running, he is an athlete. If you see a black person running, he is a thief." White Brazilians often deny the existence of racism in Brazil, Reis informed me, as they are rarely subjected to racism which is historical and structural in Brazil.

It can be argued that discrimination in Brazil is more about class and status than race and skin colour because a wealthy dark skinned Brazilian of high status would not be subjected to the same level of discrimination as a fair skinned poor Brazilian living in a *favela*. As 'black' is regularly associated with negative connotations such as poverty and uneducated, many mixed raced Brazilians prefer to disassociate themselves with the word and their blackness.

Introduction

Whether a Brazilian identifies themselves as *negro* (black), *mulatto* (mixed-race), or *moreno* (brown), they will face similar discriminatory behaviour. An expression commonly used by Brazilians from the Black Movement is, "If you want to know who is black in Brazil, ask a police officer?"[64] Carlos Santana, a Workers' Party legislator who represents Rio de Janeiro and heads the National Congress' Parliamentary Group to Promote Racial Equality, says that the perception that Brazil is the summit of racial harmony and equality is so pervasive that it makes the discussion of discrimination all but impossible.[65]

A well-known Brazilian expression accurately captures the attitude of many white Brazilians to racism, "There's no racism in Brazil, the blacks know their place." George Reid Andrews suggests that the denial of racism in Brazil, where race-relations are apparently so cordial, is because non-whites do not challenge it.[66] When non-whites stand up to racism, change is more likely to occur, as it has done in other racist countries. Author of *The Brazilians,* Joseph A. Page aptly says "white Brazilians need to acquire a greater sensitivity to racial issues and stop viewing them solely from a white perspective."[67]

"Racial prejudice in Brazil lies in the insistence that there is no racial prejudice," Joseph A. Page, a law professor at Georgetown University in Washington, wrote in *The Brazilians,* a 1995 book based on research conducted during sixteen visits to Brazil over three decades. "It's necessary that we stop this silliness of being scared to confront racism," said former President of Brazil, Luiz Inácio Lula da Silva, known popularly as Lula in a speech in November 2006, a month after his re-election for a second four-year term. "We have to confront it with claws out and teeth bared," he added.[68] Veteran African-American black activist, James Meredith commented:

> Unlike the United States and South Africa, Brazil established a system of white supremacy without the obvious signs like segregation or apartheid. Until Brazilians start to face up to this reality the legacy of slavery will continue.[69]

---

64 Brazilian police are notorious for corruption and brutality, but predominately against mixed-race and black males.
65 http://www.bloomberg.com/apps/news?sid=aIezjRWRd5Tk&pid=newsarchive
66 Warren, 2001, p. 276
67 Page, 1995, p. 83
68 http://www.bloomberg.com/apps/news?sid=aIezjRWRd5Tk&pid=newsarchive
69 http://www.theguardian.com/media/2005/nov/21/race.brazil

Garrincha, Pelé and Muḥammad 'Alī

The denial of racism amongst some of Brazil's non-white population is in stark contrast to African-Americans' attitude to racism in the United States. The difference between Afro-Brazilians and African-Americans' approaches to racism can be found in a comparison of the racial approaches of the United States' and Brazil's most celebrated athletes, Muḥammad 'Alī and Pelé. Whilst the former boxer 'Alī's outspoken political stances and proclamations of racial pride are considered by many to be the epitome of black athletes and social consciousness, in contrast the black Brazilian football icon Pelé, has over the years, "earned the scorn of many Afro-Brazilians who have voiced their extreme disappointment in the *futebol* (football) King's stance on racial issues. Pelé's non-position and even denial of racial problems in Brazil negatively influenced many black Brazilians in much the same way that 'Alī's outrageous bragging was symbolic of African-American pride during antagonistic racial relations in the 1960s and 70s."[70] Many black Brazilians would argue that Pelé is more loved by white Brazilians than by black Brazilians. For Brazil's white elite, Pelé was the ideal black: unthreatening, polite and clean-cut. In contrast to Garrincha, another black Brazilian football icon, he was the acceptable black Brazilian. Though an alcoholic and a reputed womaniser, Garrincha was embraced more warmly by Brazil's black community, as he was "one of us", an Afro-Brazilian informed me whilst at the Afro-Brazil museum in São Paulo.

To be fair, Pelé has done a lot for the black movement in Brazil and has spoken out against the country's anti-black attitudes, but chooses to adopt a more passive approach. An example of this was when Pelé publicly disagreed with a black Brazilian football player who reacted after being racially abused by fans in a football match in August 2014. The incident caught the attention of the media and, when asked about the matter, Pelé said it would have been better if the player, Aranha, had ignored the abuse like another Brazilian football player, Dani Alves, had done when a banana was thrown at him whilst playing for F.C.

---

70 http://blackwomenofbrazil.co/2014/12/13/in-brazil-ferguson-happens-everyday-but-where-is-the-widespread-protest/ Pelé is not the only high-profile black Brazilian who has received the scorn of black Brazilian activists. Joaquim Barbosa, the first black Justice of the Supreme Federal Court in Brazil, is another high-profile black who several black activists I spoke to felt that Barbosa has not done much to help the black cause despite having the means to do so. Ironically it is more lesser known black Brazilians like the black Brazilian footballer Garrincha who black activists spoke more warmly about than the iconic Pelé, as Garrincha "was one of us" I was informed.

Barcelona in Spain. Maintaining his composure, Alves nonchalantly picked up the banana, peeled it and took a bite and then carried on with the game.[71] Alves' poignant moment sparked a social media campaign in which a number of football players, including Alves' fellow Brazilian and Barcelona teammate Neymar, posted photographs of themselves with bananas to show solidarity with Alves in the fight against racism.[72]

Although Pelé admitted that he was subjected to racial abuse every time he played in Brazil, his approach to the issue was silence. Not wanting to give publicity to racists, he did not speak about racism on a regular basis, as he believed that that would make it more likely to happen again. For Pelé, repudiation in a public manner is not the best way to fight racism.[73]

Paulo César, a black Brazilian football player of the illustrious Brazilian national football team that won the 1970 FIFA World Cup, criticised his former teammate for not using his position to speak about racism in Brazil. In a 1977 interview given to *Jornal do Brasil*, headlined, "I am a black man who didn't ask permission from the whites," Paulo César considered himself to be condemned as a player due to his colour. Paulo César's outspoken comments caused outrage. He explained why his comments had irritated people so much:

> Because I am black! A black man who didn't ask for permission from whites, but demanded what I had a right to.
>
> Reporter: You think, then, that you have been a victim of racial prejudice?
>
> Paulo César: Of course I do. In Brazil things are even worse than in the United States. There, prejudice is declared, and blacks get together to free themselves from oppression. Here, no one admits that prejudice exists. Blacks themselves prefer to go through life trying to lighten their skins, instead of struggling for their rights. Prejudice is so great, that mulattoes don't like to be called black.
>
> Reporter: But have you suffered any declared discrimination?
>
> Paulo César: When I was a kid, I was invited to a party here in

---

71 The incident took place in April 2014 in a football match between F.C. Barcelona and Villarreal in Spain.
72 Many notable Brazilian footballers of various skin complexions joined the social media campaign "We are all monkeys" including; Oscar, David Luiz, Willian, Hulk, Philippe Coutinho, Fernandinho and the female footballer Marta.
73 https://www.youtube.com/watch?v=sX8FK3zUXpk

> Fluminense [football club] and they barred me at the door; they said Negroes couldn't enter the club. Even after I was well known, I was barred from clubs in Porto Alegre and Santa Catarina. The truth is that whites don't allow a black man into an elevated social position. We can only be porters, workers or truck drivers.
>
> Reporter: But, what about Pelé? He doesn't suffer this type of discrimination?
>
> Paulo César: Pelé is different. He's the "good guy," he never had the "audacity" to frequent nightclubs and restaurants in style, he never dressed extravagantly, he never tried to level himself with a white man. It's only been now, in the United States, that he's been seen dining in such-and-such a place, dancing I don't know where. I don't criticise anyone, but if I were him, I'd have been different. The truth is that Pelé has never contributed to help the black race. That's what irritates me, the black Brazilian cowers, he omits himself, he doesn't struggle for anything.[74]

Thirty seven years later Paulo César vehemently criticised the "athlete of the century" again in the mainstream media for not using his status to speak about the issue of racism in football and Brazilian society. He remarked:

> If Pelé had some notion of sensitivity, he would make a revolution for the issue [of racism]. He has more impact than political and religious leaders. But no, he prefers to speak about nonsense. We should speak about [figures like] Muhammad 'Alī, Martin Luther King and Nelson Mandela. These were great leaders who took advantage of their status to fight for blacks. They gave up their lives and fought serious fights, which Pelé should do but never has.[75]

In contrast to Pelé's soft approach in tackling racism, African-American Muḥammad 'Alī spoke of the race issue repeatedly when given the opportunity. Like many black-American Muslims in the face of oppression, 'Alī boldly confronted the fallacy of America's "equal opportunities", while Pelé, like many Christian Afro-Brazilians, became a passive symbol of Brazil's false "racial democracy", which, perversely, denied equality to Afro-Brazilians, yet all the while proclaiming that

---

74 Nascimento, 1989, pp. 84-85

75 http://esporte.uol.com.br/futebol/ultimas-noticias/2014/04/10/paulo-c-caju-diz-que-pele-tambem-tem-culpa-por-racismo-no-futebol.htm#fotoNav=3

Brazilians are treated equally. In reality, they most certainly are not. Black Brazilian footballers are regularly targeted with racial abuse. Former national team goalkeeper and World Cup winner, Dida, is one of the few players who has complained about the racial slurs from the stands. Historian Marcel Dieso Tonini, who wrote his doctorate at the University of São Paulo on black Brazilians in football, said, "The number of black players on the pitch is increasing, but among the coaches and club bosses, the number of Afro-Brazilians is in the minority." Tonini added that many of Brazil's black players who are committed Christians avoid speaking publicly about racism because they're concerned that it will damage their careers.[76]

As in nineteenth century Brazil, Islam (*Islão*) is the religion of the black rebels who jealousy guard their religious beliefs and fight for their freedom, unlike Christianity, which was often used to pacify African slaves so that they would not revolt but turn the other cheek to the persecutions of the Europeans. Islam, on the other hand, was a constant threat to Brazil's Catholic elite because the Qur'ān permits self-defence:

Fight in the way of Allah those who fight you but do not transgress. Indeed Allah does not like transgressors.[77]

FIGHTING RACISM THROUGH EDUCATION AND ACTIVISM

Education is arguably the most effective method of fighting racial discrimination. As a way of combating racism, many activists have fought to instil racial pride and celebrate blackness by teaching the history of black people. No one is born a racist. Racism is a learnt behaviour and, like any learnt behaviour, with correct education and tutelage it can be unlearnt. In traditional multicultural Muslim societies, which had their own issues with racism, classical Muslim scholars would use education as a means to eradicate this problem. Scholars such as Amr al-Jāḥiẓ, 'Abd ar-Raḥmān al-Jawzī and Jalāl ad-Dīn as-Suyūṭī produced valuable treatises in the Islamic literary genre called 'virtues of the blacks' in which they would address misconceptions regarding black people, catalogue their admirable qualities and provide biographies of laudable black/African people in history. Because the *racismo cordial* (cordial racism) in Brazil is similar to the racism that is prevalent in many Muslim communities, which was part of the inspiration behind my first book *Illuminating the*

---

76 http://www.dw.com/en/brazilian-football-plagued-by-racism/a-17646244
77 Qur'ān 2:190

Darkness, I felt drawn to explore the issue of racial discrimination and colour prejudice in Brazil.

In this book I will explore the black-consciousness movement in Brazil and examine the reasons for the growing number of conversions to Islam amongst Brazilians, particularly those of African descent. I will also share my insights into the complexities of race in Brazil and draw comparisons with the racial histories of the pre-modern Muslim world, including a comparative analysis of the East-African Zanj slave rebellion in ninth-century Baghdad with the West-African *Malê* (Yoruba) slave rebellion in nineteenth-century Bahia. I will demonstrate that the black experience in multicultural Brazil is similar to the black experience in multicultural Muslim societies by presenting a comparison of Brazil's race relations with race relations in Muslim societies, which may provide some useful insights into how to combat racial discrimination and colour prejudice.

WHO IS BLACK? WHAT IS BLACKNESS?

Who is black in Brazil is a complex question which cannot be answered adequately without explaining the racial history of the country. The same can be said about what is blackness from a Brazilian perspective as it is very different to the United States which has its own understanding of what constitutes blackness due to the 'one drop rule.'

Brazil is a racially mixed country made up of white Europeans and black Africans as well as brown indigenous peoples. Prior to the racial quotas that the Brazilian government introduced in the twenty-first century, Brazilians did not categorise themselves by race but by skin colour. The racial quota caused a change in those amongst mixed-race Brazilians who used to identify themselves by colour but who now have to specify their race. Darker-skinned Brazilians are 'African-looking,' and are largely identified as *negro* (black). 'African-looking' is a problematic term because Africans range from very fair to very dark in complexion. What defines being 'African' and what is 'African-looking' are open to debate. However, in general usage the terms refer to individuals who possess 'traditional' or stereotypical West- and Central-African features such as flat noses, large buttocks, thick lips, dark skin complexions and Afro-textured kinky hair.

In the 2010 federal census, ninety-seven million of Brazil's 190 million either identified themselves as *pardo* (brown) or *preto* (black), thus making Brazil the second-largest 'black' country in the world after Nigeria. The figures reflect the changing attitudes about race and skin colour in

Introduction

Brazil as many of those who self-identified as *pardo* or *preto* in the most recent census may have self-identified as branco (white) in previous censuses. The growing black consciousness movement has led to more Brazilians not only self-identifying as black but demonstrating a greater appreciation in their African heritage.

Black (Negro)
Etymologically, the English word 'black' is of Germanic origin. According to the Oxford dictionary, the noun 'black' refers to "black colour or pigment" or [also spelt Black] refers to "a member of a dark skinned people, especially one of African or Australian ancestry". The adjective 'black' means "of the very darkest colour owing to the absence of or complete absorption of light; the opposite of white". Second, it means "belonging to or denoting any human group having dark-coloured skin, especially of African or Australian Aboriginal ancestry". Third, it means "characterized by tragic or disastrous events; causing despair or pessimism". Fourth, it means "denoting a covert military procedure". In Portuguese the word *negro*, denoting 'black', is derived from the Latin word, *niger*, which is said to derive from a Proto-Indo-European root word, *nek*, which means "to be dark", akin to *nok* (night).

The question, 'who is black?' will produce various answers depending on who is asked and what is understood by 'black'. The word's meaning has evolved over time and varies amongst peoples. Different societies have their own criteria in classifying someone as 'black'. A 'black' person in the United Kingdom may not be considered (*negro*) 'black' in Brazil. Similarly, a 'black' person in the United States may not be considered 'black' in South Africa. The term can be deemed inappropriate or offensive as most people referred to as 'black' are not literally black in skin complexion but various shades of brown. Despite this, 'black' has historically been used to refer to people in one of four ways: descriptively, ethnically, culturally and politically.

In pre-modern times when the concept of race did not exist, 'black' was used descriptively to refer to an individual. The descriptive use of the term was also used relatively, as was the case amongst early Arabs, who at times would describe themselves as 'black', in comparison to the fairer-skinned Persians, or as 'white', in comparison to the darker-skinned black Africans. In modern times, 'black' may be used descriptively to refer to someone whose complexion is brown or dark brown, irrespective of whether they are of African descent or not.[78]

---

78 i.e. a dark-skinned Asian (Indian or Arab person) can be described as 'black'.

Ethnically, 'black' can be used to refer to someone of African, African-American,[79] sub-Saharan African or Afro-Caribbean heritage, but excluding East Africans who are not deemed 'black' by some people due to their mixed Arab ancestry and fine hair texture.[80] Amongst West-African peoples such as the Yorubas, 'black' is also used ethnically, as 'black' (*dudu*) refers to peoples of African descent. Non-Africans are referred to as white (*fufu* or *oyinbo*), irrespective of their hue or ethnic background, but *oyinbo*, in Yoruba, can also be used to refer to a light-skinned black person. The terms 'melanoid' and 'melanese', which derives from the word melanin (dark brown or black pigment), have also been used ethnically to refer to 'black' people of African descent.

Culturally, 'black' may also refer to someone who has lived the 'black experience'. It is also used loosely at times to refer to people who enjoy 'black' music or culture.[81] It may also be used to refer to people who understand the 'black struggle' of resistance, hardship and ghetto.

[79] In the United States of America, some within the Black community use 'black' to refer to African-Americans only. Dark-skinned people from Haiti or Puerto Rico, for example, are referred to by their country of origin or as Latino or Hispanic. I was made aware of this whilst speaking to an African-American woman about race. She said I would not be considered 'black' in the United States, but African or Black-British. Initially shocked when I heard this, especially as the woman was much lighter in complexion than me, after speaking to other African-Americans I found out that what she was saying was true, though there were some who said I would be considered black in the United States. Senegalese-American singer and recording artist, Akon, who was born in America but raised in Senegal, considers himself "an African raised in America". Akon said he was treated differently by black Americans while growing up in the United States because he was dark skinned and an African.
http://www.aljazeera.com/programmes/talktojazeera/2015/01/akon-america-built-black-people-150123151008241.html

[80] For instance in the Black British community, people who are of West African and Caribbean origin are normally referred to as 'black', whereas East Africans are referred to as 'Somali', 'Eritrean' or 'Ethiopian', depending on their country of origin. This is because some East Africans identify themselves as Arabs instead of as blacks. It is also said that East Africans such as the Somalis are not considered 'black' because of differences in hair texture and culture from West Africans and Caribbean people. Interestingly, even a fair-skinned person of mixed heritage from the Caribbean is more likely to be considered 'black' by members of the Black British community than a dark-skinned Somali of pure African stock.

[81] Black music is a term encompassing music produced or inspired by people of African descent. The term is also referred to euphemistically as 'urban music', 'ghetto music' or 'street music'. Popular genres of black music include: Hip-hop (United States), Reggae (Jamaica), Samba (Brazil), Afrobeats (Nigeria and Ghana) and Grime (UK).

Introduction

Cultural definitions of blackness are commonly used in countries of the African Diaspora such as the United States of America and parts of Europe that have large communities of African-descent.

Politically, 'black' may be used to refer to non-white people or anyone who is defined as 'black' by others. The United States' 'one drop of Negro blood' rule defined any individual with any African ancestry whatsoever as black, regardless of their hue or ethnic make-up. The 'one-drop rule' was based on the hypo-descent law in which children of mixed ancestry were classified as belonging to the subordinate 'race' or ethnic group i.e. in this case, the black race. The one-drop rule has caused a number of mixed-race people, who may even have stronger European ancestry than African, to be defined as 'black' in the United States.

Black In Brazil (*Negro No Brasil*)
In Brazil, racial identity is complex. Unlike the United States, which has historically defined itself as a biracial society in which people of African descent and people of mixed heritage have been classified as black, in Brazil people identify themselves using over a hundred and thirty descriptive categories. Race (*raça*) and, more specifically *negro* (black), is not widely used in Brazil in the way that it is in racially-conscious countries such as the United States.[82] The classification of *pretos* as *negros* (blacks) in the government's census is rarely employed by blacks themselves. Blacks and mixed-race Brazilians prefer to use the term *moreno* for themselves, which literally means 'tanned' or 'dark-haired'.

In recent times, black Brazilian activists have argued for the term *negro* to be used for all non-white Brazilians, which would give Brazil the second largest black population in the world after Nigeria. The term *negro* implies a certain political consciousness in those who recognise black identity as a historical, political identity. In this sense, as Jones de Aleida argues, the term *negro* is similar to 'African-American' or to the capitalised term 'Black' used in the United States.[83]

According to the American sociologist Edward E. Telles, in Brazil there are three different systems of 'racial classification' along the white-black (*branco-negro*) continuum: first, the national census system, which has five racial classifications; second, the system of self-identification that Brazilians use, which employs many different terms to describe their skin colour; third, the Black Movement's system that has two

---

82 See Appendix 1 for skin tone categories in Brazil
83 Jones de Almeida, *2003, pp. 41-63*

racial classifications – *negro* (black) and *branco* (white).⁸⁴ More recently, the terms *afrodescendente* and 'Afro-Brazilian' have been brought into use. The Afro-Brazilian, according to historian Abdias do Nascimento, may be *negro* (black), mulatto, *moreno* (brunette), *pardo* (brown), *escuro* (dark), *crioulo* (black Brazilian), or any combination of those euphemisms of African descent in various gradations of epidermic colour and ethnic classification.⁸⁵

In his travelogues on the racial history of Brazil, American-American professor Henry Louis Gates Jr, observed that the definition for 'black' in Brazil lies in self-identification with over a hundred categories used. Very dark blacks are *preto* or *negro azul* (blue black). Medium-dark blacks are *escuro*. *Preto desbotado* refers to light-skinned blacks. Light-skinned blacks, who are light enough to 'pass for white,' may be described as *mulatto disfarçado*. Gates Jr did notice in his travels that Brazilians who identified themselves as black, did so either with a certain defiance or apologetically.⁸⁶ In many cases, 'poor person' is used euphemistically to refer to a black person whilst 'middle-class' is used euphemistically for whites. White is the colour of achievement and success as reflected in the popular saying "money whitens", which many impoverished blacks and browns aspire to realise. Fleeing blackness was a consistent theme that professor Gates Jr noticed in his travels in Brazil and other Latin American countries. The same can be said in many societies around the world where the American phrase remains true, "If you're white, you're alright. If you're brown, stick around, but if you're black, get back!"⁸⁷

The United States' 'one drop rule' of defining blackness has influenced Brazilian sensibilities towards racial identity and the notion of blackness. Leaders of Brazil's black consciousness movement, which began in the 1970s under the influence of the Black Power movement of the United States, insisted on using the term *negro* (black) for non-white Brazilians. Mixed-race Brazilians were classified as black because, according to the movement's leaders, they were subject to the same form of discrimination as blacks.

Black in Brazil is also defined by facial features and hair texture just as much as by the darkness of skin.⁸⁸ A person with prominent 'African'

---

84 Telles, 2006, pp. 81-88
85 Nascimento, 1989, p. 180
86 Gates Jr., 2011, p. 39
87 The phrase was taken from Big Bill Broonzy's song 'Black, Brown and White' about Jim Crow's racial segregation law.
88 Angela and Onik'a Gilliam argue in their work that hair-type often becomes the

Introduction

features[89] such as a *nariz chato* (broad nose), thick lips, *cabelo pixaim* (kinky hair) and *bunda grande* (large buttocks) is commonly referred to as *negro* (black).

Generally speaking in Latin America, what is considered black is without value and carries negative connotations.[90] Recently there has been a pushback amongst Afro-Latinos, who are starting to identify themselves as *negro* (black). Hair texture is a defining factor in categorising blackness in many countries such as Brazil, where a person with curly and kinky, Afro-textured hair is more likely to be recognised as black. At the same time, some brown-complexioned women with Afro-textured hair do not consider themselves 'black' because they do not possess typical African traits such as a large derrière. One dark-complexioned Brazilian woman of visible African ancestry told me that she does not consider herself black because she does not have large buttocks like an African woman.

Political correctness is another matter that complicates black self-identification. In English-speaking Western countries like the United States and the United Kingdom, the terms 'negro', 'mulatto' and 'coloured', although previously acceptable, are now considered unacceptable in description of 'black' people of African descent. In contrast, the terms mulatto and *negro* are acceptable to describe black people in Spanish and Portuguese speaking countries, and 'coloured' is considered an inoffensive term with which mixed-race people in South Africa identify themselves. Matters are further complicated when some blacks, particularly those from the United States, distinguish between the words 'nigger' and 'nigga'. The former (nigger) is said to be a racist slur, whilst the latter (nigga) is said to be a term of endearment used by black people themselves. Though many of the blacks who use the N-word (nigga) would feel offended if whites were to use it. The issue is further complicated: what type of 'white' person can use the N-word without causing offence? Is a 'Latino' with pale skin not white, and thus permitted the use of the N-word because they have lived in impoverished areas with blacks? Similarly is a person of North-African descent not considered

---

primary signifier of race in Brazil, particularly for women. See Caldwell, 2007, p. 8, Gilliam, A. and Gilliam O., 1998, pp. 60-84

89 Of course, these stereotypical 'African' features would in Africa itself be seen as markers for particular tribes rather than for the inhabitants of the continent in its entirety, whose physiognomy, skin colour and other features display wide variations. Ed.

90 Sansone, 2003, p. 8

white because they are from Africa thus making it permissible for them to use the N-word or even identifying themselves as black?

The complexities of who is black continue to fuel debates and cause controversy. As a black man myself, I cannot say for certain who is 'black' as there are such widely varying definitions. Historically, people of European descent have policed the matter of who qualifies as 'black' in the modern world, and have set up a racial system of oppression in a society where skin colour has been a dividing line for opportunity. Due to this, many people of African descent have struggled with identifying themselves as black and with the very notion of blackness.

Blackness (*Negritude*)

Blackness is defined as the state of being black, or the state of being a black person or negritude (the historical, cultural and social heritage considered common to black people collectively).[91] It can also refer to the quality of being very dark.[92] For some people, the definition of blackness is restricted to a person who does not have the option to be anything but black. What is meant by this definition or experience of 'being black' is that a person who is dark in complexion with strong African features would not be mistaken for anything but black. In contrast, an individual who may be black (ethnically African) but fair in complexion or have traditional European features such as an *nariz fino* (aquiline nose) or *cabelo fino* (natural straight 'good' hair) may be identified as black or non-black. Regardless of how a person feels about themselves being 'black,' other people will inform an individual of their blackness. A dark-skinned person with prominent African features cannot escape their blackness whereas many lighter-skinned blacks can use their blackness as a form of self-identification when it suits them.

The concept of blackness in Western countries has been described as the degree to which one associates themselves with mainstream black culture, politics and values. Blackness is the antithesis of 'white privilege' and 'acting white'. Blackness or 'being black' or 'acting black' is often used to refer to someone with whom the following terms have been associated: physically strong, muscular, sensual, musical, having rhythm, knowing how to dance, entertaining, uneducated, poor, from the ghetto, hip-hop, urban, struggles, African, ebonics, large penis, curvaceous, promiscuous, nigga, nigger, loves chicken, slave, oppressed, ugly, cheerful, flamboyant,

---

91 Dictionary.com
92 Cambridge Dictionaries online

weave,[93] has an attitude, aggressive, intimidating, thief, unorganised, drug dealer, single mother, welfare, fraudster, corruption, animalistic, monkey, uncivilised, barbaric although many of the above have also been applied to poor whites in the West.

African-American scholar Charles Mills discusses the concept of blackness in African-American philosophy in his article "An Illuminating Blackness". Mills argues that the concept of blackness can be better appreciated when it is not viewed from a Eurocentric worldview, since that is inherently biased.[94] The same can be true of the concept of Africanness, which is often viewed subconsciously as being primitive and uncivilised. The idea that Africans are uncivilised stretches back to racist ideologies that were concocted by white European apologists for colonialism who depicted black Africans as being inferior to whites.

In his critical analysis of race-relations in Brazil, African-American writer and frequent traveller to Brazil, Mark Wells noticed "the negative image of blackness in Brazil has been so influential upon the people that many don't accept the fact that they are of African descent." Wells continues, "This is one of the main reasons why Brazil has lacked any kind of strong, mass black movement for equal rights in the same way as the Civil Rights Movement in America and the wars of independence in many African countries of the 1960s."[95] The growing increase in black consciousness is now changing this as more *moreno/mulatto/pardo* (brown/mixed-race/mestizo) Brazilians are starting to identify themselves as *negro* ('black').

Afro-Brazilian Perspectives On Race-Relations And Blackness
According to many of the leading Afro-Brazilian actors from the film City of God, Brazil's black population had not improved despite the country's economic growth in recent years. The 2013 documentary, *City of God - 10 Years Later*, shows what has changed in the lives of the actors and Brazil's Afro-descendants since the feature film was released.

> "Black people in Brazil? There has been no evolution for black people in Brazil. Nothing. Nothing has happened. Women's rights have improved. They are strong now, growing. That's great. Gays too, they are also growing

---

93 Weave is a form of hair extension which is woven or glued into the hair. Weave is commonly associated with black women of African descent, but women of all ethnic groups wear weave. 'Brazilian weave' is very popular amongst black women in the United States and the United Kingdom.
94 Mills, Charles, "An Illuminating Blackness" in *The Black Scholar*, pp. 32-37
95 http://www.brazzil.com/blajun01.htm

and getting their civil rights, and that's important. But black people? There has been no improvement."
SEU JORGE

"If you're black and come from a favela, and you don't have a diploma then you will be last in the line."
JONATHAN HAAGENSEN

"We (blacks) are the majority in Brazil, but we are not the majority in the market [for jobs and opportunities]…Everybody keeps saying this whole thing [racism] about black people is getting annoying. And then I think about it and I say 'It's only annoying if you don't go through it.'"
ROBERTA RODRIGUES

"I think we need more black people telling their own story."
LEANDRO FIRMINO

Marina Rocha, a mixed-raced Brazilian woman I met in Rio de Janeiro gave me an insight to race-relations in Brazil and gave me her perspective of blackness. Fluent in English and studied for a year in Ireland, Marina explained, "I would say we still don't consider all ethnicities here as equal and need to work out about the general acceptance of ethnic differences in many aspects. In Brazil, we know that, mostly, we are a mix of ethnicities but probably if you are "black," people would treat you slightly different and principally, think about you differently. This is what we usually call "false racial democracy," meaning that since our country consists in a great number of mixed people, we denied the existence of racism here, but in fact it still exists." She later went on to compare Brazil's race-relations with Ireland, where she studied, "I have to say that we are more accepting than Irish people. Not because we are more evolved than them, but because we are more open to miscegenation and are used to it. Even if you disagree about race relations, here you probably wouldn't say anything against it.

For instance, during my year studying abroad in Ireland, people usually asked me if I was 100% Brazilian or if my mother and my father are both Brazilian as well. Other than that, in Brazil no one ever asked me that, and I truly believe they never will because we are so familiar with the concept of miscegenation that is common sense here to assume most people had at least one black person in their family tree. Actually, it is not common to discuss from where we are from or if your family came from Europe or Africa. Presumably, because it is too mixed up to track it down."

As for schooling in Brazil, Marina said, "in relation about how ethnicity is discussed in my schooling in Brazil, first I would like to say

Introduction

that, according to the education I received in Brazil, it bothers me to write "black or white people" and "race", in Portuguese we'll probably say "afro descendant or Caucasian people" and "ethnicity", but I will explain why.

For many years, the Brazilian government and education institutions were/are working to eradicate expressions that could be consider pejorative and offensive, such as "black or white people" and "race", for example. Besides that, since we have a history of decades and decades of miscegenation, there are a great variety of skin colours. As there are different "levels" of black people, if one of our parents is afro descendant and the other is Caucasian, the children can be: light skin colour, *moreno claro, moreno, mulato, pardo, negro* (*negro*, is like dark skin colour, the same of black people, however we consider less pejorative than the expression "black", because seems less related with colour difference or slave Brazilian history and more related with people). So those are concepts every child learns from the beginning of school in Brazil.

But to be clear: we are used to identifying ourselves as a unit, as Brazilians, not as afro descendants or *moreno* or Caucasian. Those concepts come up just if we really need to describe our colour.

Secondly, in Brazilian history we learn Portuguese and African people related in Brazil, slave history (about African and American Indian) and due to it, the existence of racial quota/affirmative action [policies] in public school and universities for them, since historically they suffer from discrimination and have less opportunity to study than Caucasian people, for example. Brazil was the last country to abolish slavery in America and when it did there was no policy about insertion of those people enslaved in Brazilian society, which can be a major cause of social inequality here, by the way.

Also, unfortunately, it is worthy to highlight that despite this, when we study history in school, it is 90% about Europe and 10% about African history even known the latter is very important to understand our own [Brazilian] history."

The Seattle Globalist published an online video in September 2015 by freelance journalist Katherine Jinyi Li who went to the famous Avenida Paulista in São Paulo's to ask Afro-Brazilians what it means to be black in Brazil. Some of their responses were:

"Being black in Brazil is difficult and complicated."
"Being black in Brazil means suffering a lot of prejudice from childhood up to 70 years of age.

"We still get looked down at because of our hair, for having dreads or braids."
"I'm proud to be black in this country even if it doesn't give us education for us to declare our identity."
"We have to always be twice as good to prove that we deserve to be in that place. This is our fight, our resistance."

Carolina Sant'Ana da Silva Dias, a twenty year old aspiring model from Rio de Janeiro spoke to me about the difficulties non-white models face, "Brazil prefers for women to be white, even black models are expected to have white features in order to be successful." Classified on her birth certificate as *parda*, the golden complexioned beauty said that she does not know her race due to her racially mixed background but understands that in Brazil, blackness is not the ideal beauty form in the eyes of mainstream Brazil, citing the white supermodel Gisele Bündchen is the example which Brazilian society wants to project to the masses. A number of black and mixed-raced models said that it is easier to find work abroad than in their own country because of Brazil's preference for whiteness in the entertainment industry.

Maurício Arcanjo, a 28 year old black Brazilian from Salvador, gave me his perspective of what it is like to be black in Brazil, "You suffer but people do not see that you are suffering, because here in Brazil the racism is invisible. We suffer racism in childhood, adulthood and will continue to suffer racism for all our lives. Some black people think that there is no racism here. so we really have a huge job to do here to make black people conscious about what racism is and how we have to fight it."

Carla Santos Santana, a black Brazilian lady from Salvador echoed Maurício comments and added that there is a lot of discrimination against blacks in the education system and employment. Blacks are heavily discriminated against in Salvador despite the fact that the majority of its residents are blacks. Organisations like *Centro de Estudos Afro-Orientais* (CEAO) are working to help eradicate the perception of black inferiority which currently resides in Brazil, Adilson Silva informed me. An employee of CEAO, Silva a dark skinned black Brazilian elderly man of visible African features, explained the various political, economic and social barriers Brazil's Afro-descendants have to overcome to gain an equal footing with whites. An Afro-Brazilian activist summed it up to me when he said, "being black in Brazil is very difficult. Whites have all the money and power. They own everything and the police kill blacks. They neglect us just like how they neglected our African forefathers who built this country."

Introduction

AFRICAN INFLUENCES ON BRAZILIAN CULTURE

In no other country in the world has African slavery had such an enormous impact as in Brazil. At the beginning of the nineteenth century, two out of every three Brazilians were of African descent.[96] From the early days of the slave plantation, through decades of slave revolts and the return to West Africa, to the abolition of slavery and the foundation of the Brazilian Republic, Africa has been woven into the fabric of Brazilian society and culture.[97] Slavery, knowledgeable historians agree, "moulded the contours of Brazilian life" and strongly influenced its culture.[98] The large number of Afro-Brazilians that Portuguese Jesuit missionary, Frei Antonio Vieira saw when he visited Brazil in the seventeenth century, led him to remark that Brazil is "a country with the body of America and the soul of Africa". Four centuries later, Vieira's words still hold true; according to the 2010 national census, Brazilians of African descent make up the majority of the country's population. Brazil's debt to Africa is inestimable, as the aspects of Brazilian culture which it prides itself upon have been strongly influenced by their African ancestors.

Like modern day Brazilians, West Africans are known for their cheerfulness and love of dance. Much of Brazil's cultural heritage stems from West African slaves, who have been in Brazil since the seventeenth century. The Africans brought their rich and vibrant culture along with them to the 'New World'. A religious people, the Africans frequently prayed for help during the horrific ordeal of their slavery and would seek solace in music to maintain their good cheer. The infectious cheerfulness of the Africans, particularly the Yorubas, soon found its way into the Brazilian lexicon, music, cuisine and culture.

Afrobeats
Afrobeat rhythms have percolated through contemporary Brazilian music for decades. The upsurge in the interest of Afrobeats in Brazil stemmed from the music of Nigerian recording artist and political activist, Fela Kuti. Popular Brazilian musicians and bands, such as Gilberto Gil and Nação Zumbi, took inspiration from Afrobeats, which increased interest in the African musical genre in Brazil. A number of contemporary Brazilian musicians from various genres use elements of Afrobeats in their music.

---

96 Levine, 1997, p. 14
97 Dawson, 2014, p. 145
98 Levine, 1997, p. 14

Black Consciousness Day (*Dia Da Consciência Negra*)

Black Consciousness Day (also known as Black Awareness Day) was inaugurated by poet, professor and researcher Oliveira Silveira (d. 2009) from the Brazilian state of Rio Grande do Sul. According to the United Nations Educational, Scientific and Cultural Organization (UNESCO), the day is meant to "celebrate a regained awareness by the black community about their great worth and contribution to the country [of Brazil]".[99]

Black Consciousness Day is celebrated annually on the 20th November, in honour of the death of Zumbi from Palmares. The day was originally celebrated on the 13th May, the day that slavery was officially abolished in Brazil. In 2003, the Brazilian government passed Law 10/639, requiring public and private schools to teach "the black struggle in Brazil, black Brazilian culture and the role of blacks in social, economic and political aspects of the history of Brazil". The law mandated that schools celebrate a "National Day of Black Consciousness". This initiative sparked a wave of research and subsequently advocacy of a case for acknowledging Afro-Brazilian figures in the history textbooks.[100] The day is used by members of the *Movimento Negro* (Black Movement)[101] to reflect upon the injustices of slavery and also to celebrate the contributions that Brazilians of African descent have made to Brazilian society. The main focus of many in the Black Movement is to change the perception of Africans' inferiority in society and address misconceptions about African culture and peoples.[102] Proponents of the Black Movement in Brazil argue that there is more to black history than slavery and the United States' civil rights movement. Some Afro-Brazilians celebrate the whole month of November as *Novembro Negro: mês da consciência negra* (Black November: a month of Black Consciousness).

Despite its importance, Black Consciousness Day is still not recognised as a national holiday by the Brazilian government. All too often, blackness, African culture and religion have been undermined by

---

99 http://www.unesco.org/new/en/brasilia/about-this-office/single-view/news/unesco_launches_campaign_for_black_awareness_day_20_november/#.VFY8dDSsVrV

100 Aidi, 2014, p. 36

101 The Black Movement (*Movimento Negro*) is a generic name given to diverse Afro-Brazilian social movements that occurred in 20th-century Brazil, particularly those that appeared in post-World War II Rio de Janeiro and São Paulo.

102 http://lexnoir.org/2011/11/brazil-dia-da-consciencia-negra-the-day-of-black-awareness/

Introduction

white Brazilians of European ancestry. It was not until white voices spoke of the value of African culture that it was recognised by the Brazilian populace. Samba and capoeira are examples of Afro-Brazilian practices that were considered abhorrent until they received white approval. Resisting white hegemony, black activists argue that they do not need white validation to give credence to their cultural and religious practices.

Brazilian Portuguese Language
Like many other languages, Brazilian Portuguese has a history entwined with its people and those who speak it. The presence of African slaves in Brazil speaking their own languages meant that some of their vocabulary and syntaxes found their way into the Brazilian Portuguese language. Etymologists have found that the African influence on the Brazilian Portuguese language is primarily from the (Nigerian) language of Yoruba and the (Angolan) language of Quimbundo. Brazilian-Portuguese words which are Yoruba in origin mainly relate to religion and cuisine. Some of these words are: *ogum* (Yoruba male divinity), *orixá* (orisha, Yoruba divinity), *vatapá* (a Brazilian dish), *abará* (a Brazilian cake), *acarajé* (from the Yoruba word *akar*, a savoury fritter), *babalorisha* (male priest), *agogô* (musical instrument). From the Quimbundo (Angolan) language come words such as: *caçula* (youngest child), *moleque* (street child), *cachimbo* (pipe), *quitanda* (greengrocer), *maxixe* (cucumber), *samba* (dance) and *berimbau* (musical instrument).

Candomblé
Candomblé is an Afro-Brazilian religion practised by the *"povo de santo"* (people of the saint). It is a mixture of traditional Yoruba, Fon and Bantu beliefs, though taking many of its beliefs and religious practices from traditional Yoruba religions. Candomblé is a syncretic mix of African religion with Roman Catholicism and indigenous American traditions. The religion developed in Salvador, Bahia, during the era of slavery and continues to be practiced by many Brazilians in Bahia today. At the centre of Candomblé is the Yoruba name for God, *Oludumare*. Deities are called *orixas* (from the Yoruba word for a deity, *orisha*).

The word Candomblé means "dance in honour of the gods", which is why dance and music play important roles in the religion. *Ijexá* is the name of the rhythm of Candomblé music. The religion was instrumental in the creation of black activist groups such as *Ilê Aiyê*.[103] It is reported

---

103 *"Ilê Aiyê* was born inside the Candomblé place of worship," said Vovô, the group's founder, "This strengthens our work and helps strengthen our religion here in Bahia."

that the religion has two million followers, mainly in Brazil, but also in other Latin American countries. Today followers of Candomblé sing and pray in Yoruba, which underlines the religion's deep African roots.

Capoeira

Capoeira is a Brazilian martial art and dance art-form that was developed in Brazil by African slaves. It is said that capoeira emerged as a result of the African slaves from Angola, when preparing for an uprising, disguising their marital-arts training with dance routines in order to deceive the slave masters. Capoeira was a form of resistance but also strength-building for the African slaves, who also practiced it as a form of self-defence. Capoeira is now a global phenomenon.

Jongo

Jongo is a Brazilian dance of African origin from the Bantu ethnic people. Music was important in raising the spirits of the African slaves while they were working in the sugar plantations. They would break into song and dance to entertain themselves. Dances such as jongo are an integral part of contemporary Brazilian culture, particularly during the country's *carnaval* (carnival) parades.

Quilombo Of Palmares

Palmares (the land of the palm trees) was a *quilombo* (maroon society or settlement) founded by runaway slaves in Pernambuco, a state in northeast Brazil. At the height of its power, it consisted of a vast network of villages, ruled by a king in Macaco, the *quilombo's* capital. Because the king was elected and his power was checked by a council of elders, Palmares is often labelled a republic, but one with distinctively traditional African features. Its name derives from the generally uncharted and largely uncolonised interior of Pernambuco, beyond the official Portuguese coastal settlements, which is filled with palm trees and marked by inhospitable mountain ranges. The *quilombo* of Palmares existed for close to a century, during which time it resisted assaults by both the Portuguese and Dutch regimes in Pernambuco's capital, Recife. Researchers have assumed that the *quilombo* of Palmares was a 'pagan' African empire, but some researchers, such as Clyde Ahmad Winters, have pointed out that the *quilombo* was more likely a Muslim power-base for the Brazilian-African Palmares Republic.[104]

See *Ebony Goddess: Queen of Ilê Aiyê*

104 See Muhammaed Abdullah al-Ahari, 'The Caribbean and Latin America' in Svanberg, Ingvar and Westerlund, David, *Islam Outside the Arab World*, p. 456

Introduction

INDEPENDENT AFRO-BRAZILIAN STATE

In the beginning of the seventeenth century, a group of runaway African slaves settled in Palmares in the interior of the north-eastern state of Alagoas. The Africans formed a community, known as *quilombo*, for liberated Africans, where they could defend themselves from the Portuguese Brazilians. Along with the black majority, Palmares welcomed indigenous peoples, mixed-race (*mesticos*) people and renegade whites, ultimately becoming a refuge for the persecuted of Brazilian society and the prototype of a 'multicultural' society long before the term was coined.[105]

Palmares was economically self-sufficient, because the slaves practised the diversified agriculture they remembered from Africa rather than the monoculture characteristic of colonial Brazilian agriculture. A Portuguese chronicler, Governor Pedro de Almeida, described them as "very hard working". Palmarino kings were kings in the African rather than the European sense, not absolute monarchs but rather custodians of the common wealth. Although the penal code, especially in the later period, was harsh – legislation stipulated the death penalty for theft, homicide or desertion – the Palmarinos enjoyed basic civic and political equality.[106]

The Africans established political power in Palmares and managed to remain an independent nation in Brazil for almost one hundred years until 1695, when their inspirational leader and African warrior chief, Zumbi of Palmares, was captured and executed. The independent society was organised similarly to an African kingdom with a King of Assembly. The King was chosen from the best warriors; Zumbi was chosen this way and, under his leadership, the Palmares fought bravely for sixty-five years against the colonialists from Portugal and Holland, before it was finally destroyed in 1695. According to Cristina de Maria de Castro, African Muslims were involved in its formation. Documents had registered the role of Muslims (*Muçulmanos*) in the structuring of the *quilombos*, among them a certain Karin ibn 'Alī Saifudin, considered a builder of its fortified structures.[107]

ZUMBI DOS PALMARES

Born as a freeman in 1655 in Serra da Barriga, Palmares, a *quilombo* that is located in the Brazilian state of Alagoas, Zumbi was captured by

---

105 Stam, 2004, p. 41
106 Stam, 2004, p. 41
107 Castro, 2013, p. 16

the Portuguese at the age of six and given to a missionary as a slave in 1661. In 1670, Zumbi escaped and returned to Palmares as a warrior, where he launched an antislavery campaign and inaugurated resistance to Portuguese oppression. Along with other members of the *quilombo* and the help of a Muslim Moor from North Africa, Zumbi helped accommodate many runaway slaves and marginalised and oppressed freemen of various ethnicities.[108]

On 20 November 1695, Zumbi was beheaded by the Portuguese who took his head to the city of Recife to be publicly displayed as a warning not to challenge the authority of the Portuguese. Many Afro-Brazilians now celebrate Zumbi as a Brazilian hero and symbol of freedom, and they proclaim the day of his execution the *Dia de Consciência Negra* (Black Consciousness Day). São Paulo's Unipalmares University is also named after Zumbi and the *quilombo*. Afro-Brazilian feminists and black activists have also campaigned for the contribution of Dandara, Zumbi's wife, to be recognised because of the pivotal role she played in the slave resistance of Palmares.[109] Unfortunately little is known about other great Afro-Brazilian heroines of Palmares such as Aqualtune, the Angolan princess, general and later the maternal grandmother of Zumbi of Palmares, who had been enslaved in a Congolese war around 1605. Acotirene, the founding matriarch of Palmares, is another heroine, about whom too little is known. Historians are continuing their research into such legendary figures, because many women served important roles in the maroon society of Palmares, but are often overlooked.

The history of the *quilombo* of Palmares fascinates historians of slave resistance and continues to inspire Brazilians of African descent in their struggle for racial equality and justice. The success of Palmares was an embarrassment for colonial authorities, and most records were destroyed in an effort to suppress its memory. The records that do survive largely give the Portuguese or Dutch perspective of the story, though there has been a resurgence of the Afro-Brazilian perspective being told in feature-fiction films, documentaries and books.

---

108 According to historian Glenn Alan Cheney, author of Quilombo dos Palmares: Brazil's Lost Nation of Fugitive Slaves, a Moor from northern Africa taught Zumbi something about warfare and defense. Although the identity of the Moor is not known, he was likely to have been a dark-skinned Berber or Arab. Little is known about this Moor other than a document which refers to him as a "Moor" who was not like the other Africans and briefly noting that he had fled to Palmares and designed the fort at the Palmarian citadel of Macaco. Cheney, 2014, p 116 and p. 180
109 See Chapter 6 for more information about Dandara.

Introduction

Reggae

Jamaican reggae music has a strong following in Brazilian cities such as Rio de Janeiro, Salvador and São Paulo, which have large communities of descendants of Africans. Jimmy Cliff, during the 1970s, was the first reggae artist to make a mark in Brazil, before Jamaican reggae singer Bob Marley came to prominence in Brazil in the 1980s. After a series of albums, Cliff travelled to Africa and subsequently converted to Islam, taking the name El-Hadj Naim Bachir. Cliff later visited the mosque in Salvador, Bahia. Marley was a pan-Africanist and used his music to try and unite African people worldwide. Despite his passing in 1981, Marley and his music remain hugely popular amongst Brazil's black population.

Salvador da Bahia

Salvador da Bahia (colloquially called Salvador or simply Bahia) is the principal city of the state of Bahia, and is situated in northeast Brazil. It is the third largest city in Brazil, with a population of almost three million people. 80% of the city is of African descent, making it one of the largest black urban populations outside of Africa. Yet, despite this overwhelming majority, very few black and mixed-race Brazilians occupy positions of power.

Salvador was the first town to be founded in Brazil in 1549 and became the capital city until 1763, when it was succeeded by Rio de Janeiro. For three centuries, the city of Salvador was the principal port for the import of slaves from Africa. Described as the "African heart of Brazil", the African influence in Salvador is evident in the city's predominately Afro-Brazilian population. The religious practices, music and local cuisine have direct links to African culture. The city is said to be the birthplace of the Candomblé religion, samba music and the capoeira martial-art. Between 1807 and 1835 there were a number of slave rebellions that resulted in punishments and legislations imposed on slaves, such as the prohibition of slaves walking in the streets after dusk without the permission of their masters. Salvador is now one of the most popular tourist attractions in Brazil for people who are interested in learning about the African presence in Brazil.

ILÊ AIYÊ

Incredibly, up until the 1970s, Salvador's carnival parade was for whites, and blacks were only permitted to push the floats, not dance around them. That situation only came to an end during the 1970s when some *Blocos Afro* (Afro-Brazilian Carnival groups) came into existence influenced by the Black Power movement in the United States, reggae and Pan-

African movements. On 1st November 1974, the carnival musical group *Ilê Aiyê* ('House of Life' in Yoruba) was set up to raise the consciousness of the black community and to 're-Africanise' the city's carnival, which had become tourist-and-samba-dominated, and so they set up floats celebrating different African countries and carried signs that read 'Black Power'. "We wanted to call our group Black Power," says founder of *Ilê Aiyê*, Antônio Carlos 'Vovô,' "but the federal police and the military said no, they saw us as too radical, too American."[110] The group was persecuted by the police and the media during its first years and is still considered controversial for only allowing blacks to parade with the group. Despite this, the carnival group has been a beacon of light for Afro-Brazilians as it has generated a great deal of pride and consciousness in the black community of Salvador and throughout the world.[111] Popularly known as *o mais belo dos belos* (the loveliest of the lovely) during the carnival, the group is now considered to be a strong agent of black consciousness in Brazil.

OLODUM

Another Afro-Brazilian carnival group, *Olodum*,[112] was founded in 1979 "to create art and culture from the black-consciousness movement", said one of the group's founders, João Jorge.[113] The *Olodum* group came out of the *Ilê Aiyê* movement, although it disagreed with the latter group's "radical stance on questions of race and racial identity".[114] Like *Ilê Aiyê*, *Olodum*'s express purpose is to affirm Black identity and raise black consciousness. However, unlike *Ilê Aiyê*, *Olodum* is open to all races and was one of the first carnival groups to incorporate reggae and Caribbean culture into its music and lyrics.[115] *Olodum* is now an internationally-acclaimed multicultural organisation that highlights Brazil's African heritage and celebrates black pride through music, dance and art. An *Olodum* school was later established to teach children about Afro-Brazilian history, which had generally been excluded from official schoolbooks.[116]

In recent times, Maurico Pestana, the executive director of *Raça*

---

110 Aidi, 2014, p. 35; Gates, Jr. p. 29
111 The main objective of the group is the "expansion of African culture in Brazil".
112 Olodum takes its name from the Yoruba deity *Olodumaré*.
113 Neguinho do Samba (d. 2009) is also reported to be the founder of *Olodum*.
114 Jones de Almeida, *2003, pp. 41-63*
115 Jones de Almeida, *2003, pp. 41-63*
116 http://news.bbc.co.uk/1/hi/world/americas/719134.stm

Introduction

Brasil (Brazilian Race) magazine and cartoonist, published a number of cartoons for the *Olodum* school of the 1835 Bahia slave revolt, the story of the legendary figure Zumbi, and the *quilombo* of Palmares. The *Olodum* band received global attention when it was featured in the music video of the late African-American recording artist and philanthropist, Michael Jackson, "They don't care about us". Part of the music video was filmed in Salvador, Bahia with Jackson wearing the *Olodum* t-shirt. The internationally famous singer's music video brought global attention to *Olodum*, which dedicates itself to cultural activism in the struggle against racial discrimination and socio-economic inequality in Brazil.

Pelourinho

Through the activism of *Ilê Aiyê, Olodum* and other Afro-Brazilian *blocos*, they were able to revitalise *Pelourinho*,[117] the Historic Centre of Salvador, which was long neglected by the government, and prompted the United Nations Educational, Scientific and Cultural Organization (UNESCO) to declare *Pelourinho* a World Heritage Site in 1985.[118] In September 2008, the Nigerian government opened the *Casa de Nigeria* (Nigerian Cultural House) in *Pelourinho* to reaffirm the common ancestry and cultural affinity between the people of Bahia and Nigeria. Angola, Benin and South Africa also have cultural centres in the city of Salvador.

Samba

Samba is arguably the most popular musical genre and dance form in Brazil. It is often described as representing the heart and soul of Brazilian people. The word 'samba' is of Bantu origin, meaning 'belly button'. The dance involves a basic pattern of step-close-step-close and is characterised by a dip and spring upward at each beat of the music. Samba also refers to the music that accompanies this dance. *Pedra do Sal* (Rock of Salt) in Rio de Janeiro is said to be the cradle of samba. *Pedra do Sal* later became known as *Pequena África* (Little Africa), due to the immigration of a great number of Afro-Brazilian families from Bahia in northeast Brazil.

ISLAM IN THE HISTORY OF BRAZIL

Islam is not new to Brazil. According to some reports, the presence of Islam in Brazil dates back to the ninth century, hundreds of years before the Christian Portuguese first set foot in Brazil. It is not possible to speak

---

117 Pelourinho in Portuguese means "whipping post." The city's historic Pelourinho district is where African slaves were once auctioned and brutally punished.

118 Aidi, 2014, p. 35

about Afro-Brazilian history without speaking about Islam. Inspired by their Islamic faith, nineteenth-century West-African Muslims were influential in bringing an end to slavery in Brazil and shaping modern-day Brazilian culture. Despite the fact that the contributions of these African Muslims are often neglected in discussions of Brazilian history, there has been a resurgence of interest amongst black Brazilians wishing to enlighten people about the country's silenced Afro-Brazilian and Islamic history.

There is also a tendency for Western-trained academics to discredit the research of historians who were not trained in prestigious Western educational institutions. The findings of Afro-Brazilian and Muslim historians are dismissed for their perceived 'bias', while the same accusations are not levelled at Western-trained scholars, who are considered 'objective' in their scholarship.

The Islamic presence in Brazil can be divided into four phases: 1. African Muslims' contact with Brazil before the Portuguese; 2. the transportation of West-African Muslim slaves to Brazil in the nineteenth century; 3. the immigration of Arab Muslims to Brazil in the twentieth century; and 4. the conversion and renaissance of Afro-descendant Muslims in Brazil.

The Importance Of History
History is an important and honourable science in Islam, as articulated by the North-African Muslim historian Ibn Khaldūn, who states:

> Know that the science of history is a noble science that can be very beneficial and has a precious goal, since it gives us a proper understanding of the previous nations' morals and character, the biographies of the Prophets, and government and politics of the kings so that those who desire so will achieve the benefit of modelling themselves on them in matters of the *dīn* (religion) and the *dunyā* (ephemeral world).[119]

History, as is said, is written by the victors, thus it is important for those who were not 'victorious' to ensure that their perspective is known, as the African proverb states, "Until lions have their own historians, the history of the hunt will always glorify the hunter". This is most definitely the case in Brazil where Afro-Brazilian history is generally omitted from the educational system.

---

119 Ibn Khaldūn, 1967

Introduction

The history of Brazil's African descendants is not important for black Brazilians alone, for, as Januário Garcia said, "There is a history of black people without Brazil but there is no history of Brazil without black people." Afro-Brazilian history is vast and one which contemporary scholars are now beginning to investigate more vigorously. Slavery was not the beginning of African history in Brazil; Africans travelled to Brazil as free-persons, long before Europeans had set sail for the Americas as previously mentioned.

It is unfortunate that many Brazilians are not aware of their country's African and Muslim heritage unlike the United States where many people of African descent know of their African and Islamic heritage, due to the black-power movement and the popularity of activists such as Malcolm X, who was able to reconnect black-Americans with their African and Islamic heritage. "History is a people's memory, and without a memory, man is demoted to the lower animals." A charismatic leader and orator, Malcolm X, also known as Malik el-Shabazz and Omowale (meaning "the son who has come home" in Yoruba), was able not only to articulate himself amongst intellectuals, but equally to express the aspirations of impoverished blacks. Indeed, he was a source of inspiration for blacks and non-blacks alike.[120] Globalisation and the technological advances of the last half-century have increased his profile in black Brazil, as many Brazilians are starting to reconnect with their African and Islamic past.

Sources For The History Of African Muslims In Brazil
The bulk importation of African slaves into Brazil perpetuated a tradition of enslavement of Africans that was already deeply rooted in Portugal. The blood of Africa ran in the veins of many Portuguese colonial dynasties. As Gilberto Freyre suggests, the affection displayed by many Portuguese-Brazilian planters for their black chattels may be attributed to an ingrained respect for '*Gente de Cor*' (People of Colour) dating back to the time of the Muslim Moors. Compared with the Visigoths, who had preceded them as overlords of Iberia, the Moors – themselves of hybrid Afro-Asiatic stock – were racially colour-blind and did not discriminate against other monotheists ('People of the Book', meaning Christians and Jews) on the basis of ethnic origin or pigmentation. Moreover, as a consequence of what Iberian historians long misrepresented as five

---

120 http://blackwomenofbrazil.co/2014/03/16/why-do-black-soccer-players-who-denounce-experiences-with-racism-always-seem-to-have-white-wives/http://www.diariodocentrodomundo.com.br/o-duplo-racismo-de-que-sao-vitimas-as-mulheres-negras/

centuries of North African/Arab occupation of their former homeland, which has now been shown to have been the peaceful spread of Islam among the populace as well as felicitous relations with those of other religions, the Portuguese in Brazil were long familiar with the Islamic religion practised by many of their African slaves.

From the 1580s, the importation of Africans to Brazil increased dramatically. After the initial expansion of the sugar industry, blacks soon constituted over two-thirds of the population of the north-east. A century later, the discovery of gold in Minas Gerais further increased the demand for slave labour. Meanwhile, in the *sertao* (hinterland) of the north-east, *pretos* (blacks), *pardos* (browns) and *cafuzos* (Afro-Indians) formed the majority of what would become the state of Piauí, where the traditional ranching skills of such West-African pastoralists as the Fulani played a prominent role in the development of the region's nascent cattle industry.

During the eighteenth and nineteenth centuries, with the demand for unpaid labour undiminished, the Bight of Benin became the primary source – from whence came the late survival in Brazil of traditions rooted in the culture of the Yoruba (*Nagô*) and the Fon (*Gegê*).

Police reports from the aftermath of the 1835 slave revolt in Bahia provide information about the African Muslim community in Bahia and the religiosity of African Muslims. Testimonies of captured rebels and the court proceedings have been used by researchers in their examination of the Muslims in Brazil and the Muslim-led slave revolts.

In 1865, an Iraqi religious scholar by the name of 'Abd ar-Raḥmān al-Baghdādī travelled to Brazil, where he met African Muslims in Rio de Janeiro, Bahia and Pernambuco. Al-Baghdādī stayed in Brazil for a few years where he worked as an *imam* (cleric) and taught the African Muslims about the tenets of Islam. He documented his experiences in Brazil in a treatise entitled, *The Amusement of the Foreigner by All Kinds of Wonderful Things*. Whilst admitting his shortcomings as a social scientist, the epistle of al-Baghdādī is a useful source from which to understand the practices of African Muslims in nineteenth-century Brazil. As al-Baghdādī himself states, the epistle is "a reminder for those who have sight and a lesson to those who have insight."

A few years after al-Baghdādī's visit, there was another significant report about African Muslim communities in Bahia and Rio de Janeiro by Count Joseph Arthur de Gobineau, the Representative of France in Brazil, who published *L'Essai sur L'Inégalité des Races Humaines* (An Essay on the Inequality of the Human Races) in 1856. In his infamous

Introduction

essay, Gobineau theorised on the inferiority of the Latin races and the superiority of the Nordic. Gobineau's racial discourse gave rise to the concept of Aryan superiority in 1894. Adolf Hitler and his cohorts used Gobineau's theories as a basis for their doctrine of Aryan supremacy.[121]

Gobineau stayed in Brazil for eighteen months between 1869 and 1870 in which he noted that African Muslims were intellectually and physically superior to other African slaves, about whom he had nothing good to say. "There is nevertheless a certain category of blacks, mostly settled in Bahia and its surroundings, that stand out in a remarkable way from other individuals of the same race."[122]

In a political report to the Quai d'Orsai, Gobineau stated that almost one hundred copies of the Qur'ān were sold each year to slaves and former slaves. Gobineau's admission is surprising considering the fact that he was a proponent of scientistic racism which views blacks as intellectually inferior to whites. At the time of Gobineau's report, many white Europeans were illiterate, so the presence of literate black Africans must have been a real shock to the Count.

In the 1880s, Raimundo Nina Rodrigues (d. 1906), a criminal ethnographer and a professor at the prestigious medical school of Bahia was perhaps the first Brazilian scientist to examine the subject of race. As a follower of European eugenicists, particularly Italian criminologist Cesare Lombroso who was famous for measuring cranial capacity to determine intelligence, Rodrigues feared that miscegenation would lead to degeneracy. He predicted that Brazil's future, especially in the north, would become ethnically black or *mestizo*. In his well-known ethnographic study of the population of African origin in Brazil, Rodrigues declared unequivocally that Africans were inferior.[123]

Rodrigues was a pioneer in Afro-Brazilian ethnology, and his studies would influence later generations of students of Afro-Brazilian history and culture.[124] He went to Bahia in 1900 to study the religions of black people in Brazil. In one of his works, *Os Africanos no Brasil* (The Africans in Brazil), written between 1890 and 1905 and published posthumously in 1932, Rodrigues dedicated a chapter to African Muslims.[125] In it, Rodrigues identified two distinct African 'cults', which he termed

---

121 Diouf, 2013, p. 135
122 Raeders, 1934, pp. 75-76
123 Telles, 2006
124 Ethnology is the scientific description of different races and cultures.
125 The book was originally published in 1900 in *Jornal do Comércio* of *Rio de Janeiro*.

Iorubanos and *Malês*. *Iorubanos* were the followers of the traditional Yoruba religion and *Malês* were Muslims.[126]

In his *O Animismo Fetichista dos Negros Baianos* (The Fetishist Animism of Bahian Blacks), Rodrigues talks about slave insurrections in the state of Bahia during the first half of the twentieth century. According to Rodrigues, African Muslims, influenced by the prevailing political context in the heart of Africa, were the true protagonists of the insurrections. The continuation of trade with Africa's coast kept Africans in Brazil informed about the political and religious victories of Hausa Muslims on that continent.[127] In 1825 they founded a Muslim government in Ilorin, an old province of the Yoruba kingdom. Hausa insurrections in Bahia preceded the famous 1835 *Malê* (Yoruba) revolt. Despite rivalries between the Yoruba and the Hausa in Africa, the second Hausa struggles, both in Africa and in Brazil, influenced the Yorubas, who later led the great revolt of 1835.[128]

Rodrigues' student, Arthur Ramos, further stimulated research into the country's African heritage with the publication of his work, *As Culturas Negras no Novo Mundo* (Black Cultures in the New World).[129] Ramos' ethnology widened that of Rodrigues considerably, as he knew more about research conducted on the African continent, which was generally overlooked in previous studies. Ramos broadened Rodrigues' Bahian studies to include other cultural areas of Brazil, particularly the *macumba* (polytheists) of Rio de Janeiro.[130]

Brazilian journalist João do Rio (d. 1921), real name Paulo Barreto, supported Gobineau's assessment of African Muslims in his observations of the Muslims in Rio de Janeiro, which were published in a series of journalistic articles on the various religions of Rio de Janeiro. João do Rio was a mixed-race Brazilian of African descent and also a prolific writer. In 1904, he wrote a series of news articles entitled *As Religiões do Rio* (The Religions of Rio). The articles were later collected and published in book form. According to Alberto da Costa e Silva, João do Rio was a very good journalist who "had no respect or liking for the religious practices of the Africans and their descendants in Rio de Janerio".[131]

---

126 http://www.englisharticles.info/2012/04/29/raimundo-nina-rodrigues/
127 The Hausas are a West African ethnic group who were amongst the most knowledgeable Muslims of West Africa.
128 Castro, 2013, p. 16
129 See Arthur Ramos' *The Negro in Brazil*
130 Bastide, 2007, p. 22
131 Silva, *2001, pp. 72-82*

Introduction

Thus, João do Rio reported what he saw and what he was told. Alberto da Costa e Silva writes:

> This fact gives his writings on Islam in Rio de Janeiro a special touch of truthfulness. We cannot doubt his words when he says that the young people had to study hard in order to become a scholar or *alufá,* and that there were people in town able to teach and to examine students on knowledge of the Qur'ān. One of his informants said to him that, after the exams, the approved candidate would be taken in triumph on horseback, followed by the faithful, along the streets of a distant suburb.[132]

German naturalist, Karl Friedrich Philipp von Martins, also stressed the importance of acknowledging and evaluating the African contribution to the economy and civilisation of Brazil. Martins' essay on this hitherto neglected subject was published in 1844. This need was also emphasised by the Brazilian literary critic, Sílvio Romero (d. 1914), who concluded that, "We owe much more to the Negro than to the [American] Indian; he entered into all aspects of our development".[133] In his essay, *O Negro – Objeto de Ciência* (The Black – Object of Science), Romero calls for a study of black Brazilians that will surpass European ethnography.[134] Romero wrote that it is "a shame for science in Brazil not to have devoted any of its efforts to the study of African languages and religions".[135]

Few negative comments on the Muslims have been recorded, and those that exist deal almost exclusively with their rebelliousness rather than any supposed inferiority. The exceptions are two renowned French scholars. According to award-winning historian of the African diaspora Sylviane A. Diouf, "in an amazing display of gross ignorance", the French historian, Roger Bastide, stated in 1961 that African Muslims in Brazil were "passive; Moslems, i.e. Islamised blacks, converts, not pure Semites" – as if Semites were genetically Muslims who had never converted to Islam.[136] Another scholar, Etienne Ignace, a professor at the Seminary of Bahia, had a very low opinion of the Muslims he met at the turn of the century:

> With their thick intellect full of nonsense, the *Malês* are swollen with a stupid pride. They are full of hate for the Whites and the

---
132 Silva, 2001, pp. 72-82
133 Giepel, 1997
134 Isfahani-Hammond, 2014, p. 173
135 Rodrigues, José Honório, 1965, p. 102
136 Diouf, 2013, pp. 134-135

Christians. Their ignorance is 'crass and supine', they cling with fanaticism to bland and exterior practices.[137]

Despite the discordant voices of the aforementioned French scholars, historians' general perception of African Muslims was positive, acknowledging their contribution to the development of Brazil.

CONTRIBUTIONS OF AFRICAN MUSLIMS TO BRAZIL

It should be stressed that the idea of an African diaspora developed first among Africans and their descendants, a point not sufficiently recognised in many Western academic discussions on the subject.[138] In Brazil, the leading figure in raising awareness of the contribution of Africans to the development of Brazil is believed to be Manuel Querino (d. 1923), an intellectual and historian of African descent. He was instrumental in raising awareness of the African contribution to Brazil's growth with his ethnographic essay, *A Raça Africana e Seus Costumes na Bahia* (The African Race and its Customs in Bahia). In the essay, Querino exhibited various photographs of Africans and used socio-evolutionist terminology to highlight the contribution of African people to Bahia's cultures. He also wanted to inform white Brazilians of the inestimable debt that the nation owed Africans who helped build the country. In his *Costumes Africanos no Brasil*, Querino mentioned the contribution of the *Malê* to Brazilian history. Querino brought an Afro-Brazilian perspective to Brazilian historiography, which previously had viewed history solely from a white European-Brazilian perspective.

Despite the wide criticism that Querino faced, he insisted that Brazil was the result of a fusion of the Portuguese, Amerindian, and African, but that the contribution of Africans had gone unheralded. He sought to redress the balance in his suggestive essay *'O Colono Prêto como Fator da Civilização Brasileira'* (The African Contribution to Brazilian Civilisation) (1918). Though his ideas were largely ignored, Querino belongs in the pantheon of great Brazilian intellectuals and historians. Fortunately, Querino's insightful works have been the subject of study by later scholars and historians who wanted to further understand the African contribution to Brazil's history.

Latin-American professor Bradford Burns said that subsequent scholars expounded Querino's work and emphasised that Africans had possessed the skilled and unskilled labour necessary to develop

---

137 Ignace, 1909, p. 100
138 Kristin Mann in 'Shifting Paradigms in the Study of the African Diaspora and of Atlantic History and Culture' in *Rethinking the African Diaspora*, 2001, p. 3

Introduction

Brazil for the industrial age.[139] At the time, Brazil's white elite felt that Europeans were more equipped for such sophisticated work due to what was perceived as their 'superior' racial disposition. In a racial climate that was at best condescending and at worst genocidal towards blacks, Querino helped pioneer the study of Afro-Brazilian history and awaken black consciousness in Brazil. Manuel Querino writes in 'The African Contribution to Brazilian Civilisation':

> The African slave was hardworking, thrifty, and provident, qualities which his descendants did not always conserve. He sought to give his offspring a licit occupation and, whenever possible, he saw to it that his children and grandchildren had mastered a skill. The work of the Negro for centuries sustained the grandeur and prosperity of Brazil. It was the result of his labour that Brazil could afford scientific institutions, literature, art, commerce, industry, and so forth. He thus occupies a position of importance in the development of Brazilian civilization.
>
> Whoever takes a look at the history of this country, will verify the value and contribution of the Negro to the defence of national territory, to agriculture, to mining, to the exploitation of the interior, to the movement for independence, to family life and to the development of the nation through the many and varied tasks he performed. Upon his well-muscled back rested the social, cultural, and material development since, without the income which he provided and which made everything possible, there would have been neither educators nor educated: without that wealth, the most brilliant aspirations would have withered; the bravest efforts would have been in vain. With the product of the Negro's labour, the wealthy masters sent their sons to European universities and later to our own universities, from which, well instructed, came our venerable priests, able statesmen, notable scientists, excellent writers, brave military officers, and all the rest who made of first colonial and then independent Brazil a cultured nation, strong among the civilized peoples.
>
> The black is still the principal producer of the nation's wealth, but many are the contributions of that long suffering and persecuted race, which has left imperishable proofs of its singular valour. History, in all its justice, has to respect and praise the valuable

---

139 See E. Bradford Burns' *A History of Brazil*,

services which the black has given to this nation for more than three centuries. In truth, it was the black who developed Brazil.[140]

Sociologist, anthropologist and historian, Gilberto Freyre (d.1987) was credited with the creation of Brazil's official identity as a racial democracy that is proud of its African heritage. He argued that Brazil has a unique racial democracy based on the "slack balance of antagonisms" between European masters and African slaves that is the legacy of the North-African Moorish domination of the Iberian Peninsula.[141]

Born in 1900, white Brazilian scholar Freyre spent much of his childhood on a sugar plantation owned by his mother's relatives. In his revolutionary work *The Masters and the Slaves*, Freyre spoke highly of the African contribution to Brazil:

> Every Brazilian, even the light-skinned, fair-haired one, carries about him on his soul, when not on soul and body alike, the shadow or at least the birthmark of the aborigine or the negro, in our affections, our excessive mimicry, our Catholicism which so delights the senses, our music, our gait, our speech, our cradle-songs, in everything that is a sincere expression of our lives, we almost all of us bear the mark of that influence.

Freyre's highly extolled work was a turning point in the analysis of Brazil's African heritage, as the government began to promote the nation's racial mixture. The acclaimed sociologist also spoke of the significant contribution that African Muslims had made to Brazil.

Academic studies on the religion of Africans in Brazil primarily focused on the traditional Afro-Brazilian religions of Candomblé and Umbanda until Brazilian historian João José Reis' pioneering work on the important role that Islam played in nineteenth-century Bahia. Originally published in Portuguese in 1986, Reis' highly acclaimed work *Rebelião Escrava no Brasil* (Slave Rebellion in Brazil) put Islamic history in the forefront in academic circles.[142] Reis meticulously explored the role of Islam, and specifically the slave revolts, in Afro-Brazilian history. Un-

---

140 Manuel Querino, *O Colono Preto como Factor da Civilização Brasileira* (Salvador: Imprensa Official do Estado, 1918). The essay is reprinted in Querino, *A Raça Africana*, pp. 123-152, under the title 'O Africano como Colonisador'. Source: Bibliographical Essay: Manuel Querino's Interpretation of the African Contribution to Brazil, Burns, 1974, pp. 78-86.

141 See Alexandra Isfahani-Hammond's *Slave Barracks Aristocrats: Islam and the Orient in the Work of Gilberto Freyre*

142 Austin, 1997, p. 42

Introduction

like previous historians, Reis incorporated the perspective of enslaved Africans, about whom history had hitherto been largely mute, in his study. The book has been described as "a magnificent example of interpretative historical analysis" based on rigorous archival research. The expanded English translation, which was released in 1995, was later revised and published in Portuguese (2004) to accommodate a large volume of new Brazilian documentation and Africanist literature. Although the arguments did not change fundamentally, Reis states that he continued to "emphasise the ethnic factor in the 1835 revolt without losing sight of the critical role of Islam".

Recent historians such as Michael A. Gomez (*Black Crescent: The Experience and Legacy of African Muslims in the Americas*), Muḥammad Shareef (*The Islamic Slave Revolts of Bahia, Brazil: A Continuity of the 19th Century Jihad Movements of Western Sudan*), Sylviane A. Diouf (*Servants of Allah: African Muslims Enslaved in the Americas*), Allan D. Austin (*African Muslims in Antebellum America: Transatlantic Stories and Spiritual Struggles*), Alberto da Costa e Silva and Paul Lovejoy also made valuable contributions to the study of the *Malê* revolt in their respective works.

Yoruba Muslim leaders of the 1835 *Malê* revolt planned the insurrection to take place in the month of Ramadan, and rebel participants dressed in Muslim clothing and wore amulets. Despite its religious overtones, the rebellion, Reis asserts, was not a *jihād* (sacred war), as other contemporary scholars have suggested, since the African Muslims knew that they needed non-Muslim participants in order to succeed. Because the African-Muslims who initiated the struggle sought to create a rebellion uniting Africans, they encouraged the participation of non-Muslims by propagating the notion that the rebellion was an uprising for Africans. The attempt at ethnic solidarity never succeeded as the uprising was eventually quelled. Its ringleaders were either executed or exiled to Africa. In 1850, fifteen years after the *Malê* revolt, the slave trade was officially abolished in Brazil, the last of the former European colonies in the Americas to do so.[143] Within a hundred years of the revolt, there was hardly a trace of Islam among Brazil's African descendent populations.

Why Did Islam Not Survive In Brazil?
Despite Muslims making up a large number of African slaves in late nineteenth century Bahia, their presence had almost entirely vanished within a century of the Muslim-led revolt of 1835. Abdias do Nascimento observed that the disappearance of Muslims in Brazil after the slave

---

143 Giepel, 1997

revolts was because the leading exponents of Islam in Brazil were killed in retaliation for the revolts or deported to Africa, and their followers were largely absorbed into other groups.[144]

The reasons why Islam did not survive in Brazil was something French sociologist and anthropologist Roger Bastide (d. 1974) deliberated on in his study, *The African Religions of Brazil: Toward a Sociology of the Interpenetration of Civilisations*. Bastide asks if the Muslims were so proud of their faith and so resistant to Catholic proselytising, "is it not paradoxical that it [Islam] should have so suddenly died out or undergone such profound adulteration?"[145] Some enslaved and free Bahian men complained of the Muslims' arrogance and standoffishness: "The *Nagô* who can read," commented one man, "and took part in the insurrection, would not shake hands with nor respect outsiders. They even called them *gavere* [*kafir* - disbeliever]."

There are several explanations for the disappearance of Islam in Brazil. First, the number of Hausa Muslims diminished considerably after the 1814 rebellion, when rebel leaders were either massacred or deported to Africa.[146] Those Muslims who remained made few converts, largely because of their "racial and religious snobbery, which caused them to hold aloof from the other Africans,"[147] going to bed early while the other black Africans preferred to stay up late to celebrate their pagan rituals."[148] Though it has been reported that many Muslims secluded themselves from non-Muslim Africans, it does not mean that this was due to snobbery as Bastide asserts. It is more likely that it was out of fear of being influenced by pagan practices or for some other plausible reason. By establishing Catholicism as the religion of the masters and Islam as the religion of the rebel leaders, slavery tended in early times to promote Islam, especially within groups that retained their African languages, thus disproving any claim to snobbery on the part of African Muslims.[149]

Just as an animal species becomes extinct when its last representatives die out, Islam in Brazil, having lost all potential for renewal or propagation, died out along with its old adherents. A Muslim cleric called Luís told Brazilian physician Nina Rodrigues how painful it was

---

144 Nascimento, 1989, p. 100
145 Bastide, 2007, p. 146
146 Ramos, 1946, p. 337
147 Ramos, 1946, p. 345
148 Querino, *Costumes*, pp. 111-112
149 Bastide, 2007, p. 146

Introduction

for him to see children of Muslims embracing pagan sects or Christianity rather than holding fast to the Islamic faith of their ancestors.[150]

The sociological explanation for why Islam triumphed over paganism and Christianity in West Africa in contrast to Brazil, where Islam did not survive amongst Afro-Brazilians who opted for Catholicism or Candomblé, according to Bastide, was that African Muslims in Brazil were passive, and failed to try and propagate their way of life. In people's minds Islam came to represent a kind of puritanism especially because of its prohibition of intoxicants, which was particularly hard on wretched slaves seeking an escape from their harsh reality in the sugar-cane brandy known as *cachaça*. It also should not be forgotten that Christianity was imposed on Africans in Brazil, which is why many of their descendants were raised as Christians and remained so. Subsequent generations were not able to maintain their Islamic faith, particularly after the 1835 revolt when the Portuguese punished Muslims and confiscated their religious documents.

African Muslims were not comrades of other slaves in slavery, except in an insurrectionary situation, where they could become leaders. Conversely, the white man represented the world of liberty to the slaves, a world to which manumission gave access. But the *sine qua non* of such access was to imitate whites. Hence the attraction of Catholicism.[151]

The Portuguese-Brazilians tried to erase all traces of Islam and Muslim identity from Brazil. They perceived Islam as a threat to the Christian establishment, a threat they were very aware of from their history of battles with North-African Muslims in the Iberian Peninsula. Portuguese-Brazilians feared African Muslims, who were in many cases literate, experienced in warfare and more civilised than them. By the mid-twentieth century the Islamic presence in Brazil was pretty much wiped out in much the same way as the indigenous peoples of Brazil were wiped out when the Portuguese settled in Brazil in the 1500s.

THE ISLAMIC REVIVAL IN BRAZIL

It wasn't until the early 1990s that a revival of Islam took place. Although at that point there were some Arab-Muslim communities in Brazil, there were hardly any converts. According to professor of anthropology Paulo Pinto, the rise of Islam in Brazil is due more to waves of immigrant Arab Muslims in the 1970s and 1980s, when communities organised and

---

150 Bastide, 2007, p. 146; Nina Rodrigues, *Os Africanos*, p. 101
151 Bastide, 2007, p. 154

constructed mosques, than to conversion.[152] The second generation of Arab-Brazilian Muslims, who were fluent in Portuguese, also helped propagate Islam, as they could speak to their fellow Brazilians in a language that they understood, unlike many of their parents' generation. Cristina Maria de Castro and Paul Amar examined the Arab Muslim presence in Brazil in their respective works, *The Construction of Muslim Identity in Brazil* and *The Middle East and Brazil: Perspective on the New Global South*. They show that although there was an Islamic presence in Brazil, it was mainly restricted to Arabs. It wasn't until the 1990s, and the immigration of African Muslim students and workers to Brazil, that Islam began to rise again in Brazil, and Brazilian-born people started to accept Islam.

Muslim Community in São Paulo

Conversion to Islam was particularly strong in São Paulo, Rio de Janeiro, Recife and Salvador. The Muslim community in São Paulo is the largest in Latin America. The majority of Muslims are of Syrian and Lebanese descent, dating back to the 20th century. The Muslim community is steadily growing due to the conversion of a number of Brazilians and African and Arab Muslims immigrating to the country in search of a better life.

The important thing is that the "faith is accepted" says a leading religious scholar in the area, Abdelhamid Metwally, an Egyptian graduate of the al-Azhar University. Arriving in Brazil in 2007, Metwally has witnessed the growing interest in Islam, "Brazil is a country of tremendous tolerance, where we can express our beliefs with great freedom, which is not the case anymore in some European countries."

A Brazilian female Cristiane Bertolino, converted in 2008, at the Do Pari mosque in São Paulo, "I come from a Catholic family and have never had a problem since I began wearing a headscarf, even at work," she says. "It is good to be a Muslim in Brazil. It could even be the best place for a Muslim, I'm not saying there are no prejudices or frictions, but there is no conflict."

Some Muslims have found life as a Muslim a challenge due to the country's liberal attitude and the difficulty in finding halal meat in some areas. A 26 year old language student from Syria, Dana al-Balkhi, arrived in Brazil with her sister in September 2013 but her sister returned to Syria after a few days, "Brazil was too liberal for her. I am a believer too, but

---

152 http://www.theislamicmonthly.com/immigrants-and-converts-muslims-in-brazil/

less rigid," Dana said. "Brazil is an extremely welcoming country but it's difficult to practice Islam here. Halal food is expensive and difficult to find. And even if you're not viewed with hostility, you feel very different."[153]

Although the Muslim community is growing, there appears to be a significant cultural gap between converts and Arabs, who make up the majority of Muslims in São Paulo. according to Kaab Abdul, a Brazilian convert from São Paulo. A former rapper, Kaab embraced Islam in 2008 after hearing the *adhan* (call to prayer) online. The sound of the *adhan* had an intense impact on him, and he started researching Islam online before his conversion. Kaab like many converts focuses much of his time at the mosque as he sees it as a place where converts can come together and develop their own identity. "A staunch supporter of the spread of Islam, he also hopes that more people in Brazil discover and embrace the religion, especially those form less-privileged socioeconomic backgrounds" [154]

Muslim Community in Salvador

The Muslim community in Salvador, the place of the 1835 revolt, is particularly strong and close-knit since the establishment of its mosque and cultural centre. A wealthy Arab-Brazilian Muslim from São Paulo established the *Centro Cultural Islâmico da Bahia* (Islamic Cultural Centre of Bahia), also known as *Mesquita Salvador* (Salvador Mosque), in 1991. He wanted to revive the African-Muslim heritage of the city. Initially it was a small place that he rented for Muslim students to come and meet, and in time it became the Islamic Cultural Centre.[155] With the help of Misbah Wale Akanni, a Muslim entrepreneur and the current Nigerian Liaison Officer of Bahia, the Islamic Centre was created, also serving as a mosque for daily prayers. Akanni came to Brazil from Nigeria in the late 1980s as a student but, after being requested by some Muslims from Saudi Arabia to help recreate the 'lost glory' of Salvador's Islam, he returned in 1990 to help build the Islamic community in Salvador.

Now settled in Salvador with his family, Akanni and his wife run the Irawo Hotel and Restaurant[156] specialising in African and Brazilian

---

153 http://www.worldcrunch.com/culture-society/muslim-and-happy-in-...-brazil/imam-conversion-islam-charlie-hebdo-catholic-race-headscarves/c3s18548/
154 http://theeyeinislam.com/islam-in-the-slums/
155 http://www.thenational.ae/sport/world-cup-2014/brazilian-city-salvador-linked-to-a-storied-islamic-past
156 *Irawo* is a Yoruba word meaning 'star'.

cuisine, which is situated in Pelourinho, the cultural and historic heart of Salvador. He also has a shop nearby selling African merchandise. Akanni is one of the key figures who have helped to recreate the African-Muslim link with Brazil. "It's a nice place to live, nice people and it's a beautiful country. They are very hospitable and they welcome Africans," Akanni said. "Here [in Salvador] it's like an extension of Nigeria."

In 1992, a year after the Islamic Centre in Bahia was established, the Nigerian-Muslim cleric who studied at the al-Azhar University in Cairo, Shaykh[157] Abdul Hameed Ahmad, was invited to become the *imam* (religious leader) of the centre and to lead prayers at the mosque. The centre holds weekly classes in Arabic for Muslims and non-Muslims, as well as hosting seminars about Brazil's African Muslim heritage and the religion of Islam. Ahmad takes part in hosting annual seminars in universities and in the Islamic Centre about slavery, Brazil's African Muslim heritage and the religion of Islam. Non-Muslim academics and prominent speakers, such as João José Reis, also take part in the seminars by giving talks about the history of Islam in Brazil. The seminars usually take place at the *Centro de Estudos Afro-Orientais* (CEAO) (Centre for Afro-Oriental Studies), where the Shaykh also teaches Arabic language and civilisation in conjunction with the Islamic Cultural Centre of Bahia.

The Nigerian shaykh informed me of the growing interest Brazilians have in their African-Muslim heritage, as many, he said, had been unaware of the African-Muslim presence in Brazil and of the impact that they had in shaping Brazilian society. "They don't know [about the history of the African Muslims in Brazil]. They just know about *Ilê Aiyê* and *Olodum*. They think it's just part of the social programme [in Brazil]. But they do not know why it's [called] *Ilê Aiyê*, or *Olodum*." He also delivers lectures and workshops at various schools, colleges and universities. "Here [in Brazil] we have freedom of speech," he said. One thing he did emphasise during our meeting is the need to continue having social programmes for Brazilian Muslims, programmes that are able to identify and meet their needs and are in harmony with their customs. "Many people think in Islam there are no social programmes," he said. The Islamic Centre currently serves an estimated five-hundred Muslims in Salvador, and there are plans for another mosque to be built in the city due to the growing number of Brazilians embracing Islam. Akanni said about the Muslim community in Salvador, "The Muslim community is gradually

---

157 Shaykh (also spelt Sheikh) is an honorific title used for religious scholars within the Muslim community.

Introduction

growing and we are holding the Islamic flag here, *inshā'Allāh* (God-willing)."

WHY ARE BRAZILIANS EMBRACING ISLAM?

In modern-day Brazil, the view of Islam as the foreign religion of Arab immigrants and their descendants is being challenged by the growing number of Brazilians of African descent embracing Islam (*Islão*).[158] Some reports estimate that there are a million Muslims currently living in Brazil, though the national census of 2010 counts a hugely lower population of 35,167.[159] The greatest concentrations of Muslims coincide with the largest Arab-Brazilian communities, in the state of São Paulo, followed by Paraná, Rio Grande do Sul, Rio de Janeiro and Minas Gerais. Most of the Muslims are from Syria and Lebanon and of Arab descent. Brazil's Syrian-Lebanese community, estimated to be seven million strong, is affluent, influential, and largely Christian. As is the case in the United States, Arab Brazilians are wealthy, educated and own multi-million pound businesses.[160] The states which have the largest number of Muslim converts are São Paulo, Rio de Janeiro and Salvador.

There is no single reason for conversions, but a plethora of theological, emotional and cultural motivations. For some new Muslims, Islam gives their lives meaning and has woken them from a spiritual malaise. Equally, some female converts said they were attracted to the Islamic focus on modesty, which liberated them from the sexualisation of the woman and Brazil's rampant fashion-driven consumerism.[161] Hip-hop

---

158 Castro, 2013, p. 1.

159 In most mosques, new Muslims are still remembered by name and can be counted by hand. "Muslims are listed in the 'other' category, along with Buddhists, for example," said Paulo Pinto of Fuminense Federal University, who estimated that Brazil is home to almost a million Muslims. The 2010 national census counted the Muslim population as less than 50,000. The reason for the large discrepancy is that Muslims do not feel confident enough to proclaim their faith and because the census is just inaccurate. Islam has grown in Brazil, which cannot be denied. The best indicator of this is the rapid increase in the number of mosques in Brazil, according to Pinto. Speaking in 2011, he said that there are now 127 mosques in Brazil, four times as many as there were back in 2000. http://www.dawn.com/news/653677/islam-takes-root-in-land-of-bikinis-and-carnival According to the IGBE Census, the number of Muslims in Brazil rose by 29.1% from 27,239 in 2000 to 35,167 in 2010. http://www2.anba.com.br/noticia/18828937/special-reports/muslim-population-grows-29-in-brazil/

160 Aidi, 2014, p. 11

161 http://www.theguardian.com/commentisfree/belief/2009/oct/05/black-muslims-islam

music, black American Muslim activists and the September 11ᵗʰ attacks have also been mentioned as reasons for the acceptance of Islam. Other Brazilians embrace Islam simply because they believe in the religion's uncompromising *tawḥīd* (monotheism): "*la ilaha illallah* – there is no god but Allah".

Black People Accepting Islam

Black people's acceptance of Islam is not new; it has been taking place in the African diaspora since time immemorial, as Richard Reddie mentions in his article, *Why are black people turning to Islam?*[162] The phenomenon of black people's acceptance of Islam is also taking place in Brazil, which is usually considered a Catholic country. "Islam is not new to Brazil," Jewish South-African historian and anti-apartheid activist Ronald Segal said, "numerous slaves brought from west and central Africa, mainly to Brazil, were Muslims already and converted others."[163] "Muslims who came to Brazil as slaves laid the foundation of the country," said President Luiz Inácio Lula da Silva, popularly known as Lula, in an address to Brazilian Muslims.[164]

Some Afro-Brazilian Muslims rejected Christianity in favour of Islam after discovering that Jesus has been misrepresented as a white European-looking man. Despite the fact that, according to a number of historical reports and Islamic texts, Jesus was a man of colour, European Christians have used the image of a 'white god' for centuries to justify enslavement, colonialism and the genocide of indigenous and African peoples. In contrast, Islam is seen by some who are drawn to it as the 'true religion' of coloured people and the oppressed, though in reality, it embraces all races and ethnicities.[165]

Some researchers have said that Islam is being embraced as a form of protest against the Catholic establishment. The discipline which Islam imparts is also seen as a way of curbing the harvest of fatherless children, unemployment, violence, drugs and sexual crimes of the *favelas*. Disillusioned with the concept of a 'white Jesus' and Christianity as a 'European religion,' some Afro-Brazilian Muslims find comfort in Islam's teaching of racial equality and the concept of a faith-based community

---

162 http://www.theguardian.com/commentisfree/belief/2009/oct/05/black-muslims-islam
163 Segal, 1995, p. 437
164 Aidi, 2014, pp. 36-37
165 In Islam, Jesus is considered to be a prophet of God and not the son of God.

(*ummah*) in which believers of all races and economic and social strata are brothers and sisters to one another.

Mahmoud, an Afro-Brazilian living in Salvador who embraced Islam five years ago, told me, "I would like to follow the principles of the *Malês*, who fought for freedom and liberty." After reading books and seeing Shaykh Ahmad on Brazilian TV, the history of the *Malês* was what made him curious to know more about Islam. He also said that he increased his knowledge of Islam from the Internet, by means of which he also discussed the religion on various internet forums with Muslims from the UK. For Mahmoud, the history of the *Malês* is potentially a source of inspiration for black Brazilians, adding that he thinks the country's elite would prefer people knew little about their African-Muslim ancestors: "They [i.e. Brazil's elite] do not want us to be aware of who the *Malês* were, as they are scared that we are going to tell people who may then mount an insurgency and take power for ourselves. So they prefer to keep the history of the *Malês* hidden."

Hip-Hop Music And Malcolm X

Hip-hop music was influential in the rise of Islam amongst people descended from Africans in Brazil's *favelas*.[166] The hip-hop scene in Brazil was born out of 1980s *favela* street parties, at which DJs played the latest American hip-hop and soul records to largely Afro-Brazilian crowds.

When the first hip-hop records came out, they naturally made it into circulation, but they had very different impacts in Rio de Janeiro and São Paulo. When hip-hop arrived at Brazilian funk parties, Rio de Janeiro took the electro influence of the genre, which led eventually to Miami Bass and the *baile funk*. Whereas Rio's *baile funk* became known for its party lyrics, curvaceous women and violence, the hip-hop scene in São Paulo was revolutionary, socially conscious and fiercely political in nature.

In the *pereferia* (the vast urban outskirts of São Paulo), which have been hard hit by crime and unemployment, hip-hop music introduced many Afro-Brazilians to Islam. Some Afro-Brazilians use this musical art-form to inform their Brazilian brothers about Islam and the African Muslims who led rebellions in Brazil's past. Many Afro-Brazilians living in *favelas* identify with African Muslim rebels in their fight against the country's establishment.[167] Hip-hop has become a powerful tool not only

---

166 Hip-hop is a music genre of U.S. Black and Latino origin. The genre is also referred to as 'rap music.'
167 'Islam on the rise in favelas,' France 24 report

to inform but also to inspire blacks to leave a life of crime and violence. MV Bill and Anderson Sa are two of a number of Afro-Brazilian hip-hop artists from the *favelas* who have used their music to empower Brazil's impoverished black community through their lyrics and social activism.[168]

According to Hisham D. Aidi, author of *Rebel Music: Race, Empire, and the New Muslim Youth Culture,* America's export of hip-hop and its occasional black power affections are "triggering that interest" in Islam in Brazil. African-American hip-hop groups and rappers, such Public Enemy and Tupac Shakur (d. 1996), still resonate amongst black Brazilian Muslims. Black American revolutionary rappers and poets like Tupac Shakur have been influential in awakening the black consciousness of later generations as well as their own. Shakur famously said, "I'm not saying I'm gonna change the world, but I guarantee that I will spark the brain that changes the world."

Hip-hop's ghetto music appeals to impoverished blacks, not only in Brazil, but across the world. Though not all themselves Muslims, many of the African-Americans rappers used Islamic references, had Arabic names and spoke highly of Muslims like Malcolm X and Muhammad 'Alī, which created more interest in the religion. Islam is viewed as the religion of the oppressed and revolutionaries, which resonates with many black Brazilians. Professor Vitória Peres de Oliveira in his article *O Islã no Brasil ou o Islã do Brasil?* (Islam in Brazil or the Islam of Brazil?) said that a number of black Brazilian Muslims "are attracted [to Islam] by something they read or from the film Malcolm X and the black-American Muslim movement or rap music."[169] Spike Lee's film, Malcolm X, sparked an interest in Islam among *favela* youth. Malcolm X remains

---

168 Anderson Sa was one of the founders of the AfroReggae cultural movement. The not-for-profit organisation is internationally recognised for its work in combating violence through social, musical and cultural projects to keep young people away from drug trafficking. The organisation was established in 1993 in Rio de Janeiro's Vigário Geral favela as non-profit newspaper on black culture for the communities of the favelas. Later, the organisation evolved to include musical groups in which young people could learn to express their creativity. The group has strict ground-rules for young people who want to join one of the subgroup musical bands, membership of which precludes drinking alcohol, taking drugs and smoking. See Favela Rising by Jeff Zimbalist.
MV, Bill real name Alex Pereira Barbosa, is a leading Brazilian hip-hop artist and social activist. In 2006, he produced *Falcão – Meninos do Tráfico* (Falcon – Traffic Children), a documentary of young favela-dwellers involved in the world of drug trafficking. MV Bill also featured in African-American historian Henry Louis Gates Jr's documentary *Black in Latin America,* in which he discusses the issue of Brazil's racism.
169 Peres, 2006

Introduction

hugely popular and influential in the lives of many black Brazilians who want to know more about their African and Islamic heritage. Freelance journalist Taylor Barnes, based in Rio de Janeiro, also noted the impact that the activist had on the conversion of black people in Brazil. Barnes said in her article "Immigrants and Converts: Muslims in Brazil" that an Angolan immigrant living in Brazil told her that he accepted Islam after reading *The Autobiography of Malcolm X*.

The connection between the revolutionary figure of Malcolm X and the *Malê* revolt was made when *Época* magazine ran a cover story with the headline 'Islam is Growing in the Periphery of Brazil's Cities,' adding, "Young blacks are becoming Muslim activists in response to racial inequality, What do they think and what do they want – the Muslims of the ghetto?"[170] Honorê al-Amin Oaqd, the founder of Brazilian hip-hop Posse Hausa, said, "Through the [rap] music I discovered Malcolm X, and then the history of the *Malês*. I saw that Muslim slaves were at another level, They were learned, didn't drink, didn't smoke, knew how to write."[171] Another new Muslim, recording artist 'Alī Jamal Shabazz who moved from eastern Brazil to join the hip-hop group in São Paulo, said, "When I discovered the history of the *Malês*, what caught my attention was the form of resistance, and their connection with God. It was this form of worship, which is unique that faced repression." He added, "We [black Brazilians] have problems that go all the way back to the plantation. And honestly those who die young in Brazil are those who never knew their history."[172]

Like al-Amin Oaqd, many Afro-Brazilian Muslims living in the slums (*favelas*) were introduced to Islam by the revolutionary lyrics of rappers from the United States who spoke about Islam. Afro-Brazilians identified with the rappers' socially-conscious lyrics about being downtrodden in society and found aspiration in their music. In São Paulo's outskirts, which are ridden with crime and unemployment, Islam is seen as a form of resistance to the Brazilian state. Hip-hop is often used as a tool for conversion of Afro-Brazilians. Although many middle-class converts in Brazil reportedly encounter Islam through Sufi organisations and higher-education establishments, in the *favelas* it's African-American music and culture that initially made Afro-Brazilians aware of Islam.[173] The same phenomenon exists in Europe and the United States, where

---

170 Aidi, 2004, p. 32
171 Aidi, 2014, p. 30
172 Aidi, 2014, p. 31
173 Aidi, 2014, p. 34

many white and middle-class Muslim converts embrace Islam through Sufism, whereas many black and working-class Muslims found out about Islam through hip-hop music.

September 11 Attacks
The vice president of the São Bernardo do Campo-based World Assembly of Muslim Youth (WAMY), Sheikh Jihad Hassan Hammadeh, attributes the growing acceptance of Islam amongst Brazilians to the 2001 'September 11th attacks' in New York. A Syrian-born Brazilian, Hammadeh said that more Brazilians investigated Islam after the attacks and subsequently embraced the faith.

Whilst speaking to a number of Brazilian converts at the Salvador mosque, I was also told that a number of Brazilians converted to Islam after wanting to find out about the religion after hearing about it in the aftermath of the attacks. Portrayed as a terrorist religion by many media outlets, many Brazilians found that this was not true after learning about the religion themselves, subsequently leading to their conversion.

Women Accepting Islam
In regards to Brazil's reputation both for carnival and for being a fervently Christian country, Hammadeh said that Brazilian Muslims can co-exist with non-Muslim Brazilians but "it depends on your conviction".[174] Paulo Pinto of Fuminense Federal University echoed Hammadeh's comments, adding "Islam is seen as a new form of resistance".[175] The Islamic teaching of modesty is also seen as a form of empowerment for Brazilian women who embrace Islam from the highly sexualised Brazilian society. In saying that, there is a misconception that all Brazilians are promiscuous and are unable to coexist with conservative Muslims. There is a "tendency to believe that the Brazilian lifestyle with its sensuality and liberalism would object to the rules of Islam," Paulo Pinto argued. He continued, "But in fact there are many conservative moral and sexual codes that regulate behaviour here in Brazil."[176]

According to the World Assembly of Muslim Youth (WAMY), seven out of ten new Muslims in Brazil are women, though the number is

---

174 http://www.theislamicmonthly.com/immigrants-and-converts-muslims-in-brazil/

175 http://www.dawn.com/news/653677/islam-takes-root-in-land-of-bikinis-and-carnival

176 http://www.dawn.com/news/653677/islam-takes-root-in-land-of-bikinis-and-carnival

debatable.[177] Female acceptance of Islam was the subject of an interesting documentary by Luiz Carlos Lucena called *Sob o Véu do Islam* (Under the Veil of Islam) in 2012. The documentary featured a number of Brazilian Muslim women who spoke candidly about their Islamic faith, lives and personal experiences of wearing the *ḥijāb* (headscarf) in Brazil.[178] According to a new Muslim woman who wears the *ḥijāb*, "Brazil is a mix, made up of several different cultures. This mix makes Brazilians very adaptable and tolerant."[179] The secretary of the Salvador mosque, Cristina Karima said that many Brazilian Muslim women, particularly those living in Salvador wear *ḥijāb*s around the city and do not suffer much discrimination. One of the reasons for this I was told was because *baianos* (people of Bahia) think that the Muslim women are followers of Candomblé, whose white attire and head tie is similar to traditional Muslim clothes. Some people think that the white clothes worn by the followers of Candomblé is due to the African Muslim presence in nineteenth century Bahia but there is no clear evidence to support this.

The Internet And Books

Recently, studies have been carried out by Brazilian sociologists, Vera Lúcia Maia Marques and Vlademir Lúcio Ramos in 2003 and 2000 respectively, about the growing number of Brazilians who embrace Islam. According to the research of Ramos, Brazilian converts' first contact with Islam came through books published by *O Centro de Divulgação do Islam para a América Latina* (CDIAL).[180] Ramos also cited the influence

---

177 Shaykh Ahmad disagreed and said that the majority of converts in Salvador are male. According to Shaykh Aḥmad, many Brazilian women are reluctant to become Muslims because of a dearth of suitable spouses and because of the pressure they are under from non-Muslim boyfriends and husbands. In Salvador and São Paulo there are a number of Brazilian Muslim women who are unable to marry to a lack of suitable marital partners. It is an issue amongst non-Arab Brazilian women in particular, as the Brazilian Muslims of Arab descent tend to marry each other. "It is not common to find an Arab [Brazilian Muslim] marrying a [non-Arab] Brazilian [Muslim]," Shaykh Ahmad said. "Here in Salvador, Recife and Rio de Janeiro, the [Muslim] population are black. Especially in Salvador and Recife, Brazilian Muslims converts are black."

178 A number of Brazilian Muslim women do not wear the *ḥijāb* (headscarf), which is something that the mosque does not make an issue of. Unveiled Muslim women are welcome in the mosque of Salvador and are active participants in Islamic propagation work

179 http://www.dawn.com/news/653677/islam-takes-root-in-land-of-bikinis-and-carnival

180 Castro, 2013, p. 1. Brazil hosts the largest Muslim community of Latin America, and

of Muslims of Arab descent and that curiosity to learn Arabic was also influential in Brazilians embracing Islam. Marques, on the other hand, emphasises that conversions usually occur in more influential Islamic communities such as among the Arab Muslims of São Paulo. Professor of sociology, Cristina Maria de Castro, adds that there are many Brazilians who accepted Islam through the Internet, with no Islamic community nearby. In her book *The Construction of Muslim Identities in Contemporary Brazil,* Castro also mentioned Brazilian Muslims who told her that they had embraced Islam after learning about it whilst at university and through Muslim friends. Many of the new Muslims Castro met said that they took the initiative of embracing Islam after learning about it for themselves.[181]

Two brothers whom I met at the Islamic Culture Centre of Bahia converted to Islam in September 2014, four months prior to our meeting. Ismail, the elder of the two, informed me that he embraced Islam after accidentally finding out about the religion. After years of no contact with his family, he now speaks to them, for which he credits Islam. His younger brother Adam said they came across Islam after reading the book of a non-Muslim neighbour about "the message of Islam". At the back of the book there was the address of the Salvador mosque, so the brothers went there, where they met Shaykh Ahmad whom Adam described saying that he "had so much wisdom and was a nice guy. He gave us some books [about Islam]." Despite living fifteen minutes walking distance from the mosque, they did not know anything about Muslims or Islam prior to coming across their neighbour's book. Ismail said, "We read the books [that the Shaykh gave us] and by the time I read the third book, I knew I was a Muslim!" He told me that the description of the one God is what warmed him to become a Muslim. "I thought I knew God until I learnt about Islam."

Originally from São Paulo, the much-travelled brothers lived in Spain and the United States for about three years each. Despite living in Spain and the United States, the brothers did not know about Islam and had not even heard about it from their friends or in school because "we weren't ready." "Allah had a plan for us to learn about Islam when we were ready, which is why we embraced it without hesitation when we did," they said.

Another convert I met at the Salvador mosque was a man called Mustapha, a Brazilian of Lebanese origin, who accepted Islam few years

---

publishes literature on Islam that is distributed throughout South America.
181 Castro, 2013, p. 26.

Introduction

ago. Mustapha had some Muslim relatives, but did not know much about Islam prior to his conversion. Formerly a Christian, he started to study different religions and eventually embraced Islam after years of private study. "When you find out what Islam is really about, not what the media or TV shows, in terms of the message of Islam in the Qur'ān and life of the Messenger of Allah, it is heart-fulfilling," he said. Another new Muslim, born Nascimento, now goes by the Arabic name of Ibrahim, accepted Islam after finding out about the "truth of Islam." Ibrahim's father was Catholic and his mother a Christian spiritualist. Ibrahim's mother and wife have also accepted the Islamic faith. Ibrahim also gives *khutbahs* (sermons) for the Friday congregational prayer at the mosque when the shaykh is unavailable.

Situated in Tijuca, north of Rio de Janeiro, the *Mesquita da Luz* (Mosque of Light) also serves as a community centre where Muslims attend to learn and study about their religion. The mosque is home of the *Sociedade Beneficente Muculmana* (Beneficent Muslim Society) – the SBMRJ – which was formed in 1951.[182] Sami Isbelle, a spokesperson for the SBMRJ, said, "The number of Muslims continues to grow, and most are Brazilians who are converting." Isbelle added that 85% of new Brazilian Muslims have no Arab links.[183] A 31-year old former Brazilian Catholic, who accepted Islam in 2009 and frequently prays at *Mesquita da Luz,* said:

> It happened during my adolescence. I continued to believe in God but not religion. I first came across Islam through a Muslim friend and while at university I began to study the religion myself in greater detail. It explained things to me better than any other religion had.[184]

Sexual Morality
Juma, a Tanzanian-born Muslim living in Salvador for the past few years spoke of the growing Muslim community in Brazil's most populated city of people of African descent. Amongst the number of converts who have embraced Islam. Juma informed me of a number of Brazilians who found solace in Islam because of its morality. One such example I was informed of was a man who trained as a priest for six years before becoming a

---

182 http://riotimesonline.com/brazil-news/rio-entertainment/rio-muslims-prepare-for-eid-at-tijuca-mosque/

183 http://www.dawn.com/news/653677/islam-takes-root-in-land-of-bikinis-and-carnival

184 http://riotimesonline.com/brazil-news/rio-travel/discovering-islam-in-rio-and-brazil/

Muslim. Islam's strict code of ethics in regards to sexual conduct appealed to the former priest who had become disillusioned with the Church's laissez-faire attitude towards promiscuity and homosexuality in modern day Brazil. Another convert I met not too far from the Salvador mosque informed me that Islam's stance regarding homosexuality and the firmness of Muslims' beliefs in regards to sexual conduct impressed him a great deal as he felt the Islamic way of life would help curb some of the decadent lifestyle which is the cause for the spread of venereal disease in Brazil. The new Muslim who did not want to disclose his full name did say that he felt that many Brazilians are growing disillusioned with what he described as "the constant promotion of alternative sexual lifestyles such as homosexuality and cross-dressing, which is destroying the traditional family unit." In saying that, he did say that Brazil is still a very tolerant country which may seem to accept such practices but he felt that many conservative Brazilians actually agree with Islam's views on sexual morality which is why a number of men and women are drawn to the faith.

Belief In One God And The Hereafter
During my visit to the Muslim community to Salvador, some of the Brazilian Muslims told me that the message of Islam and the Qur'ānic descriptions of the Hereafter (Paradise and Hell) were the primary reasons for their conversion. One Muslim I met was in tears as he told me how moved he was knowing that he could have died without knowing about Islam. Another man in Rio de Janeiro, who previously officiated as a Catholic priest, said Islam's strict monotheism was the reason for his conversion:

> I found all the answers to my questions in Islam. I found all that I was looking for. I discovered God as He is, without any modifications.[185]

THE STRUCTURE OF THE BOOK

The aim of this book is to introduce the history of Brazil's race-relations and African-Muslim heritage to readers who are neither specialists nor seeking exhaustive detail. The book is divided into two parts. Part I presents the history of race-relations in Brazil, exploring the issue of race, anti-black racism, white supremacy, colourism, black beauty and affirmative action in contemporary Brazil. Part II examines reports of African Muslims' travels to Brazil before the Portuguese, analyses African

---

185 http://www.dawn.com/news/653677/islam-takes-root-in-land-of-bikinis-and-carnival

Introduction

Muslim slave revolts in Bahia and presents an insight into the African Muslim communities and personalities in nineteenth century Brazil.

As more people are becoming conscious of both the issue of blackness and of the religion of Islam, I hope this book will a useful source to anyone who is interested in Afro-Brazilian and Islamic history.

The source for the material for much of Part I will be Afro-Brazilian studies and articles undertaken to understand race-relations from the Afro-Brazilian perspective. I will also draw upon research I have gathered from academic studies on race relations as well as empirical data from discussions with Brazilians during my visits to Rio de Janeiro, Salvador and São Paulo in 2014 and 2015. Acclaimed North African historian Ibn Khaldūn (d. 1406) said:

> This subject [of history] is dependent on studying numerous sources, understanding diverse subjects, having the best insight and analysis, and being able to verify the truth of sources, as they can deviate and be filled with mistakes. Historical research must not be dependent on mere copying of all reports. It should instead be based on an understanding of local customs, politics, the nature of civilization, and the local conditions of where humans live. You must also be able to compare primary and secondary sources, as they can help you differentiate between the truth and falsehood, helping derive conclusions that are believable and honest.[186]

The central aim of this book is to illuminate the darkness of Brazil's anti-black racism and celebrate the contributions of African Muslims to Brazil. The resistance to anti-black racism in Brazil can manifest itself in various forms, one of which is by education. Perhaps this book may help eradicate some misconceptions about both blackness and Islam. I hope this book can help instil black pride in hitherto downtrodden black people, but in addition contribute to further racial studies and Islamic history in Latin America.

In the chapters that follow, I will explore the racial history of Brazil and its African Muslim heritage. Chapter one outlines the complexities of race, ethnicity and skin colour in Brazil. I examine the evolution of race in Brazil from the miscegenation of Portuguese men with African and Amerindian women during the era of slavery, the national policy of 'whitening' (*branqueamento*) and the mass immigration of Europeans to Brazil from the 1880s to the 1920s, to the racial democracy ideology of the 1930s. The chapter also looks at Brazilian racial categories according

---
186 Ibn Khaldūn, 1967

to the national census and compares them to the racial classifications of the United States and South Africa.

In chapter two, I discuss ideals of beauty in Brazil and the impact they have had on black Brazilian women. I examine colourism, interracial marriage, the politics of black hair, the media and the fashion industry. Brazil's mass media are very influential in projecting a white Eurocentric ideal of female beauty, by which black and mixed-race women are often marginalised. The chapter concludes by discussing the importance of black people understanding their history and thus controlling their own self-image in order to appreciate the beauty of their blackness.

Chapter three provides an analysis of affirmative action in Brazil, citing the advocates and adversaries of racial quotas in Brazil. Maria Amelia Rocha Lopez, editor-in-chief of *Raça Brasil* magazine, said:

> On the surface, racism and prejudice doesn't exist in Brazil…you might see a lot of blacks in our football team, or in music, but how many do you see in politics, government, business leadership? The image of equality is a farce. In reality, it's a lot different. We blacks call it *racismo cordial* (cordial racism).[187]

Cordial racism, also referred to as passive racism and everyday racism, is not overtly expressed; it is subconscious. The problem with cordial racism is that although difficult to prove it nevertheless exists. Based upon negative perceptions of black peoples' intellectual capabilities, many people believe that blacks are not suited for managerial or leadership roles in business and politics. While blacks and mixed-race Brazilians are trusted by the nation's elite to be footballers and musicians, there does not seem to be the same level of trust in blacks occupying managerial and leadership roles that are based on intellectual capabilities rather than athleticism.

Part two, commences with chapter 4, examining historical reports of African Muslims' travels to the Americas before the arrival of the Portuguese in the 1500s. I will analyse the African-Muslim experience in Brazil and reveal the significant role Islam played in inspiring African Muslims to rebel against their European slave masters.

Chapter five analyses the military slave revolts in Bahia that occurred in the early nineteenth century. A number of slave revolts took place in the state of Bahia involving both slaves and free-persons. The Hausa-led uprisings of 1814 shook the Portuguese as did the 1835 *Malê* (Yoruba)

---

187 http://www.independent.co.uk/news/brazilian-blacks-need-not-apply-1177609.html

Introduction

revolt. The chapter concludes with a comparison of the 9th century Zanj rebellion in Baghdad, Iraq with the *Malê* rebellion of 19th century Bahia, Brazil.

In the penultimate chapter (six), I provide an analysis of 19th century African Muslims in Rio de Janeiro, Pernambuco and Alagoas, based on anthropological reports by Brazilian anthropologists, historians, journalists and a Muslim traveller from Iraq. The chapter also draws comparisons between the 19th century Iraqi traveller's visit to Brazil with the North African Berber scholar Ibn Baṭṭūṭah's travels to West Africa in the 14th century.

The final chapter presents a brief biography of the lives of three African Muslim personalities: two former African Muslims slaves who bought their freedom, pursued their religious education, and a female anti-slave activist and trader.

I conclude the book with a discussion of the racial democracy of Islam in Brazil which examines the current day Muslim communities in Rio de Janeiro, Salvador and São Paulo.

Part One

RACE-RELATIONS IN BRAZIL

CHAPTER I

RACE, ETHNICITY AND SKIN COLOUR IN BRAZIL

"The problem of the twentieth century is the problem of the color line."

W.E.B. DU BOIS

RACE (RAÇA) IN BRAZIL refers mostly to skin colour or physical appearances rather than to ethnicity. Although race does not exist biologically as a genetic fact, it exists as a social and cultural construct in modern-day societies like Brazil. European scientists first developed the concept of race, and it was used to promote white supremacist ideology, according to which non-white people are considered inferior in their racial typology. This 'scientific' concept of race was used to categorise human beings in distinct groups with inherent characteristics and features. In premodern societies, for whom the 'scientific' concept of race did not exist, tribal affiliation was of more importance in categorising groups, and racial categories did not function as they now do in the modern racialised world in which people are considered to belong to certain racial groups. In premodern multi-racial Arabian society for example, people used colour categories, such as 'black,' 'white' and 'red', relatively in their description of individuals.[188]

In contrast, in modern-day North America and Europe, people are all too often categorised according to their race and/or ethnicity. Historically, race and ethnicity have often been used interchangeably, and used to indicate the racialisation process in which 'race' is one of many ways to express and experience ethnicity — one that places an emphasis on phenotype (skin colour, shape of head, nose, etc).[189]

---

188 See my *Illuminating the Darkness: Blacks and North Africans in Islam* for further discussion of the early Arabs' understanding of race.

189 Sansone, 2003, p. 6

In Brazil, people are generally classified descriptively rather than racially or ethnically. This is due to complexities in race-relations in the country. The complex racial system of Brazil is rooted in the ideology of white supremacy and the miscegenation that has occurred between white Europeans, brown indigenous Brazilians and black Africans since the sixteenth century, which produced Brazil's racially-mixed offspring. The nation's official whitening policy was later introduced to eradicate the country's black race, who were seen as a hindrance to progress.

Despite famed sociologist Gilberto Freyre's claim that Brazil is a racial democracy, race continues to be an elusive and complex concept in Brazil, as the latest (2010) census report of racial classifications demonstrates. Although Brazilian people are characterised by a colour continuum, the national census uses five ethno-racial categories; *branco, preto, pardo, indigena* and *amarelo*. We will look at the different racial categories later in this chapter.

THE MISCEGENATION IDEOLOGY

Miscegenation (*miscigenação*) is defined as "the interbreeding of people considered to be of different racial types".[190] It can also refer to cohabitation, sexual relations or marriage between persons of different races, especially in historical contexts where it was considered a transgression of the law according to which the practice was prohibited. Miscegenation has existed since time immemorial, generally between a male slave master and his concubine, though such relations were generally coercive in the history of Western slavery. Most of the Portuguese who initially settled in Brazil were young unmarried men, criminals and miscreants whom the Portuguese government did not want in the country. Many of the female slaves suffered the horrors of rape at the hands of their Portuguese slave masters. The miscegenation that is popularly celebrated in Brazil as evidence of the nation's racial democracy was actually due to the rape of African, *crioulo* (Afro-Brazilian) and indigenous women by Portuguese men, something which is often omitted from discussions of Brazil's racial tolerance.[191]

Women of colour had few choices when white men expressed sexual desire for them. When a master sought sex, defiance was often futile and could bring severe retribution. Given the power that white men had, it

---

190 Oxford dictionary
191 Hawthorne, 2010, pp. 173-207

should not be surprising that many brown and black women in Brazil submitted to such relationships out of fear of further abuse.[192]

Race was not a barrier to sexual relations in early Brazil, as was the case in the rest of the premodern world, particularly amongst men. Race was, however, a barrier to marriage and sustaining a long-term relationship. In Brazil, sex was colourblind but marriage in most cases was most certainly not, as Portuguese men would have sexual intercourse with black and indigenous women but would almost certainly not marry them.

The absence of Portuguese women in Brazil was one of the reasons that miscegenation was so popular amongst the Portuguese men who settled in Brazil. Native Brazilian and mulatto women were highly desired for their sensuality but were not considered suitable wives, as the nineteenth-century Brazilian adage encapsulates white Brazilian males' sexual and marital attitudes towards women:

Branca para se casar. Mulata para fornicar. Preta para cozinhar (*White women for marriage, mulattos for fornication and black women to cook*).

In three short phrases, the popular saying describes and ascribes the social identities of white, mulatto and black women. The phrase still remains true for many Brazilians, for whom white women are assigned the role of legitimate and honourable sexuality as wives, mulatto women are associated with illegitimate and dishonourable sexual practices, and black women's sexuality is not mentioned and they are associated with domestic service and labour.[193] The notion that mulattos are suitable for sexual relations, demonstrates the sexual attitudes of white Brazilian men, which found nothing wrong with enjoying sexual relations with non-white women, even though they were not considered suitable for marriage. Slave women were taken at whim by their masters, or turned into prostitutes for their owners' profit. During the eighteenth and early nineteenth centuries, some whites believed that intercourse with a virgin black girl was a remedy for syphilis.[194]

The Portuguese differed enormously from the North Americans and the British in relation to their mixed-race offspring: the children were recognised as legitimate and were incorporated into the colonisers' families. The racial mixing which occurred in Brazil between the three races

---

192 Hawthorne, 2010, pp. 192-193
193 Caldwell, 2007, p. 50
194 Levine, 1997, p. 15

was not illegal nor was it socially discouraged. Miscegenation was also encouraged by some in the Catholic Church as a way of spreading Christianity. Slave owners were obliged by law to baptise their children and workers.

The high number of mixed-race (*mestiços*) offspring resulted in the non-white population of Brazil exceeding the white population in the late nineteenth century. The offspring of relationships between white men and indigenous women, *mamelucos*, often tried to pass as white. Those who could not do so were, like the indigenous population, discriminated against.[195] *Cafuzes*, the offspring of relationships between black and indigenous people, and *mulatos*, the offspring of relationships between white men and black women, were also discriminated against and frequently abused by whites.[196] Troubled by increasing high brown and black populations, Brazil's white elite sought to whiten the population to eradicate the country's "negro stain".

As early as 1755, the king of Portugal had encouraged his Brazilian subjects to "populate themselves" and "join with the natives through marriage". In the same year, the Marquis of Pombal rose to power in Portugal as minister for war, eventually becoming prime minister. During his twenty-two years in power, he went to great lengths to encourage such intermarriages. The Portuguese crown, however, did not encourage intermarriages of white colonists with blacks and mulattos, and the Catholic Church condemned miscegenation in general, and so interracial marriages were simply not recognised by the church. Such prohibitions of race mixture were easily ignored, especially given a highly uneven ratio between the sexes among the colonisers. In the early historical period, the Portuguese colonisers were mostly males in search of wealth rather than settlement (as in the U.S. case), and Portuguese women were often forbidden to migrate, creating a very high gender imbalance in the white colonial population. This led Portuguese colonisers to seek out Amerindian and African mates, and the number of progeny from these mixed unions grew throughout most of the colonial period.

Given the racial hierarchy imposed by the slave-based economy, relationships between the white colonisers and non-white Brazilian women were highly unequal. White men frequently raped and abused African, indigenous, and mixed-race women. Indeed, mixed-race Brazilians were largely spawned through sexual violence throughout the period of slavery, although cohabitation and marriage between whites and non-whites

---

195 Hawthorne, 2010, p. 195
196 Hawthorne, 2010, p. 197

were not uncommon. Thus, a tradition of race mixture was established in Brazilian society through both violent sexual relations as well as informal and formal unions. Although the relative frequency of the different forms of miscegenation is not clear from the historical record, by the 1872 census before slavery was completely abolished – when the male-female balance had been largely restored – 5.1% of marriages in the federal district of Rio de Janeiro were between whites and mulattos, and another 0.8% involved whites and blacks.

Brazil's first formal nationwide census in 1872 classified 20% of the population as blacks and 42% as mixed-race. *Mulatos* (mulatto men) were considered unstable, but *mulatas* (mulatto women) were thought of as sexually desirable. Dark-skinned people were generally deemed slothful, prone to violence, uncontrollable and stupid. They were invariably excluded from desirable housing, employment, and social opportunities. Distrust in turn led authorities to enact new measures of social control. Brazil's government encouraged scientists to study the latent characteristics of Brazil's racial types and miscegenation.[197]

White Supremacist Views Of Miscegenation
As slavery was being abolished throughout the Americas in the nineteenth century, science would be used to validate white racial domination by claiming that Caucasians were inherently superior to non-white people. Prior to that, when race usually described one's descent rather than a hierarchy of biological types, the subjugation of Amerindians and Africans proceeded on the basis of moral and religious reasoning rather than by means of a scientific argument. Scientific interest in the issue of race in Brazil began in the late nineteenth century, and concern grew over how race would affect Brazil's future development. This was especially true in the emerging science of eugenics, which set out to discover "the social uses to which knowledge of heredity could be put in order to achieve the goal of better breeding". Eugenics, at the time, viewed blacks as inferior and mulattos as degenerate. Furthermore, eugenicists believed that tropical climates such as Brazil's weakened human biological and mental integrity, and that therefore the Brazilian population exemplified biological degeneracy.

A notable example of this thinking was Count Arthur de Gobineau, who published *L'Essai sur L'Inégalité des Races Humaines* (An Essay on the Inequality of the Human Races) in 1856, and who was appointed to serve as the Representative of France in Brazil from 1869 to 1870. He would

---

197 Levine, 1997, p. 10

come to detest Brazil, commenting that its miscegenation had affected all Brazilians across all classes and even "in the best families" (except the emperor whom he befriended), making them ugly, lazy, and infertile. His obsession would lead him to openly identify ministers and other members of the Royal Court as mulattos. For him and other Europeans, as well as for North Americans of the time, Brazil typified the perils of miscegenation by producing a degenerate people that would doom the new country to perpetual underdevelopment. Such a view of the Brazilian population by highly respected Europeans would leave its mark for many years to come.

Nina Rodrigues embraced theories of scientific racism and social Darwinism broadly held by the Brazilian intellectual elite of his time. Rodrigues viewed racial mixing and the black presence in Brazil as a hindrance to the nation's progress. His views greatly influenced the country's 'whitening' policy, which encouraged the mass immigration of white Europeans to reduce the 'degenerate' blacks and indigenous Brazilians, whom he believed to be inferior races.

Rodrigues died at a young age in 1906, while he was in the midst of developing his ideas. He had advocated for separate criminal laws for each race, which was about as close as any influential Brazilian had ever come to proposing legal racial segregation. Whereas a principle of *livre arbitrium* (free will) was part of the Imperial Penal Codes, Rodrigues proposed to eliminate the principle for blacks since he believed that they were not free to choose between lawful behaviour and crime because of their diminished mental and moral capacities. Reflecting his uncertainty about mulattos, however, he encountered difficulty in placing them within his conceptual scheme. He divided the mulatto population into superior, ordinary, and degenerate or socially unstable types.

Rodrigues' uncertainty over the classification of the mulatto may have reflected his own mixed-race identity, as well as the general sentiments of the Brazilian elite, since many of them could be classified as mulatto. Miscegenation had presented a dilemma, and consequently Brazilian eugenicists and other intellectuals had begun to waver in their conclusions about mulattos. Mulattos were perceived as clearly distinct from pure-blood blacks and Amerindians, and there was often an optimistic sense that they were more like the whites. Rodrigues' ambivalence about the status of the mulatto and the need to distinguish them from the whites may have kept him and other members of the elite from taking the extreme segregationist route chosen by the United States and South Africa in the late nineteenth and early twentieth centuries. Moreover, it would have been difficult to determine who was white in Brazil, so the imposition of segregation was impractical, as it would potentially have excluded many influential members of the Brazilian elite, as Gobineau had disparagingly described them. Although most members of the Brazilian elite would likely have been classified as white in their own country, their status as whites in the eyes of Europeans and North Americans was not so certain. This fact is likely to have influenced their own visions of race mixture and their development of a national project.

Literary critic Silvio Romero, an important Brazilian intellectual in his time, equivocated in his response to the determinist dilemma posed by Gobineau, other Europeans and, to a large extent, by Rodrigues. Although Romero agreed that blacks, especially Amerindians, were inferior to the Portuguese, who themselves were inferior to the "Germano-Saxons", he also considered the possibility that miscegenation could produce vigorous growth, and thus that Brazilians might benefit racially in their future development. Romero's uncertainty about the consequences of miscegenation would certainly add to the Brazilian elite's climate of racial insecurity, but by 1888 he began to be more confident in his optimism about miscegenation and Brazil's future.

Whitening As The Solution
Eugenics promoted social policies that would apply the new scientific understandings of heredity to improve human populations. Brazil developed their own brand of eugenics that subsequently influenced ideology and social policy.

These eugenicists accepted the racist postulation of black and mulatto inferiority, but thought this inferiority could be overcome by further miscegenation. Based on their interpretation of eugenics and their own sensitivities to theories about racial and tropical degeneracy, Brazilian scholars used a theory of constructive miscegenation and proposed "whitening" through the mixing of whites and nonwhites as the solution. Based on higher white fertility rates and their belief that white genes are dominant, these eugenicists concluded that mixing the races would eliminate the black population, eventually resulting in a white or mostly white Brazilian population. Brazilian eugenicists also successfully countered scientists' claims that tropical climates are unhealthy for whites, a prejudice that had originally limited their ability to import European labourers.

Whitening, as prescribed by the eugenicists, became the basis of Brazil's immigration policy. To accelerate the whitening goal, Brazilian elites and policy-makers looked for workers in Europe, where a demographic transition was producing surplus labour. In Brazil, as in other Latin American countries, the elites sought out and subsidised European immigrants to "improve the quality" of its work-force and replace the former slaves. In particular, the state of São Paulo, in collusion with coffee planters, encouraged, recruited, and subsidised European immigration, while the federal government restricted Asian immigration until 1910. This new supply of labour supplanted the former African slave population in places like São Paulo and, at the same time, acted as a "civilising agent" by whitening the Brazilian gene pool. These white settlers were eventually expected to mix with the native population, thereby diluting Brazil's large black population.[198]

THE WHITENING IDEOLOGY

In the aftermath of the official abolition of slavery in 1888, Brazil's white elite were concerned with the country's large non-white population. For them, the problem was how to save the white race from the threat of deterioration posed by the presence of black blood. The dominant elite felt threatened, and feared that the blacks would become a menace to society, so they spent a great deal of time mulling over how to best solve the so-called 'Negro problem'. The solution that Brazil along with other countries found was the ideology of racial whitening (*branqueamento*).[199]

Proponents of whitening believed that black Africans were less sophisticated and civilised than white Europeans. The political elite eagerly embraced the eugenicist ideas that were circulating in nineteenth century Europe as both diagnosis of and remedy for the country's socio-economic backwardness. The mixed-race and black population were regarded as a hindrance to the nation's development and evolution into a First-World nation.[200]

A conscious and systematic effort was made by the white ruling elite to de-Africanise Brazil by encouraging the immigration of white Europeans

---

198 Telles, 2006, pp. 26-29

199 Cuba, Haiti, Peru and the Dominican Republic are examples of Latin American countries that adopted the whitening ideology as a solution to their demographic problems with the mass importation of European immigrants. See Henry Louis Gates Jr.'s *Black in Latin* America. Jamaica, Australia and South Africa are examples of non-Latin American countries that imported Europeans to 'whiten' their nation.

200 https://www.academia.edu/2573184/_Confronting_Whitening_in_an_Era_of_Black-Consciousness_Racial_Ideology_and_Black-White_Marriages_in_Rio_de_Janeiro_

(from Portugal, Italy, Germany, and Spain) in the late nineteenth and early twentieth centuries. The Brazilian government subsidised the relocation of the European immigrants, and most of them settled in southern Brazil. A large number of the Europeans that immigrated were the destitute of Europe, not the skilled labourers Brazil's government envisioned. Politician João Pandiá Calógeras declared:

> The black stain is destined to disappear in a relatively short space of time because of the influx of white immigration in which the heritage of Ham is dissolving. [Theodore] Roosevelt rightly pointed out that the future has reserved for us a great boon: the happy solution of a problem fraught with tremendous, even mortal, dangers – the problem of a possible conflict between the races.[201]

A decree of June 28, 1890 conceded "free entry by persons healthy and able to work, except natives of Asia and of Africa, who can be admitted only by authorisation of the National Congress".[202] The concept of whiteness was expanded later, as white European immigrants were soon followed by newly classified 'white' Arab (Syrian and Lebanese) and 'white' Asian (Japanese) immigrants, who were given access to the nation's resources, while the recently manumitted mixed-race and black Brazilians were excluded from society and left in poverty. There were no reparations for the centuries of enslavement, nor were they given land or any means of employment except for the most menial urban jobs.

The large number of Europeans immigrating to Brazil, coupled with ongoing miscegenation, made several Brazilian intellectuals and eugenicists confident that their nation was successfully whitening.[203] Many of the thinkers, who were white, served the dominant powers by 'objectively' endorsing the 'facts' of black inferiority and the soon-to-be disappearance of the black race.[204] Prominent writer Paulo Prado wrote:

> ... in the continuous mixture of our life since the colonial era the Negro is slowly disappearing, being transformed into the deceptive appearance of a pure Aryan.[205]

---

201 Skidmore, 1974, p. 205
202 Skidmore, 1974, p. 193
203 Telles, 2006, p. 29
204 Nascimento, 1989, p. 79
205 Skidmore, 1974, p. 204

Another outspoken Brazilian intellectual, Arthur Neiva, lauded the racist whitening ideology: "Within a century the nation will be white!"[206] In 1911, João Batista Lacerda, the sole Latin American delegate to the first Universal Races Congress in London, thought that the black race would be extinct in Brazil by 2012:

> In virtue of this process of ethnic reduction it is logical to expect that in the course of another century the *metis* (half-breed) will have disappeared from Brazil. This will coincide with the parallel extraction of the black race from our midst.[207]

Lacerda and Neiva's hypothesis was widely criticised in Brazil by worried white Brazilians who were outraged by their estimate of the time it would take to purify Brazil of the black race.[208] The government's policy of mass white European immigration to Brazil in the late nineteenth and early twentieth centuries in order to dilute the black blood of the country is referred to as the "whitening (*branqueamento*) process".

Whitening (*branqueamento*) can be considered in both a symbolic and biological sense. Symbolically, whitening represents an ideology that emerged from the legacy of European colonialism in Latin America that catered to white dominance. Biologically, whitening is the process of having children with lighter-skinned individuals in order to produce lighter-skinned offspring. The belief in white supremacy was supported by 'scientific' theories of race and religious interpretations of the Divine curse on dark-skinned peoples known as the "Curse of Ham" or "Curse of Canaan".[209] The Biblical story of Noah's curse on his son's (Canaan) descendants was invoked by Christian thinkers to justify slavery. The story was used as Divine mandate for the trafficking of African slaves and the ownership of plantations. The Catholic Church also supported mass enslavement of the 'heathen' black Africans. The natural-slave theory of the ancient Greeks was also used to support the 'scientific' theory of race on the notion of white supremacy.

---

206 Skidmore, 1974, p. 193
207 Skidmore, 1974, p. 66
208 Skidmore, 1974, p. 76
209 http://lesleyannewarner.wordpress.com/2012/05/19/brazils-growing-relations-with-africa-through-the-lens-of-its-african-heritage/

Curse Of Ham

The Catholic Church validated Brazil's anti-black racism and treatment of its African subjects and legitimised the enslavement of 'heathen' black Africans. Christian thinkers endorsed the whitening ideology as a way to bring the blacks out of the darkness of heathenism to the light of Christianity.

Spanish artist Modesto Brocos y Gómes best captured Brazil's whitening ideology in his 1895 painting *A Redenção de Cam* (The Redemption of Ham), which was used to propagate the whitening ideology for the "betterment of the race" in Brazil. The painting portrays a mulatto woman holding her phenotypically white baby while the baby's white Portuguese father looks on. The baby's black grandmother is standing at her daughter's side with her hands in the air, seemingly praising God because her grandchild is white. The painting reflects the pathological desire of many black and mulatto Brazilians to be white. A realisation of Brazil's dominant elite, the title of the painting, *The Redemption of Ham*, is based on the biblical 'curse of Ham' story reported in Genesis[210]:

> The sons of Noah who went forth from the ark were Shem, Ham, and Japheth. Ham was the father of Canaan. These three were the sons of Noah; and from these the whole earth was peopled.
>
> Noah was the first tiller of the soil. He planted a vineyard; and he drank of the wine, and became drunk, and lay uncovered in his tent. And Ham, the father of Canaan, saw the nakedness of his father, and told his two brothers outside. Then Shem and Japheth took a garment, laid it upon both their shoulders, and walked backward and covered the nakedness of their father; their faces were turned away, and they did not see their father's nakedness. When Noah awoke from his wine and knew what his youngest son had done to him, he said:

> "Cursed be Canaan;
> a slave of slaves shall he be to his brothers."

He also said,

> "Blessed by the Lord my God be Shem;
> and let Canaan be his slave.

---

210 Genesis 9: 18-28. No reliance can be placed on Biblical stories involving disparagement of the Prophets from an Islamic perspective.

God enlarge Japheth,
and let him dwell in the tents of Shem;
and let Canaan be his slave."[211]

The "curse of Ham" legend has multiple versions. Also known as the "curse of Canaan", the story was been interpreted by Christian scholars both to explain the origins of human differentiation and as authorisation for the enslavement of black Africans.[212] Ham was later reinterpreted as the father of dark-skinned peoples of the world, as Ham was incorrectly understood to mean "black or dark", as David M. Goldenberg explains, in his definitive study of the story in the Abrahamic faiths. He explains that in the seventh century the expressions *Banū Ḥām* and *bnei ḥam* (children of Ham), in Arabic and Hebrew respectively, were used synonymously for "black Africans".[213]

In regards to the 'curse', according to Goldenberg four factors were at play during the first five or six centuries of the Common Era: explanation (an attempt to understand the Bible), error (a mistaken recollection of the Biblical text), environment (a social structure in which the black had become identified as slave) and etymology (a mistaken assumption that Ham meant "black, dark"). The combination of these four factors led to the birth of the fable in which Ham, the father of the black African, was cursed with eternal slavery along with his descendants.[214]

Although the Bible makes no explicit mention of the curse of blackness, the story was used by Christian Europeans to justify the colonisations of non-white 'heathens', particularly black Africans, who were considered the descendants of Ham. The white elite in Brazil, who were largely Catholic, used the assumed Biblical justification for the enslavement of black Africans for over four hundred years.

Scientistic[215] Racism
Scientistic racism ruled Western thought during the 'Age of Enlightenment', when human beings were classified into three races: the Caucasoid, Mongoloid, and Negroid. Scientistic racism advocated improving

---

211 Genesis 9:18-28
212 Gomez, 2005, pp. 44-45. See David M. Goldenberg's *The Curse of Ham: Race and Slavery in Early Judaism, Christianity and Islam*
213 Goldenberg, 2005, pp. 166-167
214 Goldenberg, 2005, pp. 166-167
215 'Scientistic' derives from 'scientism' defined as: thought or expression regarded as characteristic of scientists. Excessive belief in the power of scientific knowledge and techniques. (Oxford Dictionary) Scientistic racism is also known as 'scientific racism.'

the human race through maintaining the genetic purity of the races, particularly Caucasoids such as the Anglo-Saxons. Brazilian elites, like other Latin American intellectuals, were, however, influenced by Lamarckian eugenics according to which white genes were considered 'stronger' than their black or indigenous counterparts.[216]

Supporters of scientistic racism believed that the Negro race would advance culturally and genetically, or, on the other hand, disappear within a few generations of miscegenation. The two now-discredited beliefs that the Brazilian elite based their whitening ideology upon were: Social Darwinism, which applied Charles Darwin's natural selection theory to a society or race, and Aryanism, the belief that the 'white' Caucasoid Aryan race was superior to all others. The two racist ideologies under the umbrella of scientistic racism were used by the Brazilian power elite to further their plans to 'whiten' Brazil and thus 'improve' the nation.[217]

In 1945, a series of laws were passed by the Brazilian government subsidising European immigration and prohibiting African immigration, in order to increase the country's white population and dilute the country's black blood:

> In the admission of immigrants, the need to preserve and develop, in the ethnic composition of the population, the more convenient features of their European ancestry shall be considered.[218]

The mixture of races in Brazil consisted of three 'inferior' races according to scientific racists: the white Portuguese, the brown indigenous Brazilians, and the black Africans.[219] Although the Portuguese were considered 'white', they were at the lower end of the white race due to their mixed ancestry with North African Moors.[220] Northern Europeans were considered the 'pure' superior white race and a decision was made

---

216 https://www.academia.edu/2573184/_Confronting_Whitening_in_an_Era_of_Black-Consciousness_Racial_Ideology_and_Black-White_Marriages_in_Rio_de_Janeiro_
217 Brazil's neighbouring country, Argentina, has been able to eliminate black Africans from their nation, so much so that many people are unaware of the presence of black Africans in the history of Argentina.
218 http://atlantablackstar.com/2014/03/10/5-black-nations-that-imported-europeans-to-whiten-the-population/2/
219 See David Haberly's *Three Sad Races: Racial Identity and National Consciousness in Brazilian Literature*
220 For Gilberto Freyre, the civilising legacy of the Moors transformed the Portuguese into Afro-Europeans. Isfahani-Hammond, 2014, p. 167

to 'improve' the racial make-up of the Brazilian nation by encouraging the mass immigration of more white Europeans.

After the mass white immigration, the whitening policy officially came to an end, as Brazil had effectively whitened its population, which was reflected by the racial change in the population from 1872 until 1940. According to the Brazilian Institute of Geography and Statistics, the black population decreased from 19.9% in 1872 to 14.6% in 1940. In contrast the white population grew from 38% in 1872 to 63.5% in 1940. The figures show the clear decline in the black population, which was noticed by Clayton Cooper, a visiting statesman from the United States, who commented in 1917:

> An honest attempt is being made here [in Brazil] to eliminate the Negroes and mulattoes through the infusion of white blood.[221]

THE IDEOLOGY OF RACIAL DEMOCRACY

By the 1930s, the racial paradigm of Brazil shifted from whitening (*branqueamento*) to the ideology of racial democracy. Racial democracy (*democracia racial*) is a term used to promote the idea that Brazil is a post-racist society in which racism and racial discrimination do not exist. Those who believe in Brazil's racial democracy say that social inequalities are due to other factors such as class, education and financial resources but not race or skin colour. The myth of Brazil's racial democracy originated in the theory of Brazilian sociologist Gilberto Freyre, author of *Casa Grande e Senzala* (The Masters and the Slaves).

Freyre's theory was that with all of the racial mixing in Brazilian history, the country is void of racism because most Brazilians have some indigenous or African blood. Freyre compared the miscegenation in Brazil to the United States, where there was a separation of races. Freyre and other intellectuals who believe that Brazil is a racial paradise are, unsurprisingly, white Brazilians who are not subject to the country's institutional racism.

Freyre asserted that Brazil's miscegenation of its three races (white Portuguese, black Africans and brown Amerindians) created a hybrid race, which has made the country free of racism. According to what Freyre had observed in Europe, the United States, and Africa, in terms of race-relations, Brazil is the most advanced country in the world.

---

221 Skidmore, 1974, p. 91

Brazil's white elite embraced Freyre's ideology of racial democracy, and promoted the notion that all Brazilians live in racial harmony, and that any discrimination black Brazilians suffer is a function of social class, not of race.

Racial mixture became a central feature of Brazilian national identity, largely due to a single publication, selected by leading academics as the most influential nonfiction book of twentieth-century Brazil, Gilberto Freyre's *Casa Grande e Senzala* transformed the concept of miscegenation from its former pejorative connotation into a positive national characteristic and the most important symbol of Brazilian culture. Under the influence of his mentor, anti-racist anthropologist Franz Boas – who proposed that racial differences were fundamentally cultural and social rather than biological – Freyre effectively proposed a new national ideology.

Although he did not coin the term, and elements of the concept were being promoted well before him, Freyre fully expressed, developed, and popularised the idea of racial democracy, to the point where it dominated Brazilian racial thinking from the 1930s to the early 1990s. Freyre argued that Brazil is unique among Western societies for its smooth blending of European, Amerindian, and African peoples and cultures. As a result, he claimed that Brazilian society is free of the racism that affects the rest of the world. Although the notion that Brazil had a more benign system of slavery and race relations than the United States had a long history, Freyre turned this distinction into a central aspect of Brazil's emerging national identity, granting it a scientific, literary, and cultural status that would endure at least until well into the 1980s.

Freyre characterised the extended patriarchal family of the large rural slave plantations (*latifundios*) in the sixteenth and seventeenth centuries as a cauldron for interracial mixing that harmonised differences and diluted conflicts, thus enabling extraordinary assimilation, and creating a new "Brazilian people". In later publications, he would extend this argument into the modern period.

Freyre would generally downplay whitening and rather focus both on miscegenation's effects on diffusing racial differences and the contribution of African cultural influences to the white elite. This association of miscegenation and racial democracy with whitening would later lead black activist Abdias do Nascimento to accuse Freyre's ideas of contributing to a campaign of genocide against Brazil's black population, through which the Brazilian elite sought to eliminate black people and black culture.

Freyre's optimistic analysis of Brazilian race relations was largely based on the distinction he repeatedly made with the racial situation in the United States.

Freyre's work would later be criticised by black Brazilian activists for its romanticised portrayal of race relations in Brazil. One of those critics was the prominent black Brazilian activist and historian Abdias do Nascimento (d. 2011). Arguably Brazil's greatest modern day black leader, Nascimento strongly advocated the case for Afro-Brazilians and tackling racial inequality in contemporary Brazil. Although he did not receive the international attention of renowned black activists like Marcus Garvey, W.E.B. Du Bois, Malcolm X, Martin Luther King, or Nelson Mandela, nevertheless, Nascimento was an active militant for the black cause. "Give me the right words to get at these racists who have been in power for five hundred years!" Nascimento said, "The right words to tell Brazil, to tell the world that the black people are aware, that the black people are awake!"[222] An actor, poet and former politician, Nascimento was instrumental in galvanising Brazil's Black Movement into studying African history, religion, and culture.

In contrast to Freyre's depiction of the miscegenation which occurred in Brazil, Abdias do Nascimento said:

> There is the myth that slavery in Brazil was very gentle, very friendly, even ... These are all fabrications. Slavery here was violent, bloody. Please understand, I am saying this with profound hatred, profound bitterness for the way black people are treated in Brazil – because it's shameful that Brazil has a majority of blacks, a majority that built this country, that remain second-class citizens to this day.[223]

Argentine sociologist Carlos Hasenbalg described the devastating effects of Freyre's racial democracy ideology on Brazil's antiracist organisations:[224]

> By stressing the positive contribution of Africans and Amerindians to Brazilian culture he subverted the racist assumptions of contemporary social analysis such as Oliviera Vianna. At the same time, Freyre created the most formidable ideological weapon against antiracist activists. His emphasis upon the plastic character of the Portuguese colonizers' cultural background and the widespread

---

222 Gates, Jr., 2011, p. 49
223 Gates Jr., 2011, p. 48
224 Twine, 2005, p. 6

miscegenation among the Brazilian population led him to the notion of a racial democracy.[225]

According to Dave Treece, the populist politics of racial democracy and social integration did not become reality for many non-white Brazilians:

> Any attempts by black or working class organisations to represent their own experience and interests independently of the state, or against its rhetoric, were met with outright totalitarian repression. The country's first black political party, the Black Brazilian Front, was outlawed in 1937. So the apparently liberal ideology of mixture, integration and racial democracy went hand-in-hand with violent hostility towards those who challenged their oppression in terms of race or class.[226]

Racial democracy has never existed in Brazil according to many Afro-Brazilians, who are often subjected to discrimination and racial profiling. White Brazilian professor Idelber Avelar from Tulane University argues that many white Brazilians have fooled themselves into thinking that discrimination is only due to socio-economic status. The fact that Brazil's richest areas are overwhelmingly white and the prisons are overwhelming black, are indicative of the country's racial divide, Avelar asserts.

Brazil's prison system, in which the majority of those incarcerated are black and poor, is notoriously overcrowded. Brazilian society criminalises the poor. Many of the country's prisoners have been arrested for petty crimes, and many others are abandoned in the overcrowded prisons despite the fact that they have not been sentenced. Remand prisoners can languish for years, mixing with hardened criminals. The result is that prisons are "schools of crime", where many prisoners reoffend committing more violent crimes after their release. In many respects, the penitentiary system is a modern form of slavery, an institution that is motivated by economics and which targets non-whites. Brazil's overcrowded black and brown prisons illustrate the myth of racial democracy, because middle-class white Brazilians who commit crime are often able to avoid going to prison. A well-known saying within the *Movimento Negro,* illustrates attitudes towards race-relations in Brazil, "If you want to know who is black in Brazil, ask the police!"

---

225 Hasenbalg, 1985, p. 25
226 http://socialistreview.org.uk/313/brazil-fighting-right-be-black

In his analysis of Brazil's racial democracy ideology in the 1940s, African-American sociologist E. Franklin Frazier commented:

> Namely in Brazil there is no stigma attached to Negro blood, "One drop of Negro blood" does not make a person Negro and condemn him to become a member of a lower caste ....Moreover it is generally accepted as an unexpressed national policy that the Negro is to be absorbed into the total population. It was with this in mind that a Brazilian statesman reminded [President] Roosevelt that in a hundred years Brazil would have no Negroes whereas the U.S. would have the problem of twenty or thirty million.[227]

Brazil's Racial Democracy and the United States' Segregation Laws

If one were to compare Brazil's race-relations with those of the United States or South Africa, Brazil is undoubtedly ahead in terms of mixing of the races. However, a comparison should not be made with other racist societies merely in order to downplay the racism of the Portuguese-Brazilians. Despite Brazil's image of racial democracy, the institutionalised racism which exists in the country paints another picture. Racism in Brazil is not open and overt, it is concealed, and colour-prejudice exists in the sub-conscious of many fair-skinned Brazilians. In a report on Brazilian attitudes to racism, a large majority admitted that the country does have an issue with racism, but interestingly enough most of the respondents said they were not themselves racist.

In his study of Brazil's race-relations, Thomas E. Skidmore argues that, after embracing the racial democracy ideology, Brazil's white elites developed a sense of their moral superiority in comparison to countries like the United States.[228]

While still believing that white is better and that Brazil was becoming whiter, after 1930 elite spokesmen gained further satisfaction and confidence from the new scientific consensus that black is not inherently worse and thus that the racist claim that miscegenation must result in degeneration is nonsense. For approximately two decades after 1930, this Brazilian satisfaction at the discrediting of scientific racism led to the argument that Brazilians' alleged lack of discrimination made them morally superior to technologically more advanced countries, in which

---

227 Twine, 2005, p. 7
228 Twine, 2005, p. 6

systematic repression of racial minorities was still practised. The United States was the favourite example, and Nazi Germany became another.[229]

In the 1950s and 1960s, the United Nations Educational, Scientific, and Cultural Organization (UNESCO) funded a group of social scientists to conduct research on race relations in Brazil. The research generated a rich body of ethnographical evidence that debunked the myth that Brazil was a racial democracy. However, sociologist France Winndance Twine, author of *Racism in a Racial Democracy,* argues that, while recognising racial inequalities, scholars tended to stress socioeconomic status as the primary axis of power and de-emphasised colour and race as an axis of inequality.[230] This de-emphasis of race as an axis of power, and faith in Brazil's racial democracy is illustrated by Charles Wagley's introduction to *Race and Class in Rural Brazil*, a volume published in 1952. Wagley argues that:

> Brazil is renowned in the world for its racial democracy. Throughout its enormous area of a half-continent race prejudice and discrimination are subdued as compared to the situation in many countries.... Today it may be said that Brazil has no 'race problem' in the same sense that it exists in other parts of the world; people of three racial stocks live in what are essentially peaceful relations.[231]

During his 1994 presidential campaign, Fernando Henrique Cardoso stated in an address while visiting the northeast region of Brazil, whose population is predominantly black, that his family had *"a pé na cozinha"* (a foot in the kitchen). This popular Brazilian phrase is used to convey the idea that an individual's genealogy is linked to the "kitchen" by means of slavery and/or domestic service.[232] Though Cardoso would be considered white in Brazil, Cardoso's use of the phrase underscored the link between racial intermixture and Brazil's national identity as a *mestiço* nation in which racism does not exist.

Brazil's racial democracy is a beautiful and alluring ideal, but African-American historian Henry Louis Gates Jr. asked, "but had it ever been more than a romantic white worldview, designed to keep Afro-Brazilians in their place?" If Brazil was truly a racial democracy, there would be no need for a black-consciousness movement. The existence of Brazil's

---

229 Skidmore, 1990, p. 27
230 Twine, 2005, p. 7
231 Wagley, 1952, p. 7
232 Caldwell, 2007, p. 38

growing black-consciousness movement is a reflection of the anti-black racism that still exists in the country.

Race-relations in Brazil and other Latin American countries are very complex and fascinating. Though different from the United States, they are not necessarily better. The intermingling of blacks and whites amongst the poor in Brazil, which does not occur to the same extent in the United States, can easily give the impression that racism does not exist. This was because of the one-drop rule in the US, which created a sense of solidarity among whites, as a way of dividing them from blacks. Even though working-class whites may have been poor, they could feel a sense of superiority towards blacks who belonged to an 'inferior race'. It can, however, be argued that Latin American elites such as Brazil's are far more racist than in the United States. Until very recently, Brazil's political and social elite was white, whereas in the United States, which has a much smaller percentage of blacks, people of colour have made greater inroads into the upper echelons of society. The racial democracy which some of the country's elite promote is merely the possibility of white men having sexual relations with black women and producing mixed-race offspring without feeling guilty about it. The institutionalised racism that exists in Brazil is viciously unegalitarian and pernicious. Whites remain at the top and blacks are completely frozen at the bottom. It is like apartheid without having the apartheid laws.

THE CENSUS' RACIAL CATEGORIES

A census is an official head-count or survey, especially of a country, city or population. In the national censuses carried out in Brazil, United States of America and South Africa, racial categories differ as we shall now show.

In 1872, the Brazilian Institute of Geography and Statistics (IBGE) conducted its first national census. It was the only census conducted during the period of slavery. At the time, Brazil's population was approximately ten million. The census showed that 37% of the population were white, 44% brown, and 19% black. The brown category of 1872 consisted of *pardos* and *caboclos*, the latter referring to persons of predominantly indigenous origin. During slavery, white people were the minority, though this soon changed after the mass immigration of Europeans and Asians at the invitation of the government, thus whitening Brazil's population.

As part of Brazilian president Getúlio Vargas's modernisation efforts, the second official census took place in 1940, Brazil's first modern census, after the abolition of slavery and the mass immigration of Europeans to Brazil. Since then, the census has taken place every ten years except during the 1970s when Brazil was under military dictatorship. Thus, in 1940, after an absence of fifty years from the previous census which took place in 1890, race was reintroduced as a category in that census at the very same time that the ideology of racial democracy began to take hold. The new official belief, that race was not problematic, is demonstrated in the following quote from a Brazilian government publication in 1950:

> The preparation of the 1940 Census developed in a period in which racist aberrations appeared on the way to global predominance. Nevertheless, the national Census Commission not only wanted to remain faithful to the most honourable tradition of modern Brazilian civilisation, the equality of the races, but it also sought to eliminate any suspicion that the question on colour, introduced in the census purely with scientific objectives, was to serve as a preparatory instrument for social discrimination.

If racial discrimination were no longer believed to be important, then why ask the race question? Despite the emerging belief in racial democracy, belief in whitening also persisted among some sectors of the Brazilian elite. Concerns about Brazil's racial composition certainly remained, and the 1940 census would be an opportunity to measure the effects of massive European immigration during the previous five decades. A government document published in 1961 claimed that, as a result of the 1940 census:

> Many educated Brazilians ... were anxious to see the exact percentage of the progressive predominance of the white group in the national population, which, with triplicate impropriety, was customarily called Aryanisation, and according to the then widely diffused ideas, seemed supremely desirable.[233]

The results of the 1940 census revealed that mass European immigration had brought Brazil closer to its whitening goal. 64% of Brazilians were white in 1940. The decline in the percentage of mulattos in the population was probably the result of reduced intermarriage, due to the particularly great marginalisation of blacks and browns in this period and the relatively high levels of endogamy among the immigrant ethnic groups, whose social interactions must have been limited by their language, customs, and cultural institutions. Also, the changed categories

---
233 Telles, 2006, p. 39

for the mixed-race population, from *mestiço* and *caboclo* to *pardos,* may have led to underestimation of the change in the brown population and overestimation of the black. A shift from placing emphasis on ancestry to appearance may also have led to the reclassification of persons, who would have been considered *mestiço* but who were dark in appearance, as black in the 1940 census. Although the growth of the white population and the decrease of the brown population proportionately would have led to some optimism for supporters of whitening, such as João Batista Lacerda, the fact that the proportion of the black population did not change during this period would have surely discouraged them.

Ignoring Brazilian realities, in its 1970 report to the Committee on the Elimination of All Forms of Racial Discrimination (CERD), the military government confidently proclaimed that racial discrimination did not exist in Brazil. Brazil's foreign minister declared:

> I have the honour to inform you that since racial discrimination does not exist in Brazil, there is no need to take sporadic measures of a legislative, judicial or administrative nature to assure the equality of races in Brazil.

Even in the dark days of authoritarian rule from 1967 to 1974, the ideology of racial democracy was well entrenched and widely understood. The mere mention of race or racism was met with social sanctions, which would often result in one being labelled a racist for bringing up the issue. American sociologist Edward E. Telles was told by a reliable but confidential source, that Brazil's military government perceived black protest as a major threat to national security.[234] The *Movimento Negro* (Black Movement) of Brazil grew in the 1970s, drawing inspiration from the United States' Black Power movement and Jamaica's Rastafari movement, which caused fear amongst Brazil's elite. The two movements Afrocentricism and political activism drew international awareness, which led to a sense of pride in blackness. Brazil's *Movimento Negro* argued for non-white Brazilians to be called blacks (*negros*), as the mixed-race and black Brazilians were both treated the same as black people by the country's racist power structure.

Until 1991, Brazil's government census agency (IBGE) asked census respondents, "What colour are you?" In the 2000 census, the question read, "What colour or race are you?" The latest census, which took place in 2010, categorised Brazilians in five racial classifications, even though much of the population do not necessarily use these categories

---

234 Telles, 2006, pp. 33-41

when describing themselves.[235] The IBGE itself acknowledges that the racial classifications are disputed. The daily vernacular of the Brazilian population identifies people by colour and not by race, though this is beginning to change with black activists campaigning for non-whites to identify themselves as black.

The tables below shows Brazil's changing racial composition from its first census in 1872 until its most recent in 2010.

Brazilian Population by Race or Skin Colour from 1872 to 2010
(Census Data)

Race or Colour	Brancos (whites)	Pardos (browns)	Pretos (blacks)	Cabocios	Amarelos (yellows)	Indigenous	Undeclared	Total
1872	3,787,289	3,801,782	1,954,452	386,955	-	-	-	9,930,478
1890	6,302,198	4,638,496	2,097,426	1,295,795	-	-	-	14,333,915
1940	26,171,778	8,744,365	6,035,869	-	242,320	-	41,983	41,236,315
1950	32,027,661	13,786,742	5,692,657	-	329,082	-	108,255	51,944,397
1960	42,838,639	20,706,431	6,116,848	-	482,848	-	46,604	70,191,370
1980	64,540,467	46,233,531	7,046,906	-	672,251	-	517,897	119,011,052
1991	75,704,927	62,316,064	7,335,136	-	630,656	294,135	534,878	146,815,796
2000	91,297,042	65,318,092	10,554,336	-	761,583	734,127	1,206,675	169,875,856
2010	91,051,646	82,277,333	14,517,961	-	2,084,288	817,963	6,608	190,755,799

---

235 According to preliminary results of the 2010 census, for the first time, non-white people make up the majority of Brazil's population. Out of around one hundred and ninety-one million Brazilians, ninety-one million identified themselves as white, eighty-two million as mixed race and fifteen million as black. Whites fell from 53.7% of the population in 2000 to 47.7% last year. The once-a-decade census showed rising social indicators across Brazil as a result of economic growth, but also highlighted enduring inequalities. The census was conducted by the Brazilian Institute of Geography and Statistics (IBGE). "It is the first time a demographic census has found the white population to be below 50%," it said in its report. The number of people identifying themselves as black rose from 6.2% to 7.6%, while the number saying they were of mixed-race rose from 38.5% to 43.1%. Among minority groups, two million Brazilians identified themselves as Asian, and 817,000 as indigenous. http://www.bbc.co.uk/news/world-latin-america-15766840

Brazilian Population by Race or Skin Colour from 1872 to 2010

(Census Data by %)

Race or Colour	Brancos (whites)	Pardos (browns)	Pretos (blacks)	Cabocios	Amarelos (yellows)	Indigenous	Undeclared	Total
1872	38.14%	38.28%	19.68%	3.90%	-	-	-	100%
1890	43.97%	32.36%	14.63%	9.04%	-	-	-	100%
1940	63.47%	21.21%	14.64%	-	0.59%	-	0.10%	100%
1950	61.66%	26.54%	10.96%	-	0.63%	-	0.21%	100%
1960	61.03%	29.50%	8.71%	-	0.69%	-	0.07%	100%
1980	54.23%	38.85%	5.92%	-	0.56%	-	0.44%	100%
1991	51.56%	42.45%	5.00%	-	0.43%	0.20%	0.36%	100%
2000	53.74%	38.45%	6.21%	-	0.45%	0.43%	0.71%	100%
2010	47.73%	43.13%	7.61%	--	1.09%	0.43%	0.00%	100%

BRANCO (WHITE) — According to the census, the white Brazilians are people of European and Arab descent. People who are classified as 'white' are fair in complexion with predominant European features i.e. straight hair, aquiline noses and thin lips. In Brazil, some 'white' people define themselves as white not necessarily because of the paleness of their skin but because of their hair texture. A person with a light-brown skin complexion and perceptible African features may be considered 'white' because of their straight or curly but non-Afro textured hair. Large numbers of Brazilians who are classified as and who identify themselves as white have African and indigenous Brazilian ancestors and would not be classified as 'white' in the United States or Europe.

PARDO (BROWN/MESTIZO) — *Pardo* was a caste classification used in colonial Spanish America from the sixteenth to the eighteenth century. It means 'light-skinned' or 'mulatto', referring to people of mixed racial ancestry but also un-mixed acculturated Amerindians. Brazilians use a number of terms to describe people who would be classified as *pardo* by the census, terms such as: *moreno, mulatto, canelo, escuro, claro* and *castanho* who would all be classified as *pardo*. Those who are 'half-caste' and 'half-breed' would also be classified as *pardo,* but such terms are offensive and rarely used.

PRETO (BLACK) — The *preto* are the 'black' race and the term refers literally to the colour black. Brazilians of African descent who are dark in complexion with prominent African features are classified as *preto*. Many

Afro-Brazilians use the term *negro* (feminine form *negra*) to identify themselves rather than the word *preto*. In Salvador, the capital of black Brazil, Afro-Brazilians also affectionately refer to one another as *"preto," "pret," "pretinho"* and *"negão"*[236] as a form of endearment. Some Afro-Brazilians, particularly those affiliated with the Brazilian Black Movement, prefer the term 'Afro-Brazilian' for themselves, and would include *pardo* Brazilians in their racial classifications of blacks. Afro-Brazilians are primarily of West African (Yoruba, Hausa and Fulani ethnic group) and Central African (Bantu) origin.

The country's latest census (2010) has confirmed that, for the first time since national records began, non-whites form the majority of Brazil's population. The proportion of Brazilians identifying themselves as *negro* (black) or *moreno* (brown) increased from 44.7% to 50.7%, Brazilians of African descent being the official majority. The IBGE said in its report:

> Among the hypotheses to explain this trend, one could highlight the valorisation of identity among Afro-descendants.

The IBGE said that while its researchers had detected the trend a few years prior to the 2010 census, the results confirmed the growing increase in Brazil's non-white population. Brazil's minister for racial equality, Elio Ferreira de Araujo, attributed the change to growing pride among Brazil's black communities. People are no longer scared of identifying themselves or insecure about saying: "I'm black, and black is beautiful."

INDIGENA (INDIGENOUS) – The *indigena* (indigenous peoples of Brazil), also referred to as Amerindians and native Americans, are the original inhabitants of Brazil prior to the settlement of Europeans and Africans in the country. Many Brazilians see *indigena* as a cultural rather than a racial term, and tend to not use the term to self-identify themselves as such.

AMARELO (YELLOW) – Brazilian citizens of full or predominantly East Asian, South Asian and South-East Asian ancestry are the *amarelo* (yellow) race, according to the census. The *amarelo* are a minority amongst

---

236 *Negão* (*negona* in the feminine form) is derived from *negrão* (the augmented form of *negro*) literally "big black man." This term has several meanings depending on the context and tone of voice used. It can be used to express the notion of the black male as large, threatening, and violent; it can have a sexual connotation; or it can also be a term of endearment, as in *meu negão*. The word *negão* is sometimes translated as " nigger/nigga" which is also seen as a racially offensive term or term of endearment depending on the context of its usage in the United States. Pinho, 2010, p. 235

the five races in Brazil. The majority of *amarelo* are of Japanese origin, and are situated mainly in São Paulo and Paranā.

United States Census' Racial Categories

The United States' Census Bureau collects racial data in accordance with guidelines provided by the U.S. Office of Management and Budget (OMB), and these data are based on self-identification. In the latest Census (2010), individuals were given the option to identify themselves with more than one race. The racial categories included in the United States' census questionnaire generally reflect a social definition of race recognised in the country and not an attempt to define race biologically, anthropologically, or genetically. In addition, the Census' racial categories include racial and national origin or sociocultural groups. For instance, an individual may choose more than one race to indicate their racial mixture. Individuals who identify their origin as 'Hispanic', 'Latino' or 'Spanish' may be of any race, though 'Latino' and 'Hispanic' are cultures and not a racial group.[237] The five minimum race categories required by the OMB are as follows:

WHITE – A person having origins in any of the original peoples of Europe, the Middle East, or North Africa.

BLACK OR AFRICAN AMERICAN – A person having origins in any of the Black racial groups of Africa.

AMERICAN INDIAN OR ALASKA NATIVE – A person having origins in any of the original peoples of North and South America (including Central America) who maintains tribal affiliation or community attachment.

ASIAN – A person having origins in any of the original peoples of the Far East, Southeast Asia, or the Indian subcontinent including, for example, Cambodia, China, India, Japan, Korea, Malaysia, Pakistan, the Philippine Islands, Thailand, and Vietnam.

---

237 The terms 'Hispanic' and 'Latino/Latina' are problematic in and of themselves. The term Hispanic and/or Latino is not actually a race as is commonly understood, but a cultural heritage. In the modern usage of the word, Hispanic refers to people from Spain or Spanish-speaking countries, especially those of Central and South America. Latin is commonly used to refer to South American countries, though Brazil tends not to be included in discussions about Latin America as it is the only country in South America that speaks Portuguese as its official language.

NATIVE HAWAIIAN OR OTHER PACIFIC ISLANDER – A person having origins in any of the original peoples of Hawaii, Guam, Samoa, or other Pacific Islands.

South African Census' Racial Categories

There have been three official censuses since South Africa's first democratic election in 1994, the first conducted in 1996, the second in 2001, and the third in October 2011. The population in 1996 was 40.6 million, increasing by 10.4% to 44.8 million in 2001. The population grew by 15.5%, in the space of ten years to reach a total of 51.7 million in 2011. Despite claims of South Africa being a 'Rainbow Nation', and even though whites are a minority, they continue to control and own the vast majority of the country's land and resources, as in Brazil and the United States. *Statistics South Africa* carries out the country's census, and classifies South Africans into four main racial categories:[238]

AFRICAN – Classified as African or black, black South Africans are the original inhabitants of the country, making up 79.2% of the country's population. Black South Africans are not culturally or linguistically homogenous, as they consist of a number of ethnic groups such as the Zulu, Xhosa and Bapedi. The major ethnic groups in South Africa are predominately Bantu-speaking peoples. The word *kaffir* is a derogatory ethnic slur used in South Africa to refer to a black person. The word is derived from the Arabic word *kāfir* (unbeliever), which was adopted by Europeans to refer to black non-Muslim peoples, whom they regarded as infidels.

WHITE – Refers to white South Africans of European descent, primarily from Netherlands, Germany and France. Culturally and linguistically, white South Africans are divided into Afrikaners, who speak Afrikaans, and English speaking groups. Afrikaners are also referred to as Boers (farmers), and own over 80% of South Africa's land despite making up less than 10% of the country's population.

COLOURED – The coloured, also known as Bruinmense, Kleurlinge or Bruine Afrikaners in Afrikaans, are people of mixed racial ancestry. In Southern Africa, Cape Coloured is the name given to an ethnic group composed primarily of persons of mixed-race. The coloured population are mainly concentrated in the Cape region and come from a combination of racial and ethnic backgrounds including African, European, Chinese,

---

238 There is a fifth category called 'other', which represents approximately 0.5% of South Africa's population as of the 2011 Census.

and Indonesians (wrongly called Cape Malays). Although 'Cape Coloured' form a minority group (8.9% of the population) within South Africa, they are the predominant population group in the Western, Northern and Eastern Cape. The origins of the coloured community stems primarily from miscegenation between white European males and black South African females in the Cape Colony from the seventeenth century.

INDIAN/ASIAN — The 'Indian' race, also referred to as 'Asians,' refers to South African citizens of Indian and South Asian descent. The majority of Indians came to South Africa in the nineteenth century to work on the sugar plantations of the eastern coastal area. South Africans of Chinese, Malay and Vietnamese descent are also classified under the 'Asian' category, though some South East Asians are classified as coloured. The Indian/Asians make up approximately 2.5% of South Africa's population as of the 2011 Census.

CONCLUSION

Racial categories as shown in the Brazilian, United States and South Africa Censuses differ amongst from each other. A bi-racial person who is considered 'black' in the United States may not necessarily be considered *negro* (black) in Brazil. Similarly, the racial category *amarelo* (yellow), used to refer to a Brazilian of South Asian descent, may not be classified as an 'Asian' in South Africa.

In conclusion, race is a social construct that varies amongst peoples and cultures; to use the United States' or South Africa's experience of race to try and understand Brazil's race issues would lead to inaccuracies. Brazilians are not as race-conscious as Americans and have had a different but not necessarily a better history of race-relations. Where blacks were physically oppressed and segregated from whites in the United States, blacks in Brazil were psychologically segregated from their history and culture in an attempt to make them white or for them to become white. Race in Brazil is complex and difficult to define, and is weighted in a dramatically different way to the United States, which, nevertheless, shares a similar racial history. As an American sociologist sums up the complexities of race in Brazil, race, or skin colour for that matter, is in the eye of the beholder:

> Socially, colour or race is a continuum running from black to white and is so perceived by members of Brazilian society and, while the continuum is firmly anchored at either extreme, the intermediate

categories are flexible in that they are variously defined by different persons and may be variously applied by different persons to the same person. Thus, evaluation of colour in the intermediate is partly idiosyncratic and personal.[239]

---

[239] Saunder, 1972, p. 144 (in the original text, "colour" was spelt "color")

CHAPTER 2

BLACK BEAUTY IN BRAZIL

"People are no longer scared of identifying themselves or insecure about saying: 'I am black and I am beautiful.'"

ELIO FERREIRA DE ARAUJO

THE POLITICAL NATURE of the concept of beauty has always been a central concern of Brazil's black consciousness movement. Although Brazilian women are widely recognised for their beauty and seductiveness, mainstream Brazilian media portrays a Eurocentric ideal of female beauty with white skin, straight blonde hair, blue eyes, aquiline noses and thin lips. The denigration of features that signify African ancestry is common in Brazil, despite the fact that half of the country's population is of African descent. Afro-Brazilian women are conspicuously absent from portrayals of female beauty except for images of the carnival, where mulatto women appear to be the only acceptable image of blackness. In contrast, white Brazilian women are placed on a pedestal and valued for their beauty and elegance, whilst mixed-race and black Brazilian women are valued for their lustfulness and seductiveness. The issue of the invisibility of black aesthetics is one which resonates with women of African descent not only in Brazil, but throughout the African diaspora.

The lack of appreciation for black beauty has not gone unnoticed in Brazil. In the past few decades, Afro-Brazilian women and activists from Brazil's *Movimento Negro* (Black Movement) have taken it upon themselves to celebrate the beauty of blackness in order to encourage, inspire and uplift women of colour. The topic of black beauty has been raised in several discussions, particularly on the internet, concerning colourism, the apparent preference some show for lighter-skinned women, the politics of black hair, interracial marriages and the lack of black women in mainstream media and high-end fashion. As in the U.S., Brazil's 'Black is beautiful' cultural movement, which started in the 1970s, is challenging stereotypes of the sexuality of black Brazilian women and the Eurocentric ideal of beauty, which continues to dominate Brazil.

COLOURISM

In Brazil, while racism based on ethnic background is difficult to prove because of the country's mixed heritage, this is not the case when it comes to the topic of colourism. Colourism is skin colour categorization, usually showing favourable treatment towards those of lighter complexion amongst people of the same ethnicity or 'race'.[240] Colourism has deep roots in European colonialism and the transatlantic slave trade in which white women were idealised and perceived as elegant, virtuous and chaste and black women were classed as primitive, lustful and seductive. Thus, fair-skinned women were considered more aesthetically pleasing than dark-skinned women. The mulatto woman in Brazil is frequently held up to the world as a symbol of racial democracy, because she is considered desirable by the 'unprejudiced' Brazilian white male. The mulatto woman is placed on a pedestal above dark-skinned black women, similar to the way in which white women have been placed on a pedestal above all other women.

Portuguese-Brazilian Men And Brown Skinned Women

Brown-skinned women have been highly desired amongst the Portuguese from the time when Portuguese colonisers first set foot in Brazil in 1500. Pêro Vaz de Caminha, the literal-minded scribe of Pedro Álvares Cabral, was moved by the beauty of brown-complexioned native women. Though enamoured by the native women, in Caminha's detailed description, his attention repeatedly focused on their genitals; the Portuguese word he used, *vergonhas* (literally, "shames"), sums up the conflict of cultural patterns that both perturbed and excited him. "One of those girls," he wrote, "was all coloured from head to toe with that paint they use, and surely she was so well-formed and so rounded and her shameful parts (about which she felt no shame) were so comely that many women of our own land, seeing such perfection, would be ashamed that their parts were not equally perfect."[241]

According to Gilberto Freyre, the Portuguese males' attraction to brown-skinned women dates back to their fond memory of the 'voluptuous indolence' of the *moura encantada* (enchanted Mooress) in

---

240 Colourism (also known as shadeism) is an issue in many predominately non-white countries all over the world, such as the United States, India and Jamaica.
241 Haberly, 2010, pp. 10-11; Cortesão, 1967, p. 232

the Iberian Peninsula. The erotic impression that the African Moorish women made on the minds of the Portuguese men drove their imperial expeditions in search of brown-skinned women, Freyre asserts:

> Long contact with the Saracens had left the Portuguese the idealised figure of the "enchanted Moorish woman", a charming type of brown-skinned, black-eyed woman, enveloped in sexual mysticism, roseate in hue, and always engaged in combing out her hair or bathing in rivers or in the waters of haunted fountains; and the Brazilian colonisers were to encounter practically a counterpart of this type in the masked Indian women with their loose-flowing hair. These latter also had dark tresses and dark eyes and bodies painted red, and, like the Moorish Nereids, were extravagantly fond of a river bath to refresh their ardent nudity, and were fond, too, of combing their hair. What was more, they were fat like the Moorish women. Only, they were a little less coy and, for some trinket or other or a bit of broken mirror, would give themselves, with legs spread far apart, to the 'caraibas', who were so gluttonous for a woman.[242]

The Portuguese mens' lustful desire for the native, brown-complexioned Brazilian woman later turned towards the honey-skinned mulatto women in colonial Brazil. Regarding the position of mulattos in colonial Brazil, the maxim of the sixteenth century Jesuit, Antonil, summaries their situation: "Brazil is hell for *negros*, purgatory for whites, and paradise for *mulattos*." Other sayings such as "the lighter the better," and "white is right" are, if not voiced, in the sub-conscious of many Brazilians. Thus, in response to the prevalence of anti-blackness, many Afro-Brazilian women are finding strength in songs from the United States which celebrate the beauty of their blackness and African features, "Some say: 'The blacker the berry, the sweeter the juice'. I say the darker the flesh, the deeper the roots," by Tupac Shakur and, "Say it loud. I am black and proud," by James Brown are a few such popular sayings.

The *Mulatta*

Mulattas (mixed-race Brazilian women) have become Brazil's unofficial symbol of racial democracy and its representation of itself to the outside world. The renowned white Brazilian novelist Jorge Armado popularised the image of the sensual Brazilian *mulatta* in his novels *Dona Flor and Her Two Husbands* and *Tent of Miracles*. Though Armado's novels popularised

---

242 Freyre, 1986, p. 12

the mixed-race woman as an ideal of beauty, brown-skinned women were already highly desired amongst Portuguese plantation owners since their time in Portugal, where *café au lait* complexioned North African Berber women were highly sought after as sexual partners.

The treatment of Brazil's media of mulattos and black women also reflect attitudes of the light-skinned *mulatta* being more desirable than a dark-skinned black woman. Between 1947 and 1950, the Black Experimental Theatre promoted two annual beauty pageants, *Rainha das Mulatas* (Queen of the Mulattas) and the *Boneca de Pixe* (Tar Baby or Black Doll) celebrating the most beautiful Afro-Brazilian women in the nation's capital. The beauty pageants featuring mulatto and black women took place in order to undermine the long-standing perception that Afro-Brazilians are physically unattractive.[243]

The press coverage of the two pageants differed significantly, G. Reginald Daniel noted. One newspaper revealed its own and Brazil's qualified acceptance of mulattos and their implicit rejection of blacks when it stated that the *mulata* is "the only peaceful solution" to the racial problem in Brazil. "Only through her can the race cleanse itself." This media portrayal of the mulatto woman as Brazil's racial salvation was, however, undermined when the same newspaper referred to her as the proverbial sex object: "She is, above all, the glorification of the flesh and of the sins of the flesh."[244] As for the black pageant, the newspaper showed photographs of the contestants with the most basic factual information. There does not appear to have been any interviews with the general public concerning the national importance of the black beauty contests. Moreover, the black contestants were never portrayed in the media as being representative of Brazil's racial democracy, in contrast to their mulatto counterparts. Rather, the media gave modest praise, reaffirming stereotype views of black women as "self-sacrificing and hard working."[245]

Light Skin Vs Dark Skin
In mainstream Brazilian society, the darker the complexion, the less attractive a person is thought to be, for white media people control the portrayal of beauty. Anxiety over what white people think about black people leads to unwillingness by many in the black community to discuss the issue of colourism; they prefer to ignore it. It's an issue that divides

---

243 Reginald, 2007, pp. 74-75
244 Turner, 1992, p. 79
245 Reginald, 2007, p. 75

the black community into 'light skin vs dark skin' and online-debates about the authenticity of a person's black-identity.

Blogs like *Black Women of Brazil* are trying to raise awareness of the plight of many dark-skinned women, who are regarded as less attractive because of their hue. By raising the self-esteem of women of colour, *Black Women of Brazil* and magazines such as *Raça Brasil,* which celebrate the beauties of blackness and African features, discharge an important duty.

Changing the prejudice that whiteness is more beautiful and celebrating the beauty of blackness will lead to increased self-confidence in people's God-given skin complexion. Rather than seeing dark skin as ugly and a Divine curse, black women will think of their dark complexion and African features as the blessing they really are. Indeed there is a blessing in the struggle that people experience simply from being black in a racist society, because as the saying goes, "God gives His hardest battles to His strongest soldiers."

SKIN BLEACHING

In September 2013, Brazilian funk-singer Anitta sparked debate about the issue of skin-bleaching and race when she appeared to be noticeably whiter after signing a record deal with a major music label. Although the singer won millions of fans by taking the *favela* sound into the mainstream, anti-discrimination campaigners and social commentators accused her of sacrificing her blackness to "make it" in the predominately white middle-class market.

The controversy was prompted by the online publication of 'before and after' photographs of Anitta that show a dramatic lightening of her skin tone after she signed the record deal with Warner Music. Whether this was the result of whitening products, cosmetic surgery or the use of image-editing applications is not known. Nevertheless the apparent change in Anitta's skin complexion rekindled discussion as to whether one needs to be white to get ahead in Brazil.

Formerly *favela*'s 'mistress of funk' now turned R&B pop star, Anitta was born Larissa de Macedo Machado in Rio de Janeiro. The curvaceous, butt-shaking dancer and singer, toned down the suggestive dancing and explicit lyrics of *baile* funk or funk *carioca*, for a more mainstream sound to appeal to wider audiences. Not only did Anitta's honey-brown skin look suspiciously lighter, but she straightened her curly hair to make herself look more European. Although Anitta was projected as a cultural bridge between the predominately black community of Rio de Janeiro's shanty towns and the wealthier white communities, many outraged black activists expressed disappointment at Anitta's apparent whitening and regarded it as another example of Brazil's obsession with *branquidade* (whiteness) as the acme of beauty, wealth and success. Multicultural Brazil, like other Western countries, seems to subscribe to the ideology of white supremacy for which fair skin equates with power, access and acceptance.[246]

Skin Bleaching In Africa

Racial ambiguity can be the key to success for black and mixed-race people seeking to gain the acceptance of the mainstream community. The issue of skin-bleaching is even prevalent in Africa, where the overwhelming majority of people are black or brown in complexion. According to the World Health Organization (WHO), Nigerians are the heaviest users of skin-lightening products. According to a report published by the WHO in June 2012, 77% of Nigerian women skin-bleach, or 'tone', as it is commonly called.[247] Skin-lightening is so popular in Nigeria that women who bleach are referred to as "Fanta-face, Coca-Cola body". The term describes the overall mottled complexion of a woman who uses skin-lightening products on her face but not on her body.[248]

Nigerian writer, Sede Alonge raises an engaging argument against the emotionally-charged topic of skin-bleaching amongst dark-skinned women. According to Alonge, who is herself a dark-skinned woman but does not use skin-whitening products, women should be allowed to use skin-bleaching if they so wish, without being made to feel as if they have betrayed their race or that they have an inferiority complex towards white people. Though she admits that "there are valid health concerns as to the side effects of skin-lightening products," Alonge asserts that "it should remain an individual's prerogative to be who or what they want to be".

Addressing the hypocrisy of those who voice outrage at skin whitening, Alonge says Africa's media are infatuated by light-skinned women, and many Nigerian men who criticise women who bleach their skin prefer lighter-skinned women as marital partners.[249] "The harsh

---

246 http://www.theguardian.com/world/2013/sep/08/brazilian-funk-anitta-debate-race

247 59% of Togolese women and 27% of Senegalese women were reported to use skin-lightening products. Skin-lightening is also very popular in Ghana, South Africa, India and Jamaica.

248 http://www.economist.com/blogs/baobab/2012/09/beauty-nigeria

249 Amongst some Yoruba-speaking peoples dark-skinned women with flawless skin

truth is that in Africa, lighter-skinned girls do get more attention and are more appreciated than darker-skinned women." People's desire to have a particular skin complexion, be it darker or lighter, stems from them wanting to be more attractive and for others to take notice, Alonge argues, "And more often than not, in the case of an individual who has undergone skin lightening here in Africa, it works." Alonge concludes:

> Skin lightening should not be automatically regarded as an individual's outright rejection of their race. If a woman feels that lightening her skin will make her prettier or more confident, then society should let her be and not impose itself as judge and jury on her concept of beauty. It is high-time Africans stop being hysterical and overly-defensive about issues of their self-worth and identity.[250]

Skin-lightening creams reveal the dark side of the multi-billion dollar beauty industry. Capitalising on ideas of racial hierarchies, skin-lightening or skin-whitening cosmetics are a lucrative business, for which companies continue to promote the idea both that white skin is equivalent to beauty and that lightening dark skin is achievable and preferable. In modern-day societies where skin colour matters, fair skin comes with privileges. For women, lighter-skin is believed to be more beautiful, more 'successful' and that thus the lighter-skinned woman is more likely to marry than a darker-skinned woman. Thus, it is understandable that many darker-skinned women would want to lighten their skin despite the health risks associated with skin-bleaching.

INTERRACIAL MARRIAGES

Although Brazil is known for miscegenation in its history, interracial marriage is a recent phenomenon. In early Brazilian history, interracial marriage was not as common as many people believe. The miscegenation which resulted from interracial relationships between white Portuguese slave-masters and their African and Amerindian slaves was generally by way of rape and exploitation. The notion that harmonious relations existed between white masters and their black slaves is a romanticised image of slavery in Brazil.[251]

---

are revered. A beautiful (*odara*) dark-skinned woman is called *ādun madun* (charcoal black and shining) as a form of praise because her flawless jet-black skin resembles charcoal.
250 http://www.telegraph.co.uk/women/womens-life/10973359/Not-all-African-women-believe-black-is-beautiful.-And-thats-OK.html
251 Nascimento, 1989, p. 63

Though some white men did marry their captive women, indigenous and mulatto women were the desirable marital partners. Many of the female black slaves who married their white slave masters undoubtedly did so out of fear or for a better life. Although married, the status of black women did not change a great deal. Any improvement in treatment that they received in society was due to their marital relationship with a white man and not because blacks were looked upon more favourably in society.

Despite its national identity as a "racial democracy", many of Brazil's white elite and some black women activists still look unfavourably upon interracial marriage. The resistance to interracial romance amongst Brazil's white elite stems from belief in the inferiority of black people as marital partners.[252] A Brazilian saying reflecting such attitudes states, "*Branca para casar, Negra para trabalhar, Mulata para fornicar* (white women for marriage, black women for work and mulatto women for fornication)."[253] Another variant of the Brazilian saying: "*branca para casar, mulata para foder, negra para trabalhar,* (white women for marriage, mulatto women for fucking, and black women for work).[254] As for Afro-Brazilian women's resistance to interracial romance, this is due to some of them feeling slighted by famous and successful black men marrying white women. Black women have discussed for years black men who become successful finding love and romance with blonde white women. It is becoming an epidemic and many black women feel that they are losing 'their men' to white women, who are perceived as ideal marital partners. It is commonly believed in Brazil that, "for a black man, a blond [woman] is a trophy!"[255]

Others accuse black men of hypocrisy and question their racial pride, "They speak so much of [racial] pride, but they don't have any pride!" "Every black man...when he gets rich, gets a blond!"[256] White women in interracial relationships are also criticised, "They believe that black men are more passionate, more active and mainly more hung." Others accuse white women of being disingenuous when they say they are in love with successful black partners. The criticism directed at people involved in interracial relationships is often fuelled with exactly the same bigotry

---

252 Twine, 2005, pp. 48-53
253 Gomez, 2005, p. 93
254 Gomez, 2005, p. 93
255 http://blackwomenofbrazil.co/2013/06/16/comments-about-soccer-stars-new-white-girlfriend-show-that-brazilians-also-see-a-problem/
256 http://blackwomenofbrazil.co/2013/06/16/comments-about-soccer-stars-new-white-girlfriend-show-that-brazilians-also-see-a-problem/

that Afro-Brazilians accuse Brazil's white establishment and media of harbouring against black people.

The *Black Women of Brazil* blog reports that successful Afro-Brazilian men favouring blonde white women is a contentious issue for many Afro-Brazilian women.[257] The reasons behind the seeming preference for blonde white women is debatable as many of the respondents in the article are not the Afro-Brazilian men themselves who are involved in such relationships. Afro-Brazilian men, like other black men, may favour white women as partners for a number of reasons: personal preference, media perceptions, social status, validation from others and self-hate.

Although the media's perception of an idealised white beauty clearly influences many people's perception of beauty, it is far-fetched to claim that the media are the sole reason for black men having relations with white women. Similarly, the argument that black men do not marry black women because they hate their own colour and are ashamed of their blackness is problematic. To say that black men should only be with black women is itself a form of racism, which many black people would themselves object to if a white person were to say something similar. Although a large number of men of different ethnic backgrounds appear to have a preference for white/fair complexioned women, that does not mean that black women are any less beautiful or attractive.[258] Ironically many white Brazilians seek a lot of the natural features that black Brazilian women possess, such as prominent buttocks, full lips and chocolate-coloured skin, and in some cases they would even undergo cosmetic surgery to achieve them:[259]

---

257 "Why do black soccer players who denounce experiences with racism always seem to have white wives?" and "White women for marrying and the Brazilian solution to race: the elimination of the black race"

258 For further discussion, see my Illuminating the Difference: Black, White and Brown Women.

259 Cosmetic or aesthetic surgery is a type of surgery used to change a person's appearance to achieve what they perceive to be a more desirable appearance. Cosmetic surgery is different from reconstructive plastic surgery, which is a type of surgery used to repair damaged tissue following injury or illness. In certain situations cosmetic surgery may be needed for functional reasons. For example, breast reduction is sometimes used to alleviate back or neck pain. Cosmetic surgery is common amongst Brazilian women of various ethnicities and social classes. Buttock augmentation surgery also known as a 'Brazilian Butt Lift' or 'Fat Transfer to Buttocks' is increasingly popular amongst women who seek the 'perfect' derriere.

This question of successful black men seemingly automatically choosing white women is actually a conversation I've had with a number of black Brazilian men and women. Plenty of black women have revealed to me that they've had black men directly tell them that they won't date/marry a black woman for a variety of reasons (attitude, image, beauty and appearance of potential children).[260]

Should Black People Only Marry Black People?

The skin colour of a black person's companion has long been a measure of validating an individual's 'blackness.' The notion of whiteness being the ideal of beauty is often cited as the reason that black men have a predilection for white women. But this is not the case for many black women, who want a black man because they want to stay 'loyal to their black men'. According to African-American sociology professor George Yancey, author of the book on interracial relationships from a Christian perspective, *Just Don't Marry One*, writes "There is a call for loyalty [in the black community] that is stronger in some ways than in other racial communities."

What is noticeable is that the Brazilian media celebrate white couples and interracial couples as part of the country's national identity but rarely acknowledge black couples. This was not always the case, as the Brazilian media only recently began to portray interracial marriages, an issue the documentary *Denying Black* (2000) explores. The reason for the high number of interracial marriages in Brazil may be the nation's racist past and the ideology of whitening. In order to 'improve the race' and to gain upward mobility and acceptance in society, darker-skinned individuals often sought white marital partners.

The white European ideal is so entrenched in the minds of many Brazilians that many mixed-race Brazilians identify themselves as white despite their brown complexions and phenotypically African features. Colonialism still affects the minds of many Brazilians deeply, but Afro-Brazilian activists are trying to break the psychological chains of enslavement and the mentality of whitening. Brazilian journalist Paulo Noguiera accuses many successful black Brazilian footballers of responsibility for the 'double racism' that Brazilian black women suffer from. According to Noguiera, by their marriages with white women black Brazilian footballers perpetuate the notion that black women are unde-

---

260 http://blackwomenofbrazil.co/2014/03/16/why-do-black-soccer-players-who-denounce-experiences-with-racism-always-seem-to-have-white-wives/

sirable as marital partners.²⁶¹ Even prominent black Brazilian activists and entertainers who have campaigned and fought against racial discrimination are criticised for marrying white partners.

There are undoubtedly some black men who have identity issues with their skin complexion just as there are most definitely some white women who desire black men solely for their wealth and status, but it is deeply unfair to tar all interracial couples with the same brush.

Why Are Most Unmarried Women In Brazil Black?
Classic Brazilian scholars of race have found that darker-skinned Brazilians adopted the strategy of marrying white or lighter-skinned partners to gain social status and access to white social circles, thus producing offspring with more European physical features.²⁶²

According to the 2010 Census, 52.9% of black Brazilian women are unmarried, compared to 24.9% who are married and 2.60% divorced. The author of the book *Virou Regra?* (Did It Become the Rule?), Claudette Alves, explains: "The black woman faces loneliness independent of social stratum. This is not an exception, it is the rule, a historical symptom that indicates a real behaviour, black women (in their majority) do not have the experience of love." In the same vein, Ana Claudia Lemos Pacheco, author of *Mulher Negra: Afetividade e Solidão* (Black Women: Affectivity and Loneliness), reiterates: "Loneliness has its origin in the family structure, what do single black women have in common? Social origins and family. They are born and grow up with racism and sexism as crossed systems of oppression. Many have never experienced a fixed, lasting and healthy relationship."²⁶³

Brazilian popular culture depicts black women as highly sexualised. They are admired as sexual partners but shunned as wives. Marriage also implies having children and the responsibility for their upbringing, and many Brazilian men, both black and white, dislike their child to be dark in complexion with kinky hair. Brown skin is also a mark of poverty

---

261 http://www.diariodocentrodomundo.com.br/o-duplo-racismo-de-que-sao-vitimas-as-mulheres-negras/ http://blackwomenofbrazil.co/2014/03/16/why-do-black-soccer-players-who-denounce-experiences-with-racism-always-seem-to-have-white-wives/

262 https://www.academia.edu/2573184/_Confronting_Whitening_in_an_Era_of_Black-Consciousness_Racial_Ideology_and_Black-White_Marriages_in_Rio_de_Janeiro_

263 http://racabrasil.uol.com.br/cultura-gente/188/a-cor-do-amor-o-cotidiano-afetivo-da-mulher-308843-1.asp/

amongst many in Brazil, which is why some black Brazilian women find greater difficulty in marrying.[264]

In a discussion regarding this issue with Brazilians, it was said that Afro-Brazilian men tend not to marry Afro-Brazilian women because they are looking for a white woman. Others said that black women remain unmarried because of the increase in homosexuality, the mass incarceration of Afro-Brazilian men, their lack of financial resources, their being intimidated by black women's strong personalities and the promiscuous behaviour of Afro-Brazilian men. Some Afro-Brazilian men have said that they do not marry Afro-Brazilian women because they prefer white women, and that Afro-Brazilian women have a bad attitude whereas white women are considered more beautiful, wealthier and more compliant to their husbands.

THE POLITICS OF BLACK HAIR

Hair is a woman's crown and glory. It can also be a source of pride and prejudice within the black community who do not hold Afro-textured hair in high esteem. Since the trans-Atlantic slave trade, hair has played a significant role in defining a black woman's beauty and worth in the African diaspora.[265] Once a symbol of pride, black hair is now ridiculed and looked down upon. In Brazil, hair texture is a key marker of racial classification. The racial implications of hair texture takes on added significance for *negra* (black women) in particular, given the central role accorded to hair in racialised constructions of femininity and female beauty.[266] Black hair is a cause of debate, controversy and politics, as black women have questioned whether to 'go natural' and wear *cabelo black* (black hair or an Afro).[267] In Brazil, the natural-hair movement is expanding the definition of beauty where it was previously narrow. Writers, activists, bloggers and entrepreneurs have led a campaign to inform about natural hair, whether tightly coiled or curly, and celebrate it.

---

264 http://www.correiobraziliense.com.br/app/noticia/revista/2013/09/08/interna_revista_correio,385190/a-cor-da-relacao.shtml

265 Co-author of *Hair Story: Untangling the Roots of Black Hair in America,* Lori Tharps said, "During slavery, women with straighter hair were considered more aesthetically pleasing to their white masters, and so were more likely to become house-slaves, dramatically extending life-expectancy beyond that of coarser-haired field labourers." Tharps continues, "Straight hair was 'good' in a way that went beyond beauty. It was a matter of life and death." https://psychologies.co.uk/body/black-hair.html

266 Caldwell, 2007, p. 81

267 The phrase "go natural" refers to women of African ancestry wearing their hair as it naturally grows on their heads without chemically treated products.

Freelance writer, Dion Rabouin traces the roots of Brazil's natural-hair movement to the United States' Black Power movement of the 1970s in which iconic figures such as Angela Davis, Malcolm X[268] and James Brown[269] spoke about taking pride in one's blackness:

> Today in Brazil, when folks talk about black power, their symbol is their hair —natural hair. For Afro-Brazilians in general but black women especially, to wear an Afro or to wear their hair naturally is to wear black power.[270]

Researchers have documented extensively Afro-Brazilians' lack of access to seeing themselves presented positively in mainstream media and the education system.[271] United States' hip-hop music and Jamaica's reggae music, from artists like Lauryn Hill and Bob Marley, have played an important role in producing positive images of blackness for Afro-Brazilians. The valorisation of blackness, natural hair, dark-skin and the history of Africa in their songs helped instil black pride and black identity in Brazil's Afro-descendant population.

The 2009 music-video for the Portuguese version of the internationally popular song "Beautiful" by the American-based African singer, Akon with Brazilian singer Negra Li demonstrated how far the natural-hair movement and depiction of black beauty has come in Brazil. Akon, a dark-skinned male with strong African features, and Negra Li, a beautiful Afro-Brazilian woman wearing her hair naturally in a 'black power' (Afro) hairdo, conveyed a positive depiction of black hair and beauty to mainstream audiences in Brazil.

Renowned black Brazilian musicians, such as Seu Jorge, and musicians from the Brazilian *Música Negra* (Black Music) music genre have also

---

268 Malcolm X said in one of his most famous speeches about black people taking pride in their God-given features: "Who taught you to hate the texture of your hair? Who taught you to hate the colour of your skin? To such extent you bleach, to get like the white man. Who taught you to hate the shape of your nose and the shape of your lips? Who taught you to hate yourself from the top of your head to the sole of your feet? Who taught you to hate your own kind? Who taught you to hate the race that you belong to so much so that you don't want to be around each other?...You should ask yourself who taught you to hate being what God made you?"

269 James Brown famously sang in 1968: "Say it loud, I'm black and proud!" The song became the unofficial anthem for the 'black is beauty' cultural movement in the United States.

270 http://www.theroot.com/articles/culture/2014/06/black_power_in_brazil_means_natural_hair.1.html

271 Twine, 2005, p. 56, Pinto, 1987, and Hanchard 1994

featured black women wearing their hair naturally, which has helped to challenge the perception of *cabelo liso* (straight hair) as the ideal standard of beauty in the Brazilian media.

The Natural And Curly-Hair Movement
Despite the dominance of the portrayal of straight hair (*cabelo liso*) that swings (*balançava*) as the epitome of female hair beauty, a growing number of Afro-Brazilian women (*Afro-Brasileira*) are beginning to wear black hair or an Afro (*cabelo black*). The natural-hair movement continues to gain momentum in Brazil, as style icons and natural-hair blogs have helped inspire Afro-Brazilian women to embrace their natural hair. The Black Power 'Afro' hair-style is becoming increasing popular amongst Brazilian women of African descent, as are the various natural curly hairstyles.

Activists have campaigned against the denigration of black hair in Brazil and have organised workshops, seminars and fashion shows to celebrate the beauty of natural hair. The internet has also provided a platform for Afro-Brazilian women to speak about their hair and create online 'natural-hair communities' in which women of colour can share their experiences of maintaining and styling their tightly-curled hair. Lori Tharps, co-author of *Hair Story,* argues that there is a need for natural-hair communities to enable black women to accept and celebrate their natural hair.

> It's easy to criticise and ridicule black women for their hair obsession, but how can you expect somebody to love something they've never seen portrayed in a positive light, even in their own community?[272]

Danielle Cipriane, founder of the popular blog *Crespos e Cachos* (Frizz and Curls), added:

> Many women [who wear] black power are adhering to the culture, others for political attitude, but there are also those who wear it simply because it is stylish and on point.

Cipriane's blog is one of the most prominent platforms for Brazil's growing natural-hair movement. The blog features stories by Afro-Brazilian women about maintaining black hair as well as some of their personal experiences with using chemicals for their hair. For Cipriane, the growing popularity for Afro-Brazilians to "go natural" is beginning

---

272 https://psychologies.co.uk/body/black-hair.html

to challenge the Brazilian notion that "straight hair is beautiful". Cipriane says, "Contrary to the rules of society and straightening crazes, relaxing and stretching, many black women are discovering the beauty, the charm and femininity of black power, with or without accessory, with or without comb cream." She adds, "The texture and volume of curly hair is conquering those who are tired of chemical alteration."[273]

A number of other groups have mounted a challenge to the preponderance of straight hair and are advocating an embargo on chemicals that damage hair and scalp, one of the best-known of which is *Meninas Black Power* (Afro Girls), an organisation that fights racism in Brazil, and was founded by Elida Aquino to empower young girls to embrace their natural hair. The organisation hosts several events and has a strong online presence where it promotes the use of natural hair as a symbol of black pride. Aquino started *Meninas Black Power* while she was studying nursing and midwifery in Rio de Janeiro. Speaking about the name of the group, Aquino says, it is "a mix of femininity and the strength that we extracted from our ancestry" continuing "*Meninas Black Power* was created to bring together Afro-Brazilian women from different backgrounds who understand that naturally curly hair is also a weapon of political positioning."[274]

For years, Brazil's media has idolised straight hair as the image of beauty and has declared the natural hair movement to be a passing fashion fad. Aline Silve of *Blogueiras Negras* (Black bloggers) counters this by writing that the natural-hair movement is a choice, a rebellion, a political statement and an act of self-affirmation. The hair movement, Aline Silva writes, "[says no] to centuries of an imposition of beauty standards that do not belong to us, that mutilate us, that kill us, that deny us our rights."

Cabelo Crespo é Cabelo Bom (Kinky Hair is Good Hair) and *Cachos Estilosos* (Stylish Curls) are other popular blogs that have used social media effectively to challenge the dominant beauty paradigm in Brazil.[275] The blogs features photographs of Afro-descendant women of various complexions with curly hair. Organisations such as *Encrespa Geral, Vicio Cacheado* and *Meninas Black Power* are among those leading this campaign.

---

273 http://www.theroot.com/articles/culture/2014/06/black_power_in_brazil_means_natural_hair.html

274 http://www.theroot.com/articles/culture/2014/06/black_power_in_brazil_means_natural_hair.html

275 http://globalvoicesonline.org/2012/11/23/afro-brazilian-women-tight-curly-hair-and-black-consciousness/

Afro-Hair Empowerment Marches

In 2015 Afro-Brazilians have started to take to the streets to celebrate natural hair as a symbol of resistance against deeply-institutionalised racism in Brazil. The organisers behind the first Afro Hair Pride March (*Marcha do Orgulho Crespo*) which took place on 26th July 2015 in São Paulo, declared, "We march with pride of our afros and curly hair, holding our combing forks in our hands as a battle symbol against the social whitening process, sexual objectification of women and their silence. We believe in black empowerment and, above all, in its beauty and roots." The organisers behind the historic march, *Hot Pente, Blog das Cabeludas* (Hot Combs and Hairy Blog), added, "More than being about aesthetic, the first Afro Hair Pride March is a political act that opens in favour of a movement that celebrates afro-hair as being part of the black identity, promotes self-esteem and helps people to embrace their ancestry and the free expression of their hair, especially for women as a means of empowerment."

Since the Afro-Hair Pride March, a number of afro-hair marches have taken place across Brazil in cities such as Porto Alegre, Brasilia, Feira de Santana, Rio de Janeiro, São Gonçalo, Recife and Salvador. In downtown Recife on 13th November 2015, a vibrant march was organised by *Marcha do Empoderamento Negro* (Black Empowerment March). According to one of the event's organisers, Nathalia Rocha, the goal of the march is to educate Brazil's black population and those who are interested in discussing racism in Brazil. On 16th November, 2015, another historic march took place in Salvador, as 3,000 Afro-Brazilians held their first natural hair empowerment march, *Marcha Empoderamento Crespo,* in response to the racial prejudices against Afro-Brazilian women. As black empowerment continues to spread across Brazil further marches will continue as more Afro-Brazilians are finding pride in their blackness.

Black Hair Business

Vicio Cacheado: Estéticas Afro Diásporicas (Curly Addiction: Afro Diaspora Aesthetics), a 2014 study conducted by Ivanilde Guedes de Mattos and Aline Silva, analyses the natural-hair movement "as a phenomenon of the African Diaspora". The researchers found that recently in Brazil there has been a shift away from hair-straightening among black women, and that this had led to an increase in the market for hair-curling products.[276]

As the natural-hair movement continues to grow in Brazil, it has even become lucrative, which some Afro-Brazilian female entrepreneurs such

---

276 http://www.rioonwatch.org/?p=19495

as Heloisa Assis, popularly known as Zica, and Leila Valez, co-founders of *Instituto Beleza Natural* (The Institute of Natural Beauty) have discovered.[277] Assis and Valez, both from humble backgrounds, identified a neglected gap in the market and in 1993 they opened their first store. Offering quality services and hair products at affordable prices, *Beleza Natural* is now Brazil's leading hair-care provider specialising in "curly, curled and wavy hair".[278] As of May 2015, the company has twenty-nine salons in five Brazilian states, a factory of its own, and is estimated to be valued at 210 million reais (£66 million). The company also plans to add one hundred and twenty stores by 2020. With all her success, Leila Valez stresses that racism is still an issue for blacks trying to get into business:

> People deny [racism in Brazil]. They would never say to you, "Oh I have issues with race." But look around this restaurant. See if you can see any black woman or man who is not cleaning or serving tables. That is our reality. And if there is a black man being served, people will say, "Wow, maybe he's a soccer player, maybe he's a samba singer.' That's the truth. I experience it every day.[279]

The success of black entrepreneurs, such as *Beleza Natural* and *Prapreta*, specialising in hair and black beautification businesses demonstrates that black hair is not only beautiful but successful. Hopefully more black people can follow suit and establish themselves in positions of power, as this is where real and effective change can take place.[280]

Globally, the black haircare industry is worth billions, as black women are reported to spend more money than any other race on their hair. Mainstream Western countries largely underestimate the international market as European and Asian hair products are generally stocked in high-street stores. Although the industry is continuing to grow, as more black women are spending more money than ever before on their hair, the market is dominated by Asians businesses who control most black-hair retailers and distributors. Hopefully blacks can make more inroads into the supply and distribution of black-hair products.

---

277 http://www.forbes.com/sites/julieruvolo/2012/01/23/bye-bye-brazilian-blowouts-the-next-big-brazilian-hair-trend-is-beleza-natural/
278 http://belezanatural.com.br/en/categoria/empresa/
279 http://www.theglobeandmail.com/report-on-business/careers/careers-leadership/brazilian-hair-care-ceo-leila-velez-breaks-down-barriers/article23568496/
280 http://revistapegn.globo.com/Banco-de-ideias/noticia/2013/10/empreendedoras-criam-e-commerce-voltado-para-mulher-negra.html

Black women outside of Brazil search for Brazilian hair in particular for hair extensions, weaves, and wigs, yet most of the suppliers of Brazilian hair are not Afro-Brazilian. Blacks are primarily consumers, but whites and Asians are the producers. This inevitably leads to more and more black money leaving the black community, which in turn increases the wealth gap both in the Americas and in Europe. In the United States, East Asians, mainly from Korea, control over 70% of the black-hair supply chain, whilst in the United Kingdom, South Asians from the Indian sub-continent dominate the black-hair industry.

One of the major problems facing black distributors is that the mainly non-black distributors handpick those to whom they distribute products. This often leaves aspiring black owners disenfranchised. When black manufacturers are able to gain access to the distribution channel and supply black-owned businesses, this may help not only to employ more black people but also reduce the large wealth disparity between blacks and non-blacks. Fortunately things are starting to change in Brazil, as more black female entrepreneurs are setting up their own saloons specialising in black hair and creating employment for blacks from low-income backgrounds.[281] Leila Velez comments:

> There's a tendency here [in Brazil], when you achieve a certain amount of success, to enter a comfort zone: "It's okay, that's it." I think you can be a lot more than that. As an entrepreneur, I have a commitment to changing this country and showing that it's possible to be honest, to be serious, to have a company that is not dependent on corruption, to create jobs and create growth for people – that it's possible.[282]

Why Do Afro-Brazilians Straighten Their Hair?

Whilst every Afro-Brazilian woman's experience of hair is different, many tend to give similar reasons for why black and mulatto women choose to straighten their natural hair. Some women straighten their hair because they find it more manageable than their naturally coiled hair, others to assimilate into mainstream (white) society where straight hair is considered more attractive and professional. "[In Brazil] to be accepted by whites, we have to become like them," said Simone Santos, an Afro-Brazilian woman from Salvador. "I don't want to straighten my hair. My hair is curly!" An-

---

281 http://blackwomenofbrazil.co/2014/04/13/ethnic-consumption-heats-up-business-among-black-entrepreneurs/

282 http://www.theglobeandmail.com/report-on-business/careers/careers-leadership/brazilian-hair-care-ceo-leila-velez-breaks-down-barriers/article23568496/

other black woman added, "People criticise me a lot for my 'black power' (Afro) hairdo. Even though I know my hair was annoying them, I knew I was carrying my own identity."[283] Brazilian media and popular culture should also be held accountable for Afro-Brazilian women straightening their hair because they don't feel beautiful with their natural hair.

Humour is an important part of Brazilian culture. Racist humour and jokes are part of this culture, and Edward E. Telles alleges that people generally take them in their stride along with other types of humour.[284] Often racial humour is based on common stereotypes and naturalises popular images of blacks by downplaying their seriousness. However, as Telles points out, such humour reproduces and popularises negative stereotypes of blacks, potentially impairing their self-esteem. Historically Brazil's racist anti-black humour has long been accepted in popular culture, as Kia Lilly Caldwell explains, "Brazilian *brincadeiras* (jokes) often involve comparisons between Afro-Brazilians and animals, especially monkeys. The popular acceptance of racist humour indicates that joking provides a culturally-sanctioned means of articulating beliefs that reproduce dominant notions of white superiority and black inferiority in Brazil."[285]

Black women and their hair are often subject to ridicule, as exemplified in the racist song *Veja os cabelos dela* (Look at Her Hair), performed by Tiririca, a popular clown and children's entertainer. Written by Tiririca and distributed by Sony Music in 1996, the song was popular in Brazil and its lyrics were seen as harmless fun. Some of the song's lyrics are:

> Look, look, look at her hair.
> It looks like *bombril* (a scouring pad)
> When she passes she calls my attention
> But her hair, there's no way no
> Her *catinga* (body odour) almost caused me to faint
> Look, I cannot stand her odour
> Look, look, look at her hair!
> It looks like a scouring pad for cleaning pans
> I already told her to wash herself
> But she insisted and didn't want to listen to me
> This smelly *nega* (black woman)
> Stinking animal that smells worse than a skunk.

---

283 See *Ebony Goddess: Queen of Ilê Aiyê*
284 Telles, 2006, p. 154
285 Caldwell, 2007, p. 83

This offensive song caused an outcry amongst black activists and resulted in both Tiririca and his recording label, Sony Music, being sued for racism. The song perpetuated popular beliefs that black women are unattractive and lack proper hygiene. The notion of black women's *cabelo ruim* (bad hair) was explicitly stated in the song's lyrics. Caldwell observed that by comparing the woman's hair to a scouring pad, Tiririca made a clear statement on the coarseness of her hair that was in tune with Brazilian notions of *cabelo ruim* (bad hair).[286] The fact that the song was performed for children in a rhythmic Afro-Brazilian musical form known as Axé, may have been part of the reason that many Brazilians considered the song to be harmless fun; they believed it was performed by blacks. Whatever the case, Telles says that the song reflects the ease with which blacks are "derided to the point that explicit racism is so openly, but perhaps innocently, broadcast to children."[287] Unfortunately, Tiririca's song is not the exception in Brazilian popular culture; there are countless songs, jokes and stereotypical images about black women's hair, and thus it is no surprise that many black and mixed-race Brazilian women want to straighten their Afro-textured hair.[288]

Some black women say that they straighten their hair to attract the attention of men. The issue is a controversial one within the black community as there are many men, particularly those in the public eye, who seem to favour women with straight hair. Though many black men have expressed a dislike for wigs and weaves whose texture is different from women's natural hair texture, because they look 'unnatural' and are deceptive.[289]

Other women straighten their hair to feel beautiful or simply because of changes in fashion. If a woman straightens her hair it is ultimately her own prerogative and if she does, it does not diminish her blackness.

THE MEDIA AND THE FASHION INDUSTRY

Stereotypes of blacks in Brazil are usually negative. In a national survey conducted in 1995, 43% of Brazilians agreed that "*negroes* are only good in music and sports". Another racist stereotype is that black women are only good for sex and dancing. Other surveys have found that many

---

286 Caldwell, 2007, p. 87
287 Telles, 2006, p. 155
288 http://www.dihitt.com/barra/entrevista-jovem-que-acusa-funcionario-do-ponto-frio-de-racismo
289 Prince, 2009, p. 15

black Brazilians also held similar stereotypical images of themselves, due to the media's portrayal of non-whites.

Television exerts great influence on popular Brazilian culture and on attitudes towards beauty, mostly through the popular *telenovelas* (soap operas), which seek to portray Brazilian life and history.[290] Despite their overwhelming presence in Brazilian society, in Brazilian media non-whites are often invisible or relegated to menial roles. Television often reinforces stereotypes such as black women being highly sensual, promiscuous and/or ugly. By contrast, white women, especially blondes, are cast as the symbols of beauty, elegance and purity. "Brazilian TV has no interest in looking for diversity. It is content with promoting white superiority,"[291] Afro-Brazilian filmmaker Joel Zito Araújo said.

The Media
Mass media is a powerful propaganda tool that is used to project a worldview. There is power in the images used by advertisers, on magazine covers, and in film and television, in all of which the ideal of beauty is Eurocentric. A great deal of thought goes into the selection of images to which people will have an emotional and intellectual response. The issue that many black activists have with the Brazilian media is the very much reduced picture of black women. Many black women activists are comfortable with their female sexuality but have issues with the media's one-dimensional depiction of *mulata* and black sensuality, particularly during the Carnival. Like so many countries around the world, white beauty dominates the beauty business. Advertisers spend millions promoting this ideal, even to children.

A study, conducted by a Brazilian student of journalism for BBC Brasil, on the depiction of black people in three Brazilian teenage magazines (*Atrevida, Capricho e Todateen, Capricho* and *Todateen*), revealed a cruel picture of black exclusion. None of them had a fashion editorial with black models or a section for Afro-textured hairstyles or make-up tips for brown skin. The student of journalism, who appears to be mixed-race, remarked:

> The media sells us a reality that does not exist. We live in Brazil, the country of miscegenation. Opening a magazine, I feel as if I'm in Russia.[292]

---

290 Telles, 2006, p. 155
291 http://www.theguardian.com/world/2015/oct/07/brazil-television-mister-brau-black-couple-race-issues
292 http://www.bbc.co.uk/portuguese/noticias/2014/09/140912_isabela_artigo_

In Brazilian media, the embodiment of Brazilian attractiveness has long remained the tanned white woman not women who are naturally dark. Coffee-coloured women were described bluntly as: "*Morena da cor do pecado*" (brunette, the colour of sinning), the news magazine *Istoé's* headline read in a 1993 story about white Brazilian actress Luiza Thomé.[293] The colour brown has long been associated with sin, sensuality and immorality in Brazil, much as the way in which *negro* (black) has been associated with stupidity, ugliness and slavery.

Jacques D'Adesky found that Brazilian newspapers and magazines, which attract middle-class readership, tend to utilise European images in advertising. Among a total of 1,204 models appearing in advertising in the leading weekly magazine *Veja* between 1994 and 1995, only 6.5% were black or mixed-race. In *Cosmopolitan/Nova*, the leading magazine for a female audience, only 4% of the models used during the same two-year period were not white.[294] Though the portrayal of black and brown people is slowly improving, they are still greatly under-represented, as I found out from my trips to Brazil.

When I visited Salvador in January 2015, I noticed a similar phenomenon. Out of twenty-five debutante[295] and beauty magazines I saw at newsstands, 92% featured white females on the front cover and only 8% featured a black or mixed-race woman. Surprisingly the two magazines (*Cabelos & Cia* and *Contigo!*) that had black/mixed-race women on their front covers had the same woman, Brazilian model and actress – Taís Araújo. The January 2015 issue of *Contigo!* featured a glossy spread of the "best fashion outfits of 2014". Out of the sixty-four female celebrities featured, wearing outfits from high-end fashion designers, only five of the women (8%) were mixed-race or black. Despite black and mixed-race Brazilians comprising at least 50% of the country's population, in my

---

cq.shtml

293 Levine, 1997, p. 17

294 Telles, 2006, pp. 155-156, see Jacques D'Adesky's *Pluralismo Étnico e Multicultralismo: Racismos e Anti-Racismos no Brasil*,

295 A debutante is a young woman from an aristocratic or upper-class family who has reached the age of majority and, as a new adult, is formally introduced to society at a 'debut'. Debutante balls are very popular in Brazil, where the age of fifteen marks the age of majority. The balls are big business, and some families spend more than £100,000 on the event. See *Cinderllas of the Slums,* the BBC documentary by reporter Billie J. D. Porter, which explores fifteenth birthday debutante balls in Brazil. The documentary highlighted Brazil's social and racial inequalities, because the rich families featured in the programme were white and the 'Cinderellas from the slums' were overwhelmingly black.

study they accounted for less than 10% of coverage in beauty and fashion magazines. This is a reflection of the under-representation of black and mixed-race women in Brazilian media. Looking at the editorial boards and panellists of the magazines, the results were even more disturbing. The overwhelming majority were white Brazilian females and a couple of white Brazilian males. Black and mixed-race Brazilians comprised less than 5% of the magazine editorial boards that I reviewed.

The lack of black and mixed-race women in Brazil's beauty and fashion magazines and media is indicative of the country's obsession with whiteness and the Eurocentric ideal of beauty for which pale-skinned, blonde, blue-eyed women are highly desirable. This is an issue which receives very little coverage in mainstream Brazilian media. Fortunately in the past few decades, independent filmmakers and documentarians such as Zito Araújo have taken it upon themselves to highlight this problem.

Afro-Brazilian documentary filmmaker Joel Zito Araújo, the 'Spike Lee' of Brazil, is Brazil's most prolific documentarian and filmmaker in analysing the endemic anti-black racism in the media. *Raça* (Race), Araújo's 2013 documentary film, accompanies three black Brazilians to the front-lines of the modern battle for equal rights. In Brasilia, Paulo Paim, the nation's sole black senator, takes a stand for civil and land rights. In São Paulo, Netinho de Paula, a celebrated musician, founded a new television channel showing life from the black perspective. And in the remote countryside, *quilombo* resident Miúda dos Santos, the granddaughter of African slaves, defends her lawful claim to the land of her ancestors. In the documentary film, Araújo and the American documentarian Megan Mylan explore whether a nationality can be considered a race (i.e. the Brazilian race) and whether black Brazilians should abandon their racial identity for the sake of Brazilian unity. The filmmakers also ask if the question itself isn't already a consequence of institutional racism.[296]

Araújo also directed *A Negação do Brasil* (Denying Brazil), a critically acclaimed documentary film in which he carefully analyses depictions of blacks and race-relations in *telenovelas* (soap operas) over a span of fifty years. The documentary features candid interviews with black Brazilian actors and actresses, who speak of their experiences in Brazil's racist television industry for which black people were not considered aesthetically pleasing to white middle-class audiences. The only television roles blacks were commonly cast in were stereotypical ones

---

296 http://africasacountry.com/am-i-supposed-to-be-more-brazilian-than-black/

such as the 'Mammy', servants and henchmen, which would emphasise the notion of blacks being socially and culturally inferior to whites. Araújo found that 75% of the roles for black people were in positions of subservience. "The roles represent the way in which Brazilian society likes to see black people: as slum dwellers, domestic servants, criminals. This is still happening today."[297] Araújo further added:

> If you turn on the TV today and see a soap-opera, you're going to see that blacks aren't even 10% of the actors. The people who are valued have Germanic features. If an actor has blond hair and blue eyes, he or she will be more successful. If the actor has black characteristics, she'll probably play a domestic worker, a marginal person.[298]

The documentary also highlighted the complexities of mixed heritage, where some individuals would try to hide their black origins in order to assimilate into the white middle-class.

Araújo also found that Brazilian television writers and producers tend to portray Brazilians as white and European-looking, reinforcing the value of white skin and eliminating many popular aspects of Brazilian culture. For example, despite its centrality in the national culture, Afro-Brazilian religion is almost never presented in the Brazilian media.[299] Though there has been some progress in the past few decades with more black and mixed–race Brazilians appearing on mainstream media, non-whites continue to be poorly represented in Brazilian television and media.

The Lack Of Black Couple Representation
Another issue which is not often spoken about is the lack of black love in mainstream Brazilian media. A mainstream television show featuring a wealthy black Brazilian couple in a lead role was unheard of in Brazil until *Mister Brau* aired in September 2015. The musical sitcom starring the real life married couple, Taís Araújo and Lázaro Ramos, is significant in changing perceptions in Brazil, Joel Zito Araújo argues;

> There are a few examples of love between black people [in Brazilian media]. The expectation of Brazilian society is that the black person

---

297 http://www.theguardian.com/world/2015/oct/07/brazil-television-mister-brau-black-couple-race-issues
298 http://www.npr.org/blogs/parallels/2013/09/26/226565319/around-the-world-notions-of-beauty-can-be-a-real-beast
299 Telles, 2006, p. 155

does not have pride in being black and looks to escape blackness with a white partner.[300]

For Afro-Brazilians, the image of a rich and successful black couple is not common both on screen and in the real world. Particularly in the entertainment business, it's very difficult to find prominent black couples in Brazil. For the most part, rich and successful Afro-Brazilians tend to not marry each other. Successful black Brazilian footballers tend to marry white women and many prominent black Brazilian models and actresses also tend to marry white men. Thus, the image of Brazil's most prominent black actor and actress on the screen is "revolutionary." award-winning film-maker Joel Zito Araújo said. The couple have become a reference for Brazil's black community and one which they are fully aware of as Taís Araújo states;

> I grew up without having a black couple that represented me…So today when I see comments that I am an example for black women, that Lázaro and I are an example of a black couple, besides finding it important that this exists, I am very proud.

According to Lilian Schwartz, a professor of anthropology at the University of São Paulo, the broadcast of *Mister Brau*, is also a significant moment in Brazilian history, in which the racial question is finally coming up for discussion after decades of being ignored. Schwartz says that "Brazilians are much more aware of discrimination now."

Despite some of the stereotypical portrayals of blacks in the programme, the portrayal of a wealthy black couple in lead role should be celebrated. Given the fact that Brazilian television is overwhelmingly dominated by whites, both on and off screen, the lack of black leads is not surprising. However in a country where 81% of the population describes TV as their main source of leisure, the importance of having positive presentations of black people on TV cannot be underestimated. For that reason, the Globo TV series *Mister Brau* is truly ground-breaking.

The Media's Emasculation Of Black Men
The black male has long been considered a threat to the white establishment in Brazil. From the fear of revolts during the era of slavery to the perception of the hyper-sexualised black males "taking white women" in modern day Brazil, the dominant elite has long looked upon the black male with fear. Black activists have noticed the dominant

---

300 http://www.theguardian.com/world/2015/oct/07/brazil-television-mister-brau-black-couple-race-issues

elite's attempts to emasculate the image of the black male in Brazil, thus diminishing his power. In the *Carnaval*, it is now customary for heterosexual men to dress as women, and in the media there is a growing trend to portray black men in effeminate roles. The *Black Women of Brazil* blog traces Brazilian media's systematic attempts to feminise the traditional image of black masculinity. The growing trend for many of Brazil's most successful black actors to wear female clothes and act like women has long been a feature, the blog observes.[301]

French aristocrat Arthur de Gobineau, who developed the theory of the Aryan master race, was very well-known to Brazilian intellectuals, as were the ideas of scientific racism that Gobineau expressed. It seems that the words of Gobineau may serve to explain this trend.[302] In his 1850s book, *An Essay on the Inequality of the Human Races*, Gobineau wrote:

"What you wish to conquer or subjugate you first make feminine."

The feminisation of the black male has long been a cause for concern amongst activists in the United States' black community. As in Brazil, countless numbers of successful black male entertainers have worn female dress or played effeminate homosexual characters at some point in their careers. Black American comedian, Dave Chappelle, highlighted this issue on national television when appearing on multi-award winning talk show, *The Oprah Winfrey Show*, "I started to think about it, all the comics I have seen, men, real strong [black] brothers. Why are they always putting us in these dresses…The minute it was clear that I was adamant that I was not going to wear a dress [they left me alone]… You've got to take a stand."

In an attempt to undermine their influence within the black community, black leaders who have fought against white supremacy have also been targets for feminisation. An example of this can be found in allegations recently made, in the biography *Malcolm X: A Life in Reinvention,* that Malcolm drank wine, had extramarital affairs with a female follower and engaged in homosexual encounters. Manning Marable, the controversial book's author, based his allegations on interviews conducted with Malcolm's enemies. Marable's claims received media attention from many Western media outlets, with some newspapers reporting that Marable was a "leading black scholar", thus giving his unsubstantiated

---

301 http://blackwomenofbrazil.co/2014/11/10/the-continued-masculization-of-black-women-and-the-medias-effeminization-of-black-men-the-view-from-brazil/
302 http://blackwomenofbrazil.co/2014/11/10/the-continued-masculization-of-black-women-and-the-medias-effeminization-of-black-men-the-view-from-brazil/

accusations credence.³⁰³ Marable's book and Bruce Perry's *Malcolm: The Life of a Man Who Changed Black America*, who also "revealed the hidden gay past" of the black American militant leader, are merely attempts by white supremacists to discredit Malcolm X's legacy. Homosexual groups have even used these books' findings to further promote homosexual-rights. Homosexual activist Peter Tatchell said, "Now it is time to blow the whistle. There is not a single world-famous black person who is openly gay. Young black lesbians and gays need role models. Who better than Malcolm X, one of the great modern heroes of black liberation?"³⁰⁴ The false allegations against Malcolm are another attempt by white supremacists to emasculate him and tarnish the reputation of a man who has been and continues to be a source of inspiration for blacks in the United States, Brazil and other parts of the world.

Being Black Is Not Like Being Gay
The recent decision by the United States' Supreme Court in June 2015 to legalise same-sex marriage was met with uproar in the black community, many of whom expressed outrage not only at the legislation but at the constant attempt of lesbian, gay, bisexual and transgender (LGBT) groups to compare and equate sexual orientation with race. The comparison is not only erroneous but highly offensive, especially since blacks have no closet in which they can hide, and therefore no possibility of 'coming out'.

Muslim African-American author 'Abdullāh bin Hamid 'Alī responded to the question, 'Are Gays an Oppressed Minority?' by saying,

> This is an extremely crucial question, especially since gays have worked hard to shame and guilt African Americans into abandoning their anti-gay posture. The equation between "black" suffering and "gay" suffering I find to be extremely insulting for more than one reason. Firstly, it is because being black is not like being gay. Being black is a physical condition that the black person and everyone else cannot help but notice. Being gay, in spite of largely untenable arguments of it being an inborn condition, is still something that gays have the ability to hide. One is a fixed "condition." The other is an "act" which can easily be camouflaged.
>
> Secondly, while gays have been subjected to physical violence for placing their homosexuality on public display from time to time, when the number of those attacks are compared to incidents of

---
303 http://www.theguardian.com/world/2011/apr/07/malcolm-x-man-behind-myth
304 http://www.theguardian.com/world/2005/may/19/gayrights.usa

physical attacks on blacks by law enforcement officers, the prison industrial complex, and all other policies that have historically impeded the social progress of blacks, there is no comparison.

Thirdly, when we look closely at the gay community in the Western world, we notice three fundamental facts: 1) the overwhelming majority of gays are white which means they are members of the majority ruling group; 2) they are economically and politically privileged as a collective; and 3) because of 1 and 2, they are able to intimidate and compel many in the heterosexual community to conform to their demands. In other words, one can only be oppressed by an oppressor. When we look for who has been oppressing gays and keeping them from "marriage equality", it has been that same white majority which is complicit in the oppression of other minorities. What this means is that the gay community is neither a minority nor is it oppressed. If anything, because of their political and economic position, they are complicit in the oppression of others, especially those who refuse to accept that being a homosexual is natural.[305]

In contrast to the United States' and Brazil's long histories of racism, homosexuals have advanced much further than blacks in gaining public acceptance. In a documentary released ten years after the critically-acclaimed film *City of God*, Afro-Brazilian actor and musician, Seu Jorge, informed us that the progress which the homosexual movement has made in recent history is far greater than the progress blacks have made in Brazil's racist society.

While I was in Brazil, I found it quite strange that, despite the abundance of extremely beautiful women, there are so many homosexual men who are apparently disinterested in them. I could not understand it and was baffled by it. A number of Brazilian women I spoke to about this, expressed their frustration at the lack of male suitors because of the growing problem of homosexuality amongst men. Some of the women blamed the media for promoting their gay agenda among the Catholic masses, even though homosexuality is considered an abomination in traditional Christianity.

That said, Brazil is a very tolerant country and is becoming more gay-friendly each year, with many there claiming that homosexuality is a natural part of the human disposition. African-American psychologist and

---

305 http://www.lamppostproductions.com/reflections-on-a-supreme-court-verdict-gay-marriage/

pan-Africanist educator Dr. Umar Johnson has repeatedly refuted such claims, saying that in his direct experience with LGBT members and his research he has found no credible evidence which suggests that any African peoples are born homosexual. An advocate of traditional relationships, he argues that the deregulation of homosexuality as a mental illness in 1974 by the American Psychiatric Association (APA) was a political move, so that the LGBT movement could trump the black civil-rights movement as a primary issue in America. Most of the homosexuals Johnson came across informed him that they were victims of child molestation, which later contributed to their homosexual lifestyle. Although not all homosexuals have been victim of child abuse, Johnson wondered, why do Western academic circles rarely discuss sexual abuse as a part of the aetiology of homosexuality? He argues that homosexuality is being foisted on the black community as a strategy to reduce the black population. Whilst Johnson's theories may be dismissed as conspiracy theory by many, his work should not entirely be discounted given the historical record of Europeans' conduct towards blacks in America and Brazil.

The Fashion Industry
Fashion denotes "a popular or the latest style of clothing, hair, decoration, or behaviour".[306] The fashion industry makes and sells clothing and accessories for commercial purposes. Although fashion may theoretically be a creative art-form, the industry is a business, and as a business it finances and dominates artistic expression. Given the reality that the vast majority of affluent people in Brazil are of European ancestry, the Brazilian fashion industry is unsurprisingly Eurocentric. The imagery employed in Brazil's high-end fashion consists primarily of light-skinned, slender blonde women. The racial mix of the majority of Brazilian women is conspicuously absent from both the catwalk and fashion magazines.

White beauty is perpetually projected within Brazil and beyond. Brazilian 'supermodels', who are celebrated internationally, are usually white in complexion of European ancestry from Southern Brazil. Model scouts strategically target towns in Southern Brazil to "find the right genetic cocktail of German and Italian ancestry, perhaps with some Russian or other Slavic blood thrown in", Alexei Barrionuevo said in 'Off Runway, Brazilian Beauty Goes Beyond Blonde', a *New York Times* article. Such a mix, model scouts say, helps produce the tall, thin girls with straight hair, fair skin and light eyes that Brazil exports to the catwalks of New York, Milan and Paris with stunning success. Brazil's mixed-race

---
306 Oxford Dictionary.

and black beauties are often left to promote Brazil's highly sensual carnival. *Carnaval* is the only time when mainstream Brazilian media endorse black beauty. Eroticised mulatto *bundudo* (large buttocked) women are offered as entertainment to the foreign revellers who drive the country's lucrative tourism economy.

Female black activists reject not only the hyper-sexualised image of their bodies but also the sexualised usage of the term *mulata* (mulatto) that is automatically attached to any attractive woman visibly of African ancestry. *Preta Simoa*, northeastern black Brazilian women's group, featured an article with a group of women holding up banners in protest at the sexualisation of the black Brazilian women, "Don't call me *mulata*. I am a black woman, period! I don't want your love. I am flesh you can't have!"[307]

Ironically, while scouts search southern Brazil for women of European descent who fit their standard of beauty, European and North American men travel to the northeast of Brazil seeking sex with women of African descent whom they imagine to be hyper-sexual. Images of scantily-clad, sun-kissed women in bikinis are frequently sold to tourists in Salvador in Bahia to "sell" Brazil to the rest of the world. Historically, the *mulata* has been presented in Brazilian popular culture as the epitome of sexuality and lust, although not considered beautiful enough to be a wife. The same can be said of the way white Brazilian women are put on a pedestal as models and beauty-queens whereas mixed-race and black women are depicted as sluts.[308]

The exclusion of blacks from Brazilian Fashion Week in 2014 led to several protests by black Brazilians at the under-representation of women of African descent and indigenous models. The São Paulo Fashion Week (SPFW) responded to the outcry by introducing racial quotas in which at least 10% of models featured in the fashion week should be of African descent or indigenous. In response to the quotas, one white Brazilian designer, Glória Coelho exclaimed:

> During Fashion Week, there are plenty of black people sewing, helping the models, working behind the scenes, and making beautiful things…there are black assistants, black salespeople…why must they also be on the catwalk?![309]

---

307 https://pretassimoa.wordpress.com/2014/03/01/da-senzala-para-o-cartao-postal-minha-carne-nao-e-do-seu-carnaval/
308 http://www.nytimes.com/2010/06/08/world/americas/08models.html?_r=0
309 http://www2.uol.com.br/JC/sites/especial_joaquimnabuco/html/materia_05.html

Though shocking, Coelho's answer is a reflection of what many in the Brazilian fashion industry may not say but most definitely think, "black is not beautiful", because it doesn't sell.

The notion that "black girls don't sell" has been the recurring excuse used by high-end fashion for not employing mixed-race and black models on the front cover of magazines and advertisements. Some argue that the lack of mixed-race and black models in fashion may be due to economics not to racism per se, and that since white Brazilians are the richest ethnic group in Brazil, the fashion brands may opt for white models who resemble their target readership.

In Brazil, people of African descent are stigmatised as poor and uneducated. Inasmuch as there is no segregation between black and white, Brazil may not be considered racist, but its discrimination in the economic realm against mixed-race and black Brazilians is clear, as many international brands prefer whites to be the faces for their brands. This does not absolve the fashion industry of criticism as it remains blatantly racist. In addition, its obsession with skinniness and the fetishisation of youth are arguably just as troubling if not more.[310]

Europeans' Intimidation of the African Body
Europeans' fascination with the black body has been intimidating for black women and a source of spectacle for white people since they first made contact with black Africans. Many white men are intimidated by what they perceive as the black woman's naturally curvaceous body and the black male's sexual prowess. The elongated black male penis is legendary in European literature, as are the huge 'abnormal' buttocks of black African women, both of which are gross generalisations. In the nineteenth century, exhibitions were held in some European cities in which Sarah Baartman, a black South African woman with prominent buttocks, was displayed as a "wild and savage female" because of her "abnormal" features. Her "abnormalities", as Georges Cuvier mentions in *"The Gender and Science Reader"*, made her the contrary of the myth of the white European woman of the day. Europeans viewed Baartman's protruding buttocks and extended *labia minora* as evidence of the promiscuity of the African woman and her pathological lust. Baartman and,

---

310 Obesity is a problem in Brazil. The Brazilian diet began to change in the 1980s a process that accelerated during the 1990s. Due to the consumption of processed 'junk' food instead of fresh whole food, Brazilians became increasingly overweight. Imported food that is extremely high in calories but low in nutritional value has fattened Brazil's population.

by extension, African women in general were considered abnormal in comparison to white European women who had smaller genitalia and flat buttocks. Despite being subjects of scorn and ridicule, many European males secretly desired and pursued African women for sexual relationships.

The story of Sarah Baartman remains an important example of European attitudes towards black women. Baartman's "unusual physique" attracted the curiosity of a British doctor called William Dunlop, who persuaded her to travel with him to England. Baartman was then named the "Hottentot Venus"; she was displayed as a subject of "scientific curiosity", and Europeans exploited her to make money from exhibitions of her nakedness. Astonished by Baartman's large buttocks and genitalia, the "intellectuals" of Europe wanted to "scientifically prove" that blacks were an inferior and oversexed race.

Baartman's physical features were not unusual for Khoisan woman or many other African ethnicities whose women have prominent buttocks, although it is a grossly unscientific generalisation to apply these descriptions to all the people of this vast continent, who differ vastly in both colour and physiognomy. Like many other black women, Baartman's features may be considered "unusual" or "abnormal" to whites, as they are not accustomed to such women's curvaceous physiques and are intimidated by them. For black people of African descent, a large derriere is an attractive feature in a woman. Large buttocks and chocolate-complexioned skin are some of the features black men who appreciate beauty desire in women.

APPRECIATION OF *BLACK BEAUTY*

It is interesting that whilst mainstream Brazilian popular culture does not appreciate Brazil's chocolate-complexioned beauties, they are seen as the ideal by many black American men, as reflected in hip-hop music videos and the controversial 2011 documentary *Frustrated: Black American Men in Brazil*, which explored why a growing number of black American men move to Brazil in search of black Brazilian women. Many of the black Americans featured in the film described the black Brazilian woman as the ideal in terms of her beauty and character. "Women [in Brazil] are more caring [of men] and respect them as men", one man interviewed in the documentary said. Economics was also highlighted for the breakdown in relationships between black American men and women, because many women are financially better off than their male counterparts. "Women want to be taken care of financially" one black

American woman said, "[because] women want to feel secure, that security blanket." The documentary was made in response to allegations in *Blame it on Rio*, a controversial article by Professor William Jelani Cobb in the African-American magazine Essence in September 2006, that black American men travelled to Brazil for sexual tourism. Though the article resulted in a number of books and documentary films in response to it, the issue remains a bone of contention amongst black Americans.[311]

Black Beauty Pageants
During its carnival procession, the all-black group *Ilê Aiyê* celebrates Afrocentric notions of beauty, in contrast to Brazil's prevailing white-dominated Eurocentric standards of beauty. *Ilê Aiyê* organises an annual beauty contest to select the carnival queen, *Deusa do Ebano* (Ebony Goddess), who is a key visual and symbolic element of its carnival procession. The selected carnival queen will parade during the three days of carnival with the *Ilê Aiyê* carnival group, representing the theme of the group in her costume and dance. The selection is based on Afrocentric notions of beauty in which dark skin, full lips and prominent buttocks are valued, contrary to prevailing standards of beauty in Brazil. Contestants dress in flowing African-style garments, gracefully performing traditional Afro-Brazilian dances to songs in praise of the beauty of black women.

Documentary filmmaker Carolina Moraes-Liu captured the lives of three Afro-Brazilian contestants competing for the title of Ebony Goddess, the Queen of *Ilê Aiyê*. Although Salvador's *Noite da Beleza Negra* (Night of Black Beauty) receives little media attention, the competition is more than a beauty pageant for Afro-Brazilian women. It is part of a profound and personal search by black women for identity, self-esteem and respect due them which is conspicuously absent from Brazil's society and media. "Because blacks aren't totally accepted in [Brazilian] society, I think we have to impose ourselves," said contestant Elcijane Conceição. "[The contest] is not just about beauty. It's a circle of consciousness of beauty, of dance, of search for culture, of self-elevation, of being able to pass this on to other people."[312]

According to the contest's organisers, since the creation of the *Beleza Negra* event, Brazilian black women have felt more appreciated. "To be black in this city [of Salvador] is very hard. But after *Beleza Negra* it got easier. It got easier because we were able to get women in this city to

---
311 See Jewel Woods' *Don't Blame It On Rio: The Real Deal Why Men Go To Brazil For Sex*
312 See Carolina Moraes Liu's *Ebony Goddess: Queen of Ilê Aiyê*

feel beautiful." The Afro-Brazilian woman's comments are even more surprising given the fact that the vast majority of Salvador's inhabitants are black. She continues, "*Ilê* got it right when it started the *Beleza Negra* event. Aside from this affirmation of black aesthetics, it raised our self-esteem as women. We feel extremely valued." Antônio Carlos 'Vovô, the founder of *Ilê Aiyê*, remarked in the documentary that black people did not wear colourful clothes or have a sense of pride in their African ancestry. He said, "[Black] people were ashamed of braiding their hair. All of these things we slowly changed over time." The *Beleza Negra* event and the work of Afro-Brazilian organisations such as *Ilê Aiyê* and *Olodum* have helped to promote the beauty of blackness, though black women are still fighting for recognition in mainstream media, in which they are marginalised.[313]

The Internet has served an important role in mobilising black Brazilians of similar interests to connect with one another and organise beauty pageants celebrating black aesthetics. One of these pageants, *Miss Black Power Brazil,* was organised by Paula Azeviche and Isabel Freitas of Salvador, who work promoting black business owners in the fashion sector. The winner of the 2014 contest, Maria Priscilla, identifies herself as an activist on behalf of black people's rights more than anything else. She said that she was teaching literacy and black history in a low-income community in Rio, "bringing other references to my students, aesthetic, literary and artistic references to tell the story of our people – so that these children know they have a story, and it's not a story that starts in the slave quarters. It goes much farther back than that."[314]

Michelly Ramos, an aspiring black model from Salvador whom I met echoed Priscilla's comments. An elegantly-slim young woman with chocolate-complexioned skin, she informed me of the importance of Afro- Brazilians understanding their history *"que procurer estudar mais sobre a nossa contrbuição para o mundo, não só o Brasil* – to look to study more about our contribution to the world, not only to Brazil." A finalist for the *Beleza Black* 2015 beauty pageant, she reiterated that black beauty contests were not just about celebrating black aesthetics but about restoring the self-esteem of black men and women, *"Eu uso o meu cabelo ao natural não porque 'está na moda' e sim pelo prazer de poder ser quem eu sou!* – I wear my hair natural not because 'it's trendy' but for the pleasure of being who I am!"

---

313 http://www.pri.org/stories/2014-11-20/black-brazilian-women-are-finding-their-power-and-theyre-even-showing-it-their
314 http://www.pri.org/stories/2014-11-20/black-brazilian-women-are-finding-their-power-and-theyre-even-showing-it-their

Chica Da Silva, Zezé Motta And Taís Araújo

After playing Chica da Silva (also spelt Xica da Silva) in a film which premiered in 1976, popular black Brazilian singer, actress and activist Zezé Motta, who is of Nigerian origin, realised the lack of black people in Brazilian media.[315] "It's very hard for a black person in Brazil to have a career as an actress," she told African-American historian Henry Louis Gates, Jr., "but in the case of Chica da Silva, it had to be a black woman. The producer didn't want me because I was too ugly – until very recently, in Brazil, black people were considered ugly. The producer preferred her to be a *mulatta*, a lighter actress. But the director didn't budge. It had to be a black woman."[316]

The success of the film propelled Motta to international stardom. She subsequently travelled the world, which drew her attention to the lack of blacks in the Brazilian media and fashion industry comparatively to other countries. In spite of being "considered a Brazilian sex symbol," Motta admits that many magazines were hesitant to put her picture on the cover as it was commonly believed that "blacks don't sell".[317] On her social networking site she admitted to her followers the racism that she had suffered in her adolescence.

Growing up in Brazil, Motta thought she was *feia* (ugly) and *preta demais* (too black) because of her broad nose, *cabelo ruim* (bad hair) and *bunda grande* (large buttocks). She started straightening her hair and wearing wigs as an attempt at *branqueamento* (whitening). "My dream was to put together enough money to have a nose-job and make it thinner. I thought about making my butt smaller to be accepted," she added.[318]

It wasn't until Motta travelled to the United States in 1969, during the 'Black Power' civil rights movement that she began to appreciate the beauty of her blackness. "I saw blacks in the street, with beautiful *cabelos black power* (Afros). This trip was very important to me. I got in the shower and stopped straightening my hair. It's not a criticism of those who prefer straight hair; the bad thing is the negation of (these black) characteristics." Her experiences in the United States showed her the

---

315 See Junia Ferreira Furtado, *Chica da Silva: A Brazilian Slave of the Eighteenth Century*. A documentary project called DNA Africa traced the heritage of 150 Afro-Brazilians using DNA tracing. Motta took part in the project and discovered that she is of Yoruba heritage.
316 Gates Jr., 2011, p. 47
317 Gates Jr., 2011, p. 47
318 http://blackwomenofbrazil.co/2013/10/30/long-time-actress-zeze-motta-is-competing-for-best-supporting-actress-in-brazils-most-prestigious-movie-awards/

extent of Brazil's anti-black racism – a racism that her country-people claim does not exist. Almost four decades after the release of Motta's Chica da Silva film, the appreciation of black beauty is still an issue in mainstream Brazilian media.

Similarly, contemporary black Brazilian model and actress Taís Araújo is a source of pride for many Afro-Brazilian women, for countering prejudices in mainstream Brazilian media's perception of beauty. Regularly featured in national magazines and on television, Araújo is widely recognised in Brazil much as Motta was in her heyday in the 1970s and 1980s.

Like Motta, Araújo is a beautiful and elegant woman descended from Africans, with chocolate-coloured skin and a radiant smile. Today, she is regarded as one of the most beautiful women in Brazil. Araújo became the first black actress to be a protagonist of a *telenovela* (soap opera) in prime-time Brazilian television, when she played the character Chica da Silva. Again like Motta, who originally played the most famous black Brazilian woman in history, after her success Araújo questioned the lack of *afrodescendentes* (descendants of Africans) in the Brazilian media. Despite being the daughter of educated Afro-Brazilians, Araújo admitted that inter-racial discourse and affirmation of black identity were fragile. "It's only today I feel more prepared and secure to talk about the issue of blacks," she said. As many black activists have also argued, the actress-model points out the lack of black people behind the camera as the main reason for the under-representation of black Brazilians in the media, "*Sinto falta de autores e diretores negros na televisão. A nossa história é sempre contada pelo ponto do vista do outro* – I feel the lack of black authors and directors on television. Our history is always told from the point of view of others."[319]

A primary focus of many black activists has been the need for black people to control the depiction of themselves in the media and for entrepreneurs to create black-owned media platforms. The stereotypical depiction of black people in Brazilian media is unlikely to change until black people gain ownership of media outlets so that they can control their own image and depiction. As much as there has been an improvement in the depiction of blacks on TV, it is still whites who are pulling the strings.

Black Brazilian Media
Attempting to fill the void in black representation in the media, in

---

319 http://oglobo.globo.com/cultura/revista-da-tv/ruth-de-souza-zeze-motta-tais-araujo-refletem-sobre-presenca-do-negro-nas-ultimas-decadas-na-tv-10787670

partnership with Brazilian and Angolan entrepreneurs, black Brazilian singer Netinho de Paula founded a television channel for Afro-Brazilians.[320] The TV channel, *TV da Gente* (Our TV), which was launched in 2005, aimed to showcase black people in a positive light, in contrast to their invisibility in mainstream Brazilian media and fashion. The TV channel tried to redress the racial imbalance on television and in Brazilian society as a whole. Netinho said, "Our country is marked by racial mixtures. But the actual model of TV does not represent the majority of Brazilians. We are trying to help our own people, given that nobody else seems to want to do it. This is where the real fight starts."[321] Despite its noble intentions, the TV channel closed in 2007 due to financial difficulties.

The *Instituto Mídia Étnica* (Ethnic Media Institute) is a black Brazilian media not-for-profit organisation founded by Paulo Rogerio in 2005, to make use of the power of the media to celebrate and promote Brazil's racial diversity. The NGO carries out projects to ensure the use of technological tools for socially excluded groups, especially Afro-Brazilians. The Ethnic Media Institute aims to use a conciliatory rather than a confrontational approach to tackle the underrepresentation of blacks in media organisations and the misrepresentation of blacks in news coverage and stories those organisations produce. "In Brazil we do talk about race but not in an honest way - about white privilege, concentration of power, about the importance of diversity - no, we talk about how we're all Brazilian, we're all mixed." said the Institute's founder.

"Our conversation about race is not even close to what you have in Canada or the U.S. or Europe. There are a lot of reasons - one is media. The media in this country are very concentrated - its families. There's no black radio or TV and there's one magazine with a circulation of 40,000 copies. Second, economic power - we don't have economic power in this country. Because of segregation, they had it in the U.S. - in a strange way it was helpful. There had to be black lawyers, black doctors, there was a black Wall Street in the 1950s. You can't have black media or black education, with private schools to teach the history [like the U.S. had], if nobody has any money."[322]

Raça Brasil Magazine And Photographers
In response to the invisibility of black beauty in print media, *Raça Brasil*,

---

320 The entrepreneur featured in the documentary-film *Raça* by Joel Zito Araújo
321 http://www.theguardian.com/media/2005/nov/21/race.brazil
322 http://www.theglobeandmail.com/news/world/three-personal-stories-that-show-brazil-is-not-completely-beyond-racism/article25761242/

Brazil's first monthly magazine targeting the black population, was published in 1996. The magazine's first edition was released in September of that year and received an unprecedented response. African-American anthropologist Kia Lilly Caldwell observes that the phenomenal success enjoyed by *Raça* in its first year of publication challenged several myths concerning Afro-Brazilians and the role of blacks in the Brazilian media, "first, the belief that a black middle-class capable of purchasing luxury items did not exist; second, the belief that magazines with blacks on the cover would not sell and third, the belief that Afro-Brazilians felt more shame than pride in their ethnic and cultural identity."[323]

Despite the positive depiction of blacks in the magazine, some blacks are critical of the magazine for its failure to promote "a more *negra* (black) aesthetic". Many of the Brazilians featured in the magazine, particularly in the advertisements, are *mestiços* (mixed-race) with typical European features such as thin lips and aquiline noses. Highlighting the importance of the *mestiços* and black aesthetic is an integral part of the struggle against racism in Brazil. That said, *Raça* is doing an admirable job in celebrating the beauty of Brazil's blackness, which comes in different hues, facial features and physiognomies.

Independent freelance artists and photographers from Bahia have also taken it upon themselves to capture the beauty of black women.[324] Muha Bazila, a black Brazilian artist from Bahia, said, "I find it important to appreciate the black woman aesthetically without necessarily sexualising her."[325]

Black Beauty In The African Diaspora
Black Brazil's quest for the appreciation of black beauty runs parallel with other countries in the African diaspora and in Africa itself where black women are not considered beautiful. In Nigeria for example, Taofick Okoya, a frustrated but determined Nigerian businessman wanted to manufacture African dolls because of the lack of black dolls he noticed in Nigeria. He said, "I happen to be the kind of person that doesn't enjoy complaining and criticising without taking action."[326]

Son of the Yoruba Muslim business mogul and billionaire industrial-

---

323 Caldwell, 2007, p. 93
324 http://www.mariapreta.org/2014/06/linda-e-preta-veja-o-trabalho-desse.html
325 http://nobrasil.co/odara-conheca-o-artista-que-faz-uma-homenagem-mulheres-negras-de-todo-o-brasil/
326 http://www.elle.com/culture/art-design/q-and-a/a26422/taofick-okoya-on-queens-of-africa-dolls/

ist, Razaq Akanni Okoya, who built the Eleganza Group from humble beginnings,[327] Taofick followed his father's footsteps into entrepreneurship. He created two ranges of dolls for his new project: the "Queens of Africa" and the "Naija Princesses". Dressed in traditional African attire, the dolls come in various hues and represent the three main tribes of Nigeria: the Hausa, Yoruba and Igbo. "What is really frustrating is the generalization that Africans all have to look a certain way or be a certain colour. This is stereotyping. There are slim Africans, plus-size Africans, dark Africans, fair-skinned Africans, flat-nosed Africans, and pointed-nose Africans. Our diversity is one of our greatest attributes."[328]

Okoya's inspiration for creating the dolls was his young daughter Azeezah. When she told him that she wished she was white, the Nigerian social entrepreneur decided to help her fall in love with her natural black beauty: "Even though we live in Nigeria, there was a lot of Western influence, which might have been responsible for her wishing she was white. It made me aware that I need to make her proud and happy to be a black African girl, and not limit it to her alone, as this was a common trend amongst the younger generation."[329]

Though the dolls are now successful, Okoya initially had a difficult time convincing Nigerian toy-stores to stock his dolls, as they believed that "black dolls don't sell". Okoya then embarked on an educational campaign, via various media outlets, to teach African culture and its diversity, and to inform people about the psychological impact that white dolls have on African children who have been conditioned to believe that the European standard of beauty is the ideal. The increasingly popular dolls are now outselling white Barbie dolls in Nigeria, and are in great demand in the United States and Brazil. Okoya said, "I have received a lot of interest from Brazil and in the process I have come to realise that they also suffer from discrimination or lack of self-confidence when it

---

327 Okoya did not receive any formal education above elementary level and credits his success to hard work, "I have nothing against education. But at times, education gives people false confidence. It makes people relax, trusting in the power of certificates rather than in working hard."
http://www.ventures-africa.com/2012/10/portrait-of-a-mercurial-industrialist-rasaq-akanni-okoya/

328 http://www.elle.com/culture/art-design/q-and-a/a26422/taofick-okoya-on-queens-of-africa-dolls/

329 http://www.elle.com/culture/art-design/q-and-a/a26422/taofick-okoya-on-queens-of-africa-dolls/

comes to their skin colour."[330] Speaking to Brazilian newspaper *Folha de São Paulo,* Okoya said that he intends to expand the Queens of Africa project in order to inspire more African girls around the world, whom he felt were more exposed than African boys to racial discrimination and the pressure to conform to European standards of beauty.[331]

The recent success of dark-skinned Hollywood actress Lupita Nyong'o, who was voted the most beautiful woman in the world by some high profile Western magazines, created a sense of pride amongst women of colour throughout the world. Born in Mexico, Nyong'o is of Kenyan origin. Her short-cropped hair and phenotypically African features, have added to her international fame since winning an Academy Award (Oscar) in 2013. Nyong'o has become a source of inspiration for Afro-Brazilian women in their struggle for acceptance and appreciation by mainstream society. "Thankfully our beauty is being recognised," black Brazilian actress Erika Januza said, citing Taís Araújo and Zezé Motta as her only beauty references on mainstream television when she was growing up in Brazil.[332] Black Brazilian writer Nina Silva writes, "It is very nice to see on the cover a highly pigmented black woman and outside of the standard of thin mouth and hair down to the waist. She has the phenotype of a certain region of Africa that was never appreciated as beautiful."[333]

In her powerful speech at *Essence* magazine's "Black Women in Hollywood" luncheon ceremony in February 2014, Nyong'o spoke candidly about the beauty of blackness and about how badly she used to feel about her dark skin. She described receiving a letter from a young girl who told her that she considered buying skin-whitening cream[334] before Nyong'o "appeared on the world map and saved me". Moved by the young girl's heartfelt letter, Nyong'o admitted that her "heart bled a little when I read those words". Like the young girl and many black children growing up, Nyong'o recalled how she struggled with conventional beauty

---

330 http://newsone.com/3078796/queens-of-africa-dolls/

331 http://www1.folha.uol.com.br/folhinha/2014/08/1507521-nigeriano-cria-linha-de-bonecas-negras-para-inspirar-meninas-africanas.shtml

332 http://extra.globo.com/famosos/erika-januza-encarna-atriz-negra-eleita-mais-bonita-do-mundo-revela-ter-renegado-fio-crespo-passei-vida-alisando-cabelo-12307059.html

333 http://ela.oglobo.globo.com/beleza/cultura-em-beleza/inspiradas-em-lupita-jovens-negras-falam-de-preconceito-da-valorizacao-da-propria-beleza-12453031

334 The skin whitening cream was promoted by Dencia, a popular singer from the west-African country, Cameroon.

standards when she was younger, and how she was "teased and taunted about my night-shaded skin". She would frequently ask God to lighten her skin, but would experience disappointment when she woke up "just as dark as I was the day before". Her "self-hate grew worse" when she became an adolescent, and could not be assuaged by her mother's assurances that she was beautiful. After seeing the success of dark-skinned international model Alek Wek, Nyong'o began to appreciate the beauty of her blackness. She concluded her speech to the young girl and others like her who viewed the actress as a role model:

> I hope that my presence on your screens and in the magazines may lead you, young girl, on a similar journey. That you will feel the validation of your external beauty but also get to the deeper business of being beautiful inside. There is no shade in that beauty.[335]

CONCLUSION

The origin of the belief that whiteness is more beautiful than blackness is not clear. Some researchers have linked it to the slave trade and Africa's colonial history. Black activists have taken it upon themselves to celebrate the beauty of blackness, particularly for black women.

The importance of the beauty of blackness is not a superficial issue for many black Brazilian women who feel the need for their aesthetics to be celebrated. Black activists are campaigning against the notion that white beauty or Eurocentric aesthetics is the only "beauty".

Indeed black is beautiful as are brown, white, yellow and all shades in between. The appreciation of black beauty should not be defined by anyone but black people themselves. For far too long, the acceptable image of black beauty in Brazil has been of the mulatto light-brown complexioned women with European facial features, a curvaceous African body and jet-black hair from her indigenous ancestry. The mixed-ancestry mulatto woman symbolises the fusion of Brazil's three races, thus making her the ideal to project the image of Brazil's racial democracy. Although the concept of racial democracy is a myth, Brazil is genuinely a racially mixed nation. Many lauded beautiful 'white' Brazilian women visibly have African ancestry and many beautiful 'black' Brazilian women clearly have non-African ancestry. Beauty, as the old adage states, is in the eye of the beholder and black beauty comes in different shades of darkness, facial features, hair textures, and body sizes. Brazil's black consciousness movement have taken the initiative

---

335 http://www.essence.com/2014/02/27/lupita-nyongo-delivers-moving-black-women-hollywood-acceptance-speech/

to challenge the media's narrow definition of beauty and celebrate the uniqueness of black beauty.

Ironically the white-controlled media and fashion industry of the Western world, which dominates the perception of beauty in Brazil, consists of a large number of influential and often homosexual middle-aged white men, who dictate who is beautiful and what is beauty.[336] The fashion world's obsession with skinniness and emaciated boyish woman models has been said by some to be due to homosexual fashion designers' preferences for young men. A writer for the British newspaper "The Observer" commented:

> It has long been said that fashion is a con-trick by largely gay male designers to make women look more like men: breastless, hipless, as skinny as a boy.[337]

Though this hypothesis is unproven, it is nevertheless common knowledge that many major high-end fashion designers are homosexuals. The clear preference that the fashion industry and media has for Eurocentric women of this description is the antithesis of Afrocentric beauty, whose ideal is curvaceous and brown complexioned. As the majority of Brazil's population are of African descent, aspiring to the Eurocentric ideal of beauty will continue to cause many men and women to not appreciate their own black beauty. Black activists campaign for the appreciation that black women are beautiful and should not need to take off their clothes in order to be considered beautiful. Thus, it is very important for Brazil's blacks to educate themselves regarding their history and to be in a position to control their own image in the media and fashion industry, so that they will be able to take pride in the beauty of their blackness.

Blacks must take ownership of the beauty of their blackness instead of waiting for white validation of their aesthetics. Only when blacks

---

336 Fashion historian Valerie Steele and Fred Dennis spent two years researching the extent to which homosexual men and lesbians worked in the fashion industry and the ways in which their participation shaped aesthetics in the Western world. Their findings were on display in the fashion exhibition 'A Queer History of Fashion: From the Closet to the Catwalk' in New York City, which ran from the 13th September 2013 until the 4th of January 2014. Co-curator of the exhibition Steele said, " We see how central gay culture has been to the creation of modern fashion." http://www.fitnyc.edu/21048.asp

337 http://www.theguardian.com/commentisfree/2011/aug/07/vogue-not-for-children

as a group, particularly their women, take pride in the beauty of their blackness will they be able to resolve the dilemma of aspiring to the false ideal of whiteness and the Eurocentric concept of beauty.[338]

---

[338] *Feira Preta* (Black Fair) is an example of annual event held in Brazil which promotes black business and black group economics. The fair also features a number of Afro-Brazilian entrepreneurs showcasing their businesses and selling products aimed at black Brazilians with the aim of raising the self-esteem of blacks and celebrating the contribution which African peoples have made to the country.

CHAPTER 3

AFFIRMATIVE ACTION IN BRAZIL

"If he is black and poor, he is already condemned [in Brazilian society]"

ANTONIO FIALHO GARCIA JUNIOR,
CIVIL POLICE CHIEF, ES BRAZIL.

ACCORDING TO THE Oxford Dictionary, affirmative action is an "action favouring those who tend to suffer from discrimination; positive discrimination." According to another definition, it is "the practice of improving the educational and job opportunities of members of groups that have not been treated fairly in the past because of their race, sex, etc."[339] In the case of Brazil, affirmative-action laws relate to those of African and indigenous descent.

In the early 2000s, Brazil's government enacted affirmative-action laws for public universities by legislating racial and social quotas for student admissions with the aim of reducing the country's racial and social inequalities. As higher education is often perceived to be a gateway to success, the affirmative-action laws are an attempt to redress the historical wrongs which Brazil has meted out to its indigenous peoples and those of African descent. The controversial laws outraged many Brazilians of European ancestry, who argued that the laws create a racial divide in the country. However, the affirmative-action laws do recognise that Brazil has remained far behind the ideal of "racial democracy" espoused by Gilberto Freyre, the country's influential sociologist in the 1930s.[340]

---

339 http://www.merriam-webster.com/dictionary/affirmative%20action
340 http://www.nytimes.com/2012/08/31/world/americas/brazil-enacts-affirmative-action-law-for-universities.html?_r=0

In 2003, the Brazilian government passed Law 10/639, requiring public and private schools to teach "the black struggle in Brazil, black Brazilian cultures and the role of blacks in social, economic and political aspects of the history of Brazil." The law also required that schools celebrate a "National Day of Black Consciousness". This initiative sparked a wave of research about Afro-Brazilians figures and advocacy to have them included in history textbooks.[341]

ADVOCATES AND BENEFITS

Proponents of affirmative action argue that unequal access to education is responsible for inequality of opportunity in Brazil. Affirmative-action laws are viewed as a weapon in the fight against the legacy of African slavery. Inhumane Portuguese treatment of African and indigenous slaves is often omitted in discussions of Brazilian history. Slavery was commercial, and even after the abolition of the institution and mass European immigration to Brazil in the nineteenth century, the black and brown population of the country was left destitute without reparations. Although free, they had very limited access to wealth and education.

The IBGE's 2010 national census highlighted the great disparity between whites and non-whites, with the richest 10% of the population gaining 44.5% of total income compared to 1.1% for the poorest 10%. The richest Brazilians are overwhelmingly white, whilst the majority of black Brazilians live in abject poverty. On average, white and Asian Brazilians earned twice as much as black or mixed-race Brazilians. In Salvador, a city which is predominately non-white, whites earned 3.2 times more than blacks. An economist from Rio's UFRJ University said, "Poor salaries lead to worse education, which is a barrier to getting a good job. We need public policies." A similar study carried out by the Data Popular Institute provided further evidence of the racial divide that continues to blight Brazilian society. 82% of Brazil's wealthiest group, known as Class A, are white, whereas 76.3% of Class E (the poorest group in Brazil) are Afro-Brazilian. The same study found that 31.3% of Brazil's white population had private health plans, compared with just 15.2% of the black population. The study's findings clearly showed that in Brazil, poverty and brown skin often coincide.

Ivone Caetano, a prominent Afro-Brazilian judge in Rio de Janeiro, painted the bleak picture in store for Brazil's black population: "In Brazil every black person is going to be a victim of racism, prejudice [and]

---

341 Aidi, 2014, p. 36

discrimination, whatever your position." She continued, "Our prejudice is disguised and hypocritical."[342]

Paulo Paim, Brazil's only Afro-Brazilian senator, echoed Caetano's comments and described racism in Brazil as being "half-disguised" to keep black people out of power.[343] A firm supporter of the affirmative-action laws, Paim said that, as only 10% of students graduated from public schools, most Brazilians would benefit.[344] On average those of African descent spend two years less at school than the country's white population. With less education, many Afro-Brazilians only manage to find menial work.

The extreme social inequalities between whites and non-whites can only be explained by racism, according to Mário Theodoro of the federal government's secretariat for racial equality. Afro-Brazilian activists insist that the legacy of slavery, which has caused the huge inequality amongst whites and non-whites, can only be reversed by affirmative-action policies, of the kind found in the United States.[345]

African-American historian Henry Louis Gates Jr who himself benefited from affirmative action in the United States along with President Barack Obama, said about Brazil's affirmative action:

> Supporters argued that without affirmative action, Afro-Brazilian children had no chance to achieve equality, much less become leaders who could represent their communities in society and government. Slavery and racism left blacks at a disadvantage, keeping generation after generation of black youth trapped in poverty. Only through affirmative action, and through quotas, they argued, could blacks succeed in numbers proportionate to their share of the population. And then, perhaps social equality could follow.[346]

Challenge Stereotypes And Change Expectations
According to João Feres Jr, a political scientist at the State University of Rio de Janeiro, quotas are necessary not only to level racial inequalities but also to challenge stereotypes and expectations:

> You grow up in a society where you never see a black person in a position of power or high status, so you learn to associate black

---
342 http://www.theguardian.com/world/2011/nov/17/brazil-census-african-brazilians-majority
343 http://news.bbc.co.uk/1/hi/world/americas/7596087.stm
344 http://www.bbc.co.uk/news/world-latin-america-19188610
345 http://www.economist.com/node/21543494
346 Gates Jr, 2011, pp. 54-55

people [with] menial jobs, [with] low paid-jobs. Even people who are not actively prejudiced build up this kind of expectation... I think the affirmative action breaks with that.[347]

Luiz Inácio Lula da Silva, former president of Brazil, said in an interview that he was "completely in favour" of the quotas:

> Try finding a black doctor, a black dentist, a black bank manager, and you will encounter great difficulty... It's important, at least for a span of time, to guarantee that the blacks in Brazilian society can make up for lost time.[348]

Luiza Bairros, the only black minister in current President Rousseff's cabinet, said:

> You don't see black people writing for newspapers or directing companies, so it's more difficult to convince voters to put them into office.

Professor of history at the Federal University of Bahia, João José Reis, felt that Brazil's affirmative action policy can help change the perception of dark-skinned Brazilians who are considered by many light skinned Brazilians to be less intelligent and sophisticated than Brazilians of European ancestry. For some racist white Brazilians, the *"negra's* place is in the kitchen" and not in university campuses. Many white Brazilians have vented their racist sentiments towards blacks in recent years, Reis explains, particularly on social media towards prominent black Brazilians because of the affirmative action policies as they feel black Brazilians are not "staying in their place" of servitude to whites.

In the state of Bahia which Reis lectures, 40% of the university's places are reserved for black and students from low income families. Of these *cotistas* (beneficiaries of the reserved places), 80% must be allocated to black students in proportion to their weight in the northeastern state. As a result more black and mixed raced Brazilians are aiming to go to university and climb the social ladder to provide better lives for their families as Luiza Bairros explained, "*Cotistas* take their studies much more seriously than those who thought a university place was theirs by right. They know how important this opportunity is not just for them but for their whole family."

---

347 http://www.bbc.co.uk/news/business-23862676
348 http://www.nytimes.com/2012/08/31/world/americas/brazil-enacts-affirmative-action-law-for-universities.html?_r=0

Affirmative Action Policies

"Black political struggle laid the foundation for the current debate over affirmative action, especially in the area of education," Ollie A. Johnson writes. Since the abolition of slavery, Afro-Brazilian leaders and organisations have advocated high-quality education for blacks and all Brazilians. Education has been recognised as the key to black advancement, both individually and as a group. The same black activists, politicians, and intellectuals who created black organisations, demanded inclusion in political parties and achieved pro-black initiatives, also supported affirmative action.

Abdias do Nascimento was one of the key black Brazilian leaders demanding affirmative-action policies since the 1940s.[349] Whilst serving in the Federal Senate in 1991 and 1997, Nascimento presented his affirmative-action proposals. Although the proposals were not approved by Congress, Nascimento was one of the earliest and most visible politicians to raise the question of affirmative action in Brazil.[350]

The legislation of Brazil's affirmative-action policies began after the return to democratic rule in 1985. The democratisation process slowly yielded political space to social movements that were launching public education campaigns to raise awareness of racial discrimination and the socioeconomic exclusion of Afro-Brazilians. The first public-policy change took place in 1999 in Porto Alegre, Brazil's sixth-largest city. In that year, the municipal government passed a regulation that 5% of the workforce of all publicly-funded contracts be *negro*. Similarly, the state of Bahia, where non-whites constitute 75% of the population, adopted a ruling requiring one-third of all models and actors in state publicity to be black. Changes in federal policy soon followed. Brazil began instituting affirmative-action policies on the federal level in 2001, when Raul Jungmann, the Minister of Agrarian Development, issued an executive order requiring that 20% of all administrative positions in the ministry be reserved for blacks, as well as 20% of the staff of firms contracted by the agency, and that another 20% of the firms' staffs be women. Just as in the U.S., there is an understanding that the government should act as a model employer, leading the way for fuller racial integration in the labour market.

The first programme designed to offer poor blacks a way out of poverty was launched in 2003 at the State University of Rio de Janeiro. It set aside 20% of the university's places for black students, and it was the only

---
349 Johnson, Ollie, 2008, p. 222
350 Johnson, Ollie, 2008, p. 222

programme of its kind anywhere in the country. Similar programmes have since spread throughout Brazil.[351]

Local governments have also launched affirmative-action programmes. For example, in June 2011, the state of Rio de Janeiro issued a decree that 20% of vacancies in public examinations for civil service positions in the state government should be set aside for blacks and persons of indigenous descent. By August 2010, at least eighty public universities in Brazil had adopted affirmative-action policies. The structures of current programmes vary: some only target Afro-Brazilian students from public secondary schools as a way of reaching the neediest Afro-Brazilian students; other programmes set aside seats for public secondary school graduates of any race and then establish slots proportionally by race and according to demographic percentages in each state.

Another variant establishes separate quotas for Afro-Brazilian students from public or private secondary schools in addition to a quota for public-school students of any race. A few universities award extra points to the entrance examination scores of Afro-Brazilian applicants and public secondary-school graduates. Both mechanisms ensure that middle-class Afro-Brazilians, who have in addition been under-represented in public universities and affected by racial discrimination, will not be excluded by class or socio-economic considerations. Brazil's 1888 Constitution considers education to be:

> A right that belongs to everybody; the duty of the State and of families, promoted and stimulated with the cooperation of society, with a view of the full development of the individual for the exercise of citizenship and preparation for work.

In 2012, the Brazilian state institutionalised affirmative action in all public federal universities with the *Lei de Cotas Sociais* (Law of Social Quotas). The law requires federal public universities to reserve half of all new admission places for Brazilian public high-school graduates. Half of those reserved places are set aside for students whose household family income falls below 1.5 times the minimum wage per family member. The law also requires that within that 50% set-aside, spots be reserved for persons of African descent and of indigenous ancestry, proportional to their relative populations within each state. The purpose of the law was to promote racial equality and increase the

---

351 Gates Jr, 2011, p. 54

number of students of African descent in higher education. The racial quota was to be discontinued ten years after the law was enacted.[352]

A year later in 2013, Dilma Rousseff, Brazil's president, in a meeting with twenty leading black activist groups, renewed her commitment to affirmative-action programmes for Afro-Brazilians. After the gathering, Luiza Bairros, the Racial Equality Minister, said, "The president reaffirmed that affirmative actions, and more specifically quotas, represent a central element of the struggle for equality in Brazil."[353]

In an open letter to the president, Friar David Raimundo dos Santos, the head of *Educafro*, called on the government to implement racial-quota systems and give blacks and indigenous Brazilians their rights. *Educafro* is a charity that holds university entrance-classes mainly for black people in poor areas. Friar David has emerged as one of the most important black grassroots activists, defending affirmative action and racial quotas as necessary to break the structure of white privilege in Brazil. Since 1993, Friar David has worked with an elite Catholic University in Rio de Janeiro to secure scholarships and other support for his students. Ollie A. Johnson noted in his article *Afro-Brazilian Politics: White Supremacy, Black Struggle, and Affirmative Action*, "Because of Friar David and *Educafro* more than five hundred poor and Afro-Brazilian students have gained access to prestigious universities who probably would not have otherwise."[354]

Quota For Blacks In The Brazilian Justice System
The Brazilian National Council of Justice (CNJ) issued a resolution on 9th June 2015, that establishes that 20% of the available positions in public exams designed to select people to enter the bodies of the judiciary must be filled by people who self-identify as 'black' or 'brown.'

In the 2015 racial census of the penal system, Brazil's CNJ revealed that 85% of judges and 78% of lawyers are white, convicting a prison population that is 67% black. "We have these social situations in which it is obvious that blacks are underrepresented and undervalued while whites are always in a position of great power," says Sheila de Carvalho, human rights lawyer at the Brazilian NGO Conectas. "Affirmative action policies in the justice system ensures that those in the career actually reflect our society as an entirety, thus providing for a more nuanced social judgment," says de Carvalho. "A judge [of colour] may have

---

352 http://gotothinktank.com/affirmative-action-in-brazil-is-brazil-a-racial-democracy/
353 http://www.foxnews.com/world/2013/07/19/rousseff-renews-backing-quotas-for-brazil-blacks/
354 Johnson, Ollie, 2008, p. 223

lived through certain experiences that other judges raised with greater privileges would not be able to relate to or understand, an essential diversity of life backgrounds when faced with the very population that the justice system encircles."

De Carvalho remembers being the only black law student in lecture halls of over one hundred at the prestigious Mackenzie University. "Here in Brazil, we enter a designated space for elites and there will only be white faces, an absence of blacks that we have been conditioned to think of as normal," she explains.[355] It is hoped that the quotas for black judges will help curb the disproportion of young black men who are killed and incarcerated in Brazil.

On average, police in Brazil killed six people per day between 2009 and 2013, a study by a São Paulo-based research group found. And the victims of police violence in Brazil are overwhelmingly black and poor. Amnesty International's research shows of the 56,000 murders officially committed in the country, 30,000 were between the ages of 15 and 29. Of these victims, 77% were black.[356] Blacks in Brazil are no longer keeping quiet as police terrorise their communities, even in the face of possible death. Although not widespread, more black Brazilians are taking to protests to raise awareness of the country's anti-black racism. "This country loves our black culture, our music, our bodies, but hates the fact we still exist as the majority," said one 26-year-old woman participating in a protest against police brutality in Salvador Bahia. "Salvador is the front line of the war against African people in Brazil. My people built this city — this country — through slavery. We will not be silent. Black lives have value; Africans all over the diaspora want to live."

Success Of Affirmative Action
A great deal of empirical data indicates that the Brazilian affirmative action programmes have been successful. A study of student results at the State University of Campinas found that students from socio-economically and educationally disadvantaged backgrounds performed better than those from a higher socio-economic and educational background. The study concluded that the need for hard work when striving for greater opportunity creates an "educational resilience" that improves performance once a student is admitted to university. The educational resilience of the

---

355 http://www.seattleglobalist.com/2015/09/22/black-lives-matter-movement-building-in-brazil-sao-paulo-police/41625
356 http://www.amnestyusa.org/news/press-releases/brazil-lowering-age-of-adult-criminal-responsibility-will-consign-children-to-medieval-prison-system

less-privileged students resulted in higher grades on average in thirty-one of the fifty-five possible undergraduate courses, after only one year of university study. The relative performance of the affirmative-action students was in general higher in forty-eight of the fifty-five courses. Professor Marilene Rosa of the State University of Rio de Janeiro found that her best students were those who had gained admission via the quota system.

Idelber Avelar, Brazilian professor of Latin American Literatures and Intellectual Histories, wrote in his blog about Brazil's racial quotas:

> Research results published in the Folha de São Paulo found that out of 6,264 people surveyed, 65% were in favour of the adoption of quotas for blacks in universities.
>
> That affirmative action has fulfilled its role in creating a solid black middle class and therefore would no longer be necessary. I find it hard to take seriously the argument that affirmative action "incited racial tensions" in the US. Anyone who knows the history of race relations in the US knows that the tension comes from long before.[357]

Affirmative action has increased the mixed-race and black middle class in Brazil. In 2006, after seeing the statistics that black students in higher education had doubled in number since 2001, Ivanir dos Santos, a black activist from Rio de Janeiro, exclaimed, "We're very happy, because in the past five years we've placed more blacks in universities than in the previous 500 years." Dos Santos continued, "Today there's a revolution in Brazil!"[358]

OPPONENTS AND CRITICISMS

Opponents of affirmative action have long argued that coloured people are at the bottom of the social pyramid because of economic reasons. They argue that Brazilian society is stratified not by race but by social class. They also argue that such ameliorative measures are themselves racist and will create a racial divide in a country where it does not yet exist. Critics of affirmative action argue that Brazilians are a mixed-race people who do not view themselves according to the dichotomy of black and white, as do North Americans.

White Brazilian sociologist Demétrio Martinelli Magnoli actively opposes measures of affirmative-action and racial quotas. In 2009, Magnoli authored *Uma Gota de Sangue* (A Drop of Blood), in which he argues that Brazil's affirmative action and its black movement have resulted from the ideological scam of multiculturalism which "works

---

357 http://www.idelberavelar.com/archives/2006/07/as_cotas_raciais_em_debate.php
358 http://www.economist.com/node/21543494

against the principle of equality before the law."[359] Though Magnoli acknowledges that racism does exist in Brazil, he is of the opinion that the country is stratified not by race but in socio-economic terms. According to Magnoli, Brazil is a mixed-race country that is not based on race in the same way as the United States, where Jim Crow's one-drop rule categorised anyone with African ancestry as black.[360]

Anthropologist Yvonne Maggie also argued that Brazil would not benefit from United States-style affirmative action, because the history of race-relations in Brazil is completely different from that of the United States. Maggie argues that "a Brazilian system based on group identities similar to American affirmative action would have to render separate that which is conjoined." She says that Brazil should "focus on programmes that seek to remedy past injustices towards the poor, strengthening the ideal of equality and not the idea that humanity is divided into 'races', a notion that has caused great harm the world over."[361] Like many other academics not in favour of racial quotas, Maggie believes that everyday Brazilians do not 'see' race, as most of the population are of mixed heritage – something which has become part of its national identity.

A comment made by a white Brazilian on an online article featured in the *Economist* magazine reflects the attitudes of many white Brazilians who object to the country's racial quotas.

> If there are fewer blacks in universities, it is because they don't strive to get [education].[362]

The commentator was of the view that Brazil provides opportunities for everyone, and then she drew comparisons with the ridicule she receives because of her pale skin to the lack of blacks and mulattos in Brazilian universities. Rather than focusing on race, she argues that Brazilians should have mutual respect for one another and move on from such discussions. Others who aren't in favour of racial quotas argue that the government should focus on improving the primary and secondary public education system, in which most mixed-race and blacks study, rather than legislating racial quotas, and that beneficiaries of the quotas may not be competent to finish university due to having received an inadequate education from the public school system.

---

359 http://www1.folha.uol.com.br/fsp/ilustrad/fq2609200922.htm
360 http://stream.aljazeera.com/story/201205171947-0022211
361 http://www.nytimes.com/roomfordebate/2012/03/29/brazils-racial-identity-challenge/looking-to-the-us-has-been-a-mistake-for-brazil
362 http://www.economist.com/node/21543494/comments#comments

According to IPEA, a government-linked think-tank, blacks are relatively disadvantaged in their level of education and in their access to health and other services. For example, more than half the people of Rio de Janeiro's *favelas* (slums) are black, whereas blacks comprise just 7% of the city's wealthier districts.[363]

Affirmative action policies have proved difficult to implement. Some Brazilians fear that affirmative action may engender racism, as no such legislation has been implemented before. Some Afro-Brazilian students have refused to apply to universities under the system, because they consider it to be an unfair advantage. Other Brazilians argue that it will produce racial tensions that previously did not exist. Senator Aloysio Nunes said federal universities are centres of excellence which should select the students with the best marks, regardless of race or class. "The measure straightjackets universities because it violates their management autonomy," Nunes said.[364]

Academics from some of Brazil's best universities have led a campaign against the quotas. They argue firstly that affirmative action starts with an act of racism: the division of a rainbow nation into arbitrary colour categories. Assigning races in Brazil is not always as easy as activists claim. In 2007 one of two identical twins, who both applied to enter the University of Brasília, was classified as 'black', but the other as 'white'. All this risks creating racial resentment. Secondly, opponents say affirmative action undermines equality of opportunity and meritocracy – fragile concepts in Brazil, where privilege, nepotism and contacts have long been routes to advancement.[365]

A PROBLEM FOR THE WHITE ELITE

"There is a separation of coloured people from white people in the United States [of America]. That separation is not a disease of coloured people. It is a disease of white people. I do not intend to be quiet about it."[366]

ALBERT EINSTEIN

---

363 http://www.economist.com/node/21543494
364 http://www.bbc.co.uk/news/world-latin-america-19188610
365 http://www.economist.com/node/21543494
366 The prominent German-born physicist Albert Einstein (d. 1955), who developed the general theory of relativity, among other feats, was also a strong campaigner against anti-black racism. After living in America for a little more than ten years, Einstein witnessed first-hand the racism that blacks were subjected to by whites. Reportedly calling racism "a disease of white people," and saying he did not intend to be quiet. Compounded to address this issue, Einstein published an essay in 1946 entitled, The Negro Question, in which he spoke against anti-black racism.

Affirmative action is a white problem, as the political power and responsibility to change Brazil's racial inequality rests with Brazil's white elite. That is not to say that Afro-Brazilians and ordinary people have nothing to do. Affirmative-action laws were legislated to redress historical wrongs that white Europeans inflicted upon the African and indigenous peoples of Brazil. Some white people concocted the notion of the superiority of whiteness. Rather than looking at affirmative action as the "white man's burden" to educate brown and black Brazilians because of the benevolence of white people, it is their responsibility to readdress some their forefathers' wrongs. White supremacy is a white problem, plain and simple. This particular virulent form of racism was invented by white Europeans. Although white Brazilians of today have not perpetuated the wrongs enacted against coloured Brazilians during and after slavery, they are benefitting from the injustices, and from the privilege that come from being white in a racist society.

White Privilege And White Supremacy
White privilege most definitely exists in Brazil. Robert Jensen, author of *The Heart of Whiteness* argues that the "race problem" derives from white supremacy, the idea that non-white people are inferior in intellectual or moral terms to white people.

As some white people created the concept of white supremacy, therefore by definition, they are the root of the problem of racism, says white American anti-racism activist Tim Wise. White supremacy is ultimately about power and domination. Jensen argues that Brazil, like the United States, remains materially and ideologically a racist and systematically white-supremacist society. In material terms, white Brazilians are substantially wealthier and live longer than black and mixed-race Brazilians. There is a clear racial gap between white and non-white peoples. In ideological terms, it places greater value on knowledge which comes out of white Europe than other parts of the world. The indigenous Brazilians' and Africans' perspectives are generally not reflected in the country's educational system. White intellectuals are valued more than non-white intellectuals. In the sub-consciousness of many employers, non-whites are perceived as inferior to their white counterparts, as reflected in research carried out showing Brazilian employers' clear preference for whites.

It is relevant to point out that white privilege is an issue that is not limited to the problem of access to quality education and jobs. The historically high concentration of land ownership in the hands of white elites and the regressive tax system that largely lifts the burden off the backs of the higher-income classes protect not only an economic elite, but a largely white economic elite.

The plurality of and differences in Brazilian society lie not only in the skin-colour of the population, but are also reinforced by a socio-economic stratification in which the majority of blacks and *pardos* remain lower class, while whites enjoy the effects of white privilege. To believe that Brazil is a racial paradise is, in essence, to deny the relevance of these issues of inequality and dominance.

Changing Attitudes
Despite having the largest black population in the world after Nigeria, blacks make up a minute percentage of Brazil's private educational system. Students from private schools are predominately from white upper-class families, and are more likely to gain admission into federal universities, which, paradoxically, are heavily subsidised and thus virtually free. Private-school students are usually better prepared for tough university entrance exams than pupils from the public-school system, due to the quality of education in private schools and their ability to supplement courses with costly private tuition. Not surprisingly, the lack of opportunities for black and mixed-race Brazilians results in their gravitating to menial jobs, which reinforces the notion that white people have of being intellectually superior. This may not be uttered publicly, but Brazilians think it subconsciously.

Affirmative action may be a step in the right direction in addressing Brazil's inequalities, but non-whites who have graduated from the education system may face continued discrimination when they look for employment. An Economist article points out:

> The hardest task is to change attitudes. Many Brazilians simply assume blacks belong at the bottom of the pile.[367]

Changing the mindset of people requires both theoretical and practical education, theoretical education via informative instruction in the form of books, classes, documentaries, and practical education experientially i.e. seeing black people in positions of power and responsibility that will change the stereotypical attitudes that see blacks as being unintelligent and irresponsible. A black Brazilian lawyer spoke about this problem when he said:

> The problem is that the bar is always set higher for blacks to get a job, while a white person will not need to have much credentials

---
367 http://www.economist.com/node/21543494

to be hired in Brazil, since meritocracy, Brazilian-style, is based on contacts, privilege, good-looks and a lot of deep-seated prejudice and resentment against any qualified black professional.[368]

This is evident in what occurred on Friday 3rd July 2015, when Afro-Brazilian journalist Maria Júlia Coutinho was the target of racist abuse in social media networks on the Internet. She had recently become the first black reporter/'weathergirl' for TV Globo. Affectionately known as Majú, she is a highly competent journalist, holds a degree in journalism and is more than qualified for the role. Yet, she was still subject to a torrent of abuse by ignorant Brazilians venting their anger at the sight of a black woman with natural hair on their television screens. Many of the mindless critics questioned her competence, and said that she received the job because of racial quotas.

In response to the criticism, Majú responded in a dignified manner, "*Os preconceituosos ladram, mas a caravan passa* – The prejudice barks, but the caravan passes by".[369] Born in São Paulo, she admitted that she was not surprised at the level of abuse directed at her, "*Não me abalo. Acho triste, mas sou muito consciente. Cresci numa família que militou no movimento negro. Não perco muito tempo com isso* – I am not shocked. I find it sad, but I'm very conscious. I grew up in a family that was active in the black movement. I do not waste my time with these things". Fortunately for Majú, she was brought up in a household where she was aware of her identity as a black woman and so did not let such abuse trouble her, though she did admit that she has been subjected to a lot of racial prejudice in Brazil but that her family has been there to support her.[370] Majú's case is not an isolated one in Brazil, where blacks, irrespective of their qualifications and professional experience, have to work twice as hard to be treated as equals to their white counterparts.

The Internet and Anti-Black Racism
In recent years, the number of cases of anti-black racism on the Internet in Brazil has increased considerably. An example of this can be found with Brazil's most famous Afro-Brazilian model and actress, Taís Araújo, who was subjected to a litany of racist abuse on her social media page on

---

368 http://www.economist.com/node/21543494/comments#sort-comments
369 http://www.diariodepernambuco.com.br/app/noticia/viver/2015/07/03/internas_viver,584666/ao-vivo-maju-responde-aos-comentarios-racistas-os-preconceituosos-ladram-mas-a-caravana-passa.shtml
370 http://www.correio24horas.com.br/detalhe/noticia/william-bonner-e-famosos-defendem-maria-julia-apos-ataques-racistas/?cHash=85e2080853da801998550d8a1898e3b4

1st November 2015 after she posted a picture of herself on her Facebook page. Soon afterward, the social media page was flooded with racial slurs and attacks on her hair. Comments like, "who posted this gorilla on Facebook," "how can someone find that hair beautiful," and "I did not know that the zoo has a camera" were posted under the actress' photo. The abuse prompted a national response as many Brazilians rallied in her defence. The incident illustrates how much work Brazil must do to address the issue of anti-black racism in its society.

In the same month, high profile Afro-Brazilian actress Cris Vianna has also been the target of racist comments on the internet by Brazilians, 'Have you already used this hair to clean the house today, African?!' 'You African primate,' and 'Monkey' were some of the comments she received online. Cris Vianna has since reacted to the online abuse she has been subjected to by calling for perpetrators to be prosecuted.

> "Unfortunately, we are still going through this in the middle of 2015. Recently, the victim was the competent journalist Maria Júlia Coutinho. And now, just a month after my beautiful colleague, Taís Araújo, having been shamefully and cowardlty attacked, here we are again needing to face hidden racists under the pretence of anonymity of the Internet. On Sunday night, my Facebook page received a series of prejudiced comments, immediately recorded and sent to court. I cannot remain silent."

Another prominent Afro-Brazilian actress, Sheron Menezes, has also been attacked with racist insults in social networks in December 2015. Despite being mixed-race with obvious European ancestry, like many mixed-raced Brazilian women, Menezes also endures racial abuse like black women with full African ancestry. Below a photo of the Afro-Brazilian actress with her white fiancée whilst on vacation in Europe, social media users commented: 'You went to another country just to buy that black woman! How much did she cost?' 'Do you have authorisation from the IBAMA[371] to walk with that gorilla in the street.' 'A good slave,' 'The place of a black person is the collection of cotton, not travelling to Europe.' Another user created a montage of the actress with a monkey face and the caption '*qualquer semelhança é mera coincidência*' (any similarity is purely coincidental). Menezes took to her social media website on Instagram, to respond to the racist abuse which she said "already expected" after the recent attacks to other high-profile Afro-Brazilian actresses:

---

371   The IBAMA is the *Instituto Brasileiro do Meio Ambiente e dos Recursos Naturals Renováveis* (Brazilian Institute of Environment and Renewable Natural Resources)

"No use putting a monkey mask on my face or trying to offend me because it doesn't affect me! I was trained from childhood, and I know my value! But it affects millions of people in Brazil who suffer such discrimination every day! And its for them that I decided to express myself."

In response to the online racial abuse that many Afro-Brazilian women, both black and mixed race, have been subjected to, an Afro-Brazilian civil rights group, run by women called *Criola*, started an advertising campaign called "Virtual Racism, Real Consequences". The campaign collects racist comments from social media websites Facebook and Twitter, and uses geo-location tools to find out where the perpetrator lives. Next, they hired out advertising billboard space and other forms of out-of-home media near the residence of the culprits to expose the online offence. The racist comments are pasted onto public posters in large font, albeit with pixelated names and profile pictures. Some of the online racist comments reads, 'I came home stinking like a black person,' and 'If you washed properly, you wouldn't be so dirty.'

Criola's founder, Jurema Werneck says the campaign is intended to encourage people to speak out and report racism. Werneck thinks that the Brazilian authorities have not done enough to enforce laws against racial abuse, and that many people are afraid to speak out against racial abuse. "They call [black] women monkeys. They talk about our hair. They talk about our skin colour. And they call us prostitutes." According to Werneck, racism in Brazil is actually on the rise. And that is because of the affirmative action laws in the past decade which has enabled blacks and mixed-raced Brazilians to enter universities and places of employment, "We are entering universities. We are entering many different spaces. They are very angry because we are putting pressure in their [white] privilege." As Afro-Brazilians continue to climb the social-economic ladder, racism is likely to intensify in Brazil.

CONCLUSION

The hardest task is to change attitudes. Many Brazilians simply assume blacks belong at the bottom of the pile. Supporters of affirmative action are right to say that the country had turned its back on the problem. But adopting of American policies might not be the best way to combat Brazil's specific forms of racism. A combination of stronger legal action against discrimination and quotas in higher education for hitherto excluded social classes, in order to compensate for weak public schools may work better.

Colonialist Europeans were obsessed with power and control, by means of which they usurped the wealth and resources of non-whites. Religion, science and cultural ideologies were merely means they used to achieve their insatiable greed for power and thus wealth. In Brazil this was most certainly the case with the Portuguese colonialists who used religion, science and cultural ideologies to maintain a status quo in which whites were at the top and blacks at the bottom.

The country's image abroad of cultural diversity and racial miscegenation is a myth, but affirmative-action laws are intended to bring about the racial democracy ideal. Although the ideology of miscegenation is widespread, the mixing of races and colours resulted neither in physical nor socioeconomic homogeneity. Affirmative action in and of itself will not solve Brazil's racial problems, but Brazil's black activists argue that it's a step in the right direction. Brazil's high crime rate is a result of disparities in distribution of the country's wealth, and so it is also hoped that affirmative-action laws can help the disenfranchised leave the *favelas* (slums) and the life of drugs and crime.

White Brazilian activists have also been important in awakening other white Brazilians to how much they are complicit in prevailing systems of racial inequality. It is easy for white Brazilians to remain in denial of racism, as they are not directly affected by the institutional racism that, irrespective of social class, mixed-race and black Brazilians endure. Higher education can help blacks climb the ladder of Brazil's colour-coded social hierarchy but they will unfortunately be seen as exceptions to the rule. Though controversial and with many critics, affirmative action is a step in the right direction to redress the wrongs done to its African and indigenous peoples.

Going forward, Brazil's affirmative-action quotas should not be restricted to students alone, as more quotas should could be introduced for university lecturers and the country's Eurocentric educational system. This would, perhaps, lead to a greater sense of black consciousness, which would then lead the black community to assess its needs. High on the list of those needs is undoubtedly economic empowerment. Affirmative-action laws may be a step forward for Brazil's black community in achieving this, as education is considered the route to financial success.

Part Two

BRAZIL'S AFRICAN MUSLIM
HERITAGE

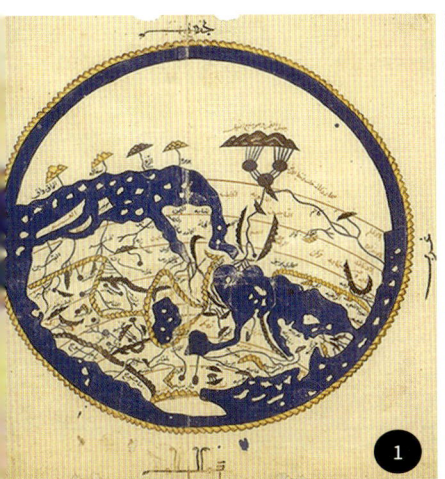
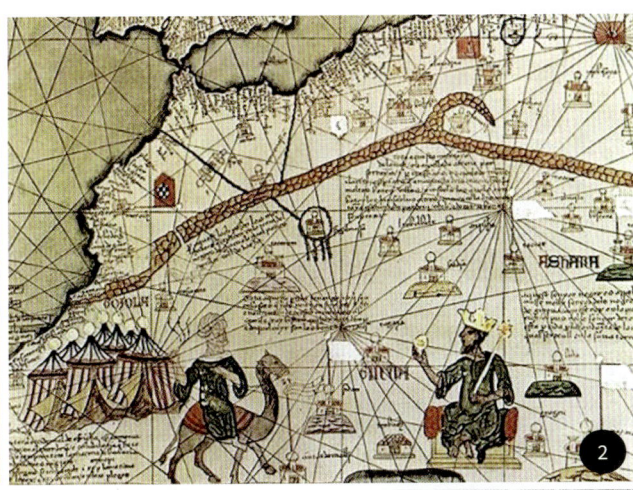

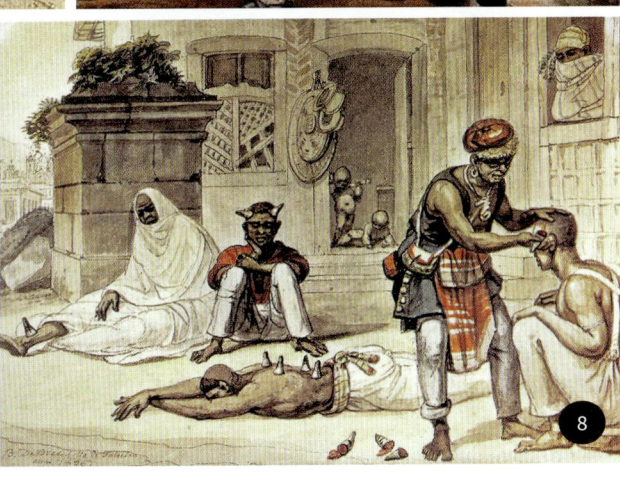

MALÊS,
do massacre à sobrevivência

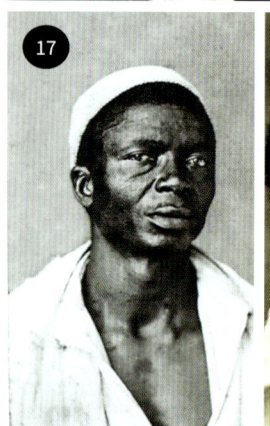

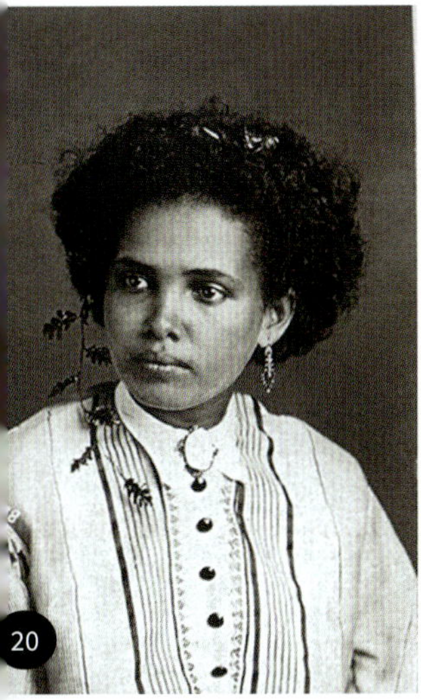
20

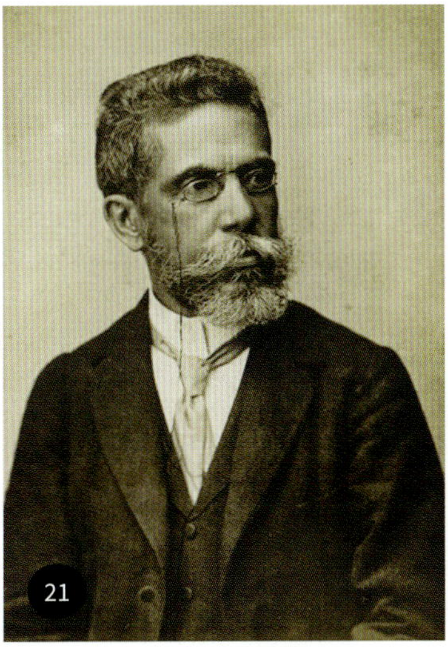
21

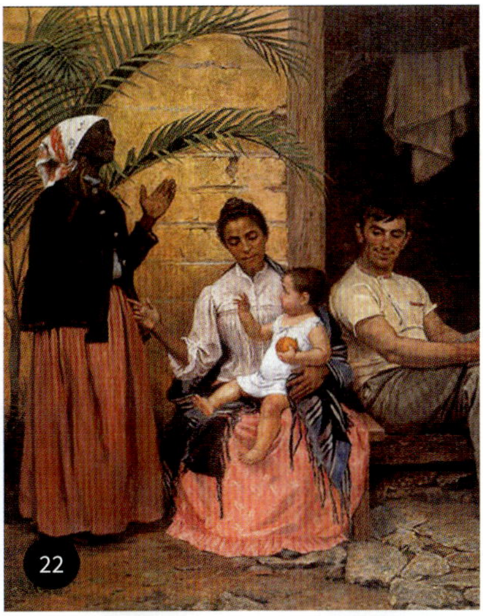
22

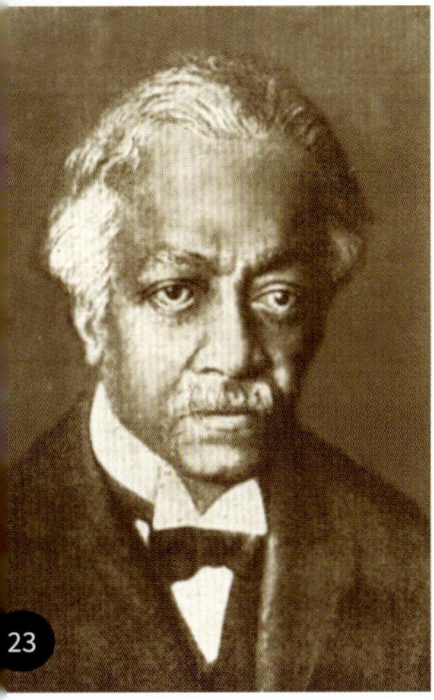
23

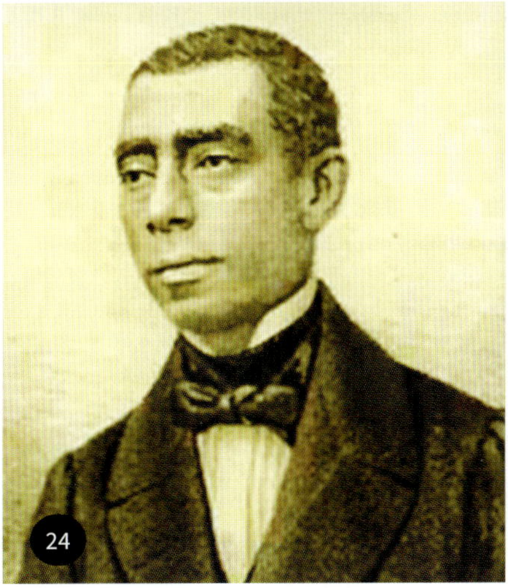
24

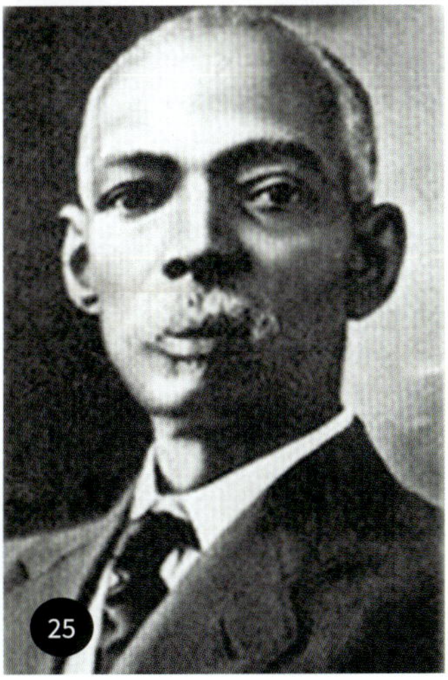
25

26

27

28

29

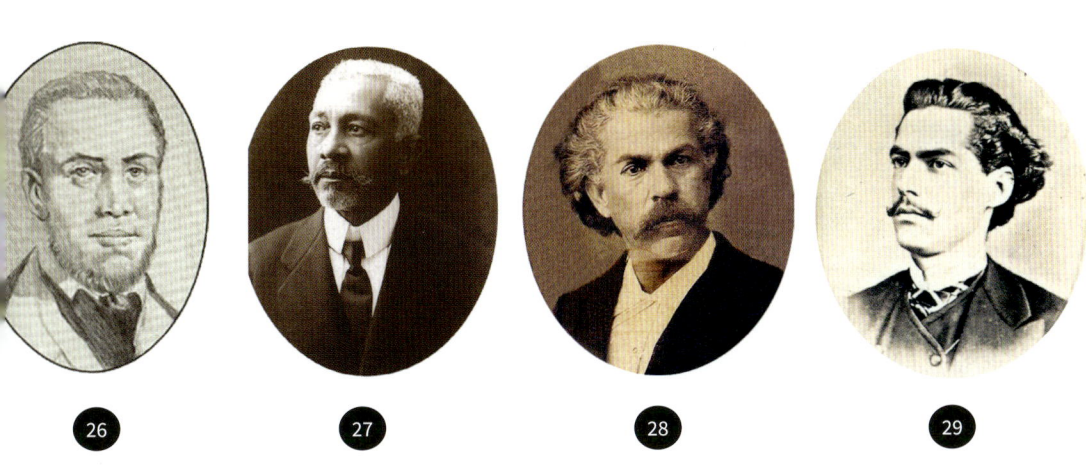

37

38

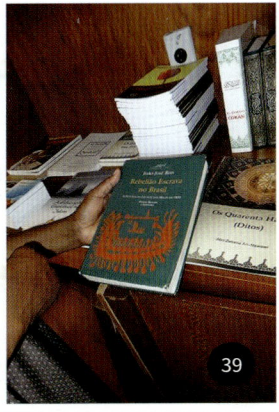

39

40

41

42

Malcolm X
Líder negro americano

Martin Luther King
Líder negro americano

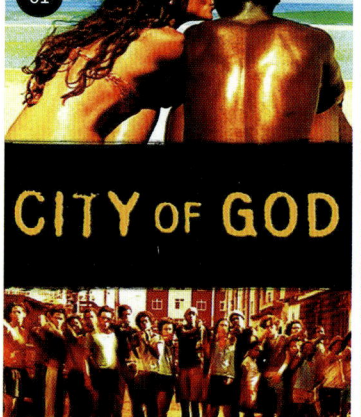
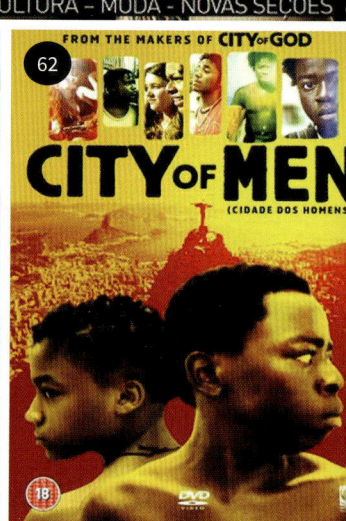
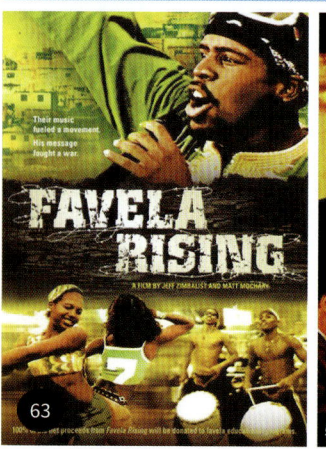
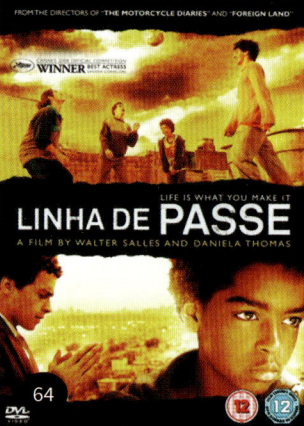

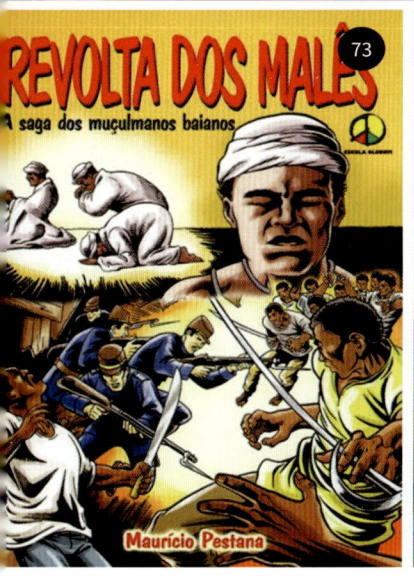

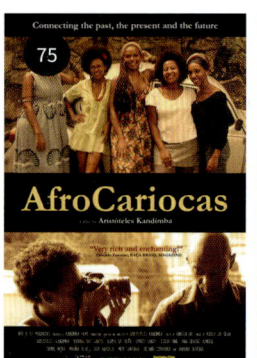

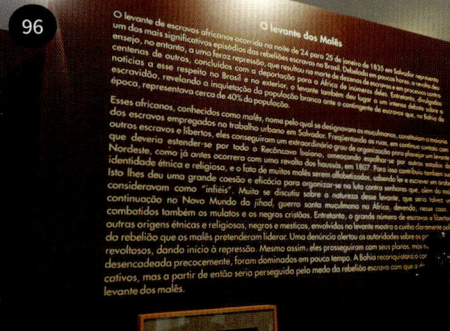

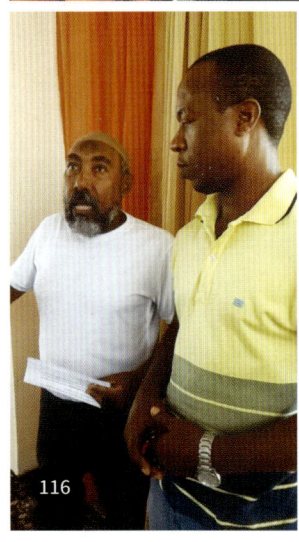

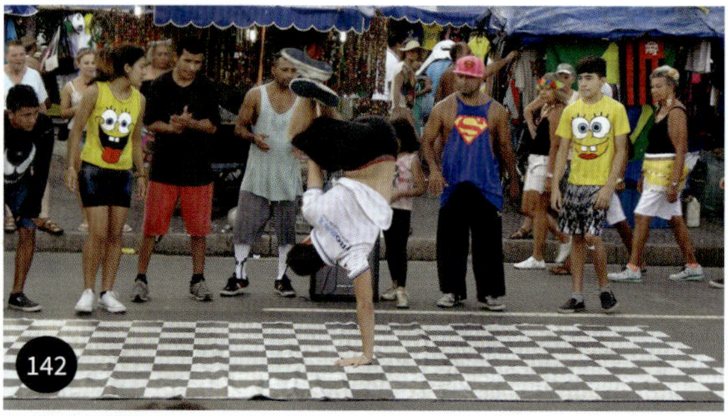
142

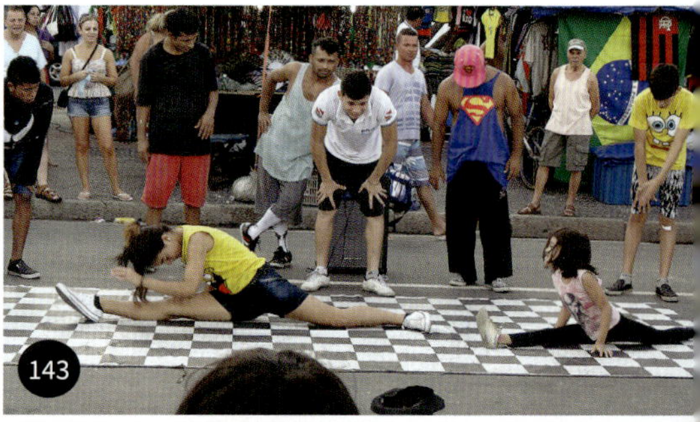
143

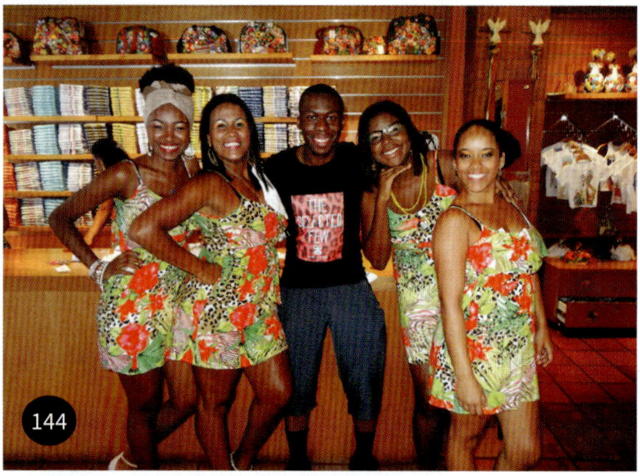
144

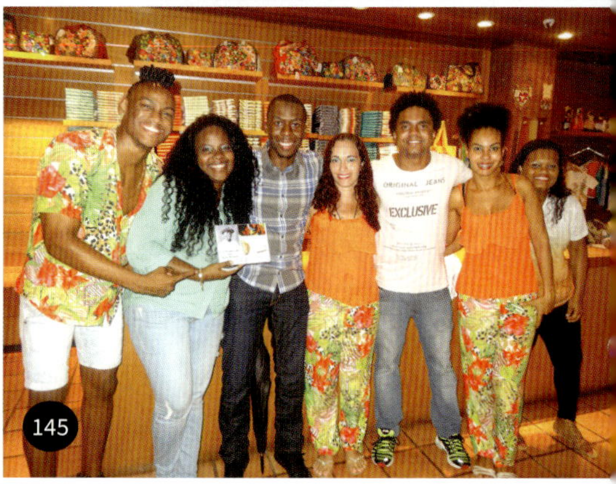

145

146

147

148

149

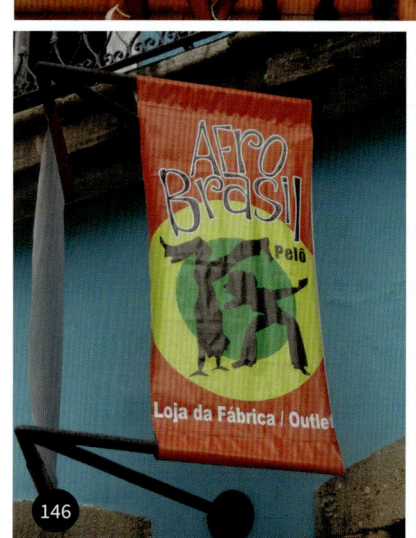

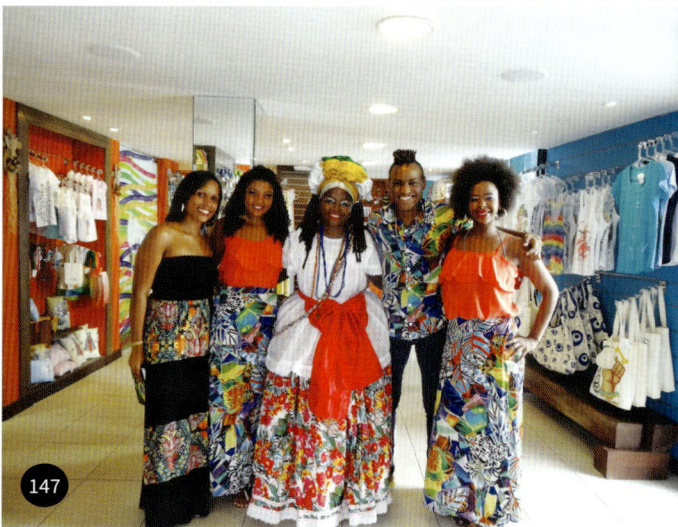

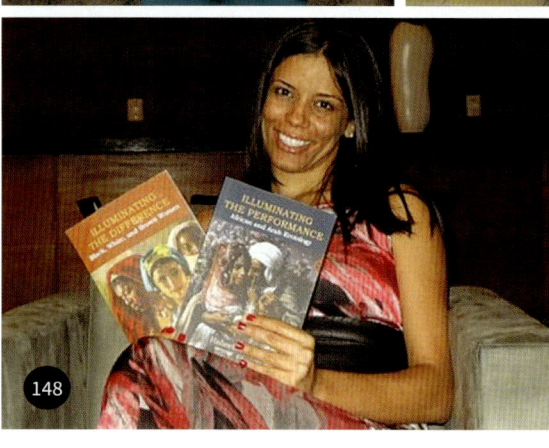

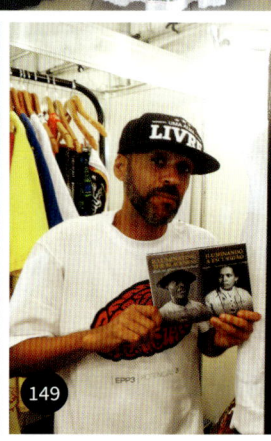

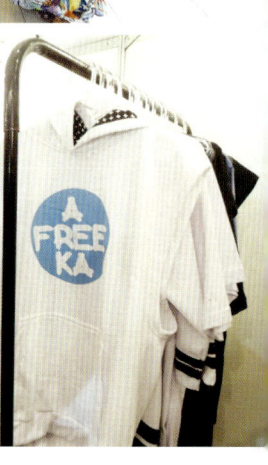

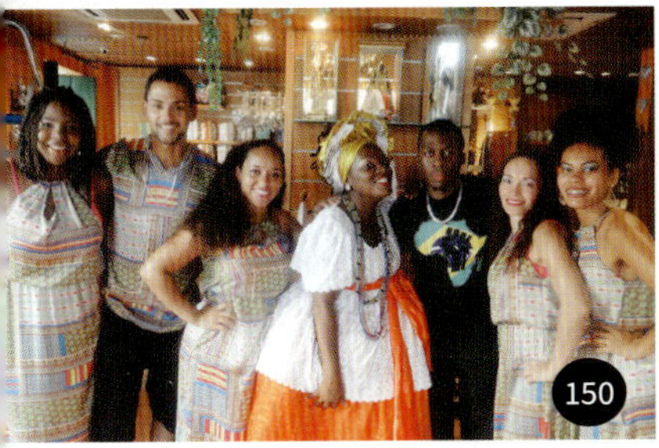

150

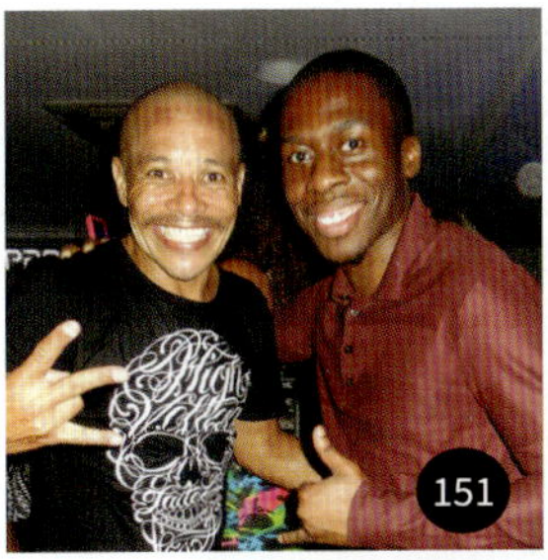

151

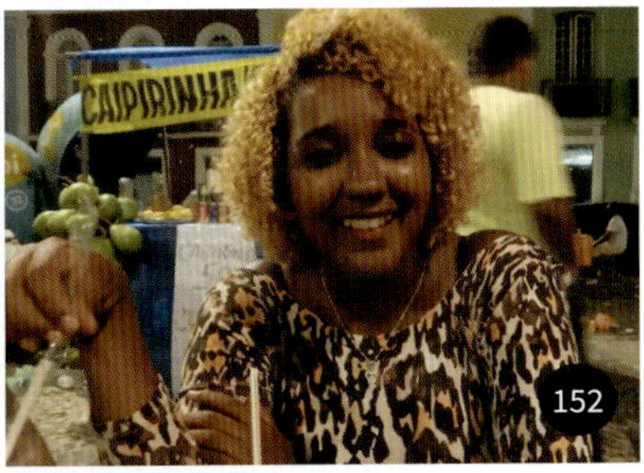

152

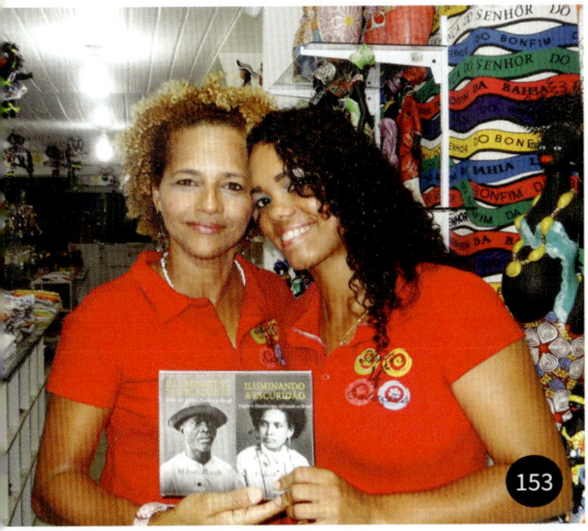

153

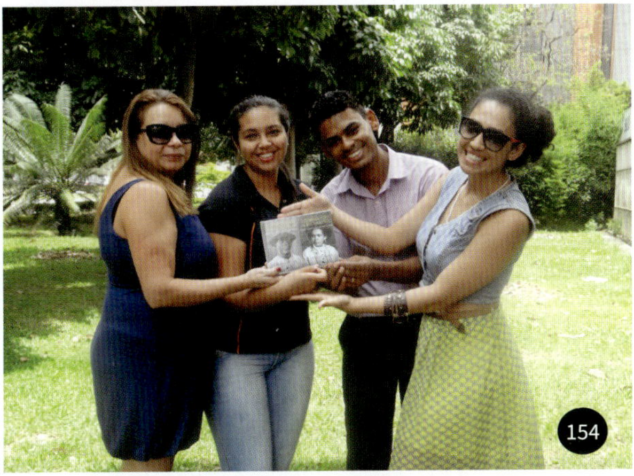

154

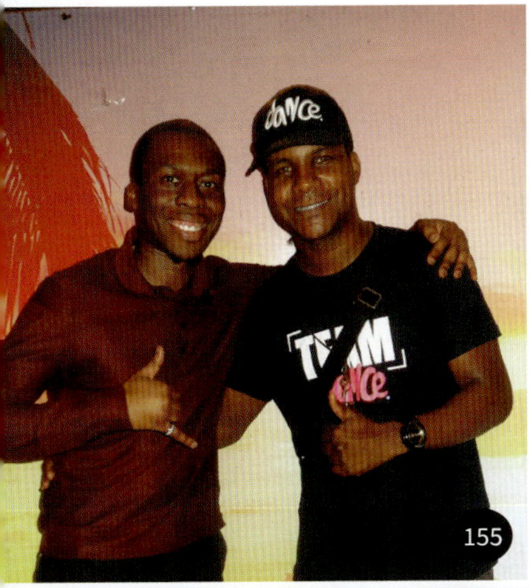

155

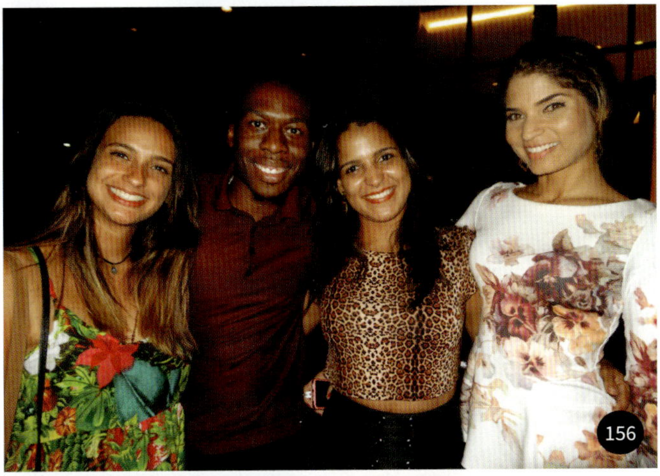

156

157

158

159

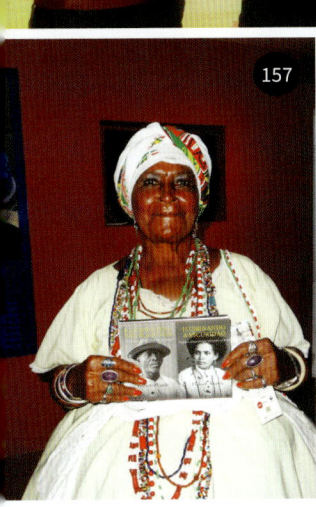

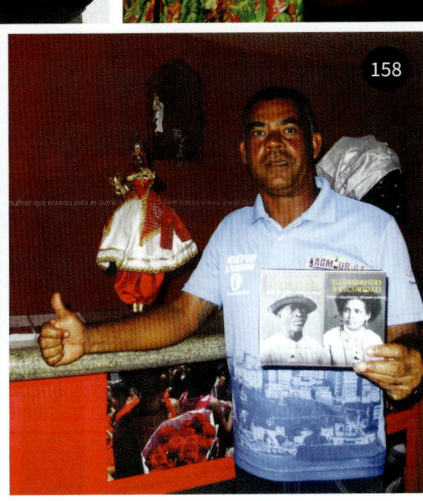

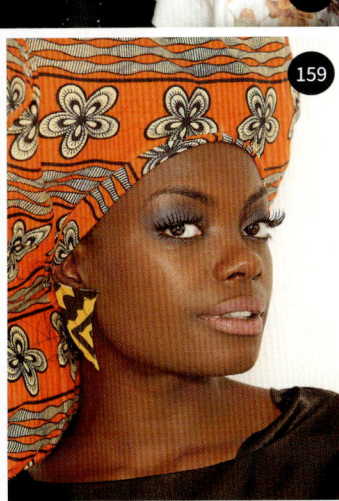

170

171

172

173

174

175

Africanos Muçulmanos na Bahia

s africanos muçulmanos eram nhecidos como malês, na Bahia, e e chegaram em grande número entre m do século XVIII e inicio do XIX, venientes da costa do Benin.

entre eles, os nagôs eram a maioria aioria dos rebeldes e dos lideres do vimento (dos seis lideres entificados com precisão, cinco am nagôs, sendo três escravos). epois deles, os hausas tiveram a ticipação mais significativa. Além nagôs e hausas, havia também os e, os tapa, os mina, dentre outros.

 escravidão urbana os cativos zavam de maior independência do e na escravidão rural, e isso facilitou ito à organização do movimento de 35. Em geral, os africanos rcorriam por toda a cidade abalhando para seus próprios nhores ou, principalmente, ntratados por terceiros para serviços entuais. Muitos trabalhadores cravizados sequer moravam na casa horial. Chamados negros ou negras ganho, e também de ganhadores ou nhadeiras, esses homens e mulheres cravizados contratavam com seus nhores entregar certa quantia diária semanal de dinheiro, e tudo que rapassasse esta quantia podiam abolsar.

O trabalhador africano sob aquele regime de escravidão que, mesmo na sua intensa jornada de trabalho, conseguisse poupar muito dinheiro podia após cerca de nove ou dez longos anos comprar sua liberdade, e muitos assim o fizeram. Os Africanos na Bahia, independentemente da situação que viviam no regime colonial (escravizados ou libertos) com frequência trabalhavam e viviam juntos, desempenhando as mesmas tarefas, morando nas mesmas casas. No trabalho de rua organizavam se em associações chamadas cantos de trabalho, nos quais se reuniam principalmente os da mesma etnia chefiados por um "capitão" encarregado de acertar os serviços desempenhados pelo grupo. Assim associados enfrentavam o trabalho diário e desenvolviam laços de amizade e solidariedade que constantemente se desdobravam em ações políticas. Esses grupos de trabalho foram essenciais na mobilização dos africanos para a revolta em 1835 e em outras ocasiões. Enquanto esperavam por serviço nas esquinas onde se reuniam, os africanos iam formulando e aperfeiçoando suas idéias de liberdade e de ataque à escravidão na Bahia.

Levante dos Malês
RESISTÊNCIA AFRICANA MUÇULMANA NO BRASIL

As Rainhas Malês do Século XIX

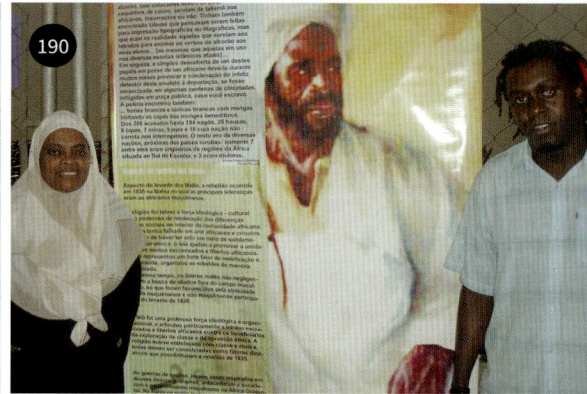

A Herança Malê
e sua influência na sociedade contemporânea

Da alimentação ao uso da roupa branca na sexta feira, da luta cotidiana a cantiga libertadora, do "Dua" guardado no bolso ou no amuleto, os malês sem dúvida deixam um legado repleto de referências para toda nossa sociedade. Sua rebeldia que, se analisada pelo âmbito religioso, teria origem na crença de todo muçulmano/muçulmana que deve se submeter somente a Deus. Dentro desta perspectiva, seria mais digno morrer lutando para se tornar um ser humano livre que viver na condição de escravo. Eles demonstraram seu poder na adversidade e sabedoria na construção de seus levantes. O domínio da língua árabe e de outros dialetos africanos frente aos senhores de engenho analfabetos, suas contínuas tentativas de se livrar da escravidão imposta e sua postura mediante a fé a qual se orientavam, os fortalece para as novas frentes de batalha que essa nova geração malê, submissa única e exclusivamente a Deus Único enfrentará, mesmo seguindo uma religião que milenarmente se encontra no continente africano sendo atualmente a religião que mais cresce no mundo com uma proporção maior relacionada ao público feminino.

Nos anos 90, com o Hip-hop no auge surge, mediante a influência histórica dos malês, a Posse Hausa (fundada em 26 de junho de 1993). Sua filosofia passa por uma postura que iria contra todos os malefícios que a sociedade impulsionava para as periferias brasileiras se abstendo delas e buscando, assim como os malês, conhecimento necessário para driblar as adversidades e buscar meios de sobressair do caus que nos era imposto. O melhor caminho adotado, na avaliação dos mesmos era o estudo. Hoje, 17 anos depois de sua fundação, a grande maioria dos integrantes concluíram o ensino superior ou estão em curso, formaram suas famílias e preservaram os valores necessários para alcançar uma vida digna. O Núcleo de Desenvolvimento Islâmico do Brasil uma realidade construída por irmãos e irmãs muçulmanas de periferia que procuram concretizar os conceitos adquiridos com a religião em algo prático objetivo para toda comunidade onde atuam. Por fim, Nossa experiência neste trabalho é reproduzir este mesmo pensamento às gerações que estão se formando e que por diversas vezes precisou de uma referência para se guiar nem sempre tiveram a sua disposição algo tão significativo como é para nós o Levante dos Malês.

Representatividade dos muçulmanos contemporâneos na política, cultura e na religião

CHAPTER 4

AFRICAN MUSLIMS IN BRAZIL BEFORE THE PORTUGUESE

Contrary to popular belief, the historical African connection to Brazil did not start with slavery. Africans travelled to Brazil hundreds of years before the Portuguese.

IT IS OFTEN said that history is written by the victors, which, in the case of Brazil, means the Portuguese. The notion that Brazil's historical relations with Africa began with Portuguese explorer Pedro Álvares Cabral's 'discovery' of it in 1500 is contested by historians and anthropologists, who have found evidence of the presence of Africans in the Americas before the sixteenth century. Pioneering work by the renowned American historian and linguist, Leo Wiener (d. 1939) of Harvard University, in his three volume work *Africa and the Discovery of America* on the presence of Africans in the Americas, which was later popularised by Guyanese historian Ivan Van Sertima, became known as the 'pre-Columbian trans-oceanic contact' theory. Afro-Brazilian historian Abdias do Nascimento mentioned that many other historians and researchers, such as Nicholas Leon, J. A. Jairazbhoy, Lopes de Gomara and Alexander von Wuthenau, found evidence of the presence of Africans in pre-Columbian America. The strongest evidence of African presence in the Americas before Christopher Columbus comes from the pen of the Italian explorer himself. Columbus noted in his journal that native Americans had confirmed that "black-skinned people had come from the south-east in boats, trading in gold-tipped spears". Researchers later found out that these gold-tipped spears were from West Africa.

According to Nascimento, the ruling elite in Brazil developed and refined myriad techniques to prevent black Brazilians connecting with their African identities and historical roots. Slavery was not the beginning of African history in Brazil, even if the country's educational system wants the masses to believe it. Nascimento and many other black activist argue that the realisation that black people from great Africans empires made contact with Brazil before white Europeans would undermine the concept of European superiority that is still taught in Brazil's educational system.

During his research, African-American historian 'Abdullāh Hakim Quick discovered that many Africans who travelled to Brazil before the Portuguese were in fact Muslims from North and West Africa. African Muslims' travels to Brazil will be the subject of this chapter, which begins by presenting reports of their travels. The chapter then concludes with a brief discussion of the African presence in Renaissance Europe at the time when the Portuguese set sail for Brazil in 1500.

NORTH AFRICAN MOORS IN BRAZIL

The Moors were the medieval North African inhabitants of the Iberian Peninsula (*al-Andalus*), present-day Spain and Portugal. The term 'Moors' is also used to refer to Muslims, particularly those of Berber and Arab descent, or to black people, irrespective of their religion.[372] The Moors are credited with bringing Europe out of the Dark Ages by their contributions to European society and its educational system. Spain was ruled by the Moors for eight hundred years and they made a lasting impact on Europe. The black African presence of the Moors in Renaissance Europe is evident in the "Flag of the four Moors" of the autonomous region of Sardinia, Italy. The flag is composed of the St George's Cross and four heads of blindfolded African-looking men. The heads are said to symbolise the defeated Moors.

What Spanish historians erroneously present as "the Moors' occupation of the Iberian Peninsula", but which really consisted of the adoption of Islam by substantial numbers of its inhabitants, began in 711 when a Muslim army, led by the North African Berber, Ṭāriq ibn Ziyād, crossed the Strait of Gibraltar that separates Spain from Morocco. The Muslim army then went on to open the whole of the Iberian Peninsula to Islam,[373]

---

372 "Moors were commonly viewed as being mostly black or very swarthy, and hence the word is often used for negro," according to the Oxford English Dictionary.

373 The Arabic verb "*fataḥa* – he opened" is incorrectly translated into English as "conquered". The Muslims always saw themselves as opening up new lands for Islam.

which Muslims ruled, sometimes in a single united political entity and sometimes as part of a patchwork of Muslim and Christian principalities, for approximately eight hundred years. During this period Spain flourished culturally and economically. British historian Basil Davidson declared that there was no land at the time that was "more admired by its neighbours, or more comfortable to live in, than a rich African civilisation which took place in [Moorish] Spain." The black African presence of the Moors is evident in the testimony of Alfonso X, the King of Castile and León, who remarked on the Moors' black skin:

> The Moors of the host wore silks and colourful clothes which they had taken as booty, their horses' reins were like fire, their faces were black as pitch, the handsomest among them was black as a cooking pot, and their eyes blazed like fire; their horses as swift as leopards, their horsemen more cruel and hurtful than the wolf that comes at night to the flock of sheep.[374]

At its height, Córdoba, the heart of Moorish territory in Spain, was the most modern city in Europe. The streets were well paved, with raised sidewalks for pedestrians. During the night, the streets were illuminated by lamps. This was hundreds of years before there was a paved street in Paris or a street-lamp in London. The city had nine hundred public baths and its inhabitants were very hygienic, so much so that it was reported that a poor Moor would prefer to go without bread rather than soap.

In Muslim Spain, education was universal and available to all, at a time when in Christian Europe the majority of the population were illiterate. In the tenth and eleventh centuries, there were no public libraries in Europe, whereas Muslim Spain had more than seventy, of which the one in Córdoba housed six-hundred thousand manuscripts. Universities in Paris and Oxford were established after visits by scholars to Moorish Spain. It was this system of education, brought to Europe by the Moors, that planted the seeds of the European Renaissance and brought the continent out of the long centuries of intellectual and physical gloom known as the Dark Ages.

Travels To The Americas

According to historian 'Abdullāh Hakim Quick, there are a number of sculptures, oral traditions, eyewitness reports, artefacts, and inscription

---

Thus, there is no evidence at all of any attempts to convert their new peoples to Islam. Ed.

374 Flesler, 2008, p. 75

which are evidence of the presence of North African Muslims in Brazil. The Arab historian and geographer al-Mas'ūdī (d. 957) made mention of Khashkhāsh ibn Sa'īd ibn Aswad, a young Moorish man from Cordoba, Spain, who in 899 sailed across the Atlantic with a number of Muslims in search of new lands. Upon their return, Ibn Aswad reported that he had discovered the '*arḍ majhūlah* (unknown land), and drew a map with the 'unknown land', which appears to be the 'New World', the Americas. Al-Mas'ūdī makes mention of Ibn Aswad's historical journey in *Murūj adh-dhahab wa ma'ādin al-jawāhir* (Meadows of Gold and Mines of Gems):

> Some people feel that this ocean is the source of all oceans and in it there have been many strange happenings. We have reported some of them in our book *Akhbār az-Zamān*. Adventurers have penetrated it at the risk of their lives, some returning safely, others perishing in the attempt. One such man was an inhabitant of Andalusia named Khashkhāsh. He was a young man of Cordoba who gathered a group of young men and went on a voyage on this ocean. After a long time he returned with a fabulous booty. Every Andalusian (Spaniard) knows his story.[375]

In the twelfth century, Arab geographer Muḥammad al-Idrīsī (d. 1155) reported on the journey of a group of North African seaman who reached the Americas:

> A group of seafarers sailed into the sea of Darkness and Fog (the Atlantic Ocean) from Lisbon, in order to discover what was in it and to what extent were its limits. They were a party of eight and they took a boat which was loaded with supplies to last them for months. They sailed for eleven days till they reached turbulent waters with great waves and little light. They thought that they would perish so they turned their boat southward and travelled for twenty days. They finally reached an island that had people and cultivation but they were captured and chained for three days. On the fourth day a translator came speaking the Arabic language! He translated for the King and asked them about their mission. They informed him about themselves, then they were returned to their confinement. When the westerly wind began to blow, they were put in a canoe, blindfolded and brought to land after three days sailing. They were left on the shore with their hands tied behind their backs, when the next day came, another tribe appeared freeing

---

375 Quick, 1998, pp. 15-16

them and informing them that between them and their lands was a journey of two months.³⁷⁶

The discovery of Arab coins in the region off the coast of South America dating back to 800 serves to validate al-Idrīsī's report on the Muslim explorers crossing the Atlantic.

Another historical report, cited in *Before Columbus: Links Between the Old World and Ancient America* by Cyrus Gordon (d. 2001), that a "Moorish ship from Spain or North Africa, seems to have crossed the Atlantic around 800 CE" further strengths the claims of the Muslim historians and geographers that African Muslim adventurers and navigators crossed the Atlantic.³⁷⁷

WEST AFRICAN MANDINKAS IN BRAZIL

The Mandinkas, also known as the Mandingos, are a West African ethnic group. The Mandinkas belong to the Mandé, West Africa's largest ethno linguistic group, who are descended from the peoples of the Mali Empire. Inscriptions found by historians and anthropologists in Bahia and Minas Gerais indicate the presence of West African Muslims in Brazil. According to anthropologist and historian Clyde Ahmad Winters, the Mandinka "made Brazil their staging area for the exploration of the New World", where they used rivers as their major mode of travel in the dense jungles of Brazil.³⁷⁸

Mansa Abubakari II's Travels To The Americas

Abubakari II (also spelt Abu Bakr II) was a fourteenth century king (*mansa*) of the Mali Empire. Abubakari II succeeded his nephew Mansa Muḥammad ibn Gao, and preceded Mansa Kankan Mūsā, the most famous ruler of West Africa. In 1311, Abubakari II abdicated from the throne in order to pursue knowledge and journeys of discovery. The ruler wanted to find out what lay on the other side of the Atlantic. With the thirst for knowledge burning inside him, the ruler of Mali set out on a lengthy voyage in search of the "New World". According to Malian historian Gaoussou Diawara, research indicates that Abubakari II landed on the northeastern coast of Brazil in 1312. Researchers discovered that the Malian emperor and his African Muslim crews landed in Recife, in the state of Pernambuco.³⁷⁹

---

376 Quick, 1998, pp. 15-16
377 Quick, 1998, p. 14; Gordon, 1971, pp. 68-70
378 http://www.academia.edu/1529630/Islam_in_Early_North_and_South_America
379 See Gaossou Diawara's *Abubakari II: Explorateur Mandingue*

Mansa Abubakari II ruled arguably "the richest and largest empire on earth – covering nearly all of West Africa". Despite the abundance of riches in West Africa, also known as the "land of gold", Abubakari gave up his power and wealth to pursue knowledge and journeys of discovery. Diawara's book also focuses on research being carried out in Mali tracing the Mansa's journey over the Atlantic.

According to Tiemoko Konate, the head of the project, the West African Muslims were not the first to cross the ocean as "there is evidence that the Vikings were in America long before him [i.e. Mansa Abu Bakar II], as well as the Chinese".[380] Syrian-born historian, Shihāb ad-Dīn al-'Umarī, mentioned the Mansa's journey to the New World in 1311. This was almost two hundred years before Christopher Columbus "discovered" America.[381]

Mansa Mūsā's Narration

Mansa Mūsā, the fourteenth century ruler of the Malian empire, informed the Governor of Cairo about Abubakari II's two expeditions into the Atlantic to discover its limits. During his famous pilgrimage to Makkah in 1324, Mansa Mūsā told of Abubakari II's voyage across the Atlantic. In 1342, Egyptian scholar, Ibn Faḍl al-'Umarī related the account of the expedition in his book *Masālik al-Abṣār fī Mamālik al-Amṣār*. During the fourteenth century at the time of the Malian Empire, a popular conception was that the end of the world lay at the other side of the Atlantic.[382] Abubakari II was far from convinced, and his quest for knowledge led him to send two hundred ships across the Atlantic, with the aim of finding out what lay beyond. It is recorded that only one ship returned, whose captain claimed that the other ships disappeared into the wild ocean. Abubakari was not convinced by the captain's testimony, and set sail from the coast of Senegambia with two thousand ships towards the coast of Brazil. Al-'Umarī narrated the story:

> I asked the Sulṭān Mūsā, said Ibn Amir Hajib [the governor of Cairo], how it was that power came into his hands. "We are," he told me, "from a house that transmits power by heritage. The

---

380 And some scholars assert that the Irish had also crossed the Atlantic long before the Vikings. See: *Two Irelands – The Irish Discovery of America* by Gunnar Thompson, Ph.D.
381 See Robin Walker's *When We Ruled*
382 Nevertheless, Ibn Khaldūn mentions the spherical nature of the earth and gives an accurate estimate of its circumference in his *Muqaddimah*, which elicited no controversy at the time or subsequently, indicating that a fixed doctrinal commitment to the idea of a flat Earth was far less widespread among Muslims than it was in Europe. Ed.

ruler who preceded me would not believe that it was impossible to discover the limits of the neighbouring sea. He wanted to find out and persisted in his plan. He had two hundred ships equipped and filled with men, and others to the same number filled with gold, water, and supplies in sufficient quantity to last for years. He told those who commanded, 'Return only when you have reached the extremity of the ocean, or when you have exhausted your food and water.'

"They went away; their absence was long, before any of them returned. Finally a solitary ship reappeared. We asked the captain about their adventures. "Prince," he replied, "We sailed a long time, up to the moment when we encountered in mid-ocean something like a river with a violent current. My ship was lost. The others sailed on, and gradually as each one entered this place, they disappeared and did not come back. We do not know what happened to them. As for me, I returned to where I was and did not enter the current."

"But the emperor did not want to believe him. He equipped two thousand vessels, a thousand for himself and the men who accompanied him and a thousand for water and supplies. He conferred power on me and, with his companions, left on the ocean. This was the last time that I saw him and the others, and I remained the absolute master of the empire."[383]

Archaeological Evidence Of West Africans In Brazil
In spite of the archaeological evidence discovered indicating the presence of Mandinka Muslims in the Americas before the Europeans, Western historians have debated the validity of their two voyages.

Even earlier evidence of a relationship between Africa and South America includes the colossal Olmec heads dating back to before 900 BC, which are often cited as evidence of African presence in the Americas before the trans-Atlantic slave period. The broad nose and thick lips of the Olmec heads indicate that they may have been African, though many Western scholars disagree with this claim.

Although there are written sources documenting the Mansa's journey to the New World, many African scholars say that the best sources on the travels of Abubakari II are the griots, West African poets, musicians and storytellers who relate tribal history and genealogies orally. Many

---
383 Quick, 1998, pp. 19-20

griots did not mention the journey of the Mansa to the New World because "the griots found his abdication a shameful act, not worthy of praise," Diawara said. "For that reason, they refused to sing praise or talk of this great African man." However there are some griots who are now beginning to divulge the lost history of Abubakari II.

There are reports that Christopher Columbus said he found black traders in the Americas. The research team cites chemical analyses of the gold tips that Columbus found on spears in the Americas, whose gold most probably came from West Africa. However, the biggest challenge that the Mali research team face is to convince "hard-nosed historians" outside of Africa that oral history can be just as accurate as written records. Diawara concludes:

> They should take an example from Abubakari II. He was a far more powerful man than any of them. And he was willing to give it all up in the name of science and discovery. That should be a lesson for everyone in Africa today.

Historian 'Abdullāh Hakim Quick adduced numerous inscriptions found in Brazil, Peru and the United States as evidence of the presence of Mandinka Muslims in the Americas before European explorers.[384] Quick writes:

> The Mandinka made contact with Brazil, the closet landmass to the West African Guinea coast. They appear to have used it as a base for exploration of the Americas. They travelled along rivers in the dense jungles of South America, and moved overland until they reached Central America. Examination of the inscriptions found in Brazil at Bahia and Minas Gerais, and on the coast of Peru at Ylo, reveal a definite presence of these African Muslims. The inscriptions were taken from ancient cities and stone tablets and were originally written in the Vai and related Mandingo scripts.[385]

For those who know West African history, West Africans' travels to the Americas are not unbelievable. West Africa was extremely wealthy at the time of Europe's Dark Ages and people specialised in numerous sciences. From the kingdom of Ghana between the ninth and thirteenth centuries, to the kingdom of Mali from the thirteenth to the fifteenth century, West Africa was known as the "land of gold".

The famous image of Mansa Mūsā holding a gold nugget testifies to

---

384 Quick, *1998*, pp. 20-21
385 Quick, 1998, p. 21,

the reputation for enormous gold wealth that his kingdom, the Mali Empire, had. Mansa Mūsā was also famed for his 1324 pilgrimage to Makkah, where the sheer volume of his lavish gifts of gold while passing through Cairo destabilised the economy of the region. The wealth of West Africa was as curse as much as it was a blessing, because it caused envy amongst Europeans, who would later invade the region in order to gain access to its resources and wealth and to obtain its people as slaves.

Timbuktu's Intellectual Heritage
Mali was a centre of excellence between the thirteenth and sixteenth centuries, reaching its peak in the fourteenth century during the reign of Mansa Mūsā when its capital city was Timbuktu. A UNESCO-listed world heritage site, Timbuktu is regarded as the spiritual capital of sub-Saharan Africa. A local saying from Timbuktu states:

> The nations formed a single line and Timbuktu was at the head. But one day, God did an about-turn and Timbuktu found itself at the back. Perhaps one day God will do another about-turn so that Timbuktu can retake its rightful place.[386]

Researchers in Timbuktu are fighting to preserve tens of thousands of ancient texts that they say prove Africa had a written history at least as old as the European Renaissance. Private and public libraries in the fabled Saharan town already contain 150,000 brittle Arabic manuscripts, some of them from the thirteenth century, and local historians believe many more lie buried under the sand. Over successive generations, proud Malian families stashed the precious texts under their mud homes and in desert caves fearing that they would be stolen by Moroccan invaders, European explorers and French colonialists. Written in ornate calligraphy, some were used to teach astronomy or mathematics, while others tell tales of social and business life in Timbuktu during its "Golden Age" in the sixteenth century when it was a seat of learning. Although most of the texts were written by men, many were written by women. Islamic education and literacy were not restricted to men in West Africa. Women also had the opportunity to excel in education, as it was seen as part of the Islamic teaching to educate both men and women.

Timbuktu's leading families are reluctant to give up their manuscripts, which they see as ancestral heirlooms, and have only recently started surrendering them. They are being persuaded by local officials that the manuscripts should be part of the community's shared culture. "It is

---

386 http://www.reuters.com/article/2006/11/10/us-mali-manuscripts-idUSL1068574520061110

through these writings that we can really know our place in history," said Abdramane Ben Essayouti, Imam of Djingarei-ber, Timbuktu's oldest mosque, built from rammed earth and wood in 1325. Experts believe that the 150,000 texts collected so far are just a fraction of those that remain hidden under centuries of dust behind the ornate wooden doors of Timbuktu's mud-brick homes. "This is just 10% of what we have. We think we have more than a million buried here," said 'Alī Ould Sidi, a government official responsible for managing the town's World Heritage Sites. Some academics say the texts will force Western academics to accept that Africa has an intellectual history as old as that of the West.[387]

Timbuktu is known for its scholarship as much as for its wealth and trade and perhaps even more. Many of the scholars of Timbuktu were also merchants. They were financially independent of the governments and rulers. "The scholar has the duty to be true to knowledge, to teach and propagate it, and to defend it when it is falsified, even when the ruler, the commercial class and the generality of people disagree," Abdassamad Clarke wrote. The Muslim scholars of Timbuktu were directly involved in keeping the market free of usury and other abuses. This also suggests an important way forward for the future, as Clarke states, "students of knowledge who go into business and hold to their knowledge, and businessmen who learn what is *ḥalāl* [permissible] and *ḥarām* [prohibited] about trade."[388]

Knowledge was highly respected in Timbuktu and the rest of the Muslim world, where scholars and even laymen were avid in their pursuit of knowledge in every field. Those who possessed it won prestige and power. Scholars were precocious readers as well as prolific writers. Ibn Baṭṭūṭah, the great Moroccan world traveller, visited Timbuktu in the fourteenth century. In his chronicles, Ibn Baṭṭūṭah noted the piety, tolerance, wisdom and justice of its inhabitants. He was also surprised by the West Africans' eagerness to learn.[389]

The Encyclopaedia Britannica states that by 1450, Timbuktu had a population of 100,000, a quarter of whom were said to have been students. Manuscripts and books were highly prized. Leo Africanus, the Andalusian Berber, who visited the city in 1510, found that books sold for higher prices than any other merchandise in the city's market.

---

387 http://www.reuters.com/article/2006/11/10/us-mali-manuscripts-idUSL1068574520061110
388 Clarke, 2014, p. 82
389 http://www.theguardian.com/world/2014/may/23/book-rustlers-timbuktu-mali-ancient-manuscripts-saved

The testimonies of Ibn Baṭṭūṭah and Leo Africanus demonstrate the importance of knowledge in West Africa and the region's intellectual history. The modern notion, enunciated in the oft-repeated saying, "If you want to hide something from a black person, put it in a book," is patently false, as is evident from the intellectual history of the great West African city Timbuktu. Recent restoration work of Timbuktu manuscripts goes a long way to correct the misconception that there was no new knowledge generated in Africa, and that Africa had primarily an oral and not a written tradition of scholarship. The vast number of Timbuktu manuscripts clearly shows that, before contact with Europeans, there was a long tradition of literacy and written scholarship in West Africa.

AFRICANS IN RENAISSANCE EUROPE

Africans On Pedro Álvares Cabral's Ship To Brazil

Spanish and Portuguese Muslims of African descent are said to have been aboard the Portuguese navigator Pedro Álvares Cabral's ship in 1500, when he ventured westward into the Atlantic, looking for winds to take him around the coast of West Africa en route to India. Cabral eventually disembarked in the land that would later be known as Brazil.

In her book, *The Construction of Muslim Identities in Contemporary Brazil*, Cristina Maria de Castro pointed cited Sheikh Muḥammad Ragip al-Jerrahi of Brasilia as saying:

> Chuhabidin bin Mājid and the navigating officer Mussa bin Sate were part of the crew that came to Brazil in 1500. In the beginning of the colonial period, Portuguese and Spanish Muslims allegedly came to the country, but were forced by the Inquisition to convert and change their names, which is why it is difficult to find records of their presence in Brazil.

According to al-Jerrahi, there are accounts of trials by the Inquisition and reports of interrogations describing the Muslims' practices and customs, which are evidence of their presence.[390] The Muslims who arrived in Brazil with the Portuguese did not constitute an organised collective of believers. Only after the seventeenth century, with the arrival of West African Muslims, did effective Muslim communities start to emerge.[391]

---

390 Castro, 2013, p. 15
391 Castro, 2013, p. 15

White Slaves

Although in our most recent history the enslavement of black Africans far outweighs the enslavement of non-black peoples, in earlier times this was not the case. Slavery was not restricted to black people. White Europeans were enslaved by Arab and Berber Muslims just as black Africans were enslaved by white Europeans, though slaves received better treatment in the Muslim world.

Indeed, the British had begun their engagement with slavery by enslaving subject Irish and Scottish populations. Historian Michael A. Hoffman explores the enslavement of white peoples in the early Americas. According to Hoffman, white slaves, particularly the Irish, were treated just as badly as black slaves,[392] but their constant rebellions eventually led to their emancipation, as the white elite considered them to be too much trouble, and concentrated on the enslavement of black Africans. The majority of white slaves in the Americas were from Britain and Ireland, a subject that Don Jordan and Michael Walsh investigate in their book, *White Cargo: The Forgotten History of Britain's White Slaves in America*. The co-authors challenge the prevailing assumption that the whites who arrived in the Americas from Britain in the seventeenth and early eighteenth centuries were indentured servants. Jordan and Walsh demonstrate that many of the exported white children and poor whites were actually slaves, thousands of whom lived and died from bondage. White slaves were also exported to Australia and North Africa.

Enslavement of whites by North Africans forms the subject of a fascinating book by Giles Milton, who asserts that one million white European were enslaved in North Africa. According to Robert Davis' study of white European slaves in North Africa, it was religion that determined who became slaves, and not race. Slavery was an institution that was not based on a person's race until the invention of race by Europeans, and the beginning of racial slavery in the Americas.[393]

Black Africans In Renaissance Europe

It is historically inaccurate to assume that all black Africans in Renaissance Europe were slaves. Historians, such as Miranda Kaufmann, have found from a variety of sources including portraits that the black African

---

392 Although enslaved in some periods, at other times free Irish and Scots suffered even more terribly than the slaves because "they were not slaves", i.e. because they did not even have the value of being someone's property. Ed.

393 See Robert Davis' *Christian Slaves, Muslim Masters: White Slavery in the Mediterranean, the Barbary Coast and Italy, 1500-1800*.

presence in Europe was not restricted to servitude. There were free black Africans who were financially independent and property-owners, such as 'Reasonable Blackman', a silk-weaver in 1590s England, who owned a cow, at that time a valuable asset.

Kaufmann found other individual Black Africans in her research who were far better integrated in European society than our modern-day prejudices about the state of blacks in Renaissance Europe. Some black Africans earned good wages and worked in respectable professions.[394] By 1550, Africans made up 10% of the city of Lisbon in Portugal, and 25% of the city's black population were free Africans. There were also African communities in Britain, Spain, Italy, the Netherlands and elsewhere in Renaissance Europe.[395] This demonstrates that the Portuguese were well accustomed to Africans when they settled in Brazil and began transporting Africans to Brazil as slaves to work on the sugar plantations.

In the case of Giulia de' Medici (d. 1588), the African presence was literally painted out of European history. Giulia, the granddaughter of an enslaved African woman named Simonetta, was portrayed in a portrait by Jacopo Pontormo in 1539 with her guardian, Maria Salviati. Guilia was the illegitimate daughter of Alessandro de' Medici (d. 1537), who was the Duke of Florence, and she was of mixed European and African ancestry.

At some point in the following century, Guilia's portrait was painted over. The child was uncovered in 1937 during the cleaning of the painting. Giulia was identified as the child in the painting in 1992. Researchers think that Guilia was painted over by a dealer before 1881 in order to increase the painting's value.[396] Art institution directors and curators show little interest in the presence of Africans in European works of art. The researcher who helped Gabrielle Langdon identify Giulia said:

> The importance [of the painting] to me is that it says to the black community that we've had extremely powerful people in European history already, and very powerful families descend from them to this day.[397]

---

394 http://www.theguardian.com/commentisfree/2012/oct/17/slavery-black-history-month
395 http://www.historytoday.com/blog/2013/05/black-face-renaissance-europe
396 http://www.ultimatehistoryproject.com/africans-in-the-renaissance.html
397 http://articles.latimes.com/2001/nov/28/news/lv-portrait28

Mario de Valdes y Cocom, a historian of the African diaspora, said the painting demonstrates the way Europeans have denigrated blackness in Renaissance Europe:

> As one of the first persons of colour in modern history whose response to racism has been recorded, Giulia de Medici's magisterial pronouncement is of utmost importance to those of us in the new world who are still suffering from the results of this ugly social phenomenon.[398]

---

[398] http://www.pbs.org/wgbh/pages/frontline/shows/secret/famous/giuliademedici.html

CHAPTER 5

SLAVE REVOLTS IN BAHIA, 1807-1835

"Muslims who came to Brazil as slaves laid the foundation of this country."
PRESIDENT LULA[399]

30% OF WEST AFRICAN slaves who arrived in Bahia in the nineteenth century were Muslims. Primarily of Hausa and Yoruba origin, African Muslims led a series of slave revolts in Bahia that led to the abolition of slavery in 1888. The notion that white abolitionists were the primary reason for the end of slavery is contested by many historians.[400] The abolitionists, who were primarily middle-class white men, did advocate the abolition of slavery, but they were not the main reason that slavery ended. Changes in the nineteenth century economic system were significant, as capitalist Western countries were moving from an agrarian slave-based economy to an industrial wage-slave economy. Agrarian slaves were no longer in demand, which is why the institution came to an end. Another major factor that brought slavery to an end, which is often not mentioned by Western intelligentsia, was the African revolts. Commonly referred to as 'slave revolts', even though they included both enslaved and free persons, Africans had to fight and shed their blood in order to attain freedom, and that culminated in the abolition of slavery as the Europeans could no longer "control their subjects".

Although there were a number of revolts in Bahia between 1807-1835 involving Muslim and non-Muslim Africans, the 1835 revolt gained the

---

399 Aidi, 2014, pp. 36-37
400 The African Muslim slaves were among the principal architects of the emancipation from slavery in Brazil though many historians tend to minimise their contribution, Professor Yusuf Nzibo argues. Nzibo, 1986, pp. 547-556. See Appendix 2 for a summary of the slave revolts in Bahia between 1807 and 1835

most attention, because of the organisation and commitment of the Yoruba Muslims (*Malê*) who led the revolt. In his report on the 1835 revolt, the chief of police observed, "Generally almost all of them [the rebels] know how to read and write using unknown characters that look like Arabic and are used by the Hausas, who seem today to have combined with the *Nagôs* (Yorubas). The former nation was the one that rebelled quite often in this Province, but has been substituted by *Nagôs*." African Muslims in Bahia were literate and determined peoples who, it is said, took their inspiration both from the successful Haitian revolution and the east African slaves who revolted against their Arab slave masters in ninth century Iraq. Symbolically, the *Malês* were the descendants of the North African Moors who brought a rich and vibrant culture to Europe that contributed to the Renaissance. At the time of the revolt, the Portuguese were semiliterate, and they feared the literacy of the African Muslims spreading amongst the other Africans, because that would be likely to culminate in an uprising like that in Haiti.

Slaves of African descent in the Americas resisted their enslavement in myriad ways, including revolts, malingering, pilferage, absconding, sabotage, arson and maroonage.[401] Slaves also found respite from the horrors of slavery in music, dance, alcohol, religion and other cultural expressions. For devout African Muslims, they found solace in prayer and reading the Qur'ān, which gave them the strength to endure the trauma of slavery and to lead a series of revolts against their European oppressors.

This chapter offers an analysis of the Bahia slave revolts and a comparison between the famous 1835 *Malê* revolt and the great Zanj slave military revolt which took place in ninth century Baghdad, Iraq.

YORUBA

Yoruba people are a large ethno-linguistic group from West Africa the majority of whom speak the Yoruba language. Yorubas are predominately found in south-western Nigeria and southern Benin. They are one of the three main ethnic groups that make up modern-day Nigeria. They can also be found in neighbouring countries: Benin, Ghana and Togo. Whilst the majority of the Yoruba people live in Nigeria, there are also substantial Yoruba communities in the United Kingdom, the United States, Brazil and parts of the Caribbean who are now indigenous. Religion plays an important role in the lives of Yorubas and their beliefs.

---

401 Maroons (from the Latin American Spanish word *cimarrón*: "feral animal, fugitive, runaway") were African refugees who escaped from slavery in the Americas and formed independent settlements.

The Yorubas were originally entirely pagans, worshipping idols (*orishas*) as intermediaries for *Olorun* (Almighty God). *Olorun,* in traditional Yoruba belief, is applied to God alone and is never used in the plural to denote *orishas*.[402]

According to West African historian, Samuel Johnson, author of *The History of the Yorubas*, it was primarily Fulani Muslim traders and itinerant preachers who introduced the Yorubas to Islam towards the end of the eighteenth century. Islam spread in the southern region of modern-day Nigeria in large numbers by peaceful means, "as it appears to be a superior form of religion to the paganism of their ancestors" as Johnson remarked.[403] The Yorubas the Portuguese enslaved were pagans or Muslims. In 1843, British missionaries from the Church Missionary Society introduced Christianity to the Yorubas.

Music also plays an important part in Yoruba culture, and Yorubas are known for their cheerfulness and love of dance. Economically, Yoruba people engage primarily in agriculture, with some working as merchants, artists and craftsmen. The Yoruba dialect spoken in Brazil is called *Nagô*.

The term 'Yoruba' itself is not known to have been used in Brazil to refer to *Nagô* slaves, the latter term being adopted by Yoruba-speaking Africans in Bahia to identify themselves. In sum, Yoruba speakers became *Nagôs* in Bahia before becoming Yorubas in Africa.[404]

The Yorubas were cosmopolitan people engaging in trade with lands remote from them, and were highly urbanised, living in small, medium, and large villages, around which they established agricultural endeavours. All of these factors contributed to the formation of a *Nagô* identity in the New World. The majority of Yoruba-speaking slaves in Bahia had come from the Oyo kingdom, and they were, therefore, the most important Yoruba subgroup in creating the local *Nagô* identity.[405]

Another important sign of identity, one that could link individuals in specific Yoruba ethnic sub-groups, was the *abaja* or facial scarification. When a person was still a child, specialists, who were usually devotees of [the *orisha*] Ogun, inscribed these marks on the body, particularly the face, with very sharp metal instruments.[406]

---

402 Johnson, 1921, p. 26
403 Johnson, 1921, pp. 38-39
404 Reis and Mamigoniam, "Nagô and Mina: The Yoruba Diaspora in Brazil" in *The Yoruba Diaspora in the Atlantic World*, p. 81
405 Reis and Mamigoniam, "Nagô and Mina: The Yoruba Diaspora in Brazil" in *The Yoruba Diaspora in the Atlantic World*, pp. 81-82
406 Reis and Mamigoniam, "Nagô and Mina: The Yoruba Diaspora in Brazil" in *The*

HAUSA

The Hausa are a Sahelian people[407] mainly found in the West African regions of northern Nigeria and southeastern Niger. There are also significant numbers found in northern regions of Benin, Ghana, Niger, Cameroon, and in smaller communities scattered throughout West Africa and on the traditional Hajj route from West Africa through Chad and Sudan. The Hausa people speak the Hausa language, which belongs to the Chadic language group, a sub-group of the larger Afro-Asiatic language family that has a rich literary heritage dating from the fourteenth century.[408]

WEST AFRICAN CULTURE

The Yoruba and Hausa were familiar with one another because they came from the same region in West Africa, which may have helped them establish relations in Bahia and to coordinate their rebellion against the government. Their shared cultural heritage, as much as religion, was what brought them together, as historian Sylviane Diouf writes:

> African Muslims and non-Muslims coming from the same cultural areas of West Africa were used to one another; but this was not the case with populations from different geographic areas. A man from the Congo was foreign to a Muslim Mandingo but he was also foreign to a non-Muslim Bambara, who came from the same area as the Mandingo and spoke the same language. The cultural differences that existed among the men and women from various parts of Africa added a layer of separation between them that had little to do with Islam and a lot to do with differences in cultures. In other words, Muslims may have remained on their own not only because of their particular religion but also because the African and American-born populations they were living with were from different cultural worlds.[409]

Religious Pride

The Yoruba and Hausa were noted for the pride they had in their Islamic faith. They believed that Islam is superior to the colonists' Christianity and the non-Muslim Africans' pagan beliefs. Allah says in the Qur'ān:

Yoruba Diaspora in the Atlantic World, p. 82

407 The Sahel is "a vast semi-arid region of North Africa, to the south of the Sahara, which forms a transitional zone at the south of the desert and comprises the northern part of the region known as Sudan." Oxford Dictionary.

408 Giepel, 1997

409 Diouf, 2013, pp. 126-127

It is He who sent His Messenger with guidance and the dīn (religion) of Truth to exalt it over every other dīn, even though the idolators detest it.[410]

Although the West African Muslims were very firm in their belief that their *dīn* (religion) was superior to those of their non-Muslim African counterparts and Christian European colonists, they did not try and force it upon others, as *"There is no compulsion where the dīn is concerned"*[411] Instead they would propagate their faith by telling non-Muslims about its tenets.

The African Muslims did not feel inferior to the white Brazilians because of their enslavement and subjugation. Some of them actually looked down on the whites because they were Christians and not of the true faith. An anecdote related by the French count Francis de Castelnau, who was stationed in Bahia in the middle of the nineteenth century, demonstrates this. The count had employed an elderly man from Nigeria called Muḥammad 'Abdullāh, who had liberated himself and become a carpenter. Muḥammad 'Abdullāh had been a *marabout* and had made the pilgrimage to Makkah.[412] According to the count, 'Abdullāh was, "very intolerant, very fanatical, he tries by every means to convert me; and though I received him as well as possible and gave him money, etc., he refuses to come back and told another Negro that he does not want to go to a Christian dog's house."[413]

Elizabeth Agassiz noted the coldness of the African Muslims, whom she observed in Rio de Janeiro, towards the white population: "They do not seem to me so affable and responsive as the Congo negroes," she stated, "but are on the contrary, rather haughty. One morning I came upon a cluster of them in the market breakfasting after their work was done, and I stopped to talk with them, asking what they had for breakfast, and trying various subjects on which to open an acquaintance. But they looked at me coldly and suspiciously, barely answering my questions, and were evidently relieved when I walked away."[414]

Despite being enslaved, the African Muslims in Brazil remained proud of their religion and their status as learned people. The Yoruba and Hausa are descendants of a long line of Muslims from great West-African

---

410 Qur'ān 9: 33
411 Qur'ān 2: 256
412 Diouf, 2013, p. 128
413 Verger, 1968, p. 328
414 Agassiz, 1969, p. 85

Muslim empires and civilisations, such as the empire of Hausaland, and before that the kingdoms of Kanem-Bornu, Songhay, Mali and ancient Ghana.

Black African Not Arab

European colonists saw a correlation between the African Muslims' intelligence and their knowledge of Arabic.[415] Sylviane A. Diouf writes:

> Muslims who distinguished themselves and were literate were thus presented as superior to the rest of the slaves on the basis that their racial origin was different. It was more acceptable to deny any Africanness to the distinguished Muslims than to recognize that a "true" African could be intelligent and cultured but enslaved nevertheless. So, gradually, the African Muslims were seen as owing their perceived superiority not to their own "genes", not even to their culture or proximity to the Arab world, but to foreign "blood".[416]

Many historians and writers attributed the "superiority" of the African Muslims to "mixed-blood" i.e. that they were partially Arabs. An example of this can be found in the statement of British naturalist George Gardner, who travelled in Brazil from 1836 to 1841:

> From the Northern parts of Africa are by far the finest races… Both the men and women are not only taller and more handsomely formed than those from Mozambique, Benguela and the other parts of Africa but have a much greater share of mental energy, arising perhaps from their near relationship to the Moor and the Arab. Among them there are many who both read and write Arabic.[417]

The idea that African Muslims' literacy and intelligence is due to Arabs, rather than their Africanicity, is another example of Europeans' anti-black racism.[418] The Brazilian elite's underestimation of the intelligence of African Muslims was what allowed the Muslims to secretly plan a series of slave revolts between 1807 and 1835.

BAHIA'S SLAVE REVOLTS

At the turn of the nineteenth century, the *jihād* (military warfare) of the Hausa-Fulani Muslim leader Usman dan Fodio in Northern Nigeria provided vast cohorts of Hausa and Fulani Muslims to the Portuguese

---
415 Diouf, 2013, p. 131
416 Diouf, 2013, p. 133
417 Gardner, 1970, p. 20.
418 Diouf, 2013, pp. 130-136

in Brazil, who were sold as prisoners of war. In addition, the Portuguese acquired thousands of Yoruba (*Nagô*) slaves from southern Nigeria. In 1807 alone, 8,307 Hausa, *Nagô* and Ewe slaves arrived in Bahia. In May of the same year, Hausa Muslim slaves and freedmen attempted an uprising near Salvador during the Corpus Christi celebrations. The insurrection did not materialise, as they were betrayed by "a slave loyal to his master".[419] The Portuguese carried out house searches of the would-be rebels and found bows, arrows, knives, pistols, a shotgun and talismans written in Arabic. Two of the Hausa leaders, one a slave and the other a freedperson, were executed, and eleven conspirators were punished publicly, receiving one hundred and fifty lashes each, to set an example for sympathisers and potential rebels. The goal of the uprising is said to have been to capture ships in the harbour with which to return to Africa.[420]

Less than two years later in January of 1809, nearly three hundred insurgents, mostly Hausa slaves but this time accompanied by Jejes (Ewe-Fon) and *Nagôs*, unsuccessfully attacked the town of Nazare das Farinhas in search of arms, ammunition and food, having participated in a massive organised collective flight from Salvador and various *engenhos* (sugar cane mills) in the Reconcavo. About a hundred men were taken prisoner. For months, the remaining maroons roamed the surrounding areas, attacking plantations, setting houses on fire, stealing, and killing.[421]

The period between 1814 and 1835 was one of incessant upheaval and unrest, often the product of African discontent. There were a number of disruptive Hausa-led revolts in 1814. In February 1814, the first of these revolts took place, with about six hundred Africans, under the leadership of a maroon Hausa *marabout,* hit the fisheries where they had been employed and the town of Itapoan. The Hausas were joined by *Nagôs* and others in the revolt. The rebel group was diverse, because they had succeeded in establishing efficient networks linking the slaves and freedmen of the Reconcavo both to those on the island of Itaparica (ten miles from Bahia) and to the maroons living in the vicinity. The insurgent Africans fought fiercely, shouting "Death to whites and mulattos", the latter constituting the backbone of Bahian regulars and its militia. The battle lasted for an hour, and the rebels were defeated, losing fifty-eight men and killing only fourteen soldiers. The repression that followed was commensurate with the gravity of the event: four men were sentenced to death, many to public floggings, two dozen died of abuse while in

---

419 Reis, 1995, p. 42
420 Reis, 1995, pp. 42-43; Diouf, 1998, pp. 153-163; Diouf. 2013, pp. 220-232
421 Reis, 1995, pp. 43-44; Gomez, 2005, p. 102, Diouf, 2013, p. 221

prison, and twenty-three freedmen were deported to the Portuguese port of Benguela, in southern Angola.[422] The rest of the captives were whipped and handed back to their owners.

Public punishments were, however, no deterrent. Less than a month later on 23rd March 1814, a group of Hausas caused havoc in Iguape, where Bahia's largest *engenhos* were. A well-conceived plan underlay the outbreak of hostilities. The revolt was eventually suppressed, but fear began to spread amongst the Brazilian elite.[423]

John Malomi was the leader of the Hausa Muslims during the 1814 revolts. His name in Hausa is said to have been Alasam Alhasan. The revolt was thought to have been inspired by the Haitian revolt that led to the abolition of slavery in Haiti. In Brazil, the enslaved Africans were aware of the Haitian slave-revolts led by Toussaint L'Ouverture,[424] the remarkable leader of the largest slave revolt in the Americas, which showed enslaved Africans that they could fight for freedom and win. Whenever Haiti was discussed at dinner, Lady Maria Nugent, wife of the governor of Jamaica, observed:

> The splendour of the black chiefs of St. Domingo, their superior strength, their firmness of character, and their living so much longer in these climates ... are the common topics at dinner; and the blackies in attendance seem so much interested, that they hardly change a plate, or do anything but listen. How very imprudent, and what *must* it all lead to![425]

Jamaica's first lady from 1801 to 1805, Lady Nugent's comments provide a rare glimpse of how enslaved Africans reacted to the news of the war for Haitian independence. Brazilian police found documents in the possession of the African slaves of the first president of Haiti, Jean-Jacques Dessalines. Inspired by L'Ouverture and the Haitian rebels, Africans in Brazil set about planning a series of revolts in Brazil to emancipate their people.

---

422 Reis, 1995, pp. 45-47
423 Reis, 1995, p. 49; Gomez, 2005, p. 102, Diouf, 2013, p. 221, Barcia, 2014, p. 112
424 Toussaint Bréda (later called Toussaint L'Ouverture) was a slave in the French colony of Saint Dominique (present day Haiti), who learned about Africa from his father, who had been born there as a free man. L'Ouverture was self-educated and an avid reader, who taught himself about military warfare, before successfully leading the slave rebellion against the French and British armies. The Haitian revolution lasted from 1791 to 1804, which culminated in the elimination of slavery there and the foundation of the Republic of Haiti in 1804.
425 Recorded in Lady Nugent's journal of her residence in Jamaica from 1811 to 1815.

Slave Revolts In Bahia, 1807-1835

The year 1816 witnessed a serious uprising in the towns of São Francisco do Conde and Santo Amaro, that led to the burning of several plantations, attacks on houses and the killing of whites.[426] The participants in the revolts were primarily African-born slaves. Three revolts erupted after the War of Independence of Bahia in 1822, followed in 1824 by an uprising on a plantation in Santana that resulted in the formation of a *quilombo* that lasted until 1828. The rebels of the 1824 revolt were reportedly Creole slaves. West Africans continued to surprise local residents and authorities with their organisational proficiency. On 25th August 1826, two years after the previous uprising in Santana, yet another revolt erupted in the Cachoeira district. Little is known about the revolt except that the leader declared himself the 'King of the Blacks,' and his wife the 'Queen of the Blacks'. In the battle, the queen fought valiantly to the death, but the king surrendered after being severely wounded.[427]

In December of that year (1826), Africans and other slaves rose in rebellion at *Urubu* (Vulture), a *quilombo* outside Salvador. The revolt was well-prepared and organised, and struck fear in the hearts of the Brazilian soldiers. According to the deposition of one of the soldiers, the rebels fought fiercely, using knives, machetes, swords and guns. The rebels' war-cry "Death to whites! Long live blacks!" rang throughout *Urubu,* and shook the authorities and local residents. The rebels consisted of nearly fifty men and some women. One of the women captured after the revolt was an extraordinary woman by the name of Zeferina, who rallied the African warriors, fighting only with a bow and some arrows. The provincial president referred to her as 'queen'. Zeferina revealed that the majority of the rebels at *Urubu* were *Nagôs* (Yorubas).[428] It is not surprising that West African women took part in battle. In Dahomey and Yoruba states such as Oyo and Ijesa, women were closely associated with war, and it was not rare for them to lead troops into battle.[429] Although some Hausa were also involved in the revolt, paraphernalia seized during the revolt's suppression were consistent with the Yoruba indigenous religion, thus suggesting that the *Urubu* rebellion was an expression of non-Muslim Yoruba indignation.[430]

Small-scale revolts continued between 1827 and 1830, which upset the delicate social balance in Bahia. With the exception of the revolt of 1830,

---

426 Gomez, 2005, p. 102
427 Reis, 1995, p. 55; Gomez, 2005, p. 103; Barcia, 2014, pp. 112-113
428 Reis, 1995, pp. 56-57
429 Barcia, 2014, p. 130
430 Reis, 1995, pp. 49-69; Gomez, 2005, p. 103

disturbances occurred outside the city of Salvador.[431] In 1827 there were at least three revolts in Cachoeira, São Francisco do Conde and Abrantes. In 1828, there were more rebellions in Itapuā, Cachoeira, Iguape and Santo Amaro.[432] In 1829, another two revolts took place in Cotegipe, a year before a daring attempt was made by the *Nagôs* (Yorubas) to stage an uprising in the heart of Salvador.

The insurgency that took place in downtown Salvador in April 1830, revealed an intricate scheme. Brazilian historian João José Reis said that "its instigators may have concluded that the only way to succeed was to attack white power at its center."[433] A group of twenty *Nagôs* attacked a number of hardware stores, where they seized swords, knives and other weapons. Once this part of the plan was accomplished, they headed for the warehouse owned by Wenceslao Miguel de Almeida, where they killed a guard and then freed newly-arrived *Nagô* slaves. Thus more than a hundred strong, the insurgents mounted an ambitious attack on the police station of Soledade, where they were eventually defeated and forced to retreat. In the battle, the rebels killed some but many of them were wounded and forty taken prisoner, while more than fifty were lynched. Some rebels managed to escape and took refuge in the bush outside the city.[434]

The 1830 revolt was meticulously planned and showed great understanding of the factors needed for success. It followed the West African pattern and their conception of how to make war.[435] According to Barcia, the *Nagô* executed their plans "in a logical, systematic and progressive manner, taking advantage of the opportunities presented to them by unprotected hardware stores packed with weapons, and by the existence of likely reinforcements-in-wait in a nearby barely-protected warehouse."[436] After the rebellion was eventually quashed, the government tightened its hold on the city. After their audacious but unsuccessful attempt, the *Nagôs* would patiently wait some years before staging another uprising in Salvador in 1835 with a large number of urban and rural slaves and freemen, with a display of courage never previously seen in Bahia.[437]

---

431 Gomez, 2005, p. 103
432 Reis, 1995, pp. 59-66
433 Reis, 1995, p. 67
434 Diouf. 2013, p. 222; Barcia, 2014, p. 113
435 Barcia, 2014, p. 113
436 Barcia, 2014, p. 113
437 Reis, 1995, pp. 67-69

The 1835 Malê Slave Revolt

The 1835 *Malê* slave revolt is arguably the most significant slave rebellion to have taken place in the history of Brazil, and consisted of some six hundred slaves and freed-persons, who are, according to Reis, equivalent to twenty four thousand people today. Inspired by religious teachers and bearing talismans containing texts from the Qur'ān, the insurgents rose up against the government in the city of Salvador.

The Night Of Power

The 1835 rebellion had been planned to begin at dawn on Sunday 25th January. The day was a Catholic holiday, which was a propitious day, since vigilance would be relaxed somewhat. The corresponding date in the lunar calendar was the 25th of Ramadan, the month in which the first *āyats* (verses) of the Qur'ān were revealed to the Prophet Muḥammad ﷺ by the archangel Jibrīl (Gabriel).[438]

> *The month of Ramadan is the one in which the Qur'an was sent down as guidance for mankind, with Clear Signs containing guidance and discrimination.*[439]

The night during which the Qur'ān was first revealed is called *Laylat al-Qadr* (the Night of Power, also known as the Night of Glory and the Night of the Decree). The exact date of *Laylat al-Qadr* is unknown, but Muslims in West Africa and elsewhere are traditionally of the view that it falls on the 27th of Ramadan or one of the odd nights in the last ten days. Thus, the Yoruba insurgents who played a central role in the rebellions are likely to have planned for the revolt to take place on the 25th, as one of the possible dates of the *Laylat al-Qadr*, hoping for Divine assistance. The Muslims prepared for the revolt by supplicating Allah for help, and most likely reading the Sūrah of The Night of Power from the Qur'ān for steadfastness:[440]

> *Truly We sent it down on the Night of Power.*
> *And what will convey to you what the Night of Power is?*
> *The Night of Power is better than a thousand months.*
> *In it the angels and the Ruh (Spirit) descend by their Lord's authority with every ordinance.*
> *It is Peace — until the coming of the dawn.*[441]

---

438 Reis, 1995, p. 73
439 Qur'ān 2:185
440 Reis, 1995, p. 93
441 Qur'ān 97: 1-5

Prior to the rebellion, the insurgents wore on their persons amulets and pieces of parchment containing *āyats* of the Qur'ān. Some amulets sent from Salvador to E. de la Rosière, the French representative in Rio de Janeiro at the time, were written addressing the plight of the oppressed and the promise of better days for hard-working believers. According to de la Rosière, an amulet read:

> In the name of God, the merciful, the compassionate! May God have compassion on our lord Muḥammad! Praised be the name of the giver of salvation, blood must be shed: we must all have a hand in it. Oh God! Oh Muḥammad! Servant of the Almighty! We hope for success if it be God in the highest's will. Glory be to God. Amen.[442]

The Revolt

In the early morning hours of Sunday 25th January 1835, the rebels took to the streets wearing white caps, turbans, robes and *abadā* (white tunics), garments peculiar to practitioners of Islam in West Africa. The *abadā*, referred to as *agbada* in Yorubaland, is considered by some Africans a symbol of social superiority, and is commonly worn by kings and nobles in Africa. In Bahia, the *abadā* was worn only in private so as not to attract attention or persecution from officers of the law, who were always on the lookout for anything out of the ordinary among the Muslims. It was only during the 1835 rebellion that the spectacle of hundreds of Muslims dressed in white occurred on the streets of Salvador. For this reason police authorities called the *abadās* "war garments".[443]

Armed with knives, lances, swords, and a few pistols, they went out to the sound of drums and attacked the National Guard barracks, the city jail and the police barracks. Alerted to the conspiracy the day before, authorities surprised the participants by attacking a group of rebels meeting in the loge or basement of a two-story house. Fighting broke out all over Salvador, and after several hours more than seventy people were dead. Gonçalves Martins, the chief of police, counted fifty Africans killed during the uprising or drowned in the sea. Some insurgents later died from their wounds and others committed suicide. As is usual in armed conflicts, the wounded are likely to have been considerably more

---

442 Reis, 1995, p. 120; De la Rosière to French Minister of Foreign Affairs, Rio de Janeiro, 13 March 1835, AMRE, *cp'Brèsil*, vol. 16, fols. 52v-53
443 Reis, 1995, p. 103

numerous than the dead. Nine people were said to have been killed by the rebels and a few wounded.[444]

On the day after the revolt, Francisco de Souza Martins, the president of the province, who was thirty years old at the time, ordered Francisco Gonçalves Martins, the chief of police, to "waste no time" in arraigning the insurgents, especially the leaders and those found "bearing arms". He told the chief to be zealous in the collection of evidence and to subpoena witnesses who could help reconstruct the movement in its entirety and to punish all the conspirators.[445]

Gonçalves Martins, who was twenty-eight years old, instructed justices of the peace to have block inspectors "enter every house and lodge belonging to black Africans and search them rigorously for men, arms and written papers." Justices of the peace followed his instructions to the letter and played a significant role in the repression of the Africans.[446] At least forty-five slaves and fifty freedmen were arrested during the two days following the rebellion. Many more conspirators were later arrested in police raids. Not all Muslims took part in the revolt, and many innocent people were arrested because they had religious writings in their houses.

The ensuing investigation, from which a wealth of information on Islam in Bahia has been garnered, consisted of over two-hundred hearings conducted in an atmosphere of widespread fear and panic.[447] Within a few months of the rebellion, over three-hundred defendants had been tried, of whom approximately 60% were slaves and the rest freed-persons. Four of the rebels were executed, forty-five flogged up to a thousand times in the course of three months, thirty-four deported, and twenty-four sentenced to prison or hard labour.[448]

Leaders Of The Revolt

In the aftermath of the revolt, the police investigation of the rebels identified seven Muslims as important leaders in the insurrection; Ahuna (or Aluna), Pacífico Licutan, Sanim, Manoel Calafate, Dandará, Nicobé, and Dassalu.

---

444 Reis, 1995, pp. 73-92; Gomez, 2005, p. 105; Diouf, 2013, p. 222
445 Reis, 1995, pp. 191-192;
446 Reis, 1995, pp. 192-196
447 Reis, 1995, pp. 73-92; Gomez, 2005, p. 105
448 Reis, 1995, p. 206

AHUNA

Ahuna was a leading scholar in Bahia who was admired by the black population. "[Ahuna] was loved by all his brethren," a freedman said. Another said about Ahuna, "he is a negro whom the others love." Ahuna has been described as being a man of "ordinary build" with four tribal marks on each cheek. The tribal marks indicate his Yoruba ancestry. Ahuna was a wanted man in Bahia during 1835. He was referred to as the "straw boss" (*maioral*) and as an extremely important link in the conspiracy's chain of command, according to the testimony of the many Africans incarcerated a few days before the uprising. Ahuna lived on a plot of land near Pelourinho Square, where he was enslaved by an unnamed man.[449]

PACÍFICO LICUTAN

Pacífico Licutan, was an enslaved *Nagô* (*Malê*), who was also a Muslim religious teacher. Licutan was of Yoruba descent and a beloved figure to West African Muslims in Salvador, Bahia. Muslims in Bahia had twice attempted to buy the freedom of the elderly Nigerian man from Antônio Pinto de Mesquita Varella, a physician who made money from Licutan's work as a tobacco-roller on Dourado Wharf in Salvador. Varella refused, and when the doctor could no longer pay his own debts, this esteemed preacher was confiscated as a piece of property to be sold to pay off Varella's creditors. Pacífico Licutan awaited his imminent sale in prison in the month of Ramadan in November 1834.[450]

In January 1835, the following year, after news that the revolt had quickly been put down, Licutan was saddened. A freed African working at the jail testified:

> He bowed his head and never raised it. He became upset and cried when the other negroes taken prisoners that morning were brought in. One of them brought him a book, or a folded piece of paper with letters on it, like those that have been found lately, and Pacífico[Licutan] read it and began to cry.[451]

Although Licutan was disappointed, he was not entirely broken. When he was interrogated by Bahian authorities on February 11, 1835, he denied his inquisitors' demands that he give up the names of his students and fellow practitioners. Licutan even refused to cooperate with a judge's

---

449 Reis, 1995, p. 129
450 Curtis, 2014, p. 111, Diouf, 2013, p. 141
451 Reis, 1995, p. 132

request for his name. When asked, he told the official that his name was Bilal. The judge became enraged, but Licutan said that "he could call himself whatever he wanted." Licutan's defiance shows that the revolt was still alive in his heart, despite its apparent failure on the battlefield.[452] Though nothing could be proved against him, Licutan received fifty lashes daily on four days in April, eleven days in May, and five days in June – one thousand lashes in all for the elderly religious leader.[453]

SANIM

Licutan was close friends with another important leader of the uprising, Luís, known to Africans as Sanim, his real name. At the time of the revolt, Sanim was an elderly man of average build with a wide forehead, white hair, thick beard, and chestnut-coloured hands. Like his friend Licutan, Sanim was a slave and worked as a tobacco-roller. Although he was born a Nupe, Sanim spoke Yoruba and Hausa fluently. He was educated, with experience of several cultures.[454]

In Africa Sanim had been an *alufá,* or scholar, and probably continued his religious teaching duties secretly in Bahia. He was a Tapa slave, and his Christianised name was Luís. Not only knowledgeable in Islam, Sanim was also a very practical person. He organised a savings fund to which each member contributed 320 reais, presumably on a monthly basis, at the time a day's pay for slave labour. The money in the pool was divided into three parts: a part for buying cloth to make Islamic garments; a part to pay masters' portions of slave wages; and a third part to be used to help buy letters of manumission.[455]

During his interrogation, Sanim said little to the authorities. In spite of the evidence that was brought against him, he denied being an *alufá*. He insisted that he had never entered the house of two African freedmen, Gaspar and Belchior da Silva Cunha, whose sartorial services he had used, although he did admit to knowing them. Pedro Ricardo, Sanim's slave master, defended Sanim's right to practice his religion, as it was a constitutional guarantee according to his attorney's interpretation of the law.[456]

---

452 Curtis, 2014, pp. 111-112
453 Diouf, 2013, pp. 224-225, Reis, 1995, pp. 130-132
454 Reis, 1995, p. 132
455 Reis, 1995, p. 133
456 Reis, 1995, p. 133

MANOEL CALAFATE

Manoel Calafate was a freed *Nagô* (Yoruba), and a caulker by trade. He lived in the house at the foot of Ladeira da Praça street where the uprising began. He lived with another freed *Nagô*, a sedan-chair porter by the name of Aprígio. Their house served as a meeting place where Muslims gathered to plan the insurrection. Manoel travelled to Santo Amaro to mobilise rebels on the eve of the uprising. The Muslims promised to die fighting alongside their leader and teacher, Manoel. "Father" Manoel, as he was known to the other Muslims, took an active part in the struggle, and he appears to have died from wounds he suffered in Palace Square a few minutes after the uprising began.[457]

DANDARÁ

Dandará, another leader of the Muslims, was also known as Elesbâo do Carmo. He was a wealthy merchant, who owned a tobacco shop in the Santa Barbara market of the Conceição da Praia Parish. The Muslims would pray together, learn Arabic and read the Qur'ān at his store. He lived with a *Nagô* slave woman, Emereciana, near the Guadalupe neighbourhood. Whilst being interrogated, Dandará admitted to having been "a teacher in his land", and he added that "he has been teaching young fellows here, but not to do evil." As later told by Luís da França, a mulatto tailor who used to spy on Dandará through the loose floorboards, Dandará used to pray regularly at night, seeking Divine guidance. Dandará was dedicated to his Islamic faith and carried the religion to the Recôncavo, which he was constantly visiting on business.[458]

NICOBÉ AND DASSALU

Nicobé (also known as Sule) and Dassalu were slaves of Englishmen living in the Vitória neighbourhood. A slave by the name of Carlos testified that "he did not know how to read, but was still learning from *mestre* Dassalu and Nicobé, as well as [from] Gustard." According to historian João José Reis, Dassalu and Gustard were probably just more advanced students in the *Malê* reading and writing classes, but Nicobé appears in the testimony of João, another slave, who referred to him as "the captain of them all". Nicobé was never captured but he, like the other religious leaders, was a great source of inspiration for the revolt of the blacks and African Muslims in Bahia.[459]

---

457 Reis, 1995, p. 133
458 Reis, 1995, pp. 133-134
459 Reis, 1995, p. 134

Religious And Ethnic Motivations Of The Revolt

The purpose of the revolt remains a subject of speculation. The work of Raimundo Nina Rodrigues, Arthus Ramos, Pierre Verger, Michael Gomez, Roger Bastide, Jack Goody, Luís Luna, Paul Lovejoy, and Muḥammad Shareef argues for a continuity of purpose between events in northern Nigeria and northeastern Brazil during the first third of the nineteenth century.[460] That is, according to Lovejoy and Gomez, the 1804-12 *jihād* of Usman dan Fodio that resulted in the creation of the Sokoto Caliphate, a theocracy in northern Nigeria modelled on the Baghdad-centred Abbasid Caliphate (750-1258),[461] was a struggle imported into Bahia along with captives from the area.[462] Jurema and João José Reis disagreed with the claim that the African Muslims were inspired by religious jihādist sentiments to wage war against *kāffirs* (unbelievers) in Brazil.

It cannot be denied that Islam played a unifying factor in the organisation of the Africans in Bahia. Africans are not a monolithic group with the same culture, language and religious beliefs. The African ethnic groups of Brazil spoke different languages and did not share the same cultural practices. The fact that a large number of the Africans were Muslims helped to unite the slaves. Islam provided them with a common language (Arabic) to communicate and brotherhood in faith. This led to greater strength and solidarity. According to Edward E. Curtis, the Muslims in Bahia made a distinction between themselves and *gaveré* (unbelievers/pagans). "Like Muslims throughout the Americas, they were known to be haughty and proud, which was partly a product of the prestige that they commanded as a result of their literacy and perceived ritual power."[463]

The Yoruba Muslims utilised their being Africans to unite with non-Muslim Africans and used their being Muslims to unite with their Muslim 'brothers' in faith. The tactic was ingenious as it led to a unified body, which would rebel against the establishment in Bahia. Historians and scholars have asserted that, though there are no explicit testimonies from the rebel leaders, the evidence does suggest that religion appears to have been a motivating factor in the African-Muslims' revolt.

In Islam, the principle of justice is universal and not restricted solely to Muslims. The African Muslims were likely to have been inspired by Qur'ānic *āyats* calling for justice, to emancipate themselves from slavery.

---

460 Gomez, 2005, p. 109
461 The Abbasid Caliphate was modelled on the prophetic Madinan model
462 Gomez, 2005, p. 109
463 Curtis, 2014, p. 121

Allah instructs the believers:

> *You who believe! be upholders of justice, bearing witness for Allah alone, even against yourselves or your parents and relatives. Whether they are rich or poor...*[464]

According to another Qur'ānic passage:

> *You who believe! show integrity for the sake of Allah, bearing witness with justice. Do not let hatred for a people incite you into not being just. Be just. That is closer to taqwā (piety).*[465]

With regards to relations with non-Muslims, the Qur'ān further states:

> *Allah does not forbid you from being good to those who have not fought you in the dīn or driven you from your homes, or from being just towards them. Allah loves those who are just.*[466]

Reis illustrates the important role both Islam and ethnicity played in the 1835 uprising. For instance, the rebellion was planned around the important month of Ramadan, and the rebel participants dressed in traditional clothing and wore amulets. Despite its religious overtones, the rebellion, Reis asserts, was not, as other historians have suggested, a *jihād,* since the African Muslims knew that they needed non-Muslim participants in order to succeed. For Reis, although the rebellion was planned by Muslims it was an African uprising,

End White Domination
Scholars have also argued that race and ethnicity were motivational factors for the rebels. The rebellion of 1835 seemed to be an attempt to overturn the political order that put whites on top and African-born blacks at the bottom, though this opinion is undermined by the fact that some blacks did not participate in the revolt.[467] One witness in the post-rebellion hearings said that the point of the uprising was to kill whites; another witness said the purpose was to kill "all whites, mulattos, and African-born blacks", another said that blacks were to be killed only if they did not side with the militants. According to another witness, the rebels "would keep the mulattos as their slaves and lackeys." Edward

---

464 Qur'ān 4:135
465 Qur'ān 5:8
466 Qur'ān 60:8
467 Curtis, 2014, p. 120

E. Curtis, author of *The Call of Bilal: Islam in the African Diaspora,* wrote that the only thing common to all the testimonies was the idea that "the rebels certainly planned to end white domination."[468]

African-Born Blacks and Brazilian Born Blacks

In Bahia, there was tension between African-born blacks and Brazilian-born blacks (*crioulo*), the former usually being given the heavier tasks.[469] Brazilian-born blacks did not participate in the revolt, which was exclusively carried out by African-born blacks from the Bight of Benin,[470] although not all African Muslims participated in the revolt.

Edward E. Curtis argues that Bahia was indeed a society characterised by strong racial divisions, in which race, defined partly by skin colour, influenced one's opportunities in life. He says, "People who were *preto*, or black, had limited life opportunities, even if they were free. Racial categories in Bahia also included the terms *pardo*, or mulatto, a person of mixed race; *cabra*, a person whose skin colour was perceived to be in between black and tan; and white." Curtis adds, "Racial identity in Bahia depended not only on physical characteristics such as skin colour but also on the continent of one's birth. Native-born blacks had their own separate category, called *crioulos*, they were considered to be different from African-born blacks, and there was significant tension between the two groups."[471] Brazilian-born blacks lived and worked in different social networks and saw themselves as having different political interests: throughout Brazilian history, they were far less willing to participate in slave revolts.

An Islamic State in Brazil?

There are also indications that some of the rebels wanted to emancipate themselves from slavery, kill their whites slave masters, create an Islamic state in Brazil and return back to Africa. However this does not appear to be the real motivation for the revolt as many historians have argued.

Abdul Hameed Ahmad, the Nigerian imam of the Salvador mosque, told me that he felt the reason why the African Muslims rose in revolt was to obtain their freedom because of the horrifying treatment they received from the Portuguese. Although he did agree that Islam played a crucial role in motivating the Muslims, he disagreed the claims of some

---

468 Curtis, 2014, p. 120
469 Sansone, 2003, p. 62
470 Gomez, 2005, p. 102; Diouf, 2013, p. 221
471 Curtis, 2014, p. 119

historians that the African Muslims wanted to establish an Islamic state in Brazil. Rather, he said, they wanted freedom and justice for themselves and their non-Muslim African brethren. Reis concurred:

> Although we have no clear idea of the rebel leaders' long-term plans, there is no doubt that they fought against the enslavement of Africans in Bahia, and that they counted on the occurrence of a general African slave rebellion as a follow-up to the actions carried on by the men who started the fight.[472]

House Negroes and Field Negroes

The authorities discovered the revolt because of an African informant who was loyal to his master. In the slave era there were usually two types of slaves Malcolm X famously said: the house negro and the field negro. The house negro lives in the house with the master, dresses well, and loves his master more than he loves himself. In contrast, the field negro lives with the masses of slaves and wants freedom from his master. The informant, a "house negro", was more concerned about the interests of the oppressor than his own people.

In Brazil, the field negroes were the African-born slaves, who rebelled against the Portuguese, and the house negroes were like many of the Brazilian-born blacks and mulattos, who remained "loyal" to living in subjugation under the Portuguese. The African Muslims in Brazil are likely to have been more prone to rise in rebellion for a variety of reasons: they were not used to living in servitude; they were warriors experienced in the art of warfare; they witnessed their women being raped by the Portuguese; and they had a strong religious conviction that it is correct to fight intolerable injustice.

Military Warfare

The African slaves in Bahia revolted numerous times before the great uprising in 1835, which remains one of the most notable slave rebellions in Brazilian history. The 1835 revolt was meticulously planned and organised by the Yoruba Muslims, who rallied their fellow African Muslims, on the basis of their shared religious beliefs, and rallied their fellow non-Muslim Africans, on the basis of their shared ancestry, to an insurrection against the Portuguese slave-owners. The armed struggle of 1835 had an intrinsically West African character. The organisation and

---

[472] Reis and Mamigoniam, "Nagô and Mina: The Yoruba Diaspora in Brazil" in *The Yoruba Diaspora in the Atlantic World*, p. 96; See works by Nina Rofrigues' *Os africanos no Brasil*, Bastide's *As religiões no Brasil*, and Verger's *Flux et reflux*

strategies of the *Nagô* leaders and the actual ways in which the battle was fought included significant elements of West African warfare from Oyo, Sokoto, Dahomey and Borno.[473]

The testimonies of West African men and women in Bahia occasionally offer clues about their familiarity with warfare, and, in some cases, go as far as mentioning their own war-related experiences in their homelands.[474]

The Yoruba were tactically astute and experienced in military warfare because of the nineteenth century Fulani-led *jihād* and civil wars in Yorubaland. Manuel Barcia explored the impact that West Africans had on the Bahia slave revolts, and demonstrates how the West Africans made use of their military skills and tactical nous, which they had developed in the wars in West Africa, to give a foundation to the Bahian slave revolts.

The Brazilian planters believed that the Africans they had imported to work on their cities and plantations were lawless savages living outside the Christian faith, who were incapable of appreciating any civilised law or technological development, and were blinded by their own prejudices and preconceptions. Consequently, in their opinion, their military actions – those revolts and insurrections they so often complained about – were heavily characterised by these backward traits and were never considered to be actual organised military actions. This poor understanding, by contemporaries and by subsequent generations of historians, of African warfare in the diaspora is problematic, since it has conveniently overlooked the fact that African warfare was precisely the "original source" of much of the population in these two slave societies.[475]

While studying these African military movements, historians have, until now, continued to use the Western vocabulary and concepts of the authorities and plantation owners while trying to understand the African side of the stories they are meant to tell.[476] By using terms such as "slave revolt" or "slave insurrection" academics continue to underestimate the vital military character of the vast majority of these movements. Barcia argues that perhaps it would make more sense to consider using more appropriate terms, such as "slave military revolt" or "African military uprising", to clarify, at least in some measure, the intrinsically martial character of each of these movements.[477]

---

473 Barcia, 2014, p. 107
474 Barcia, 2014, p. 109
475 Barcia, 2014, p. 98
476 Barcia, 2014, p. 98
477 Barcia, 2014, p. 103

In the same way that African wars associated with the transatlantic slave trade have sometimes been seen as "simply slave raids", African military actions in the Americas have frequently been considered simply revolts lacking direction, organisation, and clear objectives, when nothing could be farther from the truth. Consequently, the vast majority of scholars who have studied slave societies in the New World have perpetuated the reasoning and explanations of these violent events offered by none other than the authorities who prosecuted the Africans, and by plantation owners, their employees, and the general non-slave population, which often lived in a permanent state of panic fearing the outbreak of a massive African insurgency.[478]

Gilberto Freyre, the famous Brazilian sociologist informs us that:

> Mohammedan Fulahs and Hausas, who appear to have led the various slave revolts ... came from the kingdoms of Wurno, Sokoto, and Gando, which possessed an advanced form of political organization, a well-defined religious literature with native works composed in Arabic characters, and an art that was strong and original, superior to the anaemic Portuguese imitations of Moorish models. Slaves such as these could not be expected to conform to the role of mere artistic puppets for the Portuguese, nor could the holy water of Christian baptism all of a sudden extinguish the Mohammedan fire that was in them.[479]

According to Barcia, scholars underestimate African movements because they fought their battles in ways that were unconventional by European standards of the time. More significantly, they have also been overlooked because, in the thinking of many scholars, they failed to embody the so-called revolutionary ideas that changed the political landscape in Europe and the Americas after the last decades of the eighteenth century. This underestimation may also be related to a post-abolition backlash against Africans who refused to end slavery in Africa after the British had enforced the end of their trade in humans. This in particular created an increasingly pessimistic and negative view of Africans as barbaric, which to a certain extent seems also to have infected later historiography.[480]

The truth, however, is that many of these movements were well planned, and their leaders had clear strategies and goals that they pursued once they took up arms. They were more than simple attempts to overrun

---

478 Barcia, 2014, p. 105
479 Freyre, 1956, p.315
480 Barcia, 2014, p. 105

plantations or assassinate cruel overseers. In fact, such movements represented renewed efforts to achieve apparent and intentional goals, of which, logically, freedman, was the main one.[481]

The Aftermath Of The Revolt
After the 1835 revolt, African Muslims were stigmatised and became the target of the Brazilian authorities. They were regarded as dangerous and prone to rebellion, and therefore seen as a threat to the system. African Muslims were becoming a disruptive influence upon the country's economy, which was at the time dependent on slave labour.[482]

The slave rebellion had an enormous impact on Brazilian society. The national debate in Brazil's press following the rebellion occurred against a background of internal political turmoil and increasing pressure to end the trans-Atlantic slave trade. In his study of the debate, José T. Cairus revealed the concerns of Brazil's elite about the future of the new nation. In the nineteenth century, only a small literate elite had access to Brazil's press. Newspapers constituted a public space in which the dominant elite would express their views about politics, ideology and religion.

News about the rebellion made a great impact in Rio de Janeiro and the northeastern provinces of Brazil, due to the high concentration of enslaved Africans. The newspapers used terms like "barbarian slaves" and "semi-barbarian freed slaves", which corresponded to the traditional categorisation of slaves as *ladinos* and *boçais*. For one newspaper article published in August 1836, the process of "civilising" Africans would only be complete with their full assimilation of the Western values imposed by their European masters. The African Muslims' rebellion challenged some of the basic principles of Western slavery.[483] British anthropologist Jack Goody argued that African Muslims in Brazil came from a literate culture based on Islamic values and had what Goody called "technologies of the intellect". Islam provided the rebels with an intellectual apparatus of resistance, as demonstrated by the great amount of Islamic literature and numbers of amulets the authorities found after the rebellion. Goody compared the role of Islam in Brazil to that of the Enlightenment for the French revolutionaries in 1789.[484]

Some rebels were deported back to Africa. More than one hundred freed Africans accused of being in the revolt were deported to Lagos and

---

481 Barcia, 2014, p. 105
482 Cairus, 2014, p. 195
483 Cairus, 2014, p. 193
484 Goody, 2000, p. 197

Dahomey in West Africa. A Brazilian ship left the Africans in the Upper Guinea at their request, where they were received by the *sovah* (prince of the land). The returnees rapidly built an Afro-Brazilian Muslim community thanks to the presence of carpenters and other skilled workers among them. Given the success of this deportation, other Africans in Brazil returned to the continent on their own initiative, resulting in the issuance of more than four hundred passports. An 1836 newspaper article in Rio de Janeiro referred to approximately three trips by ship to the same area on the coast of Africa "where Africans lived peacefully, safe and free".[485] Many of the returnees built Brazilian mosques in Nigeria and Benin which still stand today.

> "Victory comes from Allah. Victory is near. Glad tidings for all the believers," promised the text on one amulet confiscated by the police. The amulets worn by African Muslim rebels were used to inspire them to victory.[486]

WAS THE MALÊ REVOLT A SUCCESS?

Whether the revolt can be regarded as a success or not will depend on one's definition of success. If the object was to overthrow the Brazilian government in Bahia, then the 1835 revolt was not a success, but, if the primary concern of the African Muslims was to preserve their faith or die as Muslims, the revolt can definitely be considered a success.

The Qur'ānic perspective is:

> *You who believe! have taqwa of Allah with the taqwa due to Him and do not die except as Muslims.*[487]

To end one's life as a Muslim and enter the Garden is the ultimate goal for every believer. Thus, African Muslims who were executed, along with those who were deported back to Africa to live the rest of their lives as Muslims, could be considered successful, as they wanted to preserve their faith or die as martyrs for their *dīn*.

The revolt could also be viewed as a success, inasmuch as it led to the abolition of slavery a few decades later. Thus the revolt is still a source of inspiration for Brazil's people of African descent in their struggle for racial and social oppression.

---

485 Cairus, 2014, p. 194
486 Reis, 1995, p. 120
487 Qur'ān 3: 102

Slave Revolts In Bahia, 1807–1835

COMPARISONS WITH THE 869 ZANJ REVOLT IN BAGHDAD

"A cloud cast a shadow upon me. Thunder crackled and lightning flashed, and a voice addressed me, saying, 'Head for Basra.'" – 'Alī ibn Muḥammad

The Zanj And The Leader Of The Zanj Revolts

Afro-Arab prose writer al-Jāḥiẓ said that the Zanj were "black people from the east coast of Africa who had been imported [to Baghdad] as slaves, at an indeterminate date." According to al-Jāḥiẓ, the Zanj were made of four ethnic groups: Qunbula, Lanjawiyya, Naml and Kilāb. The word Zanj is not of Arabic origin and scholars have debated whether it is Ethiopian, Persian or Greek. The word is also said to derive from East Africa.

Many of the early Arab writers would refer to blacks as *zanj*, *sūdān* (blacks), or *ḥabash* (Abyssinians), even though all Zanj are blacks but not all blacks are necessarily from the Zanj. The Zanj of Baghdad were Muslims. Under Abbasid rule they were treated harshly, which led to a series of revolts between 869 and 883. 'Alī ibn Muḥammad, a man who claimed to be a descendent of 'Alī ibn Abī Ṭālib, instigated the revolts. Several scholars are of the opinion that he was Persian, but others believe that he was an Arab. 'Alī ibn Muḥammad's religious doctrine has also caused disagreement amongst Sunni Muslim scholars, who have argued that he was either a Shiite or a Kharijite.[488]

The Zanj revolts were among the most significant slave rebellions in world history as well as the first major revolts in the history of the African diaspora.

The Zanj Revolts

The Zanj revolts were fomented by East African slaves, who were working in the saline areas of lower Mesopotamia to remove the salt sands and brine and open the area up to cultivation.[489] The most important sources for the history of the Zanj revolt are the works of the Arab historians: aṭ-Ṭabarī, al-Mas'ūdī and Ibn al-Athīr. Aṭ-Ṭabarī's work is the primary source. His work is highly valued for the quality as much as the quantity of information.[490] Aṭ-Ṭabarī himself was present in Baghdad during the years of the revolt, and he was thus able to construct his story from reports of numerous eyewitnesses. The result is a detailed

---

488 Popovic, 1999, pp. 33-43, Tabari's work (nine pages) and Safao's work
489 Ṭabarī, 1987, p. xiii
490 Popovic, 1999, p. 6

narrative that brings alive the main personalities and engagements of the revolt for the modern reader. The works of al-Mas'ūdī and Ibn al-Athīr are also important.

As labour-intensive activities such as mining and plantation agriculture had expanded in the Muslim domains, so the slave trade had developed, especially the commerce in African slaves. Simultaneously, cultural justifications for the enslavement of Africans multiplied, with many classical writers depicting blacks as slow-witted and bestial. Following Galen, the Arab historian al-Mas'ūdī mentions ten specific characteristics of the Zanj: frizzy hair, thin eyebrows, broad nostrils, thick lips, pointed teeth, smelly skin, black pupils, furrowed feet and hands, highly developed sexual organs and excessive merriment. The author [Galen] explains this last quality as a result of the imperfect organisation of the brain, which also causes weakness of intellect. In another work, the following characteristics were attributed to blacks: dark complexion, kinky hair, flat nose, thick lips, thin hands and feet, smelly skin, excessive petulance, sparse eyebrows, and highly developed sexual organs.

One writer who did not rehearse the stereotype was al-Jāḥiẓ of Basra, himself perhaps of African origin, who wrote:

> Everybody agrees that there is no people on earth in whom generosity is as universally well developed as the Zanj. These people have a natural talent for dancing to the rhythm of the tambourine, without needing to learn it. There are no better singers anywhere in the world, no people more polished and eloquent, and no people less given to insulting language. No other nation can surpass them in bodily strength and physical toughness. They are courageous, energetic, and generous, which are the virtues of nobility, and also good-tempered and with little propensity to evil. They are always cheerful, smiling, and devoid of malice, which is a sign of noble character.[491]

Working in intolerably humid conditions clearing the salt marshes of southern Mesopotamia, fed on a poor diet of dates and semolina, frequently racially abused, the Zanj rose in their hundreds of thousands in a revolt against the Abbasid empire that lasted for approximately fifteen years (869 – 883 CE). The Zanj conquered large parts of Iraq, Iran and Bahrain, held the city of Basra for a decade, established their own capital, and even minted their own currency.

---

491 Al-Jāḥiẓ

Guerrilla tactics and ruthless massacres, as well as the sectarian, tribal and class divisions of the Abbasid state, contributed to the quickly multiplying Zanj victories. Turkic, Slavic, Persian and Arab slaves flocked to the banner of the revolution and to the maroon city of al-Mukhtara, 'the Chosen', so that by the end of the rebellion non-Africans outnumbered ethnic Zanj in the revolutionary ranks.

In its final days, the 'republic of slaves' had become as divided by sect, class and competing centres of power as its enemies. It should be noted that ʿAlī ibn Muḥammad had promised that the liberated slaves would have slaves of their own. With Zanj unity and moral purity destroyed, it was a matter of time until revitalised Abbasi armies put down the revolt. ʿAlī ibn Muḥammad's skewered head was paraded through Baghdad. By 883 CE, the Abbasids had crushed the prolonged revolt.

The final defeat of the rebellion resulted not in the reintroduction of mass enslavement but in the incorporation of the rebels into central government forces. Slavery persisted, but there would be no further attempts at mass enslavement in the eastern Arab world until a thousand years later, when Omani-controlled Zanzibar sent slave-produced coconuts and spices to European markets.

The Zanj revolt helped Ahmad ibn Tulun to create an independent state in Egypt. It was only after defeating the Zanj Revolt that the Abbasids were able to turn their attention to Egypt, and end the Tulunid dynasty with great destruction.

Similarities With The Malê Revolt
The 1835 *Malê* revolt and the Zanj revolts in ninth century Baghdad share a number of similarities. Both were orchestrated by African Muslim slaves who were motivated by racial discrimination and who used religion as a motivational factor. The serious ramifications of the revolts for black people in Brazil and the Middle East were that anti-black attitudes intensified. Religion was used by the Christian Portuguese and Muslim Arabs to justify their ill-treatment of blacks.

Unfortunately, little is known from the perspective of the Zanj rebels as most of the historical documentation is by non-African observers. Aṭ-Ṭabarī provides little information about the aspirations, plans and ideology of the Zanj. The sources of the *Malê* revolt do provide some information about the rebels' plans and aspiration, but there is scant information from those who took part in the revolt themselves. Nonetheless, scholars of the revolts have come up with their own theories in regards to the key motivational factors for the rebels. A number of scholars cite both race and religion as primary motivational factors.

Racial And Religious Motivations Behind The Revolts

The Zanj rebels appealed to Islam, the common frame of reference of all social classes in the Abbasid empire. The Zanj thought that Islam had begun as a revolution of the dispossessed. The freed Syrian slave Zayd was the adopted son of the Prophet ﷺ and one of his military commanders. The man the Prophet ﷺ appointed to call the faithful to prayer, the first *mu'adhdhin* in Islam, was the freed Ethiopian slave Bilal. Although the Qur'ān, like the earlier Abrahamic revelations, does not prohibit slavery, it prescribes rewards for the emancipation of slaves which is also regarded as an expiation for a great number of wrong actions. The position of slaves in Islam was theoretically closer to that of well-treated serfs than that of the chattel African slaves of the Portuguese in Brazil. Islamic regulations stated clearly that a slave must be provided with food and clothing equal to his master's, and should not be tasked with work beyond his or her ability. Slaves could marry and own property. The use of violence against a slave was firmly prohibited. As for racial bases for slavery, in his final sermon the Messenger of Allah ﷺ stated that there is no difference between an Arab and a non-Arab or between a red man and a black man, except in God-consciousness. The Zanj revolutionaries saw these precepts betrayed by the merchants and land owners who had enslaved and abused them.

The Hausa and Yoruba Muslims in Brazil were well learned in Islamic history, and it is likely that they were aware of the Zanj revolt, which was documented in the work of the great Arab historian aṭ-Ṭabarī. In their revolts in Bahia, they may have drawn inspiration from the Zanj. Although the Zanj rose in revolt against fellow Muslims, their revolt may have resonated with black African slaves who were in a similar condition. The Zanj revolt also appears to have been racially motivated, though there are scholars who argue that there were other motivations behind the rebellion, which will be discussed later.

Ninth century Baghdad was not as racialised as a society as nineteenth century Bahia, but there is evidence to be found in Baghdad literature of an aversion to black Africans, in which there are disparaging portrayals of them. According to a common proverb during that time "The hungry Zanj steals, the sated Zanj rapes."[492] The Zanj revolt triggered anti-black racism among Arabs, and Prophetic traditions were fabricated that demonised blacks. "There is no good in the Zanj; when they are hungry, they steal, when they are satiated, they fornicate."

---

492 A similar saying about the Zanj was falsely attributed to the Prophet Muhammad ﷺ to give people the impression that blacks (Zanj) are animalistic by nature.

Both revolts created fear in the hearts of slave masters. Like the revolt in Bahia, the Zanj rebellion threatened the Abbasid empire, who were a world power at the time. As for the Portuguese, who also believed in 'scientific' racism, the 1835 revolt stirred up an anxiety that accelerated the abolition of slavery in 1888. The Portuguese feared further uprisings, as they were the minority ethnic group in Brazil at the time, and they arranged for some of the rebels to be executed and others sent back to Africa.

According to the jurisprudential definition, the revolts were not *jihāds*, but rather they were insurrections in order to regain freedom. The Zanj revolt signified a unique instance of solidarity among Africans in Iraq, because black soldiers of the Caliph deserted and joined the revolt. Zakariyau Oseni was of the opinion that the Zanj revolt was racially motivated. In his article, *The Revolt of Black Slaves in Iraq Under the Abbasid Administration 869-883 CE*, he writes passionately about the plight of the black man "especially black slaves whose race, more than any other, had suffered the atrocities and humiliation inherent in that ancient institution throughout the course of known history."[493] Oseni argued that the black slaves' resentment of their harsh treatment had been building up for hundreds of years before the actual revolt. According to Oseni, their discontent served as a driving force for their uprising. Theodore Nöldeke, albeit indirectly, also presents the issue of race as an influence on the revolt, as Emily Martha Silkaitis discusses in her article *Modern Takes on Motivations Behind the Zanj Rebellion*. Although Nöldeke does not specifically analyse race as a motivating factor in the Zanj revolt, he calls the rebellion the "negro insurrection".[494] Referring to it as a negro insurrection rather than a slave revolt indicates that, in his view, race was a factor if not the most important factor in the uprising.[495] In aṭ-Ṭabarī's account of the rebellion, race is also implicitly considered a factor in the uprising. Although the *Malê* and Zanj revolt consisted primarily of slaves, freemen, including Abbasid soldiers, participated in the uprisings as they empathised with the plight of the oppressed black slaves.

Religion was also used to justify the oppression and enslavement of blacks in both revolts. The Catholic Portuguese made use of Christian thinkers' interpretations of the Biblical Curse of Ham story in which Noah is reported to have said to his son Canaan, "Cursed be Canaan, a servant of servants shall he be unto his brethren." Black Africans were considered to be descendants of Canaan and thus legitimate slaves as a

---

493 Oseni, 1989, pp. 57-65.
494 Nöldeke, 1963, pp. 149-153.
495 Nöldeke, 1963, pp. 151-173.

result of this prophetic curse. The Catholic Church gave its blessing to the forced enslavement of black Africans by white Europeans, because it considered black Africans to be heathens. In the case of the Zanj revolt, some Arabs made use of weak or fabricated Prophetic traditions as well as *fatwas* (edicts) from Muslim clerics that did not disapprove of the enslavement of East Africans.[496]

The harsh treatment of African slaves under Abbasid rule highlights the change in circumstances for the disenfranchised in the Muslim world. Two centuries prior to the Zanj revolt, the treatment of slaves in the era of the Prophet Muḥammad ﷺ and the Khalifahs who took the right way (*al-Khulafā'ar-Rāshidūn*) was benign. The just treatment of slaves in the early community of Muslims is in stark contrast to the inhumane treatment they endured under the Abbasids. Oseni argues that, although the Zanj revolt was not successful, it did raise fundamental questions about the caliphate's treatment of disadvantaged members of society and about how rulers should help them in accordance with the doctrines of Islam. That said, the Zanj revolt did not bring an end to the institution of slavery under the Abbasids, whereas the *Malê* revolt was able to contribute to the abolition of the institution of Brazilian slavery in 1888.

The role of religion in the Zanj revolt was seen as a significant driving force. Oseni addresses the importance of religion in the Kharijite doctrine and draws a connection between periodic Kharijite uprisings against the Abbasids and the insurrection of the Zanj, suggesting that the slave revolt was actually a Kharijite uprising. Like Oseni, some scholars were of the opinion that, because of their egalitarian tendencies, the Zanj were followers of the Kharijite doctrine. Nöldeke also discusses the importance of religion as a motivational factor in the Zanj revolts and that Kharijite beliefs greatly influenced the leader of the Zanj, beliefs he used to appeal to the East African slaves to rise in revolt. Popovic also cites religion as a crucial factor in the Zanj revolt and claims that religion was used by the Zanj's leader to revolt, but that it may have been a political tool. Silkaities comments, "Popovic felt that religion in the Zanj revolt was no more than a means for manipulation." Religion does appear to have played a significant role in the lives of the Zanj, as they were indeed Muslims, and religion plays a fundamental role in a Muslim's life.

Race or ethnicity also appears to have been a factor in the Zanj rebellion, as is reflected in Arabs' disparaging comments about the Zanj.

---

496 The Catholic Church has since apologised to the descendants of Africans for its involvement in the slave trade, and many Muslim scholars wrote impassioned *fatwas* against the treatment blacks were subjected to.

The Arabs had no 'scientific' theories of racism, in the sense that racism is understood in the modern world, but there is evidence of discrimination against the Zanj, who were viewed as inferior to the Arabs. Similarly, as discussed earlier, black Africans were perceived to be inferior to the white Portuguese, who believed in the doctrine of 'scientific' racism. The Portuguese did not see anything inhuman about their treatment of black Africans who some thought were sub-human. In their treatment of black Africans in a manner worse than their treatment of cattle, race was clearly a motivational factor in the revolt, as is evidenced in the fact that some of the African rebels shouted "kill the whites".

Martial Qualities Of The Zanj

Bacharach concentrates on the involvement of African military slaves[497] and argues that the respective compositions of the Abbasid and Zanj fighting forces effectively led to the defeat of the Zanj. Though primary sources say nothing on the subject, Bacharach argues that the slaves commenced the uprising with little military training, yet within a few years transformed themselves into a formidable army. The Zanj rebels displayed good organisational skills and strong military tactics that were sufficient to allow them to continue the revolt against the established Abbasid army for almost fifteen years. Although the Zanj were not as experienced as the Abbasids in military warfare, they made up for this with courage and determination. They were an oppressed class, who fought valiantly against the exiting social order after years of persecution. Revolts tend to arise out of oppression and the loss of hope. Both the Zanj and Yoruba felt this, which resulted in two of the most devastating slave revolts in the history of the Muslims.

As in the *Malê* revolt, the Zanj also combined religious sentiment with social discontent. The revolts were not *jihāds* in the technical sense but many scholars argue that the spirit of *jihād*, which means to 'struggle', was ever present in their rebellions to gain their freedom.

CONCLUSION

The *Malês* were courageous, intelligent West Africans, who were dedicated to their Islamic faith. They fought valiantly not only for the freedom of their co-religionists but for their non-Muslim fellow Africans. Though many of their uprisings may not have been successful in the military sense, they were indeed successful in maintaining their faith and

---

497 See Jere L. Bacharach's 'African Military Slaves in the Medieval Middle East: The Cases of Iraq (869-955) and Egypt (868-1171)' in *International Journal of Middle Eastern Studies*, pp. 471-495

making a lasting impression on the minds of many modern-day black Brazilians and African Muslims. Just like the Zanj of ninth century Iraq, the *Malês* showed great tenacity and courage in fighting for their freedom. If it were not for the African slaves who betrayed them and informed the Portuguese of their plans, the impact of the 1835 revolt might have spread to other parts of Brazil and further accelerated the abolition of slavery. The Portuguese were particularly worried by the revolt as it was a serious threat to their economy. At the time, Brazil had an economy based on the slave trade, and, like other European slave masters in the Americas and Europe, the one thing the Portuguese feared most was loss of power, both financial and social. White supremacy is as much about power as it is about economics, and elite whites want to rule and govern poor whites and non-whites. And for power, wealth and resources are important. Any disruption to this power structure will cause a reaction from the dominant elite, who want to maintain this racial hierarchy where elite whites remain at the top and blacks at the bottom with a spectrum of shades, ethnicities and races in between.

Like previous slave revolts that occurred in Iraq and Haiti, the lesson of the *Malês* is that change to a white supremacist power-structure cannot come about without sacrifice. Some of the rebels had to sacrifice their lives for the freedom of their fellow Africans. Others had to sacrifice time, resources and wealth. For the *Malês*, who were devout Muslims, these sacrifices were immaterial if it meant that they could protect their faith. This is something that many of them were able to achieve as the 1835 revolt may not have been "successful" in a military sense, but it was most definitely a success in the Islamic sense. Their legacy remains a source of inspiration for Muslims and non-Muslims alike.

CHAPTER 6

WEST AFRICAN MUSLIMS IN RIO DE JANEIRO, PERNAMBUCO AND ALAGOAS

History, in all its justice, has to respect and praise the valuable services which the black has given to this [Brazilian] nation for more than three centuries. In truth, it was the black who developed Brazil.[498]

MANUEL QUERINO

IN 1865, IRAQI TRAVELLER 'Abd ar-Raḥmān al-Baghdādī visited Brazil and his memoirs provide a remarkable insight into the Muslim communities of Rio, Pernambuco and Bahia. A few years after al-Baghdādī's visit, the French ambassador Count Gobineau provided further insight into the Muslim community of Rio. French painter Jean-Baptiste Debret produced valuable lithographs of black and indigenous peoples in Brazil between 1816 and 1831.[499] Debret's paintings demonstrate the presence of African Muslims in Brazil. Together with the German painter Johann Moritz Rugendas (d. 1858), Debret's work is one of the most important graphic documentations of life in nineteenth-century Brazil.

---

498 Manuel Querino, *O Colono Preto como Factor da Civilização Brasileira* (Salvador: Imprensa Official do Estado, 1918). The essay is reprinted in Querino, *A Raça Africana*, pp. 123-152, under the title "o Africano como Colonisador." Source: Bibliographical Essay: Manuel Querino's Interpretation of the African Contribution to Brazil. Burns, 1974, pp. 78-86.

499 See Jean-Baptiste Debret's *Voyage Pittoresque et Historique au Brésil, ou Séjour d'un Artiste Français au Brésil* (A Picturesque and Historic Voyage to Brazil, or the Sojourn of a French Artist in Brazil)

In this chapter, I will look at the reports of al-Baghdādī, French ambassador Gobineau, Brazilian social scientist Nina Rodrigues, Brazilian journalist João do Rio and Afro-Brazilian historian Manuel Querino to gain an understanding of the various African-Muslim communities in nineteenth-century and early twentieth-century Brazil. Particular attention will be paid to the reports of al-Baghdādī, as he was learned in the religion of Islam. I will also compare al-Baghdādī's reports on the African-Muslim communities he came across with the fourteenth-century Berber traveller Ibn Baṭṭūṭah's reports on the Muslim communities he encountered in West Africa. Like al-Baghdādī, Ibn Baṭṭūṭah was well versed in the teachings of Islam, and both were shocked and amazed by the religious and cultural practices of the African Muslims they met. Although the two travel reports were centuries apart, a comparative analysis provides an insightful look at the similarities of the religious and cultural practices of West African Muslims.

MUSLIM COMMUNITIES

After the suppression of the 1835 revolt, the African Muslims fled the persecutions in multiple directions, with many winding up in Rio de Janeiro, Pernambuco, and Alagoas.[500] The fleeing Muslim insurgents found Muslims communities already there in these cities, although not as large as the Muslim community in Bahia. The African Muslims who settled in the various Muslim cities were committed to their faith and were well respected by the non-Muslims. They made a lasting impression, before a great number of Muslims returned back to Africa. As historian Sylviane A. Diouf wrote:

> Muslims strove hard to keep their religion alive, in both the enslaved community and the larger Christian society. But to be a Muslim was more than just respecting the Five Pillars of Islam. It implied a distinctive lifestyle. Especially for West Africans, with their community-based traditions, Islam is a highly communal, public, and visible religion. It dictates and regulates the daily life, material culture, and demeanour of the faithful. To be a Muslim entails following strict dietary rules, behaving in a certain way, dressing in a particular fashion, and interacting with coreligionists and non-Muslims in the manner deemed appropriate. The Africans enslaved in the Americas were no exception; they formed close-

---

500 Gomez, 2005, p. 118

knit communities and distinguished themselves in numerous ways, as they had in their homeland.[501]

Rio de Janeiro

A great number of African Muslim families from Bahia immigrated to *Pequena Africa* (Little Africa), an area of Rio de Janeiro near a well-known square called Praça 11. The Muslims were concentrated in a few streets: São Diogo, Barão de São Félix, Hospício, Núncio and América. Known as *Minas*[502] in Rio, the African Muslims managed, despite persecution by the police, to maintain their houses of prayer until the beginning of the twentieth century.

According to Alberto da Costa e Silva, what made families stay in the area was not religion, but their common origin in Salvador because of which solidarity networks were created between black Catholics, Muslims, and followers of *orishas*. Less rigorous Muslims frequented parties and samba gatherings of people from Bahia who were from other religions. Some of them married members from other religions and denominations of the Bahia Diaspora.[503]

Most of the Africans in Rio had come from the Angola-Congo region, though there were a minority of *Nagôs* (Yoruba) who were deeply involved in urban hawking and selling. According to Reis, Gomez and de Carvalho, the *Nagôs* in Rio were relatively prosperous, as reflected in the high number of manumissions among them. Although they represented nine to 15% of Rio's urban slaves, they corresponded to 50% of paid manumissions between 1840 and 1859.[504]

In 1865, the Iraqi Muslim 'Abd ar-Raḥmān al-Baghdādī wrote his illuminating commentary on the African Muslim communities he encountered during his travels to Rio de Janeiro, Salvador and Pernambuco in a treatise entitled *The Amusement of the Foreigner by all Kinds of Wonderful Things*. Similar to that other more famous Muslim traveller, the Berber Muslim Ibn Baṭṭūṭah who travelled through West Africa in the fourteenth century, al-Baghdādī was impressed by the Muslims' eagerness to learn more about their religion.

---

501 Diouf, 2013, p. 99
502 In Brazil, the term 'Mina' was broadly used to designate Africans of various ethnicities who had been brought from the Bight of Benin.
503 Castro, 2013, p. 17
504 Reis, Gomez and de Carlvalho, 'Rufino Jose Maria' in The Black Atlantic, 1500-2000, p. 68

Originally from Baghdad in Iraq, al-Baghdādī was educated in Damascus in Syria, which later became his adopted homeland. After travelling to Istanbul, which was affectionately referred to as *dār al-sa'āda* (the abode of felicity), al-Baghdādī was commissioned to travel to Basra with two sail-ships. Fate would have it that they did not arrive in Basra but Brazil, as the wind blew them far off course and brought them to Rio de Janeiro. It was in Rio that al-Baghdādī and the Ottoman Muslims first made contact with a black African Muslim, who greeted him with the Islamic greeting, *"as salāmu 'alaikum* (peace be upon you)." Because the African Muslim was dressed in the attire of a Frank [European],[505] al-Baghdādī assumed that he was not a Muslim and had only said the greeting in mockery. Given that al-Baghdādī appears to have been a learned man of Islam, his refusal to respond to the greeting of the Muslim, whom he thought was probably a Christian, is surprising, as the majority of Muslim scholars agree that Muslims should return the greeting of the People of the Book (Jews and Christians), as is reported by the hadith specialist an-Nawawī. This is understood from some Prophetic traditions and the following Qur'ānic *āyat* which informs Muslims:

> *When you are greeted with a greeting, return the greeting or improve on it. Allah takes account of everything.*[506]

After al-Baghdādī proved unable to communicate with the man in Arabic, Turkish or in signs, he felt the man was mocking him, as he only responded in Portuguese. The anecdote indicates that not all African Muslims in nineteenth-century Brazil could understand spoken Arabic, in spite of their ability to read the language, as al-Baghdādī was later to discover.

The people in Brazil were intrigued by their new guests, and requested permission to visit them on their ship, for which the captain granted permission. The *sūdān* (blacks) in particular were very curious about the Ottoman Muslims, and earnestly tried to communicate with them, but to no avail. As al-Baghdādī and the Ottoman Muslims prayed, the small contingent of blacks followed their lead:

> We stood to pray and all of them stood with us. They made their ablutions and prayed just like us. We became convinced that they were Muslims and that they believed in the unity of God. We were greatly enchanted but also astonished. We welcomed them and

---

505 Germanic tribe
506 Qur'ān 4: 86

showered them with our best attentions. Later in the afternoon, using sign language like mutes, they gratefully asked to retire.[507]

A Moroccan Jewish translator, who later accompanied an even larger group of Brazilian Muslims to the ship, explained to al-Baghdādī that "these blacks came from *Bilād al-Sūdān* (the land of the Blacks)," and went on to inform him of how they were captives from various wars in Africa. When asked, the translator said that it was estimated that there were five thousand Muslims in total.[508]

Nina Rodrigues mentions that he had been informed by *alufās* (clerics) from Bahia that in Rio de Janeiro there was a regularly organised mosque run by Arab Muslims but attended by African Muslims. Silva disagrees with Rodrigues as to the origin and upkeep of the mosque in Rio de Janeiro. According to Silva, the 3,093 Arabs who immigrated to Brazil between 1846 and 1889 were predominately Christians fleeing the oppression they were said to have suffered in the Ottoman Empire. The mosque which Rodrigues referred to was actually the house of an *imam* (Muslim leader), which served as a meeting place for Muslims for their Friday prayers.[509]

The *Mina* in Rio de Janeiro

The investigation of the *Mina* in Rio de Janeiro goes against a major trend, which focuses largely on the "Bantu" origins of the local African slave population. Hence this study suggests that the movement of Africans to Rio was more complicated than previously recognised. While the Atlantic crossing did involve two major routes, one from the Bight of Benin to Bahia and the other from Angola to Rio de Janeiro, such a simplification overlooks the lesser but nevertheless important routes from the Bight of Benin to Rio and from Angola to Bahia.[510]

A first point to be discussed is terminology. As Robin Law has observed that the words Yoruba, *Nagô*, and Lucumi have been used in different ways, in both Africa and the Americas, depending on place and time. The term Lucumi was in use as early as the sixteenth and seventeenth centuries, whereas *Nagô* appears only in the eighteenth century. Also the word Lucumi was more frequently used in Spanish America, while the Portuguese, French, and English tended to use the word *Nagô*. Law

---

507 Al-Baghdādī
508 Whether the five thousand refers to the number of Muslims in Rio de Janeiro or Brazil is not mentioned in the text.
509 Castro, 2013. p. 17
510 Soares, 2001, p. 232

found no reference to the word earlier than the mid-eighteenth century. According to Parés, the word *Nagô* first appears in Bahia in 1734.[511] According to oral tradition and several biographies, the Yoruba began to be recognised as a representative ethnic community in Rio de Janeiro in the 1830s, when the Gbe-speakers[512] were still the majority among the *Mina*. Yet, by the 1850s, the Yoruba had already become the major group. The second half of the nineteenth century witnessed the growth of a strong new Yoruba ethnic community composed of Catholics, *orixá* worshippers, and Muslims, religious divisions that apparently did not weaken ethnic identification.[513]

At the beginning of the seventeenth century, the population of Rio de Janeiro was about 3,850 people: 750 Portuguese, 100 Africans, and 3,000 Amerindians and people of mixed descent. In 1613, an epidemic decimated the indigenous population, which led to the demand for African slaves. In 1699, the Portuguese Crown officially opened commercial relations with Rio de Janeiro and the Mina Coast, which had been trading regularly with Bahia since 1670. There is little information about the origins of these slaves.[514]

In a series of articles published between 1904 and 1908, the journalist João do Rio noted that a portion of this *Mina* community could speak *Eubá*. This appears to be the first reference to the use of Yoruba language in Brazil, or at least in Rio. His guide was a man named Antônio. The Yoruba of Rio de Janeiro could be classified into two groups: *orixá* worshippers and Muslims. The first group was led by various *babalorixá* (the leader of the *orixá* houses), the second by the *lemano*, the Muslim *imām* who supervised a mosque on Barão de São Felix street. According to Antônio, the Yoruba-speaking *Mina* taught their children to speak their language and, if they could afford to do so, even sent them to Lagos for their education. As Antônio told João do Rio, "whoever can speak Yoruba (*Eubá*) can cross over from Africa and live among the blacks of Rio."[515]

A memorable character was Assumano Henrique Mina do Brasil, who died in the 1930s. He was probably the last Muslim of this African

---

511 Soares, 2001, p. 232

512 The Gbe languages form a cluster of about twenty related languages stretching across the area between modern day Ghana and western Nigeria. Gbe languages include; Ewe, Fon, Aja, Gen and Phla-Pherá.

513 Soares, 2001, p. 232

514 Soares, 2001, p. 233

515 Soares, 2001, p. 241

community. His father was Muḥammad Salim, and his mother, Fāṭima Mina do Brazil, was born in Brazil. His name provided him an identity and also revealed his diverse ancestry.[516]

Alagoas

Alagoas is a state situated in the eastern part of northeastern Brazil. Abelardo Duarte reported that a *Malê* conspiracy is said to have taken place in the state as early as 1815. The Muslim community there apparently continued into the early twentieth century, when Moraes Filho wrote about *A Festa dos Motos* (Feast of the Dead) in the city of Penedo, site of one of the largest black populations in Alagoas. Michael Gomez said that "[Nina] Rodrigues and [Abelardo] Duarte identify it as a Muslim observance (or an Islamically-influenced rite, in the view of the latter), involving as it did prayers and long periods of fasting, abstinence from alcohol, the coordination of rites with phases of the moon, the donning of long white tunics (recalling the *Nagô abadá*), and the sacrifice of sheep."[517] According to Duarte, the religious practice of Muslims was loose, as they mixed Islamic rituals with aspects of Catholicism and traditional African religions.[518] Bastide reported that the Muslim community in Alagoas continued in existence up until 1912.[519]

Pernambuco

Just as in Rio de Janeiro, most Africans living in Pernambuco had come from Angola or the coast of West Africa. There was a contingent of *Nagô* Muslims in Recife from Bahia, in addition to the influx of *Nagôs* from West Africa. Al-Baghdādī said about the African Muslims he came across whilst in Pernambuco:

> I found Muslims here more alert and dynamic then in the first town. I was happy about that. They follow two men. One is called Yusuf; he is young and very sharp. The second one is named Sulayman; he is the opposite. He did not follow us when we declared it to be *Ramadan* in Rio de Janeiro and put it at its right moment. He was still fasting the month of *Shabān*. He has his followers, and they really follow him. Their conditions in praying and fasting are like the others, except for the fact that they are more inclined to magic,

---

516 Soares, 2001, p. 242
517 See Gomez, 2005, pp. 122-123; Duarte, 1958, pp. 42-50; Rodrigues, 1982, p. 68; Mello Moraes Filho, 1946, p. 333
518 Castro, 2013, p. 18
519 Bastide, 2007, p. 145

geomancy and prophecy. Because of these practices, they hide less than the people in the first town. The Christians thus believe in them and what they show of their intentions. They give them money, and they fulfil their desires in all cases. This, even though the blacks know only the name of what they are trying to invoke. Sometimes, what they ask for coincides with destiny and providence; so, they relate it to their acts and their science. Despite this, in six months, they showed more improvement than those who did not leave me during my entire stay.[520]

LITERACY AND QUR'ĀNIC SCHOOLS

The Muslims' literacy set them apart and became as distinctive as a physical trait. A slaveholder was impressed with literate 'Samba'. In Brazil, illiteracy among men and women was not restricted to the slave quarters. Many male colonialists and most women could neither read nor write, because literacy in European cultures was reserved for wealthy males. The furthest some societies went was to allow the poor and women to read for religious reasons — so that they could have access to the Bible — but not to write. As a result, a large number of Brazilian colonialists who came from what were considered lower Portuguese classes were illiterate or barely literate. In Brazil, education was reserved for the privileged few; the movement toward mass literacy started only in the nineteenth century.[521] Prior to that, Gilberto Freyre writes, "the simplest rudiments were so little diffused that not infrequently wealthy ranchers of the interior would charge their friends of the seaboard to secure for them a son-in-law who, in place of any other dower, should be able to read and write."[522]

Because the literacy rate was high in Muslim Africa, and because of the concentration of learned Muslims in Brazil, the literacy rate among Muslims was probably higher than it was among slaveholders.[523] Thomas Ewbank, a founder and president of the American Ethnological Society, who travelled to Brazil in 1845, dined with a Bahian planter who had this opinion about the *Mina* of Bahia: "Shrewd and intelligent they preserve their own language, and by that means organise clubs and mature schemes of revolution that their Pernambuco brethren have repeatedly attempted to carry out. Some write Arabic fluently and are vastly superior to most

---

520 Al-Baghdādī
521 Diouf, 2013, pp. 159-160
522 Freyre, 1986, p. 299
523 Diouf, 2013, p. 160

of their masters."⁵²⁴ As Brazilian scholar Freyre remarked, "in the slaves' sheds of Bahia in 1835, there were perhaps more persons who knew how to read and write than up above, in the Big Houses."⁵²⁵ Reading is an inexhaustible source of knowledge and one which is respected amongst West Africans. Sylviane A. Diouf writes:

> The hostility toward the literate Africans that slaveholders expressed did not arise from the fear that the men would somehow trick them by forging passes or getting access to useful news. Even though the slaveholders discovered that the Africans' literacy in Arabic could indeed be hazardous to their safety, the animosity had another origin. In the eyes of the slaveholders, the Muslims' literacy was dangerous because it represented a threat to the whites' intellectual domination and a refutation of the widely-held belief that Africans were inherently inferior and incapable of intellectual pursuits. The Africans' skills constituted a proof of humanity and civilisation that did not owe anything to Christians' supposed civilising influence. If these men and women could read and write, if they were not the blank slates or the primitive savages they had been portrayed to be in order to justify their enslavement, then the very foundation of the system had to be questioned. This issue was so potent that some North Americans felt compelled to deny the Africanness of the "outstanding" Muslims and to portray them as Arabs.⁵²⁶

Muslim *Minas*, who were often literate, were seen as proud, courageous, and hard-working people who saved toward manumission. Rio police took the potential threat represented by the *Mina*, and particularly the *Malês*, very seriously, and tried hard to follow their activities closely in the hope of avoiding a repetition of the events in Bahia.⁵²⁷

In 1849 Rio's chief of police reported:

> Some *Mina* blacks resident in this city gathered in secret associations where, under impenetrable mystery, there were practices and rites that became suspect; they communicated among themselves through ciphered writings, and it also came to my knowledge that

---

524 Ewbank, 1856, p. 439
525 Freyre, 1986, p. 299
526 Diouf. 2013, p. 161
527 Reis and Mamigoniam, "Nagô and Mina: The Yoruba Diaspora in Brazil" in *The Yoruba Diaspora in the Atlantic World*, p. 100

the blacks of the same nation existing in Bahia corresponded with them, and so did those from São Paulo and Minas [Gerais].[528]

The police raid at one such gathering place yielded "an infinity of papers written with different inks and in unknown characters, some books also in manuscript" that, "translated, interpreted, and deciphered" by experts revealed their contents: "prayers taken from the Qur'ān, in spurious Arabic, to which were grafted words in the *Mina* and *Malê* languages." However, the chief of police, admitting that the *Malês* had the right to private worship, found no reason to keep them in prison. He decided, nevertheless, to keep an eye on them, for:

> It is natural that the spirit of religious associations will take them further, and that the followers it will gather, fanatic by its principles, will use this religion to justify and convey the ideas against slavery, for I see, in all that has been apprehended in the recent searches, exactly what had also been found in Bahia at the time of the slave uprising in 1835.[529]

African Muslims' love of knowledge stems from the Qur'ānic injunctions to read and seek knowledge. In the West African city of Timbuktu, books were one of the most valuable commodities. The Muslims of Timbuktu were precocious readers and writers, which caused the sixteenth-century Moroccan scholar Leo Africanus, during his trip to the African city, to remark on the intellectual and professional classes:

> Here there are many doctors, judges, priests, and other learned men, that are well maintained at the king's cost. Various manuscripts and written books are brought here out of the Barbarie and sold for more money than any other merchandise.

Buying And Selling Qur'āns
Al-Baghdādī relates:

> One day, I went to the market to look at the masterpieces of the Creator. I passed through a small shop where a man was selling

---

528 Cited by Carlos Eugênio Líbano Soares, 2001, *A capoeira escrava e outras tradições rebeldes no Rio de Janeiro, 1808-1850*, Campinas: Unicamp, pp. 387, 389; Reis and Mamigoniam, "Nagô and Mina: The Yoruba Diaspora in Brazil" in *The Yoruba Diaspora in the Atlantic World*, p. 100

529 Cited by Carlos Eugênio Líbano Soares, 2001, *A capoeira escrava e outras tradições rebeldes no Rio de Janeiro, 1808-1850*, Campinas: Unicamp, p. 389; Reis and Mamigoniam, "Nagô and Mina: The Yoruba Diaspora in Brazil" in *The Yoruba Diaspora in the Atlantic World*, pp. 100-101

Christian books. I entered to see if I could find an Arabic-Portuguese dictionary. I found a Qur'ān printed in France, containing no mistakes or faults, that was acceptable. I asked the owner how he had gotten it. He said: "It is my job to get books from different countries to beautify my shop in other people's eyes. This one came from France and it is been some time that it is lying here; nobody in this country wants it." I said: "How much do you want for it?" He said: "One French Lira." I said: "Can you get more of these?" He said "Yes." I paid him a deposit and after some time the Qur'āns came and the Muslims bought them and I recuperated the money I had paid the seller. People acquired copies of the Qur'ān and circulated them. This problem is solved.[530]

In 1869, just a few years after al-Baghdādī's visit to Brazil, the ambassador of Rio, Count de Gobineau wrote that the French bookshop, Fauhon and Dupont, used to sell approximately one hundred copies of the Qur'ān to black Brazilian slaves and freemen in Rio de Janeiro. A copy of the Qur'ān was very expensive (36 to 50 French francs), and the Muslims had to make great sacrifices in order to acquire one. Some of them bought the Qur'ān in instalments, often taking a full year to pay for it. The French bookshop also imported books on Arabic grammar with explanations in European languages:

> Most of these *Mina*, if not all, are outwardly Christians but actually *Mussulmans* [Muslims]. Since this religion would not be tolerated in Brazil, they practice it in secret, and most of them are baptised, with names borrowed from the calendar. Notwithstanding outward appearances, I have been able to ascertain that they faithfully cherish the beliefs they bring with them from Africa and zealously hand them on, since they study Arabic thoroughly enough to understand the Koran, at least roughly. This book is sold in Rio at 15 to 25 cruzeiros or 36 to 40 francs by the French booksellers Fauchon and Dupont, who import copies from Europe. Slaves who appear to be quite poor are willing to make the greatest sacrifices to acquire this volume, going into debt to do so and sometimes taking a year to pay off the bookseller. About a hundred copies of the Koran are sold every year .... So far as I know, the existence of a Mussulman colony in America has not previously been noted....It explains the particularly vigorous attitude of the *Mina* Negroes.[531]

---

530 Al-Baghdādī
531 Raeders, 1934, pp. 75-76

Alberto da Costa e Silva points out that the selling of copies of the Qur'ān indicates two things: first, that there were numerous African Muslims in Brazil; and second, that the African Muslims were devout, as they would not have the sacred text "written in any other language except that in which God dictated His words to [Prophet] Muḥammad."[532]

Despite the fact that copies of the Qur'ān were being sold in Rio de Janeiro and were being recited by the African Muslims, many did not understand Arabic or the basic tenets of Islam. Al-Baghdādī said that the African Muslims he met were a small community and that "their hearts are sick from ignorance. Because they left their country when they were very small, none of them have learned the religion of the Chosen Prophet [Muḥammad]." Al-Baghdādī stayed in Rio de Janeiro for a short period before travelling to Bahia and Pernambuco "in order to teach the Muslims who reside in this country for the sake of the Lord of the Worlds."[533]

Religious Learning And Qur'ānic Schools

In the early twentieth-century Brazilian journalist João do Rio's observations of the African Muslims in Rio he noted that there were African Muslim *imams* or *alufá* who were knowledgeable about the Qur'ān and taught their students the tenets of Islam in secret Qur'ānic schools. To become an *alufá* required a period of "great study", and rigorous exams.[534] After passing the exams, the student would be taken along the streets of a distant suburb on horseback in triumph, followed by the faithful.[535]

Al-Baghdādī's comments about Rio de Janeiro's African Muslims' lack of religious knowledge conflicts with João do Rio's observations. The article of João do Rio indicates that the African Muslims he came across were very studious and knowledgeable about Islam. The apparent conflict between the views of al-Baghdādī and João do Rio can be explained by surmising that al-Baghdādī may not have come across knowledgeable Muslims, whereas João do Rio appears to have done. Another explanation could be due to the fact that João do Rio was not knowledgeable about Islamic practices and so he would not know whether the African Muslims he came across were knowledgeable about the religion. A third explanation, as cited by Alberto da Costa e Silva, could be due to the fact that the number of Muslims in Rio de Janeiro

---

532 Silva, 2001, pp. 72-82
533 Al-Baghdādī
534 Gomez, 2005, p. 122
535 Silva, 2001, pp. 72-82

had diminished greatly by the time João do Rio wrote his articles about them.[536]

Interestingly, in the reports of al-Baghdādī, Rodrigues and João do Rio there isn't any mention of contact between the African Muslims and the Arab Muslims in Brazil during the era of 'whitening' the country. Nonetheless, although the African Muslims were isolated, they were also extremely eager to learn more about Islam and read the Qur'ān. Nikolay Dobronrav writes in 'Literacy Among Muslims in Nineteenth century Trinidad and Brazil' in *Slavery, Islam and Disapora*:

> Scholars have been aware of Brazil's Arabic-script tradition since the early nineteenth century. Sometime between 1819 and 1826, José Bonifácio d'Andrada, a famous Brazilian political and scholar, interviewed some Hausa people in Brazil about the geography of central Africa. In the course of the interviews, d'Andrada was informed of a Hausa man known as Francisco. He was an *imam* and teacher in Hausaland, well versed in Arabic; he could also write.

Brazilian sociologist Gilberto Freyre argued that the African Muslims were politically and culturally influential in Brazil. Recent studies by historians 'Abdullāh Hakim Quick and Paul E. Lovejoy support Freyre's assertions. Whilst not enamoured with Islam, the Portuguese had nonetheless learned to respect the religion that previously ruled the Iberian Peninsula. Thus, it is not surprising that African Muslims in Brazil were viewed differently from non-Muslim Africans.[537] Freyre informs us:

> Some of those imported into Brazil were from areas of most advanced Negro culture. This explains why some Africans in Brazil – men of Mohammedan faith [i.e. Muslims] and intellectual training – were culturally superior to some of their European, white, Catholic masters. More than one foreigner who visited Brazil in the nineteenth century was surprised to find the leading French bookseller of the Empire's capital had among his customers Mohammedan Negroes of Bahia; through him these remarkable Negroes, some of them ostensibly Christian but actually Mohammedan, imported expensive copies of their sacred books for secret study. Some of them maintained schools, and the Mohammedan in Bahia had mutual-aid societies through which a number of slaves were liberated.[538]

---

536 Silva, *2001, pp. 72-82*
537 Gomez, 2005, p. 93
538 Gomez, 2005, p. 96

Freyre continued:

> In the dark of the slave huts, with teachers and preachers from Africa to give instruction in reading the books of the Koran in the Arabic, and with Mohammedan schools and houses of prayer functioning here ... slaves who were schooled in the Koran preached the religion of the Prophet, setting it over against the religion of Christ that was followed by their white masters, up above in the Big Houses.

Arabic Documents

Rolf Reichert analysed thirty Arabic documents found in the aftermath of the 1835 slave revolt. In his book, *Os Documentos Árabes Do Arquivo Público Do Estado Da Bahia (Arabic Documents from Public Archives of the Bahia State)*, Reichert separated the documents into three types: *Cocanicos Textos* (Qur'ānic texts); *oaraçes Islamicas – não-Coranicas* (Islamic prayers – not Qur'ānic), *Amuletos, Exercicios de Escrita, etc* (Amulets and Written Documents). "In a society where even the dominant whites were largely illiterate, it was hard to accept that African slaves possessed such sophisticated means of communication,"[539] João José Reis commented. In spite of the high price of paper at that time, African Muslims used it extensively to records matters of their faith. The documents were used to help memorise prayers and Qur'ānic *āyats*. One of the flawless texts found is a copy of the opening chapter of the Qur'ān written in Arabic:

> *In the name of Allah, All-Merciful, Most Merciful*
> *Praise be to Allah, the Lord of all the worlds,*
> *the All-Merciful, the Most Merciful,*
> *the King of the Day of Repayment.*
> *You alone we worship. You alone we ask for help.*
> *Guide us on the Straight Path,*
> *the Path of those You have blessed,*
> *not of those with anger on them, nor of the misguided.*

Reichert took stock of twelve amulets that were believed to have been a source of *barakah* (Divine blessing). One of the amulets read,

> *In the name of Allah, All-Merciful, Most Merciful*
> *God will protect you from all men*
> *God will not (guide) the infidels*
> *[He] will protect you from all men, God will not [guide] the infidel*
> *God will protect you from them*

---

539 Reis, 1995, p. 106

God will not [guide] the infidels
If God wills and with God comes victory.

The Arabic documents formed the subject of a fascinating postgraduate study by Priscilla Leal Mello from the University of Fluminense. In her study, Mello traced the names of the authors of the documents, who were mainly enslaved *Nagô* (Yoruba) and Hausa men. Despite their horrific conditions, the African Muslims continued to preach the word of Allah and teach their African brethren about the importance of faith and steadfastness. The Arabic documents reflected the intelligence of the African Muslims and that they were committed to their religion and education. Reis writes, "these papers revealed that among their slaves were people highly instructed in the language of the *Koran*, people who left their marks in perfect calligraphy and correct grammar. These were Africans who, even though they were slaves in Bahia, had certainly been members of an intelligentsia in Africa, if not members of the wealthy merchant classes. They had enjoyed social privileges that allowed them to spend much of their time in intellectual pursuits."[540]

The Importance Of Education

Islam is a religion of knowledge. The first revealed Qur'ānic *āyat* instructed the Prophet Muḥammad ﷺ to *"Recite in the name of Your Lord...."* Seeking knowledge is an essential part of Islam. As Allah is the source of knowledge, those who have knowledge know the Most Knowledgeable. From the Islamic perspective, the Qur'ān is the source of Divine knowledge, thus being truly indispensable to the Muslim. This explains why African Muslims in Brazil attempted to get hold of the sacred book even in slavery.[541] As Diouf said:

> The ways in which the Muslims obtained their Qur'āns reveal not only a strong attachment to their religion and willingness to preserve their intellectual skills, but also an extraordinary spirit of abnegation, enterprise, and organisation, in the worst possible circumstances.[542]

The African Muslims showed great tenacity and were successful in their endeavours as they were able to demonstrate a large degree of autonomy. Diouf adds, "They made decisions, planned, gathered information,

---

540 Reis, 1995, p. 106
541 Diouf, 2013, p. 166
542 Diouf, 2013, p. 173

tried different avenues, built networks, and tested alternatives, all unbeknownst to white society; and they met with some success."[543]

This autonomy manifested itself in a bold way in their sustaining and sharing Islamic education. After the 1835 revolt, the Bahian Qur'ānic schools were discovered by the police. It was established that Dandará (also known as Elesbao do Caemo), an emancipated Hausa, had given classes in Arabic and conducted prayers in a tobacco shop that he owned in the Santa Barbara market. During his trial, he admitted that he was a schoolteacher in his country and that he had taught the youngest in Bahia, "but not to do evil." A native-born woman testified that Aprigio, a free African, had been writing in "strange characters" and, with others, had gathered men from their nations "to whom they taught to write with pointers dipped in ink they had in a bottle." Another witness, Lieutenant Ladislau dos Santos Titara, had observed this African group, which met in Mangueira Street, and had heard that Aprigio taught others of his nation how to read. Aprigio, the freeman, was not the only teacher; slaves, too, were involved in pedagogy. As we saw before, Sanim, a Nupe whose Christian name was Luís, gave classes in the house of an emancipated Muslim, the *Nagô* Belchor da Silva Cunha, a bricklayer. Sanim had been a teacher and a *marabout* in his country, and in addition to Nupe, he spoke Hausa and Yoruba. Even these few testimonies give an idea of the significance of the schools and the number of teachers who operated in Bahia at a time when Islam was illegal and the people of African descent were nominally Christians.[544]

Not only did schools exist in Bahia, but they were fully equipped. During the police searches, dozens of wooden slates were confiscated in the houses of Manuel Calafate, Dandará, José da Costa, Joaquim, Miguel Goncalves, and others. Besides the writing slates, the police confiscated papers written in Arabic. These have been studied and translated by different scholars, but the first to decipher them was an enslaved Hausa *marabout* named Albino. He was requested to do so by the police, who thought the papers in strange characters might be subversive propaganda. Nine pieces of paper were presented to him. The fourth document, he explained, was a sort of alphabet lesson that students used to learn how to write Arabic, and the seventh was a writing lesson.[545]

The extent of the Islamic writings by both the enslaved and free African Muslims demonstrated the Muslims' dedication to education. Thirty

---

543 Diouf, 2013, p. 173
544 Diouf, 2013, pp. 173-174
545 Diouf, 2013, p. 174

of the documents seized by the police were published in Brazil in 1970. Some of the texts were written with perfect calligraphy and grammar, and testify to the high level of knowledge attained by the Muslim intelligentsia before their deportation to Brazil. Other papers were apparently written by beginners; they copied, time and again, passages from the Qur'ān as a way of memorising them and exercising their writing skills.[546]

WOMEN AND MARRIAGE

The Africans in Brazil were polygynous because of their Islamic and African cultural heritage. The reports of al-Baghdādī indicate that the women were independent in their choice of their marital partners and practised their religion, even if it was against the wishes of their husbands.

Religious Practices

Al-Baghdādī was appalled by the fact that the African Muslim women were unveiled and that they did not adhere to the *sharī'ah* in regards to fasting and the laws of inheritance. He wrote about the Muslim women in Rio:

> Their women have no desire to fast. They do whatever they want just like Christian women who spend their time sleeping. They go to the markets without covering themselves; they drink what is forbidden. The wife inherits half of her husband's fortune when he dies; the other half is divided equally among his children, without respect to gender. It is impossible to get this problem solved. I have told them and shown them how to divide the inheritance according to Islam and the way Allah showed in His Glorious Book. I said: "The ones who accept these rules will be all right; the ones who do not conform to them and do whatever they want in taking from the Christian religion; do not argue about this and keep your affairs secret." I said this after I saw the women's opposition to the Islamic way of sharing and their total lack of acceptance.[547]

Clothes

Harvard scientist Louis Agassiz and his wife, who travelled through Brazil in 1865, left a description and two drawings of Muslim women that provide some insight into the distinctive dress of the Muslim women. Aggasiz wrote that they used to wear "a high muslin turban, and a long,

---

546 Diouf, 2013, p. 174-
547 Al-Baghdādī

bright-coloured shawl, either crossed on the breast and thrown carelessly over the shoulder, or if the day be chilly, drawn closely around them, their arms hidden in its folds."[548] This attire made an impact on the black population in general, as Gilberto Freyre remarked in the 1930s: "In Bahia, in Rio, in Recife, in Minas, African garb, showing the Mohammedan [Muslim] influence, was for a long time worn by the blacks. Especially by the black women who sold sweets and the vendors of *alua.*"[549] The women's many-layered skirts, their shawls, and their head-covers were all elements of the Prophetic customary practice (Sunnah) of covering the body modestly.[550]

Alberto Henschel (d. 1882), a nineteenth-century German-Brazilian photographer, took a number of photographs of Brazilians of African descent. Some of the women photographed wore head-ties in the traditional style of both Muslim and non-Muslim west-African women.

African Muslims used to wear white metal, silver or iron rings, as a way of identifying each other on the street, as they did not wear distinctive clothes in public out of fear of being persecuted. According to the testimony of a *Nagô* freedman from Bahia called João, "white rings ... were the badge worn by members of the *Malê* society to recognise each other." When the Muslims greeted one another, they would strike their rings as a sign of brotherhood. After the 1835 rebellion, the police confiscated dozens of rings. One witness testified that "immediately on the day after the blacks' insurrection, everyone took the rings off their fingers." Almost a century later, pioneering ethnologist Manuel Querino (d. 1923) wrote that African Muslims in Bahia wore silver rings only as wedding rings.[551]

Marriage And Sexual Relationships
The *nikāḥ* (marriage) of African Muslims in Brazil was according to the *sharīʿah* and Sunnah as practised in their native lands. Querino observed the marriage practices of Muslims in which the *imam* presided over the contract. The *imam* would begin by calling upon the couple to think carefully, so that they would never regret the action they were about to take. After giving them time to reflect, he would ask if they were marrying each other sincerely and of their own freewill. If the reply was yes, the bride, "dressed in white, her face covered with a tulle veil,"

---

548 See Louis and Elizabeth Agassiz's *A Journey in Brazil*
549 Freyre, 1986, p. 319
550 Diouf, 2013, pp. 107-108
551 Reis, 1995, p. 104

placed a silver ring on the finger of her future husband, and he, "dressed in wide Turkish-style trousers," gave his future wife a silver chain as they repeated the words *"Sadaca do Alamabi* – I give this to you in the name of God."[552] Manuel Querino writes:

> They would then kneel, and the *imām* began the ceremony. He reminded them of their duties and exhorted them to behave fittingly and not to violate their ritual obligations. In conclusion the young couple stood and kissed the imam's hand. The ceremony over, everyone adjourned to the house where the banquet was to be held. While everyone else remained seated, the bride walked to the centre of the room, clapped her hands, sang a song, and returned to her place. Then came the wedding banquet of chicken, fish, fruit etc., which included no alcoholic beverages.[553]

Querino observed that some African Muslims in Brazil openly practised polygamy, or more accurately, polygyny. Plural marriages had been widespread in Africa long before Islam, which limits the number of wives a man may have to four. Although there is not much information available about the marriages of slaves in Brazil, we are aware that polygyny was practised by some, though it must have been difficult. For Africans to find even one wife presented difficulties because of the huge imbalance in the numbers of the two sexes in the country. The shortage of women meant that many Africans could not form families, which had a decisive impact on the survival of Islam. Brazilian priests deplored the Muslims' practice of polygyny as immoral. Africans, for their part, certainly saw these unions as legitimate marriages, since their religious leaders would have sanctified them.[554] Speaking about the Muslims' polygynous marriages, Querino said it was a "hygienic measure" and regarded marriage as "a real cult, observed with rigour, in the same way as a fraternal friendship."[555]

Muslim women were subject to a strict code of honour. "Any woman who failed in her conjugal duties was a general outcast; no one would show her any favour. Nevertheless the husband could not beat her. An unfaithful wife was allowed to leave her house only in the evening, chaperoned by someone whom her husband trusted."[556] Multiple-wife

---
552 Bastide, 2007, p. 147
553 Querino, pp. 117-118; Bastide, 2007, p. 147
554 Diouf, 2013, pp. 123-124
555 Querino, *Costumes africanos*, p. 70
556 Bastide, 2007, p. 147; Querino, *Costumes*, 118

families are common practice amongst the Yorubas, and thus it is not surprising that Querino observed this practice amongst African Muslims in Brazil, many of whom are likely to have themselves been Yoruba.[557] About the sexual and marital relationships in Bahia, al-Baghdādī writes:

> In this town there are more Muslims than in the first [Rio de Janeiro]. But, they are not eager to learn. Their ignorance is the same as in the first town, with one difference. When a man wants to marry, he chooses the girl from the people who are like him. He takes her to live with him until she gives him children. If she happens to keep his secrets, runs his home, loves him, he marries her officially, and she will be called his wife. If he sees that she does not do very well, which means she did not please him, he sends her along with their children, to her father. They do not see this action either as horrible nor unwanted.
>
> The first thing I did in this city is that I cleaned up this state of degeneration. I started calling them little by little. Men came with the women they were trying out. They repented and I made a contract between them with the payment of a dowry. I informed them that divorce in the religion of Islam is allowed. I showed them how to separate, if they needed, as best I could. I fasted the month of Ramadan in this city. The Muslims wanted to pray *tarāwīḥ*. I led them in this prayer with only ten prostrations, aiming to facilitate the task for them. Their women are like the [European] Frank ones; they do not veil themselves. If a woman loses one of her family members, like her husband, father, or brother, she goes to the church, gives alms to the monks for them to read the Bible and grant forgiveness to her dead. I gathered groups of women together several times, and I defended them smoothly doing that. The majority of Muslim children turn out to be Christians because as they come to this world, they see the festivals of the Christians in the churches, with the abundance of patriarchs, clergymen, music, the beauty of dances. The child sees that only his father is different. He thinks that his father is a liar and joins the majority. He takes the path of corruption and debauchery. I suggested to some Muslims among the rich that they should not let their children go out until they reach their majority, and they should educate them. Some of them followed my instructions. I stayed in this town about a year,

---

557 Johnson, 1921, p. 113

completely occupied with teaching Muslims and improving their behaviour as best I could.[558]

Ibn Baṭṭūṭah had a similar experience of the looseness of women's dress and the apparent 'immodesty' of Africans when he visited Mali almost five hundred years before al-Baghdādī's trip to Brazil. While in Walata, Ibn Baṭṭūṭah wrote:

> Their women are of surpassing beauty, and are shown more respect than the men. The state of affairs amongst these people is indeed extraordinary. Their men show no signs of jealousy whatever; no one claims descent from his father, but on the contrary from his mother's brother. A person's heirs are his sister's sons, not his own sons. This is a thing which I have seen nowhere in the world except among the Indians of Malabar. But those are heathens; these people are Muslims, punctilious in observing the hours of prayer, studying books of law, and memorising the Koran. Yet their women show no bashfulness before men and do not veil themselves, though they are assiduous in attending the prayers. Any man who wishes to marry one of them may do so, but they do not travel with their husbands, and even if one desired to do so her family would not allow her to go.
>
> The women there have "friends" and "companions" amongst the men outside their own families, and the men in the same way have "companions" amongst the women of other families. A man may go into his house and find his wife entertaining her "companion" but he takes no objection to it. One day at Iwalatan I went into the qadi's house, after asking his permission to enter, and found with him a young woman of remarkable beauty. When I saw her I was shocked and turned to go out, but she laughed at me, instead of being overcome by shame, and the qadi said to me "Why are you going out? She is my companion." I was amazed at their conduct, for he was a theologian and a pilgrim [to Makkah] to boot. I was told that he had asked the sultan's permission to make the pilgrimage that year with his "companion" – whether this one or not I cannot say – but the sultan would not grant it.[559]

Like al-Baghdādī, Ibn Baṭṭūṭah was shocked at West African women's dress and liberal attitude towards the intermingling of the sexes. Such

---

558 Al-Baghdādī
559 See Ibn Battutah, *The Travels of Ibn Battutah*

practices are disapproved of in Berber and Arab culture as well as in Islam. The West African Muslims al-Baghdādī met are most likely to have been Yoruba, who have a more liberal attitude towards Muslim women's dress, compared to the Hausas. It is not uncommon to see Yoruba Muslim women without *ḥijāb* on a regular basis, even though they are very strict in observing their compulsory prayers and other religious duties. Despite being a religious injunction, the adoption of the *ḥijāb* is not as stringent amongst the Yorubas as it is in other Muslim communities.

Prostration

Al-Baghdādī wrote:

> One day, one of their elders, in company with another one, came to me. They started greeting me with *salām*, as was shown in the guide I had given them, because the way they used to greet was that when a man entered, he prostrated himself, taking his hat off. He threw himself to the ground, and put his face and head in the sand until he was given permission to rise. This was done only in the circles of learned people. With the grace of the Almighty, I got rid of this affair among the men but it continues among some women, I replied to their greeting stood up to welcome them and had them sit.[560]

In Yoruba culture, the prostration of reverence is a custom that is still commonly practiced amongst Yoruba peoples irrespective of their faith. The traditional Yoruba prostration of men to greet elders is called *doba'le*. The female form of the greeting is called *ikun'le*. The prostration which al-Baghdādī observed in Brazil is a modified version of the traditional Yoruba greeting. It is strictly prohibited for Muslims to prostrate to anyone other than the Creator, whether prostrating in worship or out of reverence. The evidence for this prohibition lies in an incident that occurred during the time of the Prophet Muḥammad ﷺ when one of his companions arrived from Sham and prostrated to the Prophet because he saw the people of Sham prostrating to their high priests and patriarchs out of reverence. Upon seeing his companion prostrate to him, the Prophet ﷺ informed him:

> Don't do this, for were I to instruct [anyone] to prostrate to another [person], I would instruct women to prostrate to their husbands, due to the right that they have over them.[561]

---

560 Al-Baghdādī
561 Abu Dawud, Ahmad, Ibn Majah

Prostration is for the Creator alone, and this was an issue that al-Baghdādī wanted to inform the Muslim women in Brazil about as it is a cultural practice which conflicts with the Islamic teaching about worship.

BLACK HEROINES

Many of the heroines of African descent are neglected in discussions of Afro-Brazilian history. The reason is the lack of information about them and disregard for the important role they played. Three heroines are often mentioned when discussions about great Brazilian women of African descent take place: Luísa Mahin, Maria Felipa and Dandara who have been the subjects of recent feature films, books and articles. The women's religions are unclear, as some sources indicate that they may have either been Muslim or followers of a traditional African religion. Nevertheless, they are likely to have inspired African Muslim women in Brazil in their fight against racial and religious discrimination.

Luísa Mahin

Luísa Mahin was said to be *Nagô* (Yoruba), and her religion was either Islam or the Yoruba religion. Mahin was born on the coast of Africa in the early nineteenth century, and was brought to Brazil as a slave. She was involved in the articulation of all the slave uprisings and revolts that shook the former province of Bahia in the early decades of the nineteenth century. A *quituteira* (confectioner) by profession, she was highly influential in the uprisings. If the uprising of the *Malês* had been victorious, Luísa would have been recognised as Queen of Bahia. As a black African, she always refused baptism and Christian doctrine, and one of her natural sons, Luís Gama (1830-1882), became a poet and a leading abolitionist. After being discovered, Luísa was persecuted and fled to Rio de Janeiro, where she was found, arrested and deported, possibly to Angola, although there is no proof of that.[562]

Maria Felipa

In 1823, Maria Felipa led dozens of black men and women and indigenous people in strategic escapes through the woods after burning forty-two Portuguese warships docked at Convento Beach in Itaparica, Bahia. She fought and resisted the barriers of prejudice, actively participating in forming the history of Salvador.

---

562 http://blackwomenofbrazil.co/2013/07/27/rewinding-the-clock-one-year-ago-this-month-the-luiza-mahin-and-maria-felipa-awards-honored-the-various-accomplishments-of-black-women/

Dandara

Dandara, Zumbi's wife, was a queen and warrior. She was also mother of his three children. The meaning of her name is *a mais bela* (the most beautiful). Dandara contributed throughout the growth of Palmares society to its familial, socio-economic and political organisation. Speaking about the life of Dandara, anthropologist Maria de Lourdes Siqueira said:

> Dandara is the most representative of female leadership in the Republic of Palmares. She participated in all the battles, all the fights, in everything that was created, organised, experienced and suffered there. Little is known about her origins: where she was born, where she came from. Some literature says that she had ancestry in the African nation of Jeje Mahin.[563]

A natural leader and courageous warrior, Dandara fought until her death.[564]

RETURN TO AFRICA

In the early nineteenth century, numbers of Afro-Brazilians gained their freedom and returned to West Africa. Between the 1820s and 1890s, a large number of these returnee Afro-Brazilians arrived in Lagos, Nigeria where they were known as *Aguda* (the Yoruba word for Catholic). Although the majority of the Afro-Brazilians who arrived in West Africa were reportedly Catholic, there were also Muslims amongst them. Afro-Brazilians, and Sierra Leonians (known as Saros) constituted the largest and most dominant groups of African descendants returning to Africa from the Americas. The Saros were the descendants of Yorubas from southwestern Nigeria and the Afro-Brazilians were primarily of West African and Angolan origin. In her study of Afro-Brazilian architecture, Marjorie Alonge writes;

> The Saro community lived in the Saro quarter alongside the Afro-Brazilian community in the Brazilian quarter of Lagos. Like the Afro-Brazilians, they also produced a significant genre of architecture and a distinctive creole culture during the nineteenth century. The Saro architectural style was largely based on a combination of the British colonial style and the Yoruba traditional

---

563 http://oglobo.globo.com/sociedade/historia/descrita-como-heroina-dandara-mulher-de-zumbi-tem-biografia-cercada-de-incertezas-14567996
564 http://blackwomenofbrazil.co/2014/11/20/dandara-the-wife-of-zumbi-brazils-greatest-black-leader-was-a-revolutionary-warrior-in-her-own-right/

spatial arrangement. Although the Saros contributed immensely to the development of architecture in Lagos, they were not nearly as renowned for their building design and construction skills as the Afro-Brazilians.[565]

Afro-Brazilian Architecture In West Africa

French-born ethnographer, photographer and historian Pierre Verger (d. 1996) spent a number of years studying the relations between and shared cultures of Brazil and the Bight of Benin (modern day Togo, the Republic of Benin and Nigeria). Fluent in Yoruba, Verger gained scholarly renown by publishing a series of works, including a book on the Afro-Brazilian slave trade that illuminated and explored the common threads of African and black Brazilian culture. Verger outlined four stages in the Atlantic slave trade, the fourth being the return of the former Afro-Brazilian slaves to West Africa.

In West Africa, Afro-Brazilian returnees were known as Agudas or Tabom in Ghana and Saros or Creoles in Nigeria. The freed slaves migrated to the Bight of Benin in the early 1830s. Afro-Brazilians in West Africa built a new identity by asserting their Brazilian heritage, which is still present in West Africa today. In her research of the Afro-Brazilian cultural heritage, Alinta Sara of SOAS[566] identified the influence that Afro-Brazilians had on West-African architecture. She points out that Afro-Brazilian architecture was a popular genre in West Africa from 1835 to 1950. However, "decolonisation and the subsequent adoption of new modern architectural styles generated a continued decline in Afro-Brazilian houses [and mosques]."[567]

In the late nineteenth century, Oloye Muḥammad Shitta, a wealthy Sierra Leonean-born Nigerian merchant and philanthropist, built the Shitta Bey Mosque in Lagos, Nigeria. He was of Yoruba descent and was later awarded the title 'Bey' by the Ottoman Caliph as an honour and in recognition of his rank as leader of the Muslim community in Lagos. He was later known as Muḥammad Shitta-Bey. He commissioned a mosque to be built according to the design of the Brazilian João Baptista da Costa and in 1892 it was constructed by a Nigerian builder called Sanusi Aka. Shitta-Bey financed the construction of the mosque, which was officially

---

565 See Marjorie Moji Dolapo Alonge's *Afro-Brazilian architecture in Lagos State: a case for conservation (PhD Thesis)*.
566 SOAS is the School of Oriental and African Studies University of London. It is a leading institution for the study of Asia, Africa and the Middle East.
567 http://www.pambazuka.net/en/category/features/88387

inaugurated by the Governor of Lagos in 1894. The Shitta-Bey mosque is one of several examples of religious architecture in Nigeria and Benin that were built by former slaves who returned to West Africa from Brazil. The magnificent architectural design of the Brazilian baroque mosques in West Africa is a part of the great Afro-Brazilian legacy in West Africa.

In an article about that legacy in present-day Nigeria architecture, journalist James Brooke writes:

> Nigeria's Brazilian architecture is a legacy of the thousands of freed slaves who returned to West Africa in the 19th century. Trained as carpenters, cabinetmakers, masons and bricklayers in Brazil and borrowing from the baroque styles popular in Brazil through the 18th century, these freedmen stamped their exuberant and individualistic style on doorways, brightly painted facades and chunky concrete columns.[568]

---

568 http://www.nytimes.com/1987/03/26/garden/in-nigeria-touches-of-brazilian-style.html

CHAPTER 7
AFRICAN PERSONALITIES

THE HISTORY OF Africans during the Brazilian time of slavery is largely based on police documents and autobiographies of former slaves that have been systematically examined in recent decades by researchers. The biographies of three great historical figures from Africa – Rufino José Maria, Mahommah Gardo Baquaqua, and Efunroye Tinubu – provide an insight into the lives of Africans during the Brazilian transatlantic slave trade, and are valuable in trying to understand the realities of African lives in nineteenth-century Brazil. They were all caught up in the slave trade in different capacities, but each one working admirable exploits in their struggle for freedom and justice.

RUFINO JOSÉ MARIA

In September 1853, Rufino José Maria was arrested in Recife, capital of the province of Pernambuco. A former slave, Rufino had bought his freedom and returned to West Africa to further his knowledge of Islam, before returning again to Brazil, where he fathered a child and continued to pursue his Islamic education with frequent trips to Brazil before his wrongful arrest. After his release, he settled in Recife until his death. Biographers of Rufino inform us that the African Muslim's story "reminds us that Islam had a real and vital role in the lives of millions of people African descent on all continents bordering the Atlantic Ocean."[569]

Brazilian historians João José Reis, Flávio dos Santos Gomes, and Marcus Caravalho collaborated to study Rufino's life and published their results in the fascinating biography, *O Alufá Rufino: Tráfico, escravidão e liberdade no Atlântico Negro (c. 1822 – c. 1853)* – Rufino, the Religious Cleric: Trafficking, Slavery, and Freedom in the Black Atlantic (1822 – 1853).[570]

---
569 Mamigonian, 2010, p. 65
570 A shorter version of the biography featured as an article in *The Human Tradition in The Black Atlantic 1500-2000*.

Rufino's story was gathered from police documents after his arrest, and from newspaper accounts at the time of his interrogation.

Early Life
He was born in the early nineteenth century in Oyo, one of the more powerful states in the Bight of Benin's hinterland in West Africa. Yorubaland was dominated by Oyo up until the last decade of the eighteenth century. The Oyo Empire's decline began after a rebellion against the ruler in 1796 led by a powerful military commander called Afonja. Rufino grew up at a time of political turmoil, in which there was a civil war and a major slave rebellion led by a Fulani Muslim preacher in 1817. Rufino informed the police during his interrogation that he had attended a Qur'ānic school in Oyo and that his father was an *alufa* (*imām*). It appears that Rufino stayed in Oyo up until the age of seventeen, when he was made a prisoner of war by Hausa Muslims. Despite the fact that Rufino was a Muslim,[571] he was enslaved by Muslims from a different tribe. Hausa and Yoruba were not always on the best of terms in West Africa.

In the first half of the nineteenth century, Oyo had a sizeable Muslim community formed of immigrants, primarily Hausa slaves and local Yoruba-speaking people. Literate Muslims, both local and foreign, lived by making amulets, which were very popular at the time. The Oyo Empire ruled much of Yorubaland, which had a large Muslim community composed not only of its Yoruba-speaking inhabitants but also Hausa slaves. In 1817, tensions between Muslims and Oyo traditionalists erupted in the form of a slave rebellion. It was in this context of rebellion and turmoil that Rufino was captured at the age of seventeen by Hausa Muslims and sold to Portuguese slave traders.

Enslaved In Bahia
In 1822 or 1823, Rufino arrived in Bahia during the independence struggle against the Portuguese garrison. The Portuguese occupied the capital city of Salvador, while Brazilians controlled the surrounding sugar plantations. In July 1823, Bahia joined with the rest of the country to form the Brazilian Empire under Pedro I after the Portuguese surrendered. Rufino was bought by a druggist, who lived in Salvador, and trained as a cook. He stayed in Salvador, where thousands of his countrymen arrived in Bahia as slaves as a result of the civil wars that took place in

---

571 It is not permitted for a Muslim to enslave a free Muslim.

Yorubaland. By the early 1830s, Yorubas represented close to 30% of African-born slaves in Salvador.

Rufino lived in Bahia for eight years. Between 1830 and 1831, he travelled south to the province of Rio Grande do Sul with his young master, the druggist's son. Rufino was then sold to a merchant who kept him for less than two years, when the merchant became bankrupt and moved to Montevideo to escape creditors. He was then auctioned and bought by a high-court judge called José Maria Peçanha, as part of his master's bankruptcy.

Freedom
Yorubas in Bahia were very industrious and many saved enough money to buy their freedom. Rufino obtained his freedom in November 1835, the year of the infamous slave revolt. After fifteen years as a slave, he paid 600,000 reais (approximately £210 pounds sterling) for his freedom. As was the practice for most freedmen, Rufino adopted his former master's name, becoming Rufino José Maria. He then travelled to Rio de Janeiro between late December 1835 and January 1836.

Although a minority in the capital of the Brazilian Empire, in which the majority of Africans were from the Angola-Congo region, the *Nagôs*/Yorubas were deeply involved in urban hawking and selling. Their relative prosperity is reflected in the high number of manumissions among them. Despite representing only 9% to 15% of urban slaves, they responded for 50% of paid manumissions between 1840 and 1859.

Rufino later became a cook on the transatlantic slave-trade route as a crew member aboard ship. He travelled to Angola and then returned to Brazil, arriving in Pernambuco. The transatlantic slave-trade was a risky business at that time as it had been declared illegal by the Brazilian government in 1831. In the early 1840s Rufino embarked on another trip to Africa aboard a large vessel called the *Ermelinda*.

Trips To Africa
On October 27, 1841, a British patrol-ship captured the *Ermelinda* off the coast of Angola. The ship had no slaves on board, but, according to the British, it was equipped for the slave trade. The *Ermelinda* was then taken to Sierra Leone, where it arrived on December 9, 1841. Rufino was one of the few crew members to be interrogated. Although there is no evidence of his deposition, there is a record of an accusation he made against a British officer of insulting, hitting, and wounding him. Rufino was not easily intimidated by the British and even insulted the British aggressor,

calling him a "dog". Rufino was a very self-assured man, who was proud of his heritage and religion.

The crew of the *Ermelinda* were later acquitted and the ship was returned to Pernambuco on May 1842, after a lack of evidence that the ship was equipped for the slave trade, with Rufino again on board as a cook. In Pernambuco he spent a few months working as a vendor of fabric while still on the payroll of his former employers. Then he returned to Sierra Leone, but his purpose for this trip was to further his religious knowledge.

Rufino studied in Fourah Bay, where he improved his knowledge of Islam and the Arabic language, and stayed in Sierra Leone until he was proficient in the Arabic language before returning back to Brazil.

Return To Brazil
Before Rufino eventually settled with his son in Recife in 1845, Rufino spent three months in Rio de Janeiro and Bahia, where his son was conceived. In Recife, he began his profession as a healer, practicing a type of Islam incorporating practices that reflected African religious traditions.

In September 1853, a number of freedmen in Recife, including Rufino, were arrested on suspicion of their involvement in a slave conspiracy. The authorities feared that the conspirators secretly taught slaves how to read and write in Arabic, which could lead to an uprising. During his interrogation by authorities Rufino was described as a "fat old man nearly fifty years old". Rufino had a respectable and intelligent demeanour. Despite his strong African accent, he spoke Portuguese fluently. He was very calm during his interrogation, but frowned at ironic remarks made against his religion, and smiled dryly as he answered some of their questions, showing that he had nothing to hide or fear. The Brazilian police determined that he was not a threat and released him after two weeks.

Rufino was arrested because he had numerous Islamic manuscripts in his house. The police found an old manuscript copy of the Qur'ān that he had brought from Sierra Leone in his house, prayer books, Arabic language manuals, and a notebook that he declared "teaches the medicines." According to Rio de Janeiro's newspaper *Jornal do Commercio*, in which Rufino's arrest was reported, he explained that "his religion was the one practised by [Prophet] Muḥammad and included in the Qur'ān", and explained with great knowledge and intelligence the full doctrine of that religion, which ... he said he "would not give up even if he were to be sent to the gallows."

When the Brazilian judge told him that Catholicism was the "true religion", he answered that "some learn one religion when they are born, others [learn] others, and on which [religion] was the best that was a question to be decided only when the world ends." Asked why he did not use his supposed religious power as a healer to improve his own lot, Rufino said that he was satisfied with what he owned because "some people asked God for wealth, but he only asked for knowledge, and the two precepts did not fit in the same bag."

Rufino's extraordinary story gives a glimpse of the range of possibilities open to Africans in spite of the heavy pressure of slavery. His story is even more remarkable because of his experience as a slave who obtained his freedom and worked as a trader, and then returned to Africa in pursuit of sacred knowledge, later to return back to Brazil and teach people about Islam until he passed away. It is truly an admirable and inspiring story.[572]

MAHOMMAH GARDO BAQUAQUA

Mahommah Gardo Baquaqua is the only former Brazilian slave known to have written an autobiography.[573]

Early Life

He was born in the city of Zoogoo in Central Africa in 1824, near Djougou in modern day Benin, to a Muslim merchant family. Mahommah's father was a Muslim whose manner were described as "grave and silent". He was committed to Islam and would regularly pray ṣalāh. Mahommah's mother may not have been a Muslim, although a woman of rank and wealth, as was his father, who was a travelling merchant.

Mahommah's father wanted his son to become a practising and committed Muslim like his older brother, who was a teacher, adviser, and diplomat on behalf of distant non-Muslim chiefs as well as a supplier of Qur'ānic amulets. Mahommah, however, was not interested in pursuing Islamic education like his brother. He was shielded by his mother from both father and brother.

Mahommah's mother helped her son obtain the position of messenger for a local king to whom she was related. Whilst working for the king, Mahommah participated in some unsavoury activities, as he "plundered

---

572 See João José Reis, Flávio dos Santos Gomez, and Marcus J. M. de Carvalho, 'Rufino José Maria (1820s-1850s): A Muslim in the Nineteenth-Century Brazilian Slave Trade Circuit,' in Mamigonian, 2010, pp. 65-75

573 In his own words, Mahommah gives an account of his life in the book, *The Biography of Mahommah Gardo Baquaqua: His Passage from Slavery to Freedom in Africa and America.*

for a living" and acquired a predilection for alcohol. His drink problem would get him into many misfortune later in his life.

Around 1846, when Mahommah was on his way back to Djougou to visit his mother, some supposed friends hired praise-singers to flatter him, then got him drunk, and took him to a party, from which he awakened the next day to discover himself a prisoner and a slave. Mahommah had been tricked and, in this predicament, he would cry for his mother. He was taken to the coast and shipped to Pernambuco.

Enslaved In Brazil

Originally he was sold to a local baker, but soon after was sold to a ship's captain based in Rio de Janeiro. After living in bondage for two years, in 1847 his owner took him on a voyage to New York City, where local abolitionists helped him secure his freedom. Mahommah spent the next two years in Port-au-Prince, Haiti with the Baptist Free Mission Society. In 1849 Mahommah, previously a Muslim, was baptised and converted to Christianity. The Baptist missionaries continued to hope he would return to Africa to become a Christian missionary.

Freedom

In 1849, Mahommah returned to New York State, where he enrolled in New York Central College in McGrawville, New York, remaining there until 1853. He moved to Chatham, Canada West in modern day Ontario in 1853. In 1854 Mahommah's autobiography was recorded as an oral narrative, which he narrated mostly in Portuguese, as he knew little English and no French, although he spoke fluent Dendi and Arabic, which had been his native languages in Africa. Although Mahommah's oral narrative was recorded in Portuguese while he resided in Canada, its intended audience was the anti-slavery movement in the United States.

A year later in 1855, Mahommah travelled to Britain, still intending to return to Africa one day as a missionary. In 1857, however, all records of Mahommah disappeared, and it is not known where or how he lived out his days. It is possible that he was able to get back to his birthplace in Africa, or he may, as historian Allan D. Austin states, "have reverted to the religion of his youth."[574]

---

574 See Robin Law and Paul E. Lovejoy's *The Biography of Mahommah Gardo Baquaqua*; Sylvaine A. Diouf's *Servants of Allah: African Muslims Enslaved in the Americas*; Allan D. Austin's African Muslims in Antebellum America: Transatlantic Stories and Spiritual Struggles,

EFUNROYE TINUBU

Efunporoye Osuntinubu Olumosa (often shortened to Efunroye Tinubu) (d. 1887), was a Yoruba woman trader and anti-slave activist from the Egba clan in the city of Abeokuta, the capital of Ogun State in West Africa. Tinubu was an active opponent of the British colonial government in the nineteenth century. She was a former slave trader, who, having realised the enormous differences between domestic slavery in Africa and the inhumane treatment of slaves in Europe and Brazil, became actively opposed to slave trading. In 1855, she spearheaded a campaign against Brazilian and Sierra Leonean immigrants in Lagos, whom she felt were actively trying to oppose the *oba* (king) and did not respect local customs.

Trader

Tinubu became the first *Iyalode* (First Lady) of the Egba clan, and was able to build a financial empire through trading in arms and salt with Europeans. After her first husband died, Tinubu started trading tree bark and leaves to make a living and to support her two sons. She learned valuable market skills from Osunsola, her grandmother, who traded in tree bark, roots, herbs, and leaves. She also learned business skills from her mother, Nijeede, who had been a food seller.

In 1833, after Tinubu married Adele, an exiled *oba* (king) of Lagos, she began to gain economic and political power. Moving to the coastal city of Badagry, Tinubu and her family established new connections, building a successful business, trading in salt and tobacco from Europeans for slaves from Abeokuta. After Adele returned to his throne in 1835, Tinubu moved to Lagos. Two years late, Adele died and Oluwole, his son, was made the new *oba*. During the Yoruba wars of the 1840s and 1850s, Tinubu's trade network expanded through a monopoly on slaves and palm oil, and through offering firearms obtained from the Europeans. After the accidental death of Oluwole, Tinubu arranged for Akintoye, her brother-in-law, to mount the throne in Lagos, for which he rewarded her with the ownership of valuable stores in Lagos. She made other investments in Lagos's business district and built a huge personal residence to reflect her new status. Tinubu was also rumoured to own three hundred and sixty personal slaves. By 1845, as European nations repudiated slavery and turned to commercial crops from West Africa, she expanded her empire by controlling the major new items of commerce: palm oil, coconut oil, and cotton.

Anti-Slave Activist

She then established foreign trade alliances and brokered deals with European and Brazilian political and military leaders. In Lagos, she was the major conduit between European traders and merchants from the Nigerian countryside. She fell from power in Lagos when she challenged Benjamin Campbell, the British Consul, who railed against her economic hegemony and secret slave trading with Europeans and Brazilians. She, in turn, publicly castigated Campbell for his infringement of royal authority and sovereignty in Lagos. She organised a plot to remove Campbell, but, in May 1856, before it could be implemented, Campbell confronted her with British gunboats and demanded her exile from Lagos. In the face of superior British military power, Tinubu was forced back to Abeokuta. She nonetheless remained a major trader in the interior of Nigeria until her death in 1887.[575]

---

575 See Gloria Chuku's "Tinubu, Efunroye," in *Dictionary of African Biography;* and "Tinubu, Madame (1805-1887)," in *New Encyclopedia of Africa.*

CONCLUSION
THE RACIAL DEMOCRACY OF ISLAM IN BRAZIL

THE BRAZILIAN IDEAL of racial democracy, which has been a vision of Brazilian intellectuals since the 1930s, was spoken about in principle by the Prophet Muḥammad ﷺ fourteen hundred years ago:

> *Mankind! Your Lord is one and your forefather is one. An Arab has no superiority over a non-Arab nor a non-Arab over an Arab, nor a red person over a black person nor a black person over a red person except in taqwā.*[576] *"The noblest among you in Allah's sight is the one with the most taqwā."*[577][578]

The true concept of racial equality was demonstrated in the racial harmony of the early days of Islam in the city of Madīnah, in which there was no preferential treatment given to Arabs or non-Arabs, blacks or whites. Many of the black and non-Arab companions of the Prophet ﷺ intermarried with and shared in the benefits of power with the Arabs. The believers were brothers and there was no vast wealth inequality between Arabs and non-Arabs, as there is in Brazil between whites and non-whites. Although there were instances of racial discrimination and colour prejudices, the Prophet ﷺ purified his Companions of any forms of bigotry in his general purification of their character.

Everyone harbours prejudices and may discriminate racially from time to time, but the problem lies in acting such prejudices out. From a Qur'ānic perspective, racists lack genuine discrimination in a wholesome sense, i.e. discernment:

---

576 *Taqwā* is the fearful awareness of Allah that leads to avoiding His prohibitions and complying with His commands.
577 Qur'ān 49: 13
578 Narrated by al-Bayhaqī in *Shu'ab al-īmān* from Jābir.

Among His Signs is the creation of the heavens and earth and the diversity of your languages and colours. There are certainly Signs in that for every being.[579]

As the aforementioned Qur'ānic *āyat* states, human beings' skin complexions are merely signs of the omnipotent Creator who creates whatever He wills. Those who are unaware of this, lack insight and are ignorant. Thus to be a racist is to be an ignoramus.

Mankind! We created you from a male and female, and made you into peoples and tribes so that you might come to know each other. The noblest among you in Allah's sight is the one with the most taqwā. Allah is All-Knowing, All-Aware.[580]

The perfect racial harmony of the city of Madīnah during the time of the Prophet Muḥammad ﷺ is one to which Muslim individuals and communities aspire. The Muslim community in Salvador that I visited is trying to become a faith-based community like that of the early Muslims in Madinah. Often small communities are those that embody the true spirit and message of Islam, as they do not have the political distractions with which larger communities and nations have to deal.

Indeed Islam can provide the framework for the racial harmony that Brazil has become identified with, although it is in reality a myth. Islam can provide this, as one of the new Muslims informed me: "In Islam, we are all equal in the eyes of Allah. This was how it was at the time of the Prophet and how it should be!"

Unfortunately the racial harmony of Islam that I witnessed in the Muslim community of Salvador, and which is said to be the case in Rio de Janeiro due to the large number of new Muslims, is not the case in other Muslim communities in Brazil. Vitória Peres de Oliveira reports that in São Paulo, for example, it is common for Brazilian new Muslims to complain of the 'Muslims by birth', who are mostly Arabs and are unwelcoming towards the new Muslims. She said, "It is very probable that the effort that these 'new Muslims' make to promote Islam is partly caused because they do not feel part of a close community that gives them plausibility." And she continued, "The new Muslim women of Juiz de Fora said that the Lebanese women feel that they are more complete Muslims than the new converts. Ethnic conflicts appear to exist

---

579 Qur'ān 30:22
580 Qur'ān 49:13

wherever there is an active community of immigrants."[581]

One of the biggest challenges facing Brazilian converts, particularly female converts to Islam is marriage shaykh Ahmad of the Salvador Mosque informed me. According to the Qur'an, Muslim women are only permitted to marry Muslim men. That being the case, many Brazilian Muslim women of African descent experience difficulty in finding a spouse as Arab-Brazilian men tend to favour Arab-Brazilian women as marital partners. The issue is one which is a cause of concern in Salvador, Rio de Janeiro and Recife where there are a number of Afro-Brazilian Muslim women who are unable to find suitable husbands. The issue is further exacerbated by the fact that many of the Afro-Brazilian Muslim men are not ready for marriage according to the Shaykh because of their socio-economic plight. Interestingly enough Brazilian women converts who are fair in complexion and not phenotypically African do not experience as much of a problem finding a spouse as their black Brazilian counterparts as whiteness remains the colour of female beauty in much of the Muslim communities as it does in Brazilian society at large.

The Muslim community of Salvador exemplifies one of Islam's core features, which is a celebration of and appreciation for diversity. The Qur'an states, "*Among His Signs is the creation of the heavens and earth and the diversity of your languages and colours. There are certainly Signs in that for every being.*"[582] A Brazilian Muslim residing in Salvador by the name of Abdul Waleed informed me of what he believed to be the special community of Muslims in Salvador due to the courage of the city's African Muslims legacy. Abdul Waleed, who embraced Islam ten years ago and travelled to a number of Muslim communities across the country felt that the Muslim community in Salvador is unique because of its tolerant attitudes towards other Muslims, irrespective of their appearance, gender or assumed level of faith commitment.

Adam, a recent convert living in Salvador, said that Brazilians want to hear about Islam; they are not prejudiced, and are a tolerant people who, if they hear the message, are open-minded about Islam. He said, "Brazilians think Islam is a cultural thing. They do not believe that you can be a Brazilian and a Muslim. When I tell them that Islam is not a culture specific for one type of people, they are intrigued and ask me to talk about it. In my opinion we need more active *dawah* (invitation to Islam) like how the Christians actively proselytise on TV, radio and newspapers." Adam's brother, Ismail added, "For Islam to spread in

---

581 Peres, 2006.
582 Qur'ān 30:22

Brazil, it is important to focus on who is Allah and what the message of Islam is, rather than spending time on the rules of *ḥalāl* (permitted) / *ḥarām* (prohibited)." He said that, after he read a book about the life of the Prophet Muḥammad ﷺ, he cried and said to himself, "this religion is amazing. People think that Muslims are harsh and unapproachable. It is important to focus on the message of Islamic monotheism and use wisdom in informing people about Islam." He went on to say, "When you find out about who Allah is and what He has promised us, it makes you want to do whatever you need to do to make Allah happy." Teary-eyed, he continued, "It's not [only] about the rules, Islam is a way of life. I want to be one of Allah's favourites, *inshā'Allāh* (God-willing)."

APPENDIX I
CATEGORIES OF WHITENESS AND BLACKNESS IN BRAZIL

IN 1976 IGBE conducted its *National survey by household sample* (PNAD). In the survey, Brazilians were asked to describe their own race/colour, 136 categories were given. The survey's findings reveal the richness and complexities of self-identification amongst Brazilians.

1.	Acastanhada	Somewhat chesnut-coloured
2.	Agalegada	Somewhat like a Galician
3.	Alva	Snowy white
4.	Alva-escura	Dark snowy white
5.	Alvarenta	Snowy white
6.	Alvarinta	Snowy white
7.	Alva-rosada	Pinkish white
8.	Alvinha	Snowy white
9.	Amarela	Yellow
10.	Amarelada	Yellowish
11.	Amarela-queimada	Burnt yellow
12.	Amarelosa	Yellowy
13.	Amorenada	Somewhat dark-skinned
14.	Avermelhada	Reddish
15.	Azul	Blue
16.	Azul-marinho	Sea blue
17.	Baiano	From Bahia
18.	Bem-branca	Very white
19.	Bem-clara	Very pale
20.	Bem-morena	Very dark-skinned
21.	Branca	White
22.	Branca-avermelhada	White going on for red

23.	Branca-melada	Honey-coloured white
24.	Branca-morena	White but dark-skinned
25.	Branca-pálida	Pale white
26.	Branca-queimada	Burnt white
27.	Branca-sardenta	Freckled white
28.	Branca-suja	Off-white
29.	Branquiça	Whittish
30.	Branquinha	Very white
31.	Bronze	Bronze-coloured
32.	Bronzeada	Sun-tanned
33.	Bugrezinha-escura	Dark-skinned Amerindian (derogatory)
34.	Burro-quando-foge	Disappearing donkey
35.	Cabocia	Copper-coloured (refers to civilised Amerindians)
36.	Cabo-verde	From Cabo Verde
37.	Café	Coffee-coloured
38.	Café-com-leite	Café au lait
39.	Canela	Cinnamon
40.	Canelada	Somewhat like cinnamon
41.	Cardão	colour of the cardoon, or thistle (blue violet)
42.	Castanha	Chestnut
43.	Castanha-clara	Light chestnut
44.	Castanha-escura	Dark chestnut
45.	Chocolate	Chocolate-coloured
46.	Clara	Light-coloured, pale
47.	Clarinha	Light-coloured, pale
48.	Cobre	Copper-coloured
49.	Corada	With a high colour
50.	Cor-de-café	Coffee-coloured
51.	Cor-de-canela	Cinnamon-coloured
52.	Cor-de-cuia	Gourd-coloured
53.	Cor-de-leite	Milk-coloured (i.e. milk-white)
54.	Cor-de-ouro	Gold-coloured (i.e. golden)
55.	Cor-de-rosa	Pink
56.	Cor-firma	Steady-coloured
57.	Crioula	Creole
58.	Encerada	Polished
59.	Enxofrada	Pallid
60.	Esbranquecimento	Whitening

61.	Escura	Dark
62.	Escurinha	Very dark
63.	Fogoio	having fiery-coloured hair
64.	Galega	Galician or Portuguese
65.	Galegada	Somewhat like a Galician or Portuguese
66.	Jambo	Light-skinned (the colour of a type of apple)
67.	Laranja	Orange
68.	Lilás	Lilac
69.	Loira	Blonde
70.	Loira-clara	Light blonde
71.	Loura	Blonde
72.	Lourinha	Petite blonde
73.	Malaia	Malaysian woman
74.	Marinheira	Sailor-woman
75.	Marrom	Brown
76.	Meio-amarela	Half-yellow
77.	Meio-branca	Half-white
78.	Meio-morena	Half dark-skinned
79.	Meio-preta	Half black
80.	Melada	Honey-coloured
81.	Mestiça	Half-caste/mestiza
82.	Miscigenação	Miscegenation
83.	Mista	Mixed
84.	Morena	Dark-skinned, brunette
85.	Morena-bem-chegada	Very nearly *morena*
86.	Morena-bronzeada	Sunburnt *morena*
87.	Morena-canelada	Somewhat cinnamon-coloured *morena*
88.	Morena-castanha	Chestnut-coloured *morena*
89.	Morena-clara	Light-skinned *morena*
90.	Morena cor-de-canela	Cinnamon-coloured *morena*
91.	Morena-jambo	Light-skinned *morena*
92.	Morenada	somewhat *morena*
93.	Morena-escura	Dark *morena*
94.	Morena-fechada	Dark *morena*
95.	Morenão	Dark-complexioned man
96.	Morena-parda	Dark *morena*
97.	Morena-roxa	Purplish *morena*
98.	Morena-ruiva	Red-headed *morena*

99.	Morena-trigueira	Swarthy, dusky *morena*
100.	Moreninha	Petite *morena*
101.	Mulata	Mulatto girl
102.	Mulatinha	Little mulatto girl
103.	Negra	Negress
104.	Negrota	Young negress
105.	Pálida	Pale
106.	Paraíba	from Paraiba
107.	Parda	Brown
108.	Parda-clara	Light brown
109.	Parda-morena	Brown *morena*
110.	Parda-preta	Black-brown
111.	Polaca	Polish women
112.	Pouco-clara[583]	Not very light
113.	Pouco-morena	not very dark-complexioned
114.	Pretinha	Black – either young, or small
115.	Puxa-para-branca	Somewhat towards white
116.	Quase-negra	Almost negro
117.	Queimada	Sunburnt
118.	Queimada-de-praia	Regular, normal
119.	Queimada-de-sol	Sunburnt
120.	Regular	Regular, normal
121.	Retinta	Deep-dyed, very dark
122.	Rosa	Rose-coloured (or the rose itself)
123.	Rosada	Rosy
124.	Rosa-queimada	Sunburnt-rosy
125.	Roxa	Purple
126.	Ruiva	Redhead
127.	Russo	Russian
128.	Sapecada	Singed
129.	Sarará	Yellow-haired negro
130.	Saraúba	Untranslatable
131.	Tostada	Toasted
132.	Trigo	Wheat
133.	Trigueira	Brunette
134.	Turva	Murky
135.	Verde	Green
136.	Vermelha	Red

---

583 Also Preta in other publications

APPENDIX 2

CHRONOLOGY OF SLAVE REVOLTS IN BAHIA, 1807 – 1835

YEAR (MONTH)	PLACE	LEADERSHIP	PARTICIPANTS
1807 (May)	Salvador and the Reôncavo	Hausas	7 Africans slaves and free men
1809 (January)	Nazaré das Farinhas	Hausas	More than 300 Hausa slaves
1814 (February) 1814 (March)	Reôncavo Iguape	Hausas Hausas	Estimated number of 250 rebels Slaves and freemen
1816 (January) 1816 (February)	Santo Amaro & São Francisco do Conde		African-born slaves
1822 (May) 1822 (Sept.) 1822 (Dec)	Itaparica Island São Marcos Mata Oscura & Saboeiro		280 slaves African slaves and freemen Almost 200 slaves
1824	Engenho, Santana Ilhéus		Creole slaves
1826 (Aug) 1826 (Dec)	Cachoeira Pirajá, Urubú Quilombo	African-born slaves Yoruba	African-born slaves Less than 50 slaves
1827 (Mar) 1827 (Apr) 1827 (Sept)	Cachoeira São Francisco do Conde Abrantes	African-born slaves	African slaves from different plantations Slaves from 10 plantations
1828 (Mar) 1828 (Apr) 1828 (Sept) 1828 (Nov)	Itapuã Cachoeira Iquape Santo Amaro	African-born slaves Unknown African-born slaves African-born slaves	Large number of slaves from the city and neighbouring plantations Revolts took place on 17 and 21 April Almost 40 slaves revolted on the Engenho Novo plantation Slaves on the Engennho do Tanque
1829 (Oct) 1829 (Nov)	Cotegipe Countryside		Slaves Exact location of the revolt is unknown
1830 (Apr)	Salvador	Yorubas (Nagôs)	More than 100 urban slaves
1835 (Jan)	Salvador	Yorubas (Nagôs)	600 urban and rural slaves and freemen

APPENDIX 3
INDEX OF IMAGES

Image 1 - Al-Idrisi's world map, 1154.

Image 2 - Depiction of Mansa Musa, ruler of the Mali Empire in the 14th century, from a 1375 Catalan Atlas of the known world drawn by Abraham Cresques of Mallorca. Mansa Musa is shown holding a gold nugget and wearing a crown. Mansa Musa is reportedly the richest human being in history. Mansa Musa succeeded his brother Mansa Abubakari II, who was the previous ruler of the Mali empire before he set off an expedition with 2,000 ships to cross the Atlantic, eventually landing on the coast of Brazil in 1312 in Recife, northeastern Brazil.

Image 3 - A print shows African captives being taken on board a slave ship. (Credit: Print Collector/Getty Images).

Image 4 - "Feitors corrigeant des negres" ("Plantation overseers disciplining blacks") by Jean-Baptiste Debret.

Image 5 - A Brazilian family at dinner on a coffee plantation, circa 1820. The woman feeds scraps to a small black child, whilst a female slave cools the air with a large fan by Jean-Baptiste Debret.

Image 6 - Depiction of Zumbi of Palmares, the inspirational leader and warrior chief of Palmares, an independent African kingdom situated in northeastern Brazil.

Image 7 - Painting of victorious Africans celebrating in the *quilombo dos Palmares*, an independent African state in 17th century Brazil.

Image 8 - 'Black Surgeon Applying Cupping' by Jean-Baptiste Debret in 1826 (Credit: Private Collection/Bridgeman Images).

Image 9 - *Joueur d'Uruncungo* (Player of *Uruncungo*) by Jean-Baptiste Debret.

Image 10 - Newspaper article from a Brazilian magazine of the revolt of the African Muslims in 19th century Bahia.

Image 11 - Native porter in Brazil by Jean-Baptiste Debret.

Image 12 - Islamic documents found after the 1835 *Malê* revolt (Credit:

image supplied by João José Reis)

Image 13 – Brazilian newspaper article featuring an image of a Qur'an found after the 1835 *Malê* revolt (Credit: image supplied by João José Reis).

Image 14 - Portrait of Uthman dan Fodio, the revered West African Muslim reformer of the 19th century and founder of the Sokoto Caliphate.

Image 15 - Shitta Bey mosque in Lagos, Nigeria (Credit: nationalmirroronline.net).

Image 16 - Shitta Bey mosque in Lagos, Nigeria.

Image 17 to 20 - Africans in 19th century Bahia by Alberto Henschel c. 1870

Image 21 – Mixed-race Brazilian writer Machado de Assis.

Image 22 - Spanish artist Modesto Brocos y Gómes' 1895 painting *A Redenção de Cam* (The Redemption of Ham) (Credit: Museu Nacional de Belas Artes)

Image 23 - Prominent Afro-Brazilian psychiatrist Juliano Moreira.

Image 24 - Afro-Brazilian journalist Paula Brito.

Image 25 - Afro-Brazilian historian Manuel Querino.

Image 26 - Mixed-race Brazilian writer, Teixeira e Sousa.

Image 27 – Afro-Brazilian polymath and public intellectual, Teodoro Sampaio.

Image 28 - Mixed-race Brazilian composer, Antônio Carlos Gomes.

Image 29 - Mixed-race Brazilian poet and abolitionist Castro Alves.

Image 30 to 31 -.The Islamic Cultural Centre of Bahia, also known as the Salvador Mosque. (Credit: Habeeb Akande)

Image 32 - Misbau Wale Akanni, Nigerian Muslim entrepreneur living in Salvador. (Credit: Habeeb Akande)

Image 33 - Arab- Muslim businessman who established Salvador mosque. (Credit: Habeeb Akande)

Image 34 - Yussuf, the first Brazilian to chair the Islamic Center of Bahia (Credit: Gabriela Bilo).

Image 35 to 36 - Shaykh Abdul Hameed Ahmad, *imam* of the Salvador mosque. (Credit: Habeeb Akande)

Image 37 – The author carrying out research about the history of African Muslims in 19th century Brazil with Shaykh Abdul Hameed Ahmad, *imam* of Salvador Mosque. (Credit: Habeeb Akande)

Image 38 - Islamic magazine in Arabic of a descendant of the African Muslims in Bahia being presented with a *tasbeeh* (Islamic prayer beads). (Credit: Habeeb Akande)

Image 39 - Portuguese copy of João José Reis' book on the African Muslim revolts in 19th century Brazil. (Credit: Habeeb Akande)

Image 40 to 45 - Muslim community in the Salvador mosque. (Credit: Habeeb Akande)

Image 46 to 47 - Kaab Abdul, a Brazilian Muslim convert living in São Paulo (Credit: Hasan Shahid,

Index of Images

The Eye in Islam).

Image 48 - Kaab Abdul, a Brazilian Muslim convert living in São Paulo (Credit: Gabriela Biló/ Futura Press).

Image 49 to 50 - Brazilian Muslims march in protest against the controversial anti-Islamic film, *The Innocence of Muslims* in 2012. (Credit: Reuters)

Image 51 - Second World Black and African Festival of Arts and Culture (commonly known as FESTAC) 1977 framed banner hung in *Museu AfroBrasil (Afro-Brazil Museum) in* São Paulo.

Image 52 - Nigeria Cultural House in Salvador, Bahia. (Credit: Habeeb Akande)

Image 53 - Nigerian woman, likely Yoruba, viewing Queen Elizabeth II at a Myohaung Day service in Lagos Cathedrral, Nigeria (Credit: Brian Brake).

Image 54 to 55 *Centro de Estudos Afro-Orientais* (Centre for Afro-Oriental Studies). (Credit: Habeeb Akande)

Image 56 - Framed paintings of African-American leaders, Malcolm X and Martin Luther King, in the library of the *Centro de Estudos Afro-Orientais (*Centre for Afro-Oriental Studies).

Image 57 - *Raça* film poster

Image 58 - Nelson Mandela, Martin Luther King Jr and Malcolm X t-shirts in Salvador. (Credit: Habeeb Akande)

Image 59 to 60 - *Raça* magazine.

Image 61 - *City of God* film poster.

Image 62 - *City of Men* DVD film cover.

Image 63 - *Favela Rising* DVD film cover.

Image 64 - *Linha de Passe* DVD film cover.

Image 65 - Michael Jackson in Salvador, Bahia filming the music video, "They Don't Care About Us."

Image 66 - House where Michael Jackson filmed his music video in the Historic Centre (Pelourinho) in Salvador, Bahia.

Image 67 to 70 - Afro-Brazilian Museum in Salvador, Bahia. (Credit: Habeeb Akande)

Image 71 - A protestor holds a sign reading "I support the 3rd international march against the genocide of Black people." (Credit: Facebook.com/ ReajaOuSeraMorto).

Image 72 - Salvador, Bahia. (Credit: Habeeb Akande)

Image 73 – Children's cartoon book of the history of the African Muslims' revolts for the Olodum school.

Image 74 - *Preta Simoa,* northeastern black Brazilian women's group protesting against racial discrimination and sexism in Brazil. White sign, far left: "I am a black woman and I am not yours!"; Red sign: "My blackness you don't touch and my flesh you don't have!" Green sign: "Don't call me *mulata*. I am a black woman, period! I don't want your love. I am not your sexual object."

Yellow sign (back): "I am black in colour, in my soul, in my heart; this doesn't mean I am at your disposition!" White sign: "My body belongs to me!" Yellow sign (bottom): "I am a black woman, yes, and my body is not an object of your sexual satisfaction." White sign (bottom center): "My hair doesn't deny (my origin), it affirms it!" White sign (bottom left): "Because to stop being a racist, my love, is not to fuck a *mulata*." (Credit: Preta Simoa).

Image 75 - Independent film by Angolan filmmaker about the Afro-Brazilian women of Rio de Janeiro.

Image 76 - Painting of Afro-Brazilian women in Salvador, Bahia. (Credit: Habeeb Akande)

Image 77 to 79 - Afro Fashion Day, 20th November 2015 in Salvador, Bahia. (Credit: Habeeb Akande).

Image 80 to 81 - Afro-Brazilians practising capoeira in the Historic Centre (Pelourinho) in the city of Salvador. (Credit: Habeeb Akande)

Image 82 - Antônio Carlos 'Vovô,' founder of *Ilê Aiyê* (Credit: blackwomenofbrazil).

Image 83 - João Jorge co-founder of Olodum (Credit: blackwomenofbrazil).

Image 84 to 85 - Olodum music group performing at the Historic Centre (Pelourinho), Salvador. (Credit: Habeeb Akande)

Image 86 Afro-Brazilian women in Bahia wearing Ilê Aiyê clothes (Credit: blackwomenofbrazil).

Image 87 - Afro-Brazilian women wearing traditional African attire.

Image 88 to 89 - Samba reggae music group *Swing do Pelô* with its founder Ivan Santana in Pelourinho. (Credit: Habeeb Akande)

Image 90 - Italian artists, Orticanoodles' mural of Afro-Brazilian musician and politician, Gilberto Gil in Rio de Janeiro. (Credit: Habeeb Akande)

Image 91 - Jewelry of African contintent and black American rapper and activist Tupac "2Pac" Shakur at the Afro Fashion Day in Salvador, Bahia. (Credit: Habeeb Akande)

Image 92 - The author with some of the organisers of *Eu Sou Negão* (I am Black), an Afro-Brazilian empowerment project from the Comvida Institute based in Camçari, Bahia, which focuses on providing personal and professional training for young people from low-income communities. (Credit: Habeeb Akande)

Image 93 - Booklet from *Eu Sou Negão* (I am Black). (Credit: Habeeb Akande)

Image 94 - Entrance at Afro-Brazil Museum in São Paulo. (Credit: Habeeb Akande)

Image 95 - Afro-Brazil t-shirt inside souvenir shop in the Afro-Brazil Museum in São Paulo. (Credit: Habeeb Akande)

Image 96 to 97 - The history of the African Muslim revolt in 19th century Bahia at the Afro-Brazil

Index of Images

Museum in São Paulo. (Credit: Habeeb Akande)

Image 98 - Stand of Brazilian footballers, Garrincha and Jarizinho, at the Afro-Brazil Museum in São Paulo. (Credit: Habeeb Akande)

Image 99 - Brazilian footballers, Pelé and Garrincha embracing each other after a football match between their respected teams, Santos and Botafogo.

Image 100 - Afro-Brazilian actor Lázaro Ramos and his wife, Afro-Brazilian actress and model, Taís Araújo (Credit: Sergio Zalis / Globo).

Image 101 - Afro-Brazilian actress and singer, Zezé Motta (Credit: Divulgação).

Image 102 - Afro-Brazilian historian, author and activist, Abdias do Nascimento (Credit: Agência Brasil).

Image 103 - Afro-Brazilian children (Credit: Associated Press).

Image 104 - Afro-Brazilian footballer Tinga suffered racial abuse whilst playing in Peru and spoke out against the problem of racism in his home country, "In Brazil we talk about equality, but we hide our prejudice….we pretend that everyone is equal."

Image 105 - A white Brazilian football fan racially abusing Afro-Brazilian goalkeeper, Aranha, during a football match in August 2014 between Gremio and Santos.

Image 106 - Billboard advertisement from Afro-Brazilian women activist group Criola addressing Brazil's anti-black racism. The rough translation of the billboard states, "If you washed properly, you wouldn't be so dirty." The "Virtual Racism: the consequences are real" campaign from Criola is exposing online racism, by reproducing offending remarks on billboards near where the perpetrator lives. (Credit: Criola).

Image 107 - The Instituto Beleza Natural salon in Salvador, Bahia. Beleza Natural is Brazil's largest beauty salon dedicated to black "kinky" hair. (Credit: Habeeb Akande)

Image 108 - Brazilian women of African descent took to the streets of São Paulo in the summer of 2015 for the first Afro Hair Pride March '*Marcha do Orgulho Crespo.*' Organisers behind the march said, "We march with pride of our afros and curls, holding our combing forks in the wrist as a battle symbol against the social whitening process, sexual objectification of women and their silence. We believe in black empowerment and, above all, in its beauty and roots." The organisers continued, "More than being just about aesthetic, the first Afro Hair Pride March is a political act that opens paths in favour of a movement that celebrates afro hair as being part of the black identity, promotes self-esteem and helps people to embrace their ancestry and the free expression of their hair, especially for women as a means of empowerment."

(Credit: Facebook.com/MarchadoOrulhoCrespoBrasil)

Image 109 - Painting of Afro-Brazilian women in Salvador, Bahia (Credit: Habeeb Akande)

Image 110 - Afro-Brazilian capoeiraista (a practitioner of the Afro-Brazilian martial art, capoeira).

Image 111 - Afro-Brazilian TV journalist, Maria Júlia Coutinho. In early July 2015, weather reporter Maria Júlia Coutinho, also known as Maju, experienced several racist attacks online, after her appointment in May of the same year, becoming the first black weather reporter on Brazil's most watched national television news show. When her photo was posted on the show's social media Facebook page, several people posted racist comments about her. Following the incident, a number of prominent Brazilian celebrities spoke publically to denounce the racist attacks. Glória Maria, Brazil's first black TV reporter, experienced racism for most of her broadcast career when she worked on Fantástico, a popular news magazine show. "This is proof of what I always say, that racism will never end. What (Maju) is going through, I lived through it on Fantástico. I received letters and afterwards, emails. There wasn't a public declaration and it came directly to me, hurting my soul and heart. Today, it hurts Brazil. That's the difference. I had to endure the lonely stride. What she is living through is normal in Brazil. But it never weakened me and I never gave up."

Image 112 - Afro-Brazilians speaking at a black consciousness event.

Image 113 - Nigerian hotel and restaurant in the Historic Centre (Pelourinho) in Salvador.

Image 114 - Acarajé is a popular Bahian cuisine. It originates from West Africa, where it is known as akara by the Yoruba people of south-western Nigeria. (Credit: AF Rodrigues).

Image 115 - Brazilian Muslim in the Salvador mosque speaking to the author about his conversion to Islam and the Muslim community in Brazil. (Credit: Habeeb Akande)

Image 116 - Brazilian and African Muslim in the Salvador mosque speaking about the history of Islam in Brazil. (Credit: Habeeb Akande)

Image 117 to 123 – Interviews conducted by the author in Rio de Janeiro and Salvador with Brazilians of African descent about the black experience in Brazil. (Credit: Habeeb Akande)

Image 124 - Painting of an upset Afro-Brazilian child in Salvador, Bahia. (Credit: Habeeb Akande)

Image 125 - Anti-FIFA World Cup mural by artist Paulo Ito in São Paulo (Credit: Paulo Ito).

Image 126 to 129 - The whiteness of Brazilian football fans for the World Cup 2018 qualifying match between Brazil and Peru on 17th November 2015 in Salvador, Bahia.

Index of Images

Despite having a largely black and brown population, the lack of non-white faces in the football stadium reflects Brazil's apartheid between Brazil's white (wealthy) and non-white (poor) population. The majority of Brazilian fans in the stadium were noticeably far lighter in complexion (including popular Brazilian musician Ivete Sangalo) compared to the dark-skinned Brazilians working in the kiosks and footballers on the football pitch who are mainly from humble backgrounds. (Credit: Habeeb Akande)

Image 130 - The author and Brazilian historian and professor João José Reis, author of *Rebelião Escrava no Brasil: a História do Levante dos Malês* (1835) (Slave Rebellion in Brazil: The History of the Malê Uprising 1835) in Salvador. (Credit: Habeeb Akande)

Image 131 - The author with the Director of the *MAFRO - Museu Afro-Brasileiro UFBA* (Afro-Brazilian Museum) in Salvador. (Credit: Habeeb Akande)

Image 132 to 158 – The author discussing race-relations in Brazil and the *Illuminating the Blackness* picture book with Brazilians in Rio de Janerio, São Paulo and Salvador. (Credit: Habeeb Akande)

Image 159 - Afro-Brazilian model, dancer and actress, Nayara Justino, speaking about racism and sexism in Brazil, "In Brazil there is a huge amount of prejudice against women, and against black women it's even worse." Justino was selected as the Globeleza carnival queen in 2013 after a public vote on one of Brazil's biggest TV shows. However not long after the news was announced, she was subjected to a barrage of racial abuse due to her dark complexion and African features. Justino was later dismissed for being "too black" to represent Brazil's carnival poster girl, for a lighter skinned mixed-race woman. The incident prompted outrage amongst black activists as it exposed the country's deep-rooted prejudice against dark-skinned peoples. "Black people in Brazil are ashamed of being black, There are very few people who are openly proud of being black," said Neusa Borges, an Afro-Brazilian actress. (Credit: Eduardo Só / MF Models Assessoria)

Image 160 to 166 – The author with Brazilians and Africans in Rio de Janerio, São Paulo and Salvador as part of the research of this book and for an upcoming documentary about the contribution of black people and Muslims to Brazil. (Credit: Habeeb Akande)

Image 167 - Brazilian model, Isabel Correa, was chosen to represent Brazil in Romanian photographer, Mihaela Noroc's project to photograph naturally beautiful women from around the world, to show that "beauty is everywhere." Speaking about the project, Isbael Correa said, "I was chosen because I fought for ten years to break the taboo that a black person cannot represent the beauty of our country! I wanted to change [the perception] that we are much more than the *mulatta* (mixed race) women of the carnival, sexual tourism, and that we (blacks) are inferior to the beauty of other races. And it doesn't matter if you think I'm ugly or beautiful in *The Atlas of Beauty*, I'm there! Simplicity is the real Brazilian beauty." (Credit: Mihaela Noroc)

Image 168 to 169 - Afro-Brazilians with the author in Salvador. (Credit: Habeeb Akande)

Image 170 to 171 – Map of Brazil.

Image 172 – Salvador tour guide, Ricardo with a Nigerian football jersey gifted to by the author in Salvador, Bahia. (Credit: Habeeb Akande)

Image 173 – *Mesquita do Brasil* (Mosque of Brazil) in São Paulo

Image 174 - Efunroye Tinubu, Yoruba trader and anti-slave activist.

Image 175 – Portrait of Mahommah Gardo Baquaqua, a former slave from Brazil who wrote his autobiography in which he described his African homeland and his life enslaved in Brazil before being freed in New York.

Image 176 – Shaykh Abdul Hameed Ahmad praying with Brazilian Muslims. (Credit: ademmm).

Image 177 to 179 – Brazilian Muslims in the Salvador mosque. (Credit: Habeeb Akande)

Image 180 – Afro-Brazilian Muslims in a mosque in São Paulo. (Credit: possehausa.blogspot.co.uk)

Image 181 to 182 – *Associação Posse Hausa*, an Afro-Brazilian hip-hop group and black activist not-for-profit organisation promoting hip-hop culture and Brazil's African Muslim heritage. Posse Hausa was founded by Afro-Brazilian Muslim rapper and activist Honorê al-Amin Oaqd. The group's name was inspired by the Hausa Muslims who took part in the revolts in 19th century Bahia. (Credit: possehausa.blogspot.co.uk)

Image 183 – Brazilian Muslims marching against religious intolerance in Rio de Janeiro (Credit: Amanda Dias)

Image 184 to 191 – *Exposição Levante Does Malês – Resistência Africana Muçulmana no Brasil – Sec XIX* (Exhibition of the Malê Uprising – African Muslim Resistance in 19th century Brazil). Organised by black activist and Muslim organisations, the exhibition took place during Black Awareness week in 2010. The exhibition showcased the history of Brazil's African Muslims in 19th century Bahia, their heritage and their influence on contemporary Brazilian society. (Credit: possehausa.blogspot.co.uk).

BIBLIOGRAPHY

The Holy Bible with Apocrypha. Oxford: Oxford University Press, 1995

'Alī, 'Abdullah Yūsuf. *The Meaning of The Holy Qur'an*. Maryland: Amana Corporation, 1992.

Abelardo Duarte, *Negros muçulmanos nas Alagoas (os Malês)*, Maceió, Alagoas: Edições Caeté, 1958.

Adamu, Mahdi. *The Hausa Factor in West African History*. Zaria: Ahmadu Bello University Press, 1978.

Agassiz, Louis and Agassiz, Elizabeth, *A Journey in Brazil*, New York: Praeger, 1969.

Aḥmad al-'Alī, Ṣāliḥ. *'Alī b. Muḥammad : Sāḥib al-Zinj*. Beirut: Dār Al-Midār al-Islāmī, 2006.

Aidi, Hisham, D., *Rebel Music: Race, Empire, and the new Muslim Youth Culture*, New York: Vintage Nooks, 2014.

Ajayi, J. F. Ade and Crowder, Michael (ed.). *A History of West Africa*. London: Longmans, 1971.

al-Bukhāri, Muḥammad b. Ismā'īl. *Ṣaḥīḥ al-Bukhārī*. Beirut: al-Maktabah al-'Aṣriyyah, 2005

Alkhateeb, Firas, *Lost Islamic History: Reclaiming Muslim Civilisation from the past*, London: Hurst & Company, 2014.

Alonge, Marjorie Moji Dolapo, *Afro-Brazilian architecture in Lagos State: a case for conservation (PhD Thesis)*, Newcastle: Newcastle University, 1994.

Akande, Habeeb, *Illuminating the Darkness: Blacks and North Africans in Islam*, London: Ta-Ha Publishers, 2012.

Akande, Habeeb, *Illuminating the Difference: Black, White, and Brown Women*, London: Rabaah Publishers, 2015.

Akintoye, Stephen Adebanji, *A History of the Yoruba People*, Amalion Publishing, 2010.

Amar, Paul [ed.], *The Middle East and Brazil: Perspectives on the New Global South*, Indiana: Indiana University Press, 2014.

Andrews, G., 'Black political protest in São Paulo, 1888–1988', in J.Domínguez (ed.), *Race and Ethnicity in Latin America*, New York: Garland Publishing, 1994.

Araújo, Emanoel (org.), *A Mão Afro-Brasileira: significado da Contribuição Artistica a História*, São Paulo: Tenenge, 1988.

Austin, Allah D., *African Muslims in Antebellum America: Transatlantic stories and spiritual struggles*, London: Routledge, 1997.

Bacharach, Jere L, 'African Military Slaves in the Medieval Middle East: The Cases of Iraq (869-955) and Egypt (868-1171),' in *International Journal of Middle Eastern Studies*, 13. 1981.

Barcia, Manuel, *West African Warfare in Bahia and Cuba: Soldier Slaves in the Atlantic World, 1807-1844*, Oxford: Oxford University Press, 2014.

Bastide, Roger (translated by Helen Sebba), *The African Religions of Brazil: Toward a Sociology of the Interpenetration of Civilisations*, Maryland: The John Hopkins University Press, 2007.

Bay, Edna G., and Mann, Kristin, [eds], *Rethinking the African Diaspora: The Making of a Black Atlantic World in the Bight of Benin and Brazil*, London: Frank Cass, 2001.

Bethell, Leslie, [ed], *Colonial Brazil*, University of Cambridge Press, 1991.

Bonnett, Alastair, *Anti-Racism*, London: Routledge, 2000.

Burns. E. Bradford *The Journal of Negro History*, Vol. 59, No. 1., Jan., 1974.

Burns, E. Bradford, *A History of Brazil*, New York: Columbia University Press.

Cairus, José T., 'Islamic Transnationalism and Anti-Slavery Movements: The Malê Rebellion as Debated by Brazil's Press' in Amar, Paul [ed.], *The Middle East and Brazil: Perspectives on the New Global South*, Indiana: Indiana University Press, 2014.

Caldwell, Kia Lilly, *Negras in Brazil: Re-envisioning Black Women, Citizenship, and the Politics of Identity*, London: Rutgers University Press, 2007.

Castro, Cristina Maria De, (translated by Rodrigo Braga Freston) *The*

Construction of Muslim Identities in Contemporary Brazil, Lexington Books: Plymouth, 2013.

Cheney, Glenn Alan, *Quilombo dos Palmares: Brazil's Lost Nation of Fugitive Slaves,* Hanover, CT: New London Librarium, 2014.

Childs, Matt D., *The Yoruba Diaspora in the Atlantic World (Blacks in the Diaspora),* Bloomington, IN: Indiana University Press, 2005.

Chuku, Gloria, "Tinubu, Efunroye," in Henry Louis Gates Jr., and Emmanuel K. Akyeampong, [eds], *Dictionary of African Biography,* New York: Oxford University Press, 2008.

Clarke, Abdassamad, *Follow the Money: A Muslim Guide to the Murky World of Finance.* Norwich: Diwan Press. 2014.

Clarke, Peter B., *West Africa and Islam,* London: Edward Arnold, 1982

Corrêa Do Lago, Luiz Aranha, *Da Escravidão ao Trabalho Livre: Brasil, 1550-1900,* São Paulo: Companhia das Letras, 2014.

Cortesão, J. [ed.], *A Carta de Pêro Vaz de Caminha,* Lisbon: Portugália, 1967.

Covin, David, *Unified Black Movement in Brazil, 1978-2002,* North Carolina: McFarland & Company, 2006.

Curtis, Edward, E., *The Call of Bilal: Islam in the African Diaspora,* The University of North Carolina Press, 2014.

D'Adesky, Jacques, *Pluralismo Étnico e Multicultralismo: Racismos e Anti-Racismos no Brasil,* Rio de Janeiro: Pallas, 2001.

Dannin, Robert. *Black Pilgrimage to Islam.* Oxford: Oxford University Press, 2002.

Davidson, Basil, *Africa in History.* New York: Simon & Schuster, 1995.

Davidson, Basil, *West Africa Before the Colonial Era, A History to 1850.* London: Longman, 1998.

Davis, Robert C., *Christian Slaves, Muslim Masters: White Slavery in the Mediterranean, the Barbary Coast and Italy, 1500-1800,* Palgrave School, 2005.

Dawson, Alan Charles, *In Light of Africa: Globalizing Blackness in Northeast Brazil,* Toronto: University of Toronto Press, 2014

De la Rosière to French Minister of Foreign Affairs, Rio de Janeiro, 13 March 1835, AMRE, *cp'Brèsil,* vol. 16, fols.

Doi, Abdurrahman I. *Islam in Nigeria.* Zaria: Gaskiya Corporation Limited, 1984.

Diawara, Gaossou, *Abubakari II: Explorateur Mandingue*, Paris: L'Harmattan, 2010.

Diouf, Sylviane A., *Servants of Allah: African Muslims enslaved in the Americas*, New York: New York University Press, 2013.

Diouf, Sylviane A. *Servants of Allah : African Muslims Enslaved in the Americas*. New York: New York University Press, 1998.

Dirks, J., *Muslims in American History,* Beltsville, MD: Amana Publications, 2006.

El Hamel, Chouki, *Black Morocco: A History of Slavery, Race, and Islam,* New York: Cambridge University Press, 2013.

Equiano, Olaudah, *The Interesting Narrative of the Life of Olaudah Equiano or Gustavus Vassa, the African*, New York: The Modern Library, 2004

Ewbank, Thomas, 1856, *Life in Brazil, or the Land of the Cocoa and the Palm,* New York: Harper and Brothers, p. 439.

Farid, A. A., Muhammad Shareef bin, *The Islamic Slave Revolts of Bahia, Brazil*, Pittsburgh, PA: Institute of Islamic-African Studies, 1998

Fausto, Boris and Fausto, Sergio, *A Concise History of Brazil*, Cambridge: Cambridge University Press, 2014.

Fausto, Boris (translated by Arthur Brakel), *A Concise History of Brazil*, New York: Cambridge University Press, 2006.

Figueira, Vera Moreira, 'O preconceito racial na escola,' in *Estudos Afro-Asiáticos*, 18, 1990.

Flesler, Daniela, *The Return of the Moor: Spanish Responses to Contemporary Moroccan Immigration*, Purde University Press, 2008

Freyre, Gilberto, *The Masters and the Slaves: A Study in the Development of Brazilian Civilization*, (translated by Samuel Putnam), New York: Alfred A. Knopf. 1956, p. 315.

Freyre, Gilberto, *The Masters and the Slaves: A Study in the Development of Brazilian Civilization,* Berkeley: University of California Press, 1986

Frost, Peter. *Fair Women, Dark Men: The Forgotten Roots of Color Prejudice*. Christchurch: Cybereditions, 2005.

Futlonge, Nigel D., 'Revisiting the Zanj and the Re-visioning Revolt: Complexities of the Zanj Conflict (868-883).' *Negro History Bullerin* 62, no. 4, pp. 7 – 14, 1999

Gabriel, Deborah. *Layers of Blackness: Colourism in The African Diaspora*. London: Imani Media Ltd, 2007.

Bibliography

Gardner, George, *Travels in the Interior of Brazil, 1836-1841*. 1849. Reprint, New York: AMS Press, 1970.

Gates, Jr., Henry Louis, *Black in Latin America*, New York: New York University. 2011.

Gbadamosi, T. G. O. *The growth of Islam among the Yoruba, 1841-1908*. London: Longman, 1978.

Genovese, Eugene D., *From Rebellion to Revolution: Afro-American Slave Revolts in the Making of the Modern World,* Baton Rouge: Louisiana State University Press, 1979.

Gervase-Smith, William. *Islam and the Abolition of Slavery*. Oxford: Oxford University Press, 2006.

Gibb, H. A. R. *Studies on the Civilization of Islam*. Oxford: Routledge, 2007.

Giepel, John, Brazil's African Legacy in *History Today*, Volume 47, Issue 8, 1997.

Gilliam, Angela and Gilliam, Onik'a, 'Odyssey: Negotiating the Subjectivity of Mulata Identity in Brazil,' in *Latin American Perspectives*, 26, (3), 1999.

Gilroy, Paul, *There Ain't no Black in the Union Jack*, London: Hutchinson. 1987.

Glazier, Stephen P. (ed.). *Encyclopedia of African and African-American Religions*. New York: Routledge, 2001.

Goldenberg, David M. *The Curse of Ham: Race and Slavery in Early Judaism, Christianity and Islam*. Princeton, New Jersey: Princeton University Press, 2003.

Gomes, Flávio, Xavier, Giovana, and Farias, Juliana Barreto, [eds.] *Mulheres Negras no Brasil Escravista e do pós-emancipação*, São Paulo: Selo Negro, 2014.

Gomes, Miriam, *Ilê Aiyê*, CIP: São Paulo, 2006.

Gomez, Michael A. *Black Crescent: The Experience and Legacy of African Muslims in the Americas*. New York: Cambridge University Press, 2005.

Goody, Jack, *Power of Written Tradition*, Washington, D.C.: Smithsonian Institution, 2000.

Gordon, Cyrus, *Before Colombus: Links Between the Old World and Ancient America*, New York: Crown Publishers Inc, 1971.

Graden, Dale T., An Act "Even of Public Security": Slave Resistance, Social Tensions, and the End of the International Slave Trade to Brazil" in *The Hispanic American Historical Review, no. 2*: pp. 249-282, 1996.

Griffin, John Howard Griffin, *Black Like Me*, 2009, Middlesex: Penguin, 2009.

Guimarães, Antonio Sérgio Alfredo, 'Racism and Anti-Racism in Brazil: A Postmodern Perspective,' in *Racism and Anti-Racism in World Perspective*, Benjamin Bowser, [ed.] London: Sage Publications, 1995.

Haberly, David. T., *Three Sad Races : Racial Identity and National Consciousness in Brazilian Literature*, Cambridge: Cambridge University Press, 2012.

Hamdun, Said, and Noel King. *Ibn Battuta in Black Africa*. 2nd ed. Bellew Publishing Co Ltd, 1975.

Hanchard, Michael, *Orpheus and Power: The Movimento Negro of Rio de Janeiro and São Paulo, Brasil. 1945-1988*, Princeton: Princeton University Press, 1994.

Hasenbalg, C. *Discriminação e desigualdades raciais no Brasil*. Rio de Janeiro, Graal [2 ed]. 2005, Belo Horizonte/Rio de Janeiro, Editora UFMG/Iuperj/Ucam, 1979.

Hawthorne, Walter, 2011, *From Africa to Brazil: Culture, Identity, and an Atlantic Slave Trade, 1600-1830*, New York: Cambridge University Press, 2011.

Hoffman, Michael A., *They Were White and They Were Slaves: The Untold History of the Enslavement of Whites in Early America*, Independent History, 1993.

Holloway, Joseph E. [ed] *Africanisms in American Culture,* University of Indiana Press, 1990.

Hunwick, John and Powell, Eve Troutt. *The African Diaspora in the Mediterranean Lands of Islam*. Princeton, NJ: Markus Wiener Publishers, 2007.

Hunwick, John, *Timbuktu & the Songhay Empire*. Leiden : Brill, 2003.

Hunwick, John, *West Africa, Islam and the Arab World*. NJ: Markus Wiener Publishers, 2006.

Ibn al-Ḥajjāj, Muslim al-Qushayrī, *Ṣaḥīḥ Muslim*. Beirut: Dār Iḥya' at-Turāth al-'Arabī, 2000.

Ibn Battutah, Abu Abdullah (edited by Tim Mackintosh-Smith). *The*

Bibliography

Travels of Ibn Battutah. London: Picador, 2002.

Ibn Khaldun, (translated by Franz Rosenthal). *The Muqaddimah: An Introduction to History*. Princeton: NJ: Princeton University Press, 2nd edn, 1967.

Ignace, Etienne, 'La secte musulmane des Malês du Brésil et leur révolte en 1835,' in *Anthropos* , 4, 1, 1909.

Isaac, Benjamin. *The Invention of Racism in Classical Antiquity*. Princeton, New Jersey: Princeton University Press, 2004.

Isfahani-Hammond, Alexandra, 'Slave Barracks Aristocrats Islam and the Orient in the Work of Gilberto Freyre' in Amar, Paul [ed.], *The Middle East and Brazil: Perspectives on the New Global South*, Indiana: Indiana University Press, 2014.

Jackson, Sherman A., *Islam and the Blackamerican*. New York: Oxford University Press, 2005.

Jackson, Sherman A., *Islam and the Problem of Black Suffering*. New York: Oxford University Press, 2009.

Jensen, Robert, *The Heart of Whiteness: Confronting Race, Racism and White Privilege*, 2005.

Johnson, Ollie A., 'Afro-Brazilian Politics: White Supremacy, Black Struggle, and Affirmative Action' in Kingstone, Peter R., and Power, Timothy J. [eds.], *Democratic Brazil Revisited*, Pittsburgh: University of Pittsburgh Press, 2008.

Johnson, Samuel. *The History of the Yorubas*. Lagos: CSS Limited, 1921.

Jones de Almeida, Adjoa Florência, 'Unveiling the Mirror: Afro-Brazilian Identity and the Emergence of a Community School Movement,' in *Comparative Education Review*, v47 n1 pp. 41-63 Feb 2003.

Jordan, Don and Walsh, Michael, *White Cargo: The Forgotten History of Britain's White Slaves in America*, Edinburgh: Mainstream Publishing, 2007.

Junia Ferreira Furtado, *Chica da Silva: A Brazilian Slave of the Eighteenth Century,* New York: Cambridge University Press, 2009.

Junne, Jr., George H., *Neither Christian nor Heathen: Islam among the African Slaves in the Americas,* University of Northern Colorado, 1995.

Kent, R., K., 'African Revolt in Bahia: 24-25 January 1835' in *Journal of Social History 3, no. 4: 335-356,* 1970.

Khan, Muhammad Muhsin and Al-Hilālī, Muhammad Taqi-ud-Din

(translators). *The Noble Qur'an*. Riyadh: Darussalam, 2001.

Kilson, Martin. *The African Diaspora*. Massachusetts: Harvard University Press, 1976.

Knight, Dan, *Battle for Black Beauty in Brazil and Worldwide: Our Woman is a Beautiful happy nappy woman*, CreateSpace Independent Publishing, 2014.

Law, Robin, and Lovejoy, Paul E., *The Biography of Mahommah Gardo Baquaqua*, Princeton: Markus Wiener Publishers, 2001.

Lawal, Nike S., Sadiku, Matthew N. O., and Dopamu, P. Ade, *Understanding Yoruba Life and Culture*, Africa Research & Publications, 2004.

Levine, Robert, M., *Brazilian Legacies*, London: M. E. Sharpe, 1997.

Levine, Robert M., *The History of Brazil*, New York: Palgrave Macmillan, 2003.

Lewis, Bernard. "Race and Color in Islam." in *The African Diaspora: Interpretive Essays*, by M. L. Kilson and R. I. Rotberg, 37-56. 1976.

Lewis, Bernard, *Race and Slavery in the Middle East*. New York: Oxford University Press, 1990.

Lewis I. M. [ed], *Islam in Tropical Africa*, Suffolk: Oxford University Press, 1966.

Lovejoy, Paul, *Muslim Encounters with Slavery in Brazil*, Markus Wiener Publishers, 2006.

Lovejoy. Paul, 'Background to Rebellion: The Origins of Muslim Slaves in Bahia.' in *Slavery and Abolition 15, no. 2: 151180*, 1994

Mello Moraes Filho, *Festas e tradições populares do Brasil*, Rio de Janeiro: F. Briguiet, 1946.

Miller, Randall M., Smith, John David, [eds.], *Dictionary of Afro-American Slavery*, New York: Greenwood Press, 1988.

Mills, Charles, 'An Illuminating Blackness' in *The Black Scholar*, Volume 43, Number 4, Winter 2013, Special Issue: Role of Black Philosophy, Paradigm Publishers.

Milton, Giles, *White Gold: The Extraordinary Story of Thomas Pellow and North Africa's One Million European Slaves*, London: Hodder & Stoughton, 2005.

Morgan, M., *Lost History*. Washington D.C.: National Geographic Society, 2007.

Nascimento, Abdias do, *Brazil: Mixture or Massacre?*, Massachusetts: The Majority Press, 1989.

Nishida, Mieko, *Slavery & Identity: Ethnicity, Gender, And Race in Salvador, 1808 - 1888*, Bloomington, IN, Indiana University Press, 2003.

Nöldeke, Theodore, 'A Servile War in the East.' in *Sketches from Eastern History*, [Reprint from 1892 ed.] Beirut: Khayats, 1963.

Nzibo, Yusuf A., 'The Muslim factor in the Afro-Brazilian struggle against slavery' in *Journal, The Institute of Muslim Minority Affairs*, Volume 7, Issue 2, pp. 547-556, 1986.

Ogumefu, M. I., *Yoruba Legends,* Forgotten Books, 2007

Ohtake, Ricardo [ed.], *Emanoel Araujo: Autobiografia do gesto*, Instituto Tomi Ohtake, 2008.

Oseni, Zakariyau I. 'The Revolt of Black Slaves in Iraq under the 'Abbasid Administration in 869-883 C.E.' Hamdard Islamicus 12/2, 1989. pp. 57-65, 1989.

Owomoyela, Oyekan, *Yoruba Proverbs,* University of Nebraska Press, 2005.

Page, Joseph A., *The Brazilians*, Da Capo Press: 1995.

Peres, Vitória; Mariz, Cecília.. "'Brasileiros' e 'Árabes': conversão ao islã no Brasil". Em fase de publicação como capítulo de livro, 2005.

Peres, Vitória de Oliveira, *'O Islã no Brasil ou o Islã do Brasil?'* (Islam in Brazil or the Islam of Brazil?) in *Religião e Sociedade*, Rio de Janeiro, v.26, n.1, p.83-114, 2006.

Peres, Vitória; Mariz, Cecília.. 'Conversion to Islam in contemporary Brazil.' in *Exchange 35 (1)*.p.102-115, 2006.

Pinho, Patricia de Santana (translated by Elena Langdon), *Mama Africa: Reinventing Blackness in Bahia*, London, Duke University Press, 2010.

Pinto, Regina Pahim, 'A representação do negro em livros didáticos de leitura' in *Cadernos de Pesquisa*, 63, 1987.

Popovic, Alexandre, *The Revolt of African Slaves in Iraq in the 3rd/9th Century*, (translated by Léon King), Princeton, NJ: Markus Wiener Publishers, 1999.

Prince, Althea, *The Politics of Black Women's Hair*, Ontario, Canada: Insomniac Press, 2009.

Quick, Abdullah Hakim, *Deeper Roots: Muslims in the Americas and the Caribbean From Before Columbus to the Present*, London: Ta-Ha Publishers, 1998.

Raça Brasil, Numero 159, Outubro 2011, Ano XV.

Raça Brasil, Numero 170, Setembro 2012, Ano XV.

Raeders, Georges, 1934, *Le comte de Gobineau au Brésil,* Paris: Les Editions Latines, 1934.

Ramos, Arthur, *The Negro in Brazil*, Philadelphia: Porcupine Press (original published in 1939), 1980.

Ramos, Arthur, *As Culturas Negras no Novo Mundo*, São Paulo: Companhia Editora Nacionals, 1946.

Ramos, Arthur, *O Negro Brasileiro,* Rio de Janeiro: Civilização Brasileira, 1934.

Reddie, Richard S. *Black Muslims in Britain.* Oxford: Lion, 2009.

Reginald, Daniel, G., *Race and Multiraciality in Brazil and the United States: Converging Paths*, Pennsylvania: The Pennsylvania State University Press, 2007.

Reichert, Rolf, *Os Documentos Árabes Do Arquivo Público Do Estado Da Bahia*, Bahia: Centro de Estudos Afro-Orientais, 1970.

Reis, João José, *Rebelião Escrava No Brasill: A Historia do levanter dos Malês (1835)*, São Paulo: Editoria Brasiliense, 1986.

Reis, João José, *Rebelião Escrava No Brasill: A Historia do levanter dos Malês em 1835*, São Paulo: Companhia das Letras, 2004.

Reis, João José, *Domingos Sodré, um sacerdote africano: Escravidão, liberdade e candomblé na Bahia do século XIX*, São Paulo: Companhia das Letras, 2008.

Reis, João José, 'Slave Resistance in Brazil: Bahia 1807-1835' in *Luso-Brazilian Review,* no. 1: III, 1988.

Reis, João José, Gomes, Flávio dos Santos and de Carvalho, Marcus J. M., *O Alufá: Tráfico, escravidão e liberdade no Atlântico Negro (c. 1822 – c. 1853)*, São Paulo: Companhia das Letras, 2010.

Reis, João José. 'Um balanço dos estudos sobre as revoltas escravas na Bahia,' in *Escravidão e invenção da liberdade: estudos sobre o negro no Brasil*, João José Reis, São Paulo: Brasiliense, 1988.

Rio, João do[Paulo Barreto], 'No mundo dos feitiços. Os feiticeiros,' in *As religiões no Rio,* Rio de Janeiro: Nova Aguilar, 1976.

Robinson, David, *Muslim Societies in African History,* New York:

Cambridge University Press, 2007.

Robinson, Eugene, *Coal to Cream: A Black Man's Journey beyond Color to an Affirmation of Race,* 1999.

Rodrigues, Nina. *As raças humanas e a responsabilidade penal no Brasil.* [4. ed]. Salvador, Livraria Progresso, 1957.

Rodrigues, Nina, *O animismo fetichista dos negros bahianos,* Rio de Janeiro: Civilização Brasileira, 1935.

Rodrigues, Nina, *Os africanos no Brasil.* [6 ed]. São Paulo: Ed.Nacional; [Brasília]: Ed. Universidade de Brasília, 1982.

Rodrigues, Nina, *Os Africanos no Brasil,* São Paulo: Companhia Editora Nacional, 1945.

Rodrigues, José Honório, *Brazil and Africa* (translated from *Brasil e Africa: outro horizonte*), London: Cambridge University Press, 1965.

Ryan, Patrick J. *Imale: Yoruba Participation in the Muslim Tradition.* Missoula, Montana: Scholars Press, 1978.

Sansone, Livio, *Blackness without Ethnicity: Constructing Race in Brazil,* New York: Palgrave, 2003.

Saunder, J., 'Class, color, and prejudice: A Brazilian counterpoint,' in E. Q. Campbell [ed], *Racial Tensions and National Identity,* Nashville, Tenn.: Vanderbilt University Press, 1972.

Segal, Ronald, *Islam's Black Slaves: A History of Africa's Other Black Diaspora,* London: Atlantic Books, 2001.

Segal, Ronald, *The Black Diaspora,* London: Faber and Faber, 1995

Shareef, Muhammad, *The Islamic Slave Revolts of Bahia, Brazil.* Pittsburg: Sankore Institute of Islamic-African Studies, 1998.

Silkaitis, Emily Martha, 'Modern Takes on Motivations Behind the Zanj Rebellion,' in *Lights: The Messa Journal,* Issue 3, Volume 1, Spring 2012.

Silva, Alberto da Costa e, 'Buying and Selling Korans in Nineteenth Century Brazil' in *Slavery & Abolition: A Journal of Slave and Post-Slave Studies,* Volume 22, Issue 1, 2001.

Silva, Nelson do Valle, 'Distancia social e casamento interracial no Brasil,' in *Estudos Afro-Asiáticos,* 14, 1987.

Skidmore, Thomas E., *Black into White – Race and Nationality in Brazilian Thought,* New York: Oxford University Press, 1974.

Soares, Carlos Eugênio Líbano, *A capoeira escrava e outras tradições rebeldes no Rio de Janeiro, 1808-1850,* Campinas: Unicamp, 2001.

Stam, Robert, *Tropical Multiculturalism: A Comparative History of Race in Brazilian Cinema and Culture,* Duke University Press, 2004

Svanberg, Ingvar and Westerlund, David, [eds], *Islam Outside the Arab World,* Richmond: Curzon Press, 1999.

Ṭabarī, (translated by David Waines). *The History of al-Ṭabarī : Volume XXXVI The revolt of the Zanj : AD 869 – 879 / A.H. 255 – 265.* New York: State University of New York Press, 1992.

Ṭabarī, (translated by Philip M. Fields). *The History of al-Ṭabarī: Volume XXXVII The 'Abbāsid Recovery.* New York: State University of New York Press, 1987.

'Tinubu, Madame (1805-1887),' in *New Encyclopedia of Africa,* John Middleton and Joseph C. Miller, [eds.], 2nd ed. Vol. 5, Detroit: Charles Scribner's Sons, 2008.

Trimingham, John Spencer. *A History of Islam in West Africa.* London: Oxford University Press, 1962.

Trimingham, John Spencer, *Islam in West Africa.* London: Oxford University Press, 1959.

Talhami, Ghada Hashem. 'The Zanj Rebellion Reconsidered.' in *The International Journal of African Historical Studies,* 10:3, 1977.

Telles, Edward E., *Race in Another America: The Significance of Skin Color in Brazil,* New Jersey: Princeton University Press, 2006.

Thomas, Louis Vincent and Luneao, Rene, *La Terre Africaine et ses Religions: Traditions et Changements,* Paris: L'Harmattan, 1975.

Thompson, Vincent Bakpetu, *The Making of the African Diaspora in the Americas, 1441-1900,* Longman, 1987.

Tomasson, Richard F., Crosby, Faye, and Herzberger, Sharon D., *Affirmative Action: The Pros and Cons of Policy Practice,* Rowan & Littlefield Publishers, 2001.

Twine, France Winddance, *Racism in a Racial Democracy,* New Jersey: Rutgers University Press, 2005.

Vasconcellos, Christianne Silva, *O Uso de Fotografias de Africanos no Estudo Etnográfico de Manuel Querino*

Verger, Pierre, *Flux et reflux de la traite des négres entre le Golfe de Bénin et Bahia de todos os Santos, du XVIIe au XIXe siècle,* Paris: Mouton, 1968

Vieira, Antônio, *Sermões Pregados no Brasil,* Lisbon: Agencia Geral das

Bibliography

Colonias. Cited in Oliveira 1969, 1940.

Walker, Dennis, 'Black Islamic Revolts of South America,' in *Islamic Review (03027570) 58,* no. 10/11: 9-11, 1970.

Walker, Robin. *When We Ruled.* Every Generation Media, 2005.

Warren, Jonathan W., *Racial Revolutions: Antiracism and Indian Resurgence in Brazil,* London: Duke University Press, 2001.

Wehr, Hans. *Arabic-English Dictionary.* New York: Spoken Language Services, 1976.

Weiner, Leo, *Africa and the Discovery of America,* Philadelphia: Innes and Sons, 1920.

Wise, Tim, *White Like Me: Reflections on Race from a Privileged Son,* Soft Skull Press: Berkeley, CA, 2011.

Woods, Jewel and Hunter, Karen, *Don't Blame It On Rio: The Real Deal Why Men Go To Brazil For Sex,* New York: Grand Central Publishing, 2008.

X, Malcolm and Haley, Alex. *The Autobiography of Malcolm X.* London: Penguin Books, 1965.

Yancey, George A., *Just Don't Marry One: Interracial Dating, Marriage, and Parenting,* Judson Press, 2002.

INDEX

abadā, 192, 219
abolition, xxv, 1, 8-10, 33, 80, 93, 148, 151, 181, 188, 202, 204, 209-210, 212
abolitionist, xix, xxv, 7, 9, 181, 235, 244
Abrantes, 190, 256
Abubakari II, 171-174
affirmative action, 2, 16, 31, 66, 68, 147-163
Africa,
central, 3-4, 22, 58, 97, 225, 243
east, 205
northern, 38
west, xviii, xxv, 3, 5, 33, 46, 53, 69, 97, 167, 168, 171-172, 174-175, 177, 182, 184, 191-192, 201, 214-215, 219, 236-240, 245
southern, 99
African, xiii-xvii, xix-xx, xxii-xxvi, 1-10, 10
African-American, xiv, xxvi
culture, xiv, xxiv
east, 11, 22, 24, 182, 205, 210
history, xvii
Muslim, xiii-xiv, xvii-xviii, xx, xxv, 1-2, 7
north, xvi, xxv
pan-African, xi, xiv
west, xiv, xvi-xvii, xxiii-xxv, 1-8
Afrobeats, 24, 33
Afro hair, 115-116, 118, 121
Afro-Brazilian, xix-xxi, xiv, xxv-xxvi, 2, 10, 14, 16, 18, 20-21, 25, 29, 31-34, 38-42, 48, 53, 59, 61, 67, 74, 88-89, 91, 97, 103, 105-106, 110-112, 114-118, 120-121, 123, 125, 127, 130, 135-140, 142, 148-149, 151-153, 157-158, 160-162, 167, 214, 236-238
carnival group, 39-41
culture, xxiv, 45
dance, 135
entrepreneur, 145
ethnology, 45
history, xxiv, 42-43, 45, 49-51, 66, 235
museum, xi, xiii, xviii, xix, 18
music, 122
Muslim, xxv, 20, 57-58, 61, 204, 249
religion, xiv, 35, 50, 126
state, 37
Afrodescendente, xxii, 25, 138
Aguda, 236-237
Ahmad, Abdul Hameed
Ahuna, 193-194
Aidi, Hisham D., 60
Aka, Sanusi, 238
Akanni, Misbah Wale, xi, 55-56
Akon, 24, 115
Al-Azhar university, 54, 56
Al-Baghdādī, 'Abd ar-Raḥmān, 44, 213-217, 219, 222-225, 229, 232-235
Al-Idrīsī, 170-171
Al-Jawzī, 'Abd ar-Raḥmān, 21
Al-Jāḥiẓ, Amr, 21, 205-206
Al-Umarī, Shihāb ad-Dīn, 172
Alagoas, 37, 69, 213-214, 219
Allah, xi, xiii, xxiii-xxiv, 21, 58, 64, 184, 191, 198, 204, 208, 216, 226-227, 229, 244, 247-248, 250
alufa, 47, 195, 217, 224, 240

Ali, Muhammad, 17-18, 20, 60
Álvares, Pedro, 104, 167, 177
Alves, Castro, xix,
Alves, Dani, 18-19
Andalusia, Andalusian, 170, 176
Armado, Jorge, 104
Amar, Paul, 54
amarelo, 74, 95-98, 100
Amerinidian, 3
amulet, 51, 192, 198, 203-204, 226, 240, 243
Angola, 4-5, 35-36, 38, 41
anthropology, 53, 127
anti-black racism, xv-xvi, xxvi, 1, 11, 14, 66-67, 83, 92, 125, 137, 154, 157, 160-161, 208
appropriation
   cultural, xix
white, xix
Arab, 23-24, 38, 44, 54-55, 57, 60, 63, 65, 73, 81, 96, 168, 170-171, 178, 182, 186, 205-208, 210-211, 217, 221, 247
   Afro-Arab, 205
Arab-Brazilian, 54-55, 57, 248
culture, 234
   dark-skin, 23,
immigrants, 57
Muslim, 42, 53-55, 63, 217, 225
Arabic, xiii, 56, 60, 63, 65, 84, 99, 168, 170, 175, 182, 186-187, 196-197, 202, 205, 216, 221-228, 242, 244
   documents, 226-227
Aranha, 18
Araújo, Joel Zito, xxii, 123, 125-127, 139
Araújo, Taís, 124, 126-127, 137-138, 142, 160-161
Aryan, 45, 81, 85, 128
Aryanism, Aryanisation, 85, 93
As-Suyūṭī, Jalāl ad-Dīn, 21
Assis, Machado de, xix
Austin, Allan D., 51, 244
Axé, 122

Baartman, Sarah, 133-134

Baghdad, 11, 22, 69, 182, 197, 205, 207-208, 216
Bahia, xviii, xxv-xxvi, 1-2, 5, 7-10, 22, 35, 39, 41, 44-48, 50-51, 55-56, 63, 66, 68, 132, 140, 150-151, 171, 174, 181-190, 192-197, 199-201, 204, 208-209, 213-215, 217-222, 224-225, 227-228, 230, 232, 235, 236, 240, 241, 242, 251, 255
Bahian cuisine, xviii
Baiano, 63, 251
baile funk, 59, 107
Bairros, Luiza, 150, 153
Baquaqua, Mahommah Gardo, 239, 243-244
Barcia, Manuel, 190, 201-202
Bastide, Roger, 8, 47, 52-53, 197, 219
Beauty, xx-xxi, 2, 32, 66-68, 103-109, 111-112, 114-118, 123-125, 131-132, 134-144, 232-233, 249
Benin, xiii, 5-6, 41, 182, 184, 204, 237-238, 243
Berber, 38, 69, 106, 168, 176, 178, 214-215, 234
Bight of Benin, 5-6, 8, 44, 199, 215, 217-218, 237, 240
Black
activist, activism, xix, 1-2, 10, 17-18, 35, 38, 88, 95, 108, 122-123, 127, 132, 138, 143-144, 151, 155, 163, 168,
Black Consciousness Day, 33-34, 38
   blackness, xi, xiv-xvii, xx, xxiii, xxiv, xxvi, 1, 16, 21-22, 24, 26-30, 32, 34, 66-68, 84, 94, 103, 105, 107, 111, 112, 115, 118, 122, 127, 136-137, 140, 142-144, 180, 251,
   consciousness, xx, xxvi, 2, 21-22, 26, 29, 40, 49, 60, 91-92, 103, 143, 163,
   culture, xix, 28, 46, 60, 87, 154,
   definition, 23-25
   history, xiv-xv, 136,
   movement, 2, 10, 18, 25, 29, 34, 88, 94, 97, 103, 155, 160,
bloco, xxiii, 39, 41,
boa aparência, xvi,

Index

Boas, Franz, 87
Borno, xi, xvi, 201,
branco, 22, 25, 74, 95-96
Brazil, Brazilian
    abolitionist, xix
    culture, xxiii-xxiv, 13, 32-34, 36, 42, 87-88, 113, 121-123, 126, 134, 148, 237
    elite, xxv-xxvi, 1, 3, 6, 12, 18, 21, 49, 59, 68, 76, 78-80, 83-85, 87, 90, 92-94, 110, 127-128, 154, 157-158, 168, 178, 186, 188, 203, 212,
    Empire, 240-241
film, xv
football, footballer, xv, 14-15, 18-21, 68, 112, 127
government, 22, 30, 34, 77, 81, 85, 93-94, 147-148, 204
hair, 120
media, 14, 68, 103, 106, 112, 116-117, 121, 123-126, 132, 137-140
    music, xviii, 33, 122
    police, 17, 242
    Portuguese language, 35
    sexuality, xx
    TV, xv, xx, 59, 123, 125-127, 138
    weave, 28
Burns, Bradford, 48

cabelo, 26, 28, 114, 116, 122, 136-137
Cabral, Pedro Álvares, 104, 167, 177
cachaça, 53
Cachoeira, 189-190, 256
Calógeras, João Pandiá, 81
Caldwell, Kia Lilly, 121-122, 140
Candomblé, xiv, xxvi, 35-36, 39, 50, 53, 63
Caravalho, Marcus, 239
Cardoso, Fernando Henrique, 91
Calafate, Manoel, 193, 196, 228
Capoeira, 34, 36, 39,
Caribbean, xxiv, 24, 40, 182
Carnival, xv, xvii, xxii-xxiii, 36, 39-40, 62, 103, 123, 132, 135
Castro, Cristina Maria de, 37, 54, 63-64, 177

Catholic Church, 9, 76, 82-83, 210
Catholicism, 35, 50, 52-53, 219, 242
Caucasian, 30-31, 77
census, 22, 25, 33, 57, 67, 74, 77, 92-100, 113, 148, 153
Christian, Christianity, 9-10, 20-21, 41, 43, 48, 52-53, 57-58, 62, 64-65, 76, 82-84, 112, 130, 169, 183-185, 201-202, 207, 209, 214, 216-217, 220-221, 223, 225, 228-229, 232, 235, 244, 249,
Cliff, Jimmy, 39
colourism, xxvi, 1, 14, 16, 66-67, 103-104, 106,
Columbus, Christopher, 167, 172, 174
Congo, 5, 184-185, 215, 241,
Cooper, Clayton, 86
Córdoba, 169-170
Coutinho, Maria Júlia (Majú), 160-161
crioulo, 26, 74, 199,
Cuba, xiv, 7, 80,
Curtis, Edward E., 197-199,

dawah, 249,
Dahomey, 189, 201, 204,
Dandara, 38, 196, 235-236
Dandará, 193, 196, 228
Darwin, Charles, 85
Darwinism, 78, 85
Dassalu, 193, 196
Davidson, Basil, 169
Davis, Robert, 178
Debret, Jean-Baptiste, 213,
Dessalines, Jean-Jacques, 188
Diouf, Sylviane A., 47, 51, 184, 186, 214, 221, 227
discrimination, xvi-xvii, 10-11, 13, 15-17, 19-22, 26, 31-32, 41, 63, 86-87, 89-91, 93-94, 107, 113, 127, 133, 141-142, 147, 149, 151-152, 159, 162, 191, 207, 211, 235, 247
Djougou, 243-244
divinities, xiv,
dan Fodio, Uthman, xvi, 186, 197
Du Bois, W.E.B., 73, 88
Dutch, 36, 38

entrepreneur, entrepreneurship, xv, 55, 114, 118-120, 138-139, 141, 145
Equiano, Olaudah, 3
eugenics, 77, 79, 85
Europe, European, xiv, xvi, xix, xxi, xxv-xxvi, 2-4, 6-7, 9-10, 12, 14, 16, 21-25, 28-31, 34, 37, 43, 45, 47-51, 54, 58, 61, 67-68, 73-74, 78-82, 84-87, 92-93, 96-100, 104, 107, 112-113, 119-120, 124, 126, 131-134, 139-143, 147-148, 150, 158, 161, 163, 168-169, 172-175, 177-182, 185-186, 202-203, 207, 210, 212, 216, 220, 223, 225, 232, 245-246

fashion, xviii, 57, 67, 103, 116-117, 122-125, 131-133, 136-137, 139, 144, 214,
favela, xv, xviii, 16, 29, 58-61, 107, 157, 163
femininity, xx, 114, 117,
Fon, 35, 44, 187, 218,
Freyre, Gilberto, 43, 50, 74, 85-88, 104-105, 147, 202, 220-221, 225-226, 230
Fulani, 44, 97, 183, 186, 201, 240
futebol, 18

Gardner, George, 186
Garrincha, 17-18
Gates Jr., Henry, 26, 60, 91, 137, 149
Gegê, 44
gente de cor, 4, 43
Geipel, John, 7
Gil, Gilberto, 33
Gobineau, Count, 44-45
Goldenberg, David M., 84
Gomes, Flávio dos Santos, 239
Gomes, Modesto Brocos y, 83
Gomez, Michael, 51, 197, 215, 219

Hair, xvi, xx, 24, 26-28, 31, 67, 96, 103, 105, 114-122, 131, 136-137, 142-143, 161-162, 195, 206, 253
  Afro-hair, 27, 96, 115-116, 118, 121-122
  bad, 122, 137
  curly, 107, 116-118

  good, 28
  natural, xviii, 114-118, 120-122, 136, 160
  kinky, 22, 26-27, 113
  straight, 16, 96, 103, 114, 117, 120, 137
Haiti, xiv, 11, 24, 80, 182, 188, 212, 244
  revolt, 1, 11, 182, 188
Ham, Curse of, 81-84, 209
Hanchard, Michael, xvii
Hasenbalg, Carlos, 88
Hausa, xiv, xxv, 2, 7-8, 11, 46, 52, 61, 68, 97, 141, 181-182, 184-189, 195, 202, 208, 225, 227-228, 234, 240, 256
Henschel, Alberto, 230
ḥijāb, 63, 234,
Hill, Lauryn, 115
hip-hop, xix, 24, 28, 57, 59-61, 115, 134
Hispanic, 24, 98,
Hoffman, Michael A., 178
homosexual, homosexuality, xxiii, 65-66, 114, 128-131, 144,

Iberian Peninsula, 50, 53, 105, 168, 225,
Ibn Baṭṭūṭah, 69, 176-177, 214-215, 233
Ibn Khaldūn, 42, 67, 172,
Igbo, 141,
Ignace, Etienne, 47
Ijesa, 189
Ilê Aiyê, xxvi, 1, 35, 39-41, 56, 135-136
illiteracy, 220
immigrants, xxvi, 85, 240, 245, 249
  Arab, 57, 81
  Asian, 81
  Brazilian, 245
  European, 80-81
indigena, 74, 97
inferiority complex, xvi, xxiv, 108
Islam, xiv, xxiv, xxvi, 1-2, 7, 21-22, 39, 41-42, 44, 47, 50-69, 168-169, 183-184, 192-193, 195, 197-198, 199, 203, 208, 210, 214, 216, 224-225, 227-229, 231-232, 234-235, 239, 242-243, 247-250

Jabaquara, 9
Jackson, Michael, 41
Jesus, 58,

Index

jihād, 8, 51, 186, 197-198, 201, 209, 211
Johnson, Samuel, 183
Jongo, 36
Jorge, João, 40
Jorge, Seu, 115, 130

Kaufmann, Miranda, 178-179
Kharijite, 205, 210
King, Martin Luther, 20, 88
Kuti, Fela, 33

L'Ouverture, Toussaint, 188
Lacerda, Batista João, 82, 94
Lagos, xiii, xvi, 203, 218, 236-238, 245-246
Latin America, 5, 11, 26-27, 36, 48, 54, 63, 67, 80, 82, 85, 92, 98, 155, 182
Latino, 24, 27, 59, 98,
Lebanon, Lebanese, 54, 57, 64, 81, 248
Li, Negra, 115
Licutan, Pacífico, 193-194
literacy, xiv, 1, 136, 175, 177, 182, 186, 197, 220-221, 225
Lovejoy, Paul, 8, 51, 197, 225
Lula da Silva, Luiz Inácio, 16-17, 58, 150, 181

Maggie, Yvonne, 156
Magnoli, Martinelli, 155-156
Mahin, Luísa, 235
Malês, 8, 22, 46-48, 51, 58-59, 61, 68, 182, 194, 196, 211-212, 219, 221-222, 230, 235
  definition, 8
  revolt, 10-11, 61, 182, 191, 204, 207, 209-211
Mali Empire, 171, 175
Mandela, Nelson, 20, 88
Mandinka, Mandingo, 171, 173-174, 184
Marley, Bob, 39, 115
Marriage, 67, 74-77, 93, 103, 109-110, 112-113, 129-130, 229-231, 249
  interracial, 67, 76, 103, 109-110, 112
Martins, Gonçalves, 192-193
Martins, Karl Friedrich Philipp von, 47
masculinity, 128
media, xxiv, 14, 18-20, 40, 62, 64, 67-68, 103, 106, 108, 111-112, 115-117, 121-128, 130, 132, 135-141, 143-144, 150, 160-162
Menezes, Sharon, 161
mestiço, 37, 76
Metwally, Abdelhamid, 54
Milton, Giles, 178
Mills, Charles, 29
Mina, 29, 215, 217-218, 220-223
Mina Coast, 5, 218
Minas Gerais, 4-5, 44, 47, 57, 171, 174
miscegenation, 15, 30-31, 45, 67, 74-79, 81, 85-90, 100, 109, 123, 163, 253
monotheism, 58, 66, 250
Moor, Mooress, Moorish 38, 43, 50, 85, 104-105, 168-171, 182, 186, 202,
moreno/morena, xvi, xviii, xx, 16, 25-26, 29, 31, 96-97, 124, 251-254
Motta, Zezé, 137-138, 142,
Movimento Negro, 2, 34, 89, 94, 103, 160,
mulatto/mulatta/mulata, xviii, 10, 16, 19, 26-27, 29, 31, 75-79, 83, 86, 93, 96, 103-106, 110, 120, 123, 132, 137, 143, 152, 156, 187, 196, 198-200, 254
Muḥammad, 'Alī ibn, 205, 207
Musa, Mansa Kankan, xvi, 171-172, 174-175
Muslim
  Arab, 42, 53-54, 63, 178, 217, 225
  army, 168
  Berber, 178, 215
  clothes, clothing, 51, 63
  community, communities, xii, 2, 21, 44, 53-56, 63, 65-66, 69, 177, 213-214, 219, 238, 240, 248-249
  converts, 39, 47, 52-55, 57-58, 61-65, 248-249
  empire, 186
  Fulani, 183, 186, 240
  history, xxiv, 60, 211
  historian, 42, 171
  Ottoman, 216

Portuguese, 177
scholars, 21, 176, 216
society, societies, 21-22
Spain, Spanish, 169, 177
world, 11, 22, 176
MV Bill, 59-60

Nagô, 8, 44, 52, 182-183, 187, 189-190, 194, 196, 201, 215, 217-219, 227-228, 230, 235, 241, 256
Nascimento, Abdias do, 25, 51, 87-88, 151, 167-168
Native American, 3, 97, 167
negão, 97,
negritude, 28,
negro/negra, xiv, xviii, xx, 2, 12, 16, 19, 22-23, 25-29, 31, 47, 49-50, 76, 80-81, 85-86, 90, 94, 97, 100, 105, 110, 114, 122, 124, 138, 140, 150-151, 157, 168, 185, 194, 200, 209, 223, 225, 254,
field negro, 200
house negro, 200
Neiva, Arthur, 82
Netinho de Paula, 125, 139
Neymar, 19
Nicobé, 193, 196,
Nigeria, xiii, xv-xviii, xxv, 2-3, 6, 22, 24-25, 41, 55-56, 108, 140-141, 159, 182-187, 197, 204, 218, 236-238, 246,
nigger, 27-28, 97
Nixon, Richard, 12
Nöldeke, 209-210
Nugent, Maria, 188
Nunes, Aloysio, 157
Nyong'o, Lupita, 142

Obama, Barack, 149
Ogun (state), xiii, 245
Olodum, xxvi, 40-41, 56, 136
Olodumaré, 40
Olorun, 183
orixá (orisha), xiv, 35, 183, 215, 218
Oseni, Zakariyau, 209-210
Ottoman Empire, 217
Oyo, xiii, 183, 189, 201, 240

Oyo Empire, 240

pagan, 36, 52, 183-184, 197
Pagoda, xx,
Paim, Paulo, 125, 149
Page, Joseph A., 17
Palmares, xxv, 11, 34, 36-38, 41, 236,
Papal Bull, 4
Paraná, 57, 98,
pardo/parda, xviii, 10, 22, 26, 29, 31-32, 44, 74, 92, 94-97, 159, 169, 199, 253-254
Paulo César, 19-20
Pelé, 17-20
Pelourinho, 41, 55, 194
Pernambuco, 36, 44, 69, 171, 213-215, 219-220, 224, 239, 241-242, 244
Persian, 23, 205, 207
Pestana, Maurico, 40
polygamy, polygyny, xv, 229, 231
Popovic, Alexandre, 210
Portugal, Portuguese, xiii, xxv, 1-8, 15, 23, 27, 30-31, 33-38, 41-44, 48, 50-51, 53-54, 66-68, 74-76, 79, 81, 83, 85-86, 88, 90, 98, 104-106, 109, 115, 148, 163, 167-168, 177, 179, 182-183, 186-188, 199-200, 202, 207-209, 211-212, 216-218, 220, 223, 225, 236, 240, 242, 244, 253
Prejudice, 10, 12-15, 17, 19, 21-22, 31, 54, 68, 79, 90-91, 107, 114, 118, 138, 148-150, 160-161, 179, 201, 236, 247, 249
Prado, Paulo, 81
preto, preta, pretinho, xviii, 10, 22, 25-26, 44, 74-75, 95-97, 137, 199, 253-254
prison, prisoner, xxvi, 89, 130, 153, 187-188, 190, 193-194, 222, 240, 244,
promiscuous, promiscuity, xvii, xxi-xxii, 28, 62, 65, 114, 123, 133
Prophet Muḥammad, xi, xiii, xxv, 65, 191, 208, 210, 224, 226-227, 234, 242, 247-248, 250
prostitute, xxi-xxii, 75, 162,

Index

Querino, Manuel, 48-49, 213-214, 230-232,
Quick, Abdullah Hakim, 168-169, 174, 225,
Quilombo, xxv, 9, 36-38, 41, 125, 189, 256
Qurʾān, Qurʾānic, 21, 45, 47, 65, 182, 184, 191-192, 196-198, 204, 208, 216, 220, 222-229, 240, 242-243, 247-249

racial, xiv-xv, xix-xx, xxv, 2, 3, 6, 10, 12, 14-18, 21-22, 25-26, 28, 40, 45, 49-50, 52, 61, 67, 73-80, 86-89, 91-100, 105-106, 108-110, 112, 114, 121, 124-125, 127, 131, 139, 147-149, 151-153, 155, 157-159, 161, 163, 178, 186, 199, 204, 208-209, 212, 235, 247-248
abuse, 14, 19-20, 161-162, 206
categories, 67, 73-74, 92, 98-100, 199,
democracy, xxvi, 10-11, 13, 20, 30, 50, 67, 69, 74, 86-94, 104, 106, 110, 143, 147, 163, 247
discrimination, 10, 13, 15, 21-22, 41, 86, 93-94, 113, 142, 151-152, 207, 247
equality, 2, 38, 58, 97
prejudice, 17, 19, 118, 160
quotas, 2, 22, 31, 68, 132, 147, 153, 155-156, 160
racism, xvi, xxvi, 9-21, 30, 32, 60, 68, 86-87, 90-92, 94, 104, 111-113, 117-119, 122, 130, 133, 137, 140, 148-149, 156-158, 162-163, 180, 211
anti-black, xv-xvi, xxvi, 1, 11, 14, 66-67, 83, 92, 125, 137, 154, 157-158, 160-161, 186, 208
cordial racism, 21, 68
definition, 11
institutional, 12, 86, 90, 92, 118, 125, 163
scientistic, scientific, 12, 45, 78, 84-85, 90, 128, 209, 211
systematic, xv
Ramadan, 51, 191, 194, 198, 219, 232
Ramos, Arthur, 46, 197
Ramos, Lázaro, 126,
Rape, xxii, 3, 15, 74, 76, 109, 200, 208

Rastafari, 94,
Recife, 36, 38, 54, 63, 118, 171, 219, 230, 239, 242, 249,
Reggae, 24, 39-40, 115,
Reis, João José, xi, xv, 3, 16, 50-51, 56, 150, 190-191, 196-198, 200, 215, 226-227, 239,
revolt, xv, xxv, 1-2, 7-11, 21, 33, 41, 44, 46, 50-53, 55, 61, 66, 68, 127, 181-182, 186-212, 214, 226, 228, 235, 241, 255-256
Rio, João do, 46-47, 214, 218, 224-225
Rio Branco Law, 9
Rio de Janeiro, 39, 41, 44-47, 54, 57, 59-60, 63, 65-67, 69, 77, 80, 85, 107, 117-118, 148-149, 151-153, 155, 157, 185, 192, 203-204, 213-219, 223-224, 232, 235, 241-242, 244, 248-249
Rio Grande do Sul, 34, 57, 241
Rodrigues, Raimundo Nina, 7, 45-46, 52, 78-79, 197, 214, 217, 219, 225
Romero, Sílva, 12, 47, 79,
Rousseff, Dilma, 2, 150, 153
Rufino José Maria, 239-243

São Paulo, xi, xiii, xviii, xx-xxi, 5, 13, 18, 21, 31, 34, 38-39, 54-55, 57, 59, 61-64, 67, 69, 80, 98, 118, 125, 127, 132, 154-155, 160, 222, 248
Sa, Anderson, 59-60
Salvador, xi-xii, xvii-xviii, xx-xxi, 5, 7-8, 32, 35, 39-41, 54-58, 62-67, 69, 97, 118, 120, 124, 132, 135-136, 148, 154, 187, 189-192, 194, 199, 213, 215, 236, 240-241, 248-249, 256
Samba, xx, 24, 34-35, 39-41, 119, 215, 220
Sanim. 193, 195, 228,
Santana, 118, 189, 256
Santo Amaro, 189-190, 196, 256
São Francisco, 189-190, 256
Sexagenarian Law, 9
sexual tourism, xxi-xxii, 135
sexuality, xx-xxiii, 75, 104, 123, 132
Shakur, Tupac, 60, 105

Shareef, Muhammad, 51, 197
Shitta, Oloye Muhammad, 237-238
Silva, Alberto da Costa e, 46-47, 51, 215, 224
Silva, Chica da, 137-138
Skidmore, Thomas E., 90,
skin
  bleaching, 107-109,
  colour, xxvi, 16, 22, 25, 27-28, 31, 67, 73, 86-87, 95-96, 100, 104, 109, 112, 141, 159, 162, 199,
  complexion, 19, 22-23, 96, 107, 109, 113, 248,
  slavery, xv, xxv, 1-3, 6-12, 17, 31-35, 38, 42-43, 52-53, 56, 67, 74, 76-77, 80, 82, 84, 87-89, 91-93, 109, 114, 124, 127, 148-149, 151, 154, 158, 167-168, 178, 181-182, 188, 197, 199, 202-204, 207-210, 212, 222, 225, 227, 239, 243-245
Spain, Spanish, 18-19, 64, 81, 98, 168-171, 179
Sokoto Caliphate, 197
South Africa, South African, 11, 17, 23, 27, 41, 58, 67, 78, 80, 90, 92, 99-100, 108, 133
Sufism, 61
Syria, Syrian, 54, 57, 62, 81, 172, 208, 216

Telles, Edward E., 25, 94, 121-122
Timbuktu, xvi, 175-177, 222
Tinga, 14
Tinubu, Efunroye, 239, 244-246
Tiririca, 121-122
Treece, Dave, 89
Twine, France Winndance, 91

Umbanda, 50
United States of America, xiv, xxv, 3, 6, 11-12, 14-20, 22-28, 34, 39, 43, 57, 61, 64, 67, 78, 86-88, 90-92, 94, 96-100, 104-105, 115, 120, 128-130, 137, 141, 149, 156-158, 174, 182, 244

Van Sertima, Ivan, 167
Vargas, Getúlio, 92
Velez, Leila, 119-120
Verger, Pierre, 197, 237
Veríssimo, José, 12
Vieira, Antônio, 9-10, 33
Vianna, Cris, 161
Vovô, Antonio Carlos, 35, 40, 136

Wagley, Charles, 91
Wells, Mark, 29
Weneck, Jurema, 162
white
whiteness, xxiv, xxvi, 14, 16, 32, 81, 107-108, 112, 125, 143-144, 158, 249, 251
white privilege, 15, 28, 139, 153, 158-159, 162
white supremacy, 1, 11-12, 15, 17, 66, 74, 82, 108, 128, 153, 158, 212
Wiener, Leo, 167
Winters, Clyde Ahmad, 36, 171

X, Alfonso, 169
X, Malcolm, xiv, 43, 59-61, 88, 115, 128-129, 200

Yoruba, xiii-xv, xvii-xviii, xxv-xxvi, 1-2, 5, 7-8, 11, 22, 24, 33, 35-36, 40, 43-44, 46, 51, 55, 68, 97, 108, 137, 140-141, 181-185, 187, 189-192, 194-197, 200-201, 208, 211, 215, 217-218, 227-228, 232, 234-237, 240-241, 244-245, 256
  Muslim, xiii, xv, xvii, 1-2, 8, 51, 140, 182, 197, 200, 208, 234
  religion, xiv, 35, 46, 235
Yorubaland, 8, 192, 201, 240

Zanj,
  revolt, 22, 68, 182, 205-212
Zeferina, 189
Ziyād, Ṭāriq ibn, 168
Zumbi, 11, 33-34, 37-38, 41,

ABOUT THE AUTHOR

Habeeb Akande is a British born writer and historian of Yoruba descent. He is an alumnus of al-Azhar University in Cairo, Egypt and Kingston University in the UK. He is also the author of *Illuminating the Darkness: Blacks and North Africans in Islam* and *A Taste of Honey: Sexuality and Erotology in Islam*.